D0152147

An Introduction to Microcomputer Systems

Architecture and Interfacing

John Fulcher

University of Wollongong
Australia

ADDISON-WESLEY PUBLISHING COMPANY

Sydney · Wokingham, England · Reading, Massachusetts
Menlo Park, California · New York · Don Mills, Ontario
Amsterdam · Bonn · Singapore · Tokyo · Madrid · San Juan

QA
76.5
.F853
1989

© 1989 Addison-Wesley Publishers Ltd.
© 1989 Addison-Wesley Publishing Company, Inc.

All rights reserved. No part of this publication may be reproduced, stored in a retrieval system, or transmitted in any form or by any means, electronic, mechanical, photocopying, recording or otherwise, without prior written permission of the publisher.

The programs in this book have been included for their instructional value.
They have been tested with care but are not guaranteed for any particular purpose. The publisher does not offer any warranties or representations, nor does it accept any liabilities with respect to the programs.

Many of the designations used by manufacturers and sellers to distinguish their products are claimed as trademarks. Addison-Wesley has made every attempt to supply trademark information about manufacturers and their products mentioned in this book. A list of the trademark designations and their owners appears on p. xvi.

Cover designed by Hybert Design and Type, Maidenhead.
Typeset by Columns Typesetters of Reading.
Printed in Singapore.

First printed 1989.

British Library Cataloguing in Publication Data
Fulcher, John
  An introduction to microcomputer systems:
  architecture and interfacing.
  1. Microcomputer systems. Interfaces with
  peripheral equipment
  I. Title
  004.6'16

  ISBN 0–201–41623–9

Library of Congress Cataloging in Publication Data
Fulcher, John
  An introduction to microcomputer systems: architecture and
  interfacing/John Fulcher.
    p.   cm.
  Bibliography: p.
  Includes index.
  ISBN 0–201–41623–9
  1. Microcomputers. 2. Computer architecture. 3. Computer
interfaces.   I. Title.
QA76.5.F853 1989
004.2'2–dc20   89–31530
                                                                                    CIP

Dedicated to my father,
Lee Meredith Fulcher

Preface

APPROACH

As the title suggests, this book is an *introduction* to Microcomputer Systems. Accordingly, the emphasis throughout is on *fundamental* interfacing techniques. Hopefully, this book will serve as a springboard for those readers attempting to interface real-world devices to specific microcomputers. The references and further reading listed at the end of the book should be consulted for a more detailed coverage of some of the topics presented in each chapter.

I am not claiming any of the techniques presented herein as original, rather that I have simply gathered these together into a single volume; the old adage of there being 'nothing new under the sun' (Ecclesiastes 1:9) applies to microcomputer interfacing. In order to illustrate the interfacing techniques introduced in the text, I have presented programming examples based on the two industry standard 16-bit microprocessors, namely the Intel i8086 and Motorola MC68000.

Understanding how a peripheral device works is half the battle in interfacing it to a microcomputer. Hence the approach taken in this book is to firstly describe the operation of the peripheral device in question, prior to explaining how to interface to it. For example, what does *ghosting* mean in relation to a keyboard matrix? What does *overrun* mean in relation to data communications? What function does a Character Generator ROM serve in a CRT display? What is a *seek error* in a disk drive? and so on.

In order to facilitate the interfacing of different peripheral devices, families of peripheral support chips are commonly available from the various integrated circuit manufacturers. If a standard 'off-the-shelf' microprocessor support chip is not readily available, then a custom interface can be designed and constructed for the particular application at hand. Such custom interfaces can be fabricated out of discrete logic ('TTL glue'), programmable logic devices (PLDs), or indeed dedicated microcontroller chips.

Programmable interface devices usually incorporate several internal registers for controlling their behaviour. At a bare minimum, there will be a (write-only) control register, and a (read-only) status register (both in fact

vii

could share the *same* address space). The increasing functionality of the more recent peripheral support chips means that it is more likely to find *several* such on-chip registers.

It is imperative to read the manufacturer's data sheets (as well as application notes if available), in order to become thoroughly versed with the capabilities of a particular support chip, before attempting to use it. Moreover, it is important to understand its operation down to the level of bit patterns in the various registers. Even if the device is ultimately controlled from a high-level language program, it is still essential to understand what the effect would be of changing just *one* bit in the relevant register. It might be possible, for example, to cause inadvertently the peripheral device to malfunction simply because at some stage of its operation one of its registers momentarily passes through a default state which in turn causes an unexpected condition. For example, can the serial support chip handle *overrun*, and if so how? Likewise a *seek error* in a floppy disk controller chip.

In designing new systems, it is better to stick with the one microprocessor family throughout, rather than 'mixing and matching' components. (The CRT controller used in the IBM PC is a Motorola MC6845, whereas the CPU and other peripheral support chips belong to the i8086 family. The CRT is arguably one of the PC's worst features.)

Interfacing peripheral devices to a microcomputer involves three important factors. *Firstly*, we need to know the basic operating principle of the peripheral device we're attempting to interface to the computer. *Secondly*, we need to know the characteristics of the particular peripheral support chip we're using for this task. *Thirdly*, we need to write the control software. In order to do this, we need to develop an intimate working knowledge of the language in which this is to be implemented. Throughout this book, we concentrate exclusively on assembly language programming (specifically i8086 and MC68000). In reality, we could be controlling the peripheral device via a high-level language routine. However, for time-critical applications, or where program space is at a premium, it is often necessary to optimize specific portions of the program by resorting to assembly code (particularly for ROMable code). The better high-level language compilers allow the ready linking of such assembler routines.

An intimate working knowledge of the specific processor's (assembly) instruction set is thus germane to this whole process. As a corollary to this, a good working knowledge of the software development tools available to the programmer is also essential. At the lowest level this will comprise a cross assembler on a host computer, with the assembled code downline loaded in some manner into the target machine. At the other end of the spectrum, it could involve a full Microprocessor Development System (MDS), which incorporates not only the relevant editor, assembler, linker, loader and high-level compiler, but also emulation capabilities of the hardware under development. Many MDSs also include built-in logic analysis capability, to assist in debugging hardware (timing) faults.

Another important consideration is that of interface standards. We introduce several different standards throughout the book. Some 'standards' are in reality more *de facto* industry standards, such as RS232c, whereas others have been formalized, such as Multibus (IEEE796). The thing to watch out for with standards is that different manufacturers might implement certain features in slightly different ways. Standards are also revised from time to time, so it is important to keep abreast of developments in this direction.

It is also imperative to understand the workings of the microcomputer to which the device is being interfaced. Certain assumptions as to how the existing system works could lead to disaster. For example, in the development of the Minix Operating System on the IBM PC, a 16-bit DMA Controller was used (Tanenbaum, 1987). A 4-bit latch was used to derive the four most significant bits in order to form the 20-bit address expected by the i8086 CPU. However, problems were encountered in crossing the inbuilt 640K page boundary of the IBM PC!

In summary, the five important points to keep in mind when interfacing a peripheral device to a microcomputer are:

(1) Understanding how the peripheral device works;
(2) Understanding how the peripheral support chip (off-the-shelf or custom) works (when in doubt, read the instructions!);
(3) A working knowledge of the processor's instruction set;
(4) A working knowledge of any relevant 'standards' used;
(5) An understanding of the microcomputer system to which the peripheral device is being interfaced.

READERSHIP

I have not assumed any specific knowledge in computer architecture on the part of the reader; hence the reason for the inclusion of Chapter 1, which introduces fundamental architecture considerations. Likewise, I have not assumed any background knowledge in terms of electronic hardware, beyond that of high school physics; Chapter 2 introduces the basic electronic building blocks used in interfacing peripheral devices to microcomputers. Micro-computer bus considerations are treated in Chapter 3.

This is *not* an introductory text on assembly language programming; some prior exposure to *an* assembly language is assumed (such as ACM Curriculum-78 CS3: Introduction to Computer Systems).

The bulk of the material on interfacing is presented in the remaining seven chapters. The topics covered include parallel, serial (including data communications), CRT displays, hard copy units, timer/counters, analog-to-digital and digital-to-analog converters and disk drives.

The book is suitable for teaching a one semester course on Micro-computer Interfacing, as specified in ACM Curriculum-78 CS4: Introduction to Computer Organization. Indeed it has been successfully used as such for several years now at the University of Wollongong. To this end, review questions are presented at the end of each chapter in order to test the reader's understanding of the topics presented therein.

I have always been a firm believer in the proverb 'one picture is worth more than a thousand words'. Accordingly, I have *deliberately* made extensive use of diagrams throughout this text. It is my belief that *seeing* how a particular peripheral device works is half the battle in interfacing it to a computer. Indeed this book grew out of a set of overhead transparencies used by the author to teach the third-year Microcomputer Interfacing course to Computer Science majors at the University of Wollongong.

ACKNOWLEDGEMENTS

I would like to thank Professor Juris Reinfelds who had the foresight that my CSCI334 Microcomputers Course Notes would be suitable for publication in book form. Thanks are also due to Associate Professor Greg Doherty for providing the facilities within the Department of Computing Science at the University of Wollongong for writing this book. I would also like to thank Michael Milway, David Wilson and the UK reviewer for their excellent proofreading of the original manuscript; they offered many helpful suggestions on how it could be improved. Thanks are also due to Phillip McKerrow, Ross Nealon and Stephen Troth for their help along the way. The support and understanding of my family is also much appreciated: thank you, Cassandra, Nathan, David and Kate.

I would also like to thank the following companies for permission to reproduce material from published sources: Addison-Wesley Publishing Co. Inc., Analog Devices Inc., Apple Computer Inc., International Business Machines Corp., Intel Corp., Motorola Inc., Prentice-Hall Inc., Rockwell International Corp., Texas Instruments Inc. and Western Digital Corp.

Publishers acknowledgement

The publishers wish to thank the following for permission to reproduce figures and tables: Figures 4.22–4, 5.26–7, 6.22–4, 6.35–7, 8.16–7, 10.26, B.2, B.5–9, B.11–18 and Tables 5.3, 8.2, 10.4, B.2–7 reprinted by permission of Intel Corporation, © Intel Corporation from the following publications: iAPX 286 & 386™ Programmers & Hardware Reference Manuals; Microsystems Components Handbook (1985); Data Sheets i8255, i8251, i8275, i82786, i8256, i8237, i8089, i82258, i8272 and i82380. Figures 3.13, 3.25 and 10.14: H. S. Stone, *Microcomputer Interfacing*, © 1982, Addison-Wesley Publishing Co., Inc., Reading MA. (Figures 6.11 and 7.22). Reprinted with permission of the publisher.

Contents

Trademark notice

Apple®, AppleTalk®, and Macintosh® are registered trademarks of Apple Computer Incorporated.
Laserwriter™, Lisa™ and Quickdraw™ are trademarks of Apple Computer Incorporated.
Bisync™, CGA™, IBM-PC™, PC/XT™, PC/AT™, PS/2™, PC-DOS™, MCA™, SDLC™, SNA™ and VGA™ are trademarks of the International Business Machines Corporation.
CP/M™ is a trademark of the Digital Research Corporation.
Ethernet™ is a trademark of the Xerox Corporation.
Exec™, SYS/32™ and Tri-State™ are trademarks of the National Semiconductor Corporation.
Freestyle™ is a trademark of Wang Laboratories.
HPIB™ is a trademark of Hewlett Packard.
I²C-bus™ is a trademark of Philips.
iPSC™, iRMX86™ and Multibus™ are trademarks of the Intel Corporation.
MACSYM™ and μMAC™ are trademarks of Analog Devices Incorporated.
MC68000™, MC68020™, MC68030™ and RMS68K™ are trademarks of the Motorola Corporation.
MS-DOS™ and OS/2™ are trademarks of the MicroSoft Corporation.
Nubus™ is a trademark of Texas Instruments Incorporated.
PDP-11™ and VAX™ are trademarks of the Digital Equipment Corporation.
PostScript™ is a trademark of Adobe Systems Incorporated.
Smartmodem™ is a trademark of the Hayes Corporation.
STD-bus™ is a trademark of the Pro-log Corporation/Mostek Incorporated.
UNIX™ is a trademark of AT&T.
VMEbus™ is a trademark of Mostek Incorporated/Motorola Corporation/Philips-Signetics.
Z80™ and ZRTS™ are trademarks of the Zilog Corporation.

1

Microcomputer Architecture and Interfacing

OBJECTIVES

This first chapter introduces microcomputers from the viewpoint of computer architecture. The fundamental instruction fetch–decode–execute cycle is discussed, as it relates to the classic Von Neumann architecture.

The basic CPU–memory interface is discussed, along with the organization of information within memory. Interfacing between the CPU and peripheral devices is introduced, together with the fundamental Input/Output (I/O) techniques of polling, interrupts and Direct Memory Access (DMA).

1.1 INTRODUCTION

It is possible to view microcomputers in a number of different ways, depending on a person's particular background and/or bias. To the digital design engineer, they are often viewed as programmable hardware devices which add flexibility and versatility to their designs, often at the sacrifice of speed. To the mainframe or minicomputer specialist, they are often viewed as slower, more limited subsets of 'real' computers. Programmers often regard microcomputers as primitive devices, requiring programming at the assembly language level.

These days microcomputers have become powerful enough to rival the processing capabilities of mainframe and minicomputers of just a couple of years earlier. In terms of functionality, there is really no significant difference between mainframes, mini- and microcomputers. By far the majority of computers consist of the same three main functional units: the Central Processing Unit (CPU, or simply, processor), memory, and Input/Output (I/O). These functional units are connected together via a number of parallel lines (wires). These data wires are grouped in lots of 8, 16 or 32, and constitute the system data bus.

In a mainframe computer, each functional block consists of one or more free-standing cabinets, each housing several Printed Circuit Boards (PCBs). The functional blocks within a minicomputer each comprise several PCBs, and are housed inside a couple of cabinets at most. A microcomputer, by way of contrast, can be constructed on a single PCB, or in the limit, within a single Integrated Circuit (IC) package. In a microcomputer, the CPU is usually contained within a single Very Large Scale Integrated (VLSI) circuit, the I/O interface within a couple of large scale (and/or medium scale) ICs, and memory within a bank of VLSI (or LSI) chips.

Programs are stored in memory and carry out operations on data which is also stored in memory. This stored program concept can be traced back to the times of Babbage (mid 1840s), amongst others. In the classic Von Neumann computer (circa 1945), there is no distinction between programs and data; they are both stored in the same memory. Von Neumann machines are characterized by the following:

    (1)   data and instructions share the same memory,
    (2)   memory is linear (one dimensional),
    (3)   instructions and data are indistinguishable, and
    (4)   data has no inherent meaning.

Utilizing the same memory for programs and data means that we can apportion the amounts of memory for each as required (however, it is often difficult to estimate *beforehand* how much memory space to allow for programs, and how much to allow for data). A single memory also reduces the number of data paths (highways/buses) from one section of the computer to another. Such a scheme also allows for 'self-modifying code', which can be a disadvantage if programmed incorrectly (since the CPU is capable of interpreting the same stored information as *either* instructions *or* data, depending on the context).

The internal construction of computers has changed little since the times of Von Neumann; most modern-day micro-/mini-/mainframe computers are *still* based on the Von Neumann concept. Two notable exceptions are the Intel i8048/51 single-chip microcomputer and the Motorola MC68030 microprocessor. These machines employ a Harvard architecture which separates out the program and data spaces. A Harvard machine has the advantage that the *instruction* word length is not set by the *data* word size, as it is in a Von Neumann machine. Moreover, the width of the registers need not necessarily be restricted to some multiple of the word size.

1.2   MICROCOMPUTER ARCHITECTURE

Architecture is defined as the art or science of building, including planning, designing, construction and decoration (bells and whistles). It is used in this same sense when describing both buildings and computers. In other words, a computer architect is concerned with the planning, design, construction and 'decoration' of computers.

The internal construction, or architecture, of a typical microcomputer is shown in Figure 1.1. The CPU can be likened to the conductor in an orchestra; it synchronizes the efforts of all the individual orchestra members. Contained within the CPU is a set of registers, an Arithmetic and Logic Unit (ALU) and a control unit. These three sections are connected by an internal bus, which may not necessarily be the same width as the external bus.

In conventional computers, programs are stored (in binary form) in memory as a series of sequential instructions. Program execution consists of repeatedly fetching, decoding and executing these instructions, one at a time.

Figure 1.2 shows how typical instructions are stored. Consider the case of the Intel i8086: if regarded by the CPU as an instruction, the binary pattern $F4_{16}$ would be interpreted as 'halt the operation of the CPU' (this instruction is often used for diagnostic purposes during software debugging). On the other hand, if regarded as data, this binary pattern would be simply F4H- (exadecimal).

The register set comprises both general-purpose and special-purpose types. One of the dedicated (special) registers is the program counter. This register points to the memory location where the next sequential instruction is to be found. It becomes updated automatically following the execution of the current instruction. Another special-purpose register is the Instruction Register (IR). This register temporarily stores instructions fetched from memory, and passes them on to be decoded by the control unit. Another special register is the Stack Pointer (SP), which is used as a pointer to an area analog. Such a scheme also allows for 'self-modifying code', which can be a disadvantage of programming incorrectly (since the CPU is capable of interpreting the same stored information as either instructions or data, depending on the context).

The internal construction of computers has changed little since the time of Von Neumann and most microcomputers and mainframe computers are still based on the Von Neumann model. The notable exceptions are the Intel i80-860 single chip microcomputer and the Motorola MC68030 microprocessor. These machines employ a Harvard architecture which separates out program from data spaces. A Harvard machine has the advantage that the instruction word length is not set by the data word size, but is in a Von Neumann machine. Moreover, the width of the registers need not necessarily be restricted to some multiple of the word size.

1.2 MICROCOMPUTER ARCHITECTURE

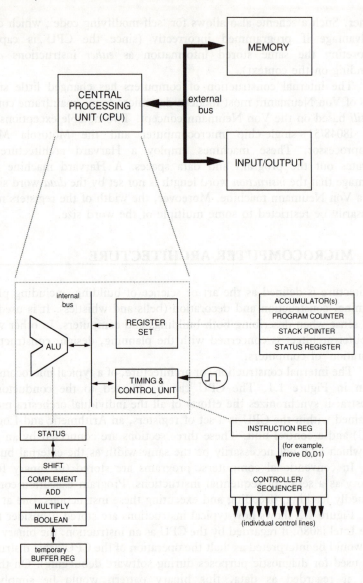

Figure 1.1 Typical microcomputer architecture.

of memory reserved as a push-down stack (a Last In, First Out queue (LIFO)), for the temporary storage of variables. The accumulator holds data fetched from memory, passes this data onto the ALU for some calculation, receives results back from the ALU and passes these results back to memory. The Status Register (SR) reflects the current state of the CPU.

Instructions fetched from memory are passed via the IR to the control

i8086	(binary) MEMORY CONTENTS	(hexadecimal) MACHINE CODE REPRESENTATION	ASSEMBLER MNEMONIC	INSTRUCTION
	1 1 1 1 0 1 0 0	F4H	HALT	causes the CPU to cease operation

MC 68000	MEMORY LOCATION		MEMORY CONTENTS		
	(binary)	(hex)	(binary)	(hex)	ASSEMBLER MNEMONIC
0001 0000 0000 0000 0000		$10000 $10002 ($10004) ⋮	0010 0000 0011 1100	$203C $ABCD ($xxxx) ⋮	MOVE.L #$ABCD,D0 (next instruction)

Figure 1.2 Binary representation of programs (and data).

unit for decoding and subsequent execution, as indicated in Figure 1.3. The instruction decoder determines what operation needs to be performed. The control unit (controller/sequencer) carries out the decoded instruction, by selecting the appropriate combination of individual control lines.

An instruction fetch involves loading the IR with the contents of a particular location, followed by incrementing the program counter to the next

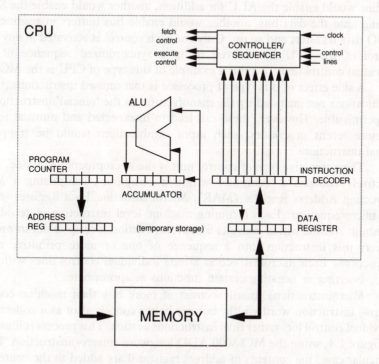

Figure 1.3 Instruction decoding within the CPU.

sequential location (unless the current instruction is a branch or jump). This sequence can be described in C as follows:

```
/* Instruction Fetch */
{
    addr_reg = Prog_Count;    /* load next address from PC → addr bus */
    bus = read;               /* set control logic for a bus read (!read
                                 = write) */
    Instr_Reg = data_reg;     /* load data bus into instruction register */
    Prog_Count ++;            /* increment program counter */
}
```

The control unit itself can be of two different types, either hardwired or microprogrammed. The advantage of the former is speed (being essentially a hardware technique), and the latter flexibility (being essentially a software technique).

Some of the earlier 8-bit processors employed a hardwired control unit consisting of a large combinational logic circuit, where, depending on the combination of input signals, the output lines are activated accordingly. The inputs to the control unit are nothing more than the machine code (binary) instructions. The control unit outputs are the individual (dedicated) control lines, used to enable or activate other sections within the CPU. For example, one line would enable the ALU for addition, another would enable the SR for reading onto the data bus, another would enable bus buffers in readiness for an I/O data transfer, and so on. Only *one* such control is activated at any time; control of the CPU is achieved using a synchronized sequence of such individual control lines. A typical example of this type of CPU is the MC6800.

A side effect of this type of processor is that unused instructions (binary combinations not included by the manufacturer in the 'official' instruction set) are permissible. However, these can lead to unexpected and unusual results. In more recent processors, such input combinations would be trapped as 'illegal instructions'.

The alternative type of control unit is the microprogrammed one, which effectively contains a 'computer within a computer', comprising a Micro-instruction Address Register (MAR), Microinstruction Data Register (MDR) and microsequencer. Each incoming machine level instruction is decoded by an inbuilt routine which consults a microinstruction lookup table, in order to convert this instruction into a sequence of one or more primitive micro-instructions. Each microinstruction affects individual control lines within the CPU, asserting or negating certain functions as appropriate.

Microinstructions usually consist of more bits than machine code (or macro-) instruction word width, but are better conceived of as a collection of individual control bits rather than instructions as such. This process is illustrated in Figure 1.4, using the MC68000 ADD longword (macro-)instruction. In this particular case, the contents of address register 0 are added to the contents of

(MC68000)
MACROINSTRUCTION

ADD.L D0,A0

MICROINSTRUCTION SEQUENCE

(i)   move contents of D0 onto Data Bus
(ii) move contents of Data Bus into ALU port-1
(iii) set ALU for addition
(iv) move contents of A0 onto Data Bus
(v)   move contents of Data Bus into ALU port-2
(vi) perform addition
(vii) move contents of ALU O/P port onto Data Bus
(viii)move contents of Data Bus into A0
[(ix) increment Program Counter]

(16 bits)

| 1101 0001 1100 0000 |

$D1C0

(much wider word length)

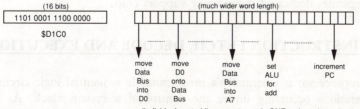

move
Data
Bus
into
D0

move
D0
onto
Data
Bus

move
Data
Bus
into
A7

set
ALU
for
add

increment
PC

(individual control line outputs - only ONE activated at a time)

Figure 1.4 Microinstruction example.

data register 0, with the (32-bit longword) result being stored in D0.

There are two main types of microcoded processors, namely horizontal and vertical. The latter type incorporates additional hardware decoding, which reduces the word length (for example, three bits can be used to select 1-of-2^3 or eight control lines, whereas horizontal microcoding would require eight bits). Most modern-day CPUs employ a compromise between these two types.

The advantage of this type of control unit is that it can be used to emulate *different* instruction sets, and can be altered by the manufacturer at some later time, in order to enhance its instruction set. This was indeed the case with the Motorola MC68010 virtual memory processor which was essentially the same as the earlier MC68000 CPU, but with its microcode altered in order to handle recovery from bus errors, in the event of attempts to access pages of virtual memory not already residing in physical memory. (Virtual memory is a technique whereby large programs residing on disk appear to the user as if they reside in memory; a Memory Management Unit (MMU) handles the swapping of program segments from disk to memory, and vice versa.)

Most microprocessors these days are microprogrammed rather than hardwired.

The third functional block within the CPU is the ALU. One function of the ALU is to perform arithmetic operations such as add, subtract, multiply and divide on operands presented to it by the control unit. Another function of the ALU is to perform boolean operations, such as NOT, AND, OR and EXclusive-OR. Other operations performed by the ALU include clear, increment, decrement, rotate and shift (in both arithmetic and logic form).

ALU operations affect flag bits in the SR. These status or control bits can be subsequently used to test for conditional jumps, which are taken depending on whether a carry, overflow, negative or zero result was obtained.

Some earlier microprocessors were not capable of more than complement, add, AND and OR, whereas these days 16- and 32-bit integer multiply and divide functions are typical. The trend in recent times has been to extend the arithmetic capability of the CPU by incorporating floating-point arithmetic in a separate, dedicated coprocessor support chip.

1.3 INSTRUCTION FETCH, DECODE AND EXECUTION

A microprocessor is essentially a programmable sequential logic circuit, with all operations occurring under the control of a system clock. As already mentioned, in a sequential machine, instructions are fetched one at a time from memory, and passed to the control unit for subsequent decoding and execution. Instructions will take up different amounts of storage space in memory, depending on what the instruction actually does. Thus fetching different instructions will take varying numbers of system clock cycles. In the case where an instruction requires operands from two different areas of memory, additional external fetches from memory will be required as part of the instruction decoding process. Memory reads and writes may take several clock cycles to execute. Thus execution times for different instructions will vary, depending on the addressing mode (namely whereabouts the CPU can find the operand(s) for the current instruction). These times can range from a single cycle for a NOP (No OPeration, or step onto the next instruction), for example, to several cycles for an instruction of the type MOVE (data from) LOC#1, (to) LOC#2, with the addresses specified indirectly in registers.

A computer with a word length of eight bits is not restricted to operands within the range 0 to 255; longer operations simply take two or three such cycles. More can be accomplished during a single instruction fetch–decode–execute cycle in a 16-bit processor, and still more with a 32-bit one. This cannot be extrapolated indefinitely however, since overhead increases with word length : why fetch 32 bits at a time when only the eight least significant bits are required most of the time? (8-bit peripheral devices still predominate in the marketplace, and transmission over serial data communications lines is usually in 8-bit blocks.)

The program counter always points to the memory location where the next instruction is to be found, and is updated automatically as part of the instruction fetch–decode–execute cycle. Usually the program counter will point to the next sequential memory location, but there are times when it does not. For example, with a JUMP or BRANCH instruction, the program counter will be set to point to a non-sequential address. Alternatively, whenever the CPU is interrupted by an external device, the contents of the

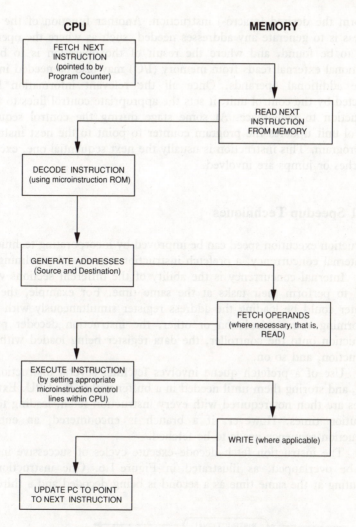

Figure 1.5 Instruction Fetch, Decode and Execute Cycle.

program counter will be overwritten with the starting address of the appropriate interrupt service routine. This has repercussions in a Von Neumann machine, where it is possible for the program counter to be inadvertently set to point to data rather than an instruction; the control unit will still attempt to decode this binary information as if it were an instruction.

Program execution consists of nothing more than repeated instruction fetches, decodes and executions. Figure 1.5 describes this process in more detail. Once an instruction has been read in from memory, it is passed to the control unit for decoding. This decoding process involves consulting a lookup table, in order to determine the sequence of microinstructions needed to perform the desired (macro-) instruction. Another function of the decoding process is to generate any addresses needed, such as where the operand(s) is (are) to be found, and where the result of the operation is to be stored. Additional external reads from memory (I/O) may also be needed in order to locate additional operands. Once all the relevant information has been collected by the control unit, it sets the appropriate control lines to allow this instruction to take place. At some stage during the control sequence the control unit updates the program counter to point to the next instruction in the program. This instruction is usually the next sequential one, except when branches or jumps are involved.

1.3.1 Speedup Techniques

Instruction execution speed can be improved by incorporating techniques such as internal concurrency, a prefetch instruction queue and pipelining.

Internal concurrency is the ability of the different sections within the CPU to perform their tasks at the same time. For example, the program counter could be loading the address register simultaneously with the ALU performing some calculation or other, the instruction decoder passing an instruction onto the controller, the data register being loaded with the next instruction, and so on.

Use of a prefetch queue involves fetching several instructions at one time, and storing them until needed in a buffer within the CPU. External bus cycles are then not required with every instruction fetch, leading to reduced execution times. However, if a branch is encountered, an entirely *new* instruction sequence needs to be fetched.

The instruction fetch–decode–execute cycles of successive instructions can be overlapped, as illustrated in Figure 1.6. One instruction can be executing at the same time as a second is being decoded and a third is being

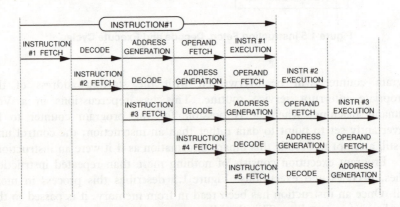

Figure 1.6 Overlapping of instruction cycles.

fetched from memory. This results in a certain degree of concurrency, which in turn leads to higher system throughput. Again, however, some mechanism must be provided for inhibiting such overlapping in the event of a branch (jump) being encountered (although the whole process can be reinitiated from a new, non-sequential starting address). Moreover, it could be possible for the second instruction to finish executing *before* the first instruction, which could produce undesirable effects. Consider, for example, the following code fragment:

```
move D1,D2      ;move contents of reg. D1 → reg. D2
not   D2        ;take the complement of reg. D2
```

If the second instruction finishes before the first, then the wrong complement value – the old value of D2 – will be stored in register D2. Thus more care has to be taken when overlapping instructions, in order to overcome such potential problems.

Apart from prefetch queues and instruction overlapping, pipelining techniques can also be employed. The MC68030 processor, for example, uses a three-stage instruction pipe. This allows for concurrent operation of up to three words of a multiword instruction, or three consecutive single-word instructions. Instructions are loaded during instruction prefetch into the first stage. The second stage will already hold any immediate data or extension words required by the control and execution units. The third and last stage of the pipe produces fully decoded and validated instructions. (The MC68020 is discussed in more detail in Appendix A.)

1.4 CPU–MEMORY INTERFACE

In the early days of computers, memories were fabricated from miniature magnetic cores, but have since been superseded by semiconductor types.

Semiconductor memories are available in two main varieties, Random Access Memory (RAM) and Read-Only Memory (ROM). (Actually it would be more accurate to describe random access memories as read/write, since both RAMs and ROMs are in fact random access. This simply means that any location can be accessed as readily as any other; which can be contrasted with *serial* access storage media such as magnetic tape.)

Programs are usually stored in ROM (so they cannot be overwritten), and data in RAM, although this is not always the case. For example, temporary workspace will often be provided in RAM; conversely, fixed data arrays and lookup tables are often stored in ROM.

Mid 1980s capacities of RAMs and ROMs were 1M × 1-bit and 16K × 8-bit respectively, but these have a habit of doubling every year or so. Memory arrays are constructed out of such chips, to form different word-width memories, as indicated in Figure 1.7. The 16 × 8-bit memory array

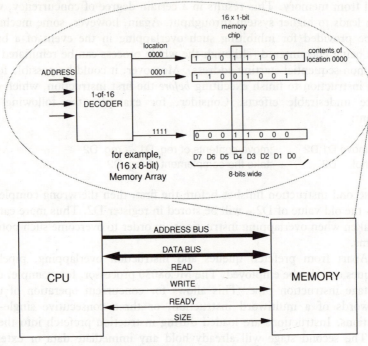

Figure 1.7 CPU-to-memory interface.

shown here is formed from eight 16×1-bit memory chips (ICs). Memory word width has increased over the years in order to support various CPU word sizes, from 8- through 16- to 32-bit processors.

Figure 1.7 also shows the usual interface signals between a CPU and memory. The various memory locations are accessed via the address bus. The contents of each memory location are transferred over the data bus, as indicated in Figure 1.8. Both the address and data buses are simply a collection of parallel wires running across the surface of a PCB between the

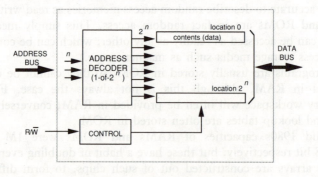

Figure 1.8 Conceptual memory organization.

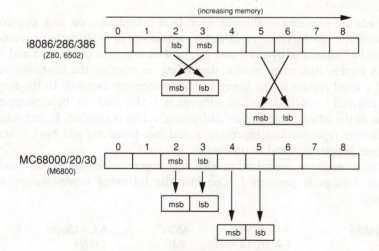

Figure 1.9 Memory alignment.

CPU chip and the memory array. The number of parallel wires that constitute each bus varies with the word size of the particular CPU in question, being typically 16-bit address and 8-bit data for an 8-bit CPU like the Zilog Z80, through 24-bit address and 16-bit data for a 16-bit processor like the MC68000, to 32-bit address and data for a 32-bit processor like the i80386.

Read and write control signals control the memory operation in progress at any time. In practice these signals can be separate, as shown in Figure 1.7 (the case for Intel family processors), or combined on a single line (as R/$\overline{\text{W}}$), as is the case with Motorola processors.

Ready is a handshake signal from the memory to the CPU to indicate that the desired memory location has been accessed, and that its contents have stabilized sufficiently for the next operation to proceed. It is an asynchronous interface signal, in that it bears no particular relation to the system clock.

Size is a signal from the CPU to indicate the current word width on the data bus. Dynamic bus sizing is supported by more recent 32-bit processors such as the MC68020, i80386 and NS32332. This means that the CPU can automatically adjust itself, on a cycle-by-cycle basis, to the bus width connected to it for any particular data transfer.

As already mentioned, memories are constructed out of the basic RAM and ROM chips to form arrays of the required word width (RAMs and ROMs are discussed in Chapter 2). Different assumptions are made by different processor families as to how this memory array is actually organized. Intel iAPX86 family processors (as well as the Zilog Z80 and Rockwell R6502), for example, expect memory to be organized as a succession of bytes; 16-bit words are stored with the least significant byte first, followed by the most significant byte, as shown in Figure 1.9. Motorola MC68000 family processors (as well as the earlier M6800), on the other hand, store words with the *most* significant byte first, as indicated. There is an additional constraint with the MC68000, in that words are required to align on even byte boundaries; no such constraint exists with the i8086. There is, however, ambiguity in i8086 systems; namely, does word#3 consist of bytes#2 and #3, or does it consist of bytes#3 and #4?

A further difference results, depending on whether the least significant byte of a word resides in the lower or higher memory location. In the former case – referred to as 'little-endian addressing' – this leads to 'byte swapping', whereas in the latter – 'big-endian addressing' – this is avoided. Either scheme has different repercussions regarding actual bus transfers, and both schemes have their supporters (and detractors).

Such memory organization also has repercussions as far as reading assembly listings is concerned. Consider the following representative code segments:

i8086:	A1 00 13	MOV	AX,#1300H
	EA 16 14	JMP	1416H
MC6800:	34 38 13 00	MOVE.W	#$1300,D2
	4E F9 14 16	JMP.W	$1416

It is readily apparent that the assembled address locations become reversed with the i8086 code, whereas they can be read directly in the MC68000 listing.

1.5 INTERFACING TO INPUT/OUTPUT DEVICES

Interfacing between a CPU and a peripheral usually involves a tradeoff between hardware and software. The advantage of hardware is speed, whereas the disadvantages are cost and inflexibility. The advantage of software is versatility, whereas its main disadvantage is its slow speed.

Interfacing can be handled entirely by the CPU (in software, with minimal hardware support), or at the other extreme, by a dedicated (intelligent) peripheral controller (in hardware, with minimal software support). Somewhere between these two extremes is the more usual master (CPU)-to-slave (peripheral) configuration, where the (dumb) peripheral support chip has a number of built-in functions, accessible by the CPU writing various bit patterns to its onboard control (command) register(s). The peripheral support chip handles many of the tasks with which the CPU would otherwise need to concern itself.

A recent trend has been the emergence of coprocessor peripheral support chips which enable the CPU and coprocessor to carry out their respective tasks concurrently, communicating with each other upon completion. In many cases, these coprocessors are so intelligent that their processing ability rivals that of the host CPU. The resulting configuration more closely resembles a multiprocessor or distributed processing system, rather than the more traditional CPU–support chip master–slave relationship.

Another trend has been the emergence of custom peripheral chips where, rather than use a standard off-the-shelf support chip, a designer programs a dedicated single-chip microcomputer to perform the desired task (for example, the i8021 used in the keyboard of the Apple Macintosh).

The success in the marketplace of specific microprocessor chips depends not only on the inherent qualities of the parent CPU, but also on the ready availability of both support chips and software for the processor in question. Ready access to data sheets, application notes and technical support (within the local geographical area) are further factors which sway a user towards one particular processor over another.

In terms of functionality, it could be argued that one specific peripheral chip is superior to another; manufacturers can supply so-called 'benchmarks' which purport to show the superiority of their products over their competitors. Such benchmarks should be regarded with a certain degree of healthy scepticism however, unless they originate from an 'independent' third party.

As a rough rule-of-thumb, designers should choose support chips from the same processor family as the CPU itself; whether they be actually manufactured by the chip designer, or by a second-source company manufacturing the chips under license. After all, such support chips are *designed* to work with that particular microprocessor (although this did not prevent Apple from using Intel, Zilog and Synertek chips to support the Motorola CPU in their Macintosh computer!).

Generally speaking, 32-bit support chips from the same manufacturer are more powerful than 16-bit support chips, just as 16-bit chips are more powerful than 8-bit support chips. Comparing 8-, 16- or 32-bit support chips from different manufacturers is not that straightforward however; a lot depends on the particular application. Independent comparisons usually show that such support chips are functionally equivalent at least. Table 1.1 provides a representative sample of the more commonly available microprocessor peripheral support chips.

Nowadays, whenever a new microprocessor is released into the marketplace, it usually incorporates the ability to utilize the already existing (and often quite substantial) support chip and software base from the previous processor generation. For example, in the case of the MC68000, Motorola designed into this processor the ability to interface to the already existing, tried and proven family of MC6800 support chips; although the MC68000 is basically an asynchronous processor, it also has the ability to interface to synchronous support chips. Newer (asynchronous) 16/32-bit support chips were subsequently developed to interface specifically to the MC68000(20,30). A similar situation applied with the Intel i80286(386), which were able to utilize the earlier i8080(86) support chips.

The Synertek/Rockwell 6502 and Motorola MC6800 families are generally interchangeable; each can be used with the opposite processor. Both use memory-mapped I/O and both rely on a synchronizing E(nable)-clock. Intel and Zilog support chips do not depend for their operation on a synchronizing clock signal from the CPU. They also assume ported I/O rather than memory mapping. In recent years, support chips have been designed

Table 1.1 Typical peripheral support chips.

FUNCTION	MOTOROLA	ROCKWELL	INTEL	ZILOG
PARALLEL INTERFACE	MC6821 (8-bit) MC68230 (16-bit)	R6520,22	i8255 i8256	Z8420 Z8036
SERIAL	MC6850	R6551	i8256	Z8440
programmable TIMER	MC6840 (8-bit) MC68230 (16-bit)	R6522,30,32	i8253,54	Z8430 Z8036
CRT CONTROLLER	MC6845 (8-bit)	R6545	i8275	
KEYBOARD			i8279	
BUS CONTROLLER			i8286,89,289 i82188,288	
FLOPPY DISK CONTROLLER	MC6843 (8-bit)	R6565	i8271	
PRIORITY INT. CONTROLLER	MC6828		i8259	
DMA CONTROLLER	MC6844 (8-bit) MC68440 (16-bit)		i8237,57	Z8410 Z8016
MEMORY CONTROLLER			i8202,3,7,8 (DRAM)	
MEMORY MANAGEMENT	MC6829 (8-bit) MC68451 (16-bit)			Z8010,15

specifically to interface to the newer 16/32-bit processors released by Intel, Motorola, Zilog, National Semiconductor and others.

Intel processors support ported I/O, whereas Motorola processors support memory-mapped I/O. Motorola borrowed the idea of memory mapping from the earlier Digital Equipment Corporation PDP-11 and VAX families of minicomputers. The advantage of memory mapping is that all I/O locations are addressed in exactly the same manner as memory locations; no special repertoire of I/O instructions is therefore required (along with the various addressing modes for each). Thus the overall size of the instruction set is reduced. The following are representative instructions for both ported and memory-mapped I/O:

i8086	MEMORY → REGISTER:	mov	AX,MEM#1
i8086	I/O DEVICE → REGISTER:	in	AL,PORT#1
i8086	I/O DEVICE → MEMORY:	in	AL,PORT#1
		mov	MEM#1,AL
MC68000	MEMORY → REGISTER:	move	MEM#1,D0
MC68000	I/O DEVICE → REGISTER:	move	DEV#1,D0
MC68000	I/O DEVICE → MEMORY:	move	DEV#1,MEM#1

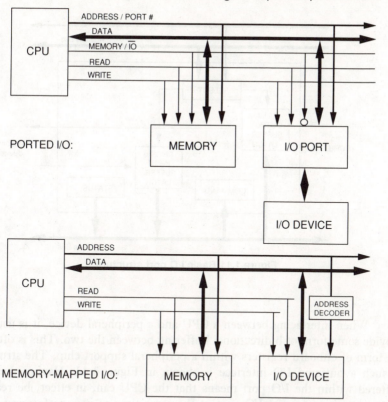

Figure 1.10 Ported versus memory-mapped I/O.

Most assemblers allow for the appropriate naming of memory and I/O ports, irrespective of whether ported or memory-mapped I/O is in use.

A disadvantage with memory mapping is that some additional external address decoding is necessary to discriminate between memory and I/O devices (this is done within the CPU for ported I/O schemes). Another disadvantage is that some of the available address space is taken up with I/O device locations; not all of it is available for memory. Note, however, that with ported I/O systems, not all of the available I/O address space is always used. This means that memory-mapped I/O is more flexible; you only ever use what you really need in any particular application.

It should be pointed out that memory mapping can be used with Intel processors, over and above the inbuilt ported I/O structure, assuming that the additional external decoding circuitry is provided.

Both types of I/O are illustrated in Figure 1.10, where it is seen that one additional interface signal is required for ported I/O, in order to distinguish between memory space and I/O space (memory and peripheral devices occupy the *same* space in systems utilizing memory-mapped I/O).

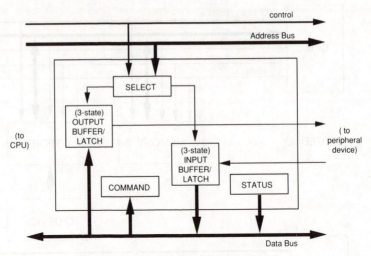

Figure 1.11 Basic I/O port structure.

When interfacing between a CPU and a peripheral device, it is usual to provide some form of bidirectional buffering between the two. This is often in the form of onboard registers within a peripheral support chip. The structure of such a buffered I/O interface is shown in Figure 1.11. Having the data buffered within the I/O port means that the CPU can, in effect, be reading from (or writing to) the I/O port at the same time as it is performing some other function. This leads to rudimentary concurrent operation. Such buffering also allows for different speeds between the CPU and peripheral device, for example, a printer will not be able to keep pace with characters reaching it from a CPU: a block of characters (say 256 bytes) is therefore buffered within the I/O section (in dedicated local memory).

Buffering is also often required between CPU and a peripheral device due to the different electrical characteristics of the two devices. The CPU usually operates at TTL logic levels (+5 V[HI] and 0 V[LO]) whereas peripheral devices can have many different voltage and current characteristics.

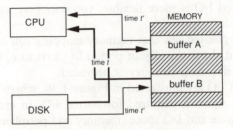

Figure 1.12 Double buffering.

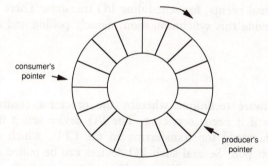

consumer's
pointer

producer's
pointer

Figure 1.13 Circular buffer.

Voltage level translation, scaling (up or down), current boosting (or limiting), or even analog-to-digital (and digital-to-analog) conversion might be required, depending on the peripheral in question.

An I/O interface can also act as a translator, adapting signals from one format (say ASCII or BCD) to another (binary).

Software input and output buffers will often be required over and above the hardware buffers just discussed. Double buffering is illustrated in Figure 1.12, while circular buffering is shown in Figure 1.13.

Double buffering allows the peripheral device to transfer a block of data into one area of memory while the CPU is simultaneously fetching data placed into another area of memory on a previous occasion. Each buffer is used alternately by the CPU and disk. At times, the disk will be transferring data into buffer A, at the same time as the CPU is fetching data from buffer B. At other times, the disk will be loading buffer B, and the CPU will be fetching data from buffer A. Double buffering thus allows for concurrent operation.

Figure 1.13 illustrates the use of a circular buffer, where a producer and consumer are simultaneously filling and removing items from the First-In-First-Out (FIFO) buffer. In practice, care must be taken to select a buffer length sufficiently large so that buffer overflow does not occur (pointer movements are restricted to modulo[buffer length]). The circular list is empty whenever the producer and consumer pointers become equal. A typical application of such a data structure is in a serial data communications link, where characters arrive at random intervals, but where the CPU removes them at regular intervals. (The circular list thus acts as a buffer between the asynchronous peripheral device and the synchronous processor.)

1.6 I/O INTERFACING TECHNIQUES

The times at which data reaches a computer from the outside world can be quite unpredictable. The processor therefore needs some means of synchronizing itself to external events, for scheduling I/O transfers. There are two main methods of achieving this synchronization, namely polling and interrupts.

1.6.1 Polling

Polling is a software technique whereby the processor continually asks a peripheral device if it needs servicing. The I/O device sets a flag in the SR when it has data ready for transferring to the CPU, which the processor notices on its next poll. Several such I/O devices can be polled in succession, with the processor jumping to different I/O software routines, depending on which flags have been set.

Polling works well if a minimum amount of processing is required in response to each set flag. For slow I/O transfers, the processor will be spending most of its time in its polling loop, asking each I/O device in turn if it has any data ready. This amounts to wasted time, during which the CPU could be carrying out other useful tasks. In applications where there is little else for the processor to do (such as in keyboard scanning, for example), this is fine, but for applications which involve substantial calculation as well, this amounts to inefficient use of the processor. The advantage of the polling technique is its simplicity.

1.6.2 Interrupts

Rather than have the CPU continually asking I/O devices whether they have any data available (and finding most of the time that they have not), a more efficient method is to have the I/O devices tell the processor when they have data ready. The processor can be carrying out its normal function, only responding to I/O transfers when there is data to respond to. On receipt of an interrupt, the CPU suspends its current operation (storing the contents of its program counter, SR and other registers), identifies the interrupting device, then jumps (*vectors*) to the appropriate interrupt service routine (interrupt handler).

The advantages of interrupts, compared with polling, are the speed of response to external events and the reduced software overhead (of continually asking I/O devices whether they have any data ready). Its main disadvantages are software commissioning and maintenance, and the additional hardware overhead required (in the form of device identification, supplying vector information and priority resolution).

A typical interrupt interface is shown in Figure 1.14. There are two handshake control lines that interface between the CPU and I/O port, namely Interrupt Request and Interrupt Acknowledge. Most systems will have more than one I/O port, with its associated set of interrupt handshake lines, so that some form of external (hardware) arbitration will be necessary in order to resolve priorities.

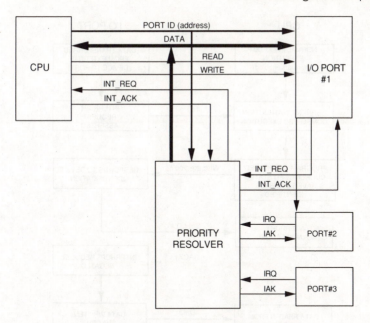

Figure 1.14 Interrupt interface.

This priority resolver decides in which order the I/O ports will be serviced in the event of multiple interrupt requests occurring. It provides the vector address, and also places the port identification number on the data bus once priority has been determined. Such priority resolvers are available in IC form, typical ones being the Motorola MC6828 and Intel i8259 Priority Interrupt Controllers (PICs).

Figure 1.15 shows the sequence of events which occurs in transferring data from an I/O device to the CPU using interrupts. Interrupts have to be first enabled both within the CPU and the device itself, after which the processor continues with its normal program execution. Data becomes ready in the external device (disk drive, say), after which the device flags this fact to the peripheral support chip. The peripheral chip then asserts the interrupt request line. Response to the interrupt is not immediate, but is made pending until the CPU can deal with it, which will typically be at the completion of the currently executing instruction. When the processor is able to respond to the interrupt, it suspends current program execution and identifies the interrupting device. This ID could either be placed on the data bus by the interrupting device, or the CPU could poll all I/O devices to determine which one interrupted. The processor may then acknowledge the interrupt.

Following recognition of Interrupt Acknowledge, the I/O device will usually negate its interrupt request line, then proceed to send data to the CPU over the system bus. After the processor has read the data, it returns to continue execution of the program it was running prior to the interrupt. The I/O device then interrupts the CPU when it next has some input data ready.

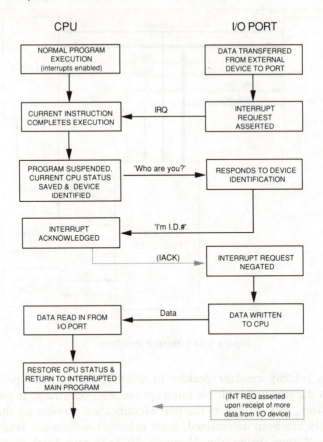

Figure 1.15 Interrupt protocol (read from I/O device).

With more than one possible interrupting device, a priority must be allocated to each. Within the CPU it will therefore be necessary to mask off lower priority interrupts, and to respond only to those of higher priority (non-maskable interrupts, however, must always be responded to by the processor, a typical example being a system control console). In cases where several devices are allocated the same priority level, additional external hardware (in the form of a PIC) will be necessary.

Figure 1.16 shows a main program being interrupted by a printer following the emptying of its printer buffer (and hence is now ready for more data). Before the printer handler is able to refill the print buffer, it is itself interrupted by the higher priority disk drive, which results in a block being transferred between disk and main memory before the printer handler can finish execution.

There will be some means within the CPU whereby interrupts can be enabled and disabled. For example, the very first function performed by the interrupt handler is to 'disable further interrupts', so that the current interrupt

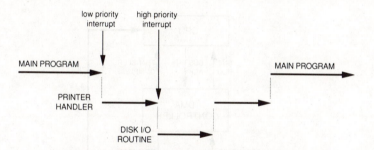

Figure 1.16 Nesting of interrupts (2 levels of nesting).

can be attended to first. Any interrupts that occur during the servicing of this first one will usually be latched into the I/O port, and remain pending until the processor is ready to deal with them (that is, providing their priority level was higher than the current mask).

Some processors also provide an autovector facility, whereby the starting location of the interrupt service routine can be set automatically within the CPU, depending on its priority level. Otherwise, the interrupting device has to place this starting address on the bus itself. This ability caters for so-called dumb peripherals, which are incapable of providing this vector information themselves. Intelligent peripherals, by way of contrast, are able to provide their own vector.

Debugging programs incorporating interrupt handlers is difficult, since the system is no longer deterministic; interrupts can arrive at any time from the outside world. Such timing-dependent bugs can prove difficult to diagnose and correct. Use of interrupts also results in *incomplete* (non-deterministic) solutions, which explains why they are not allowed in real (proven) fault-tolerant systems.

1.6.3 Direct Memory Access (DMA)

Interrupts provide fast response to a peripheral device, but the servicing of the interrupt is performed in software. Sometimes I/O transfers need to occur faster than interrupts can manage, such as with disk I/O, high-speed graphics, or interfacing to a Local Area Network (LAN). The servicing previously carried out by software can be performed faster if it is done by specialized hardware. Such a dedicated controller is designed to perform one specific task only, namely the high-speed transfer of data between the I/O device and memory (and vice versa), but bypassing the CPU. Hence the technique is referred to as Direct Memory Access (DMA).

With DMA, the device actually takes control of the system bus for the time required to transfer the data, then hands back the bus to the CPU upon completion. Figure 1.17 shows a system which uses a DMA Controller

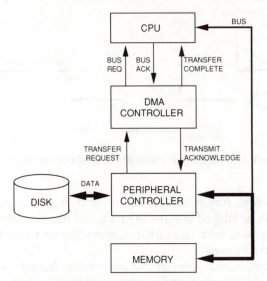

Figure 1.17 Direct memory access.

(DMAC) for data transfers between disk and memory. The disk is connected to a peripheral controller which communicates to the DMAC via the Transfer Request and Transmit Acknowledge handshake lines. The DMAC in turn interfaces to the CPU via the Bus Request, Bus Acknowledge and Transfer Complete lines.

It is important to realise that the DMAC itself is accessed by the CPU as a typical I/O device, with its own unique port ID, vector and interrupt priority. However, once the DMAC has been granted the bus, it cannot be interrupted by the CPU, at least in 'burst' mode (in this sense the DMAC has priority over the processor). With 'interleaved' or 'cycle steal' DMA, the DMAC and CPU share alternate bus cycles.

DMA transfers are inherently faster than either interrupts or polling, since they bypass altogether the imbedded instruction fetch–decode–execute cycles of the CPU. Rather than fetching instructions sequentially from memory, a DMAC has inbuilt (firmware) instructions. Moreover, these instructions can be executed concurrently, for example, transferring data at the same time as decrementing a byte counter.

The internal construction of a typical DMAC is illustrated in Figure 1.18. This particular DMAC has two independent channels. Each channel has dedicated address, command and byte count registers, and interfaces to its corresponding peripheral controller via the usual Transfer Request and Acknowledge lines. Data chain registers are provided to cater for successive block transfers; the starting address of the next successive block is stored therein.

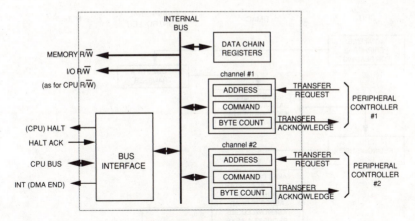

Figure 1.18 DMA controller.

Apart from the address and data buses, the usual CPU interface signals are also provided, namely Read/Write, Halt and Interrupt Request. In the case of a DMA transfer, Interrupt Request serves as an indication to the CPU that the DMAC has finished with the bus (thanks very much!). The Halt and Halt Acknowledge lines are the means whereby the DMAC synchronizes its operation with the processor.

Figure 1.19 shows the sequence of events involved in transferring a single byte from disk to memory using DMA. The CPU first sets up the disk controller for a read, initializes (by setting the number of bytes to be transferred, and setting the DMAC for a read or write operation) and starts the DMAC. The disk controller then requests a transfer from the DMAC. The DMAC does not respond immediately, but waits until the peripheral device actually has some data ready to transfer. Once it has, the DMAC requests the system bus from the processor. Unlike the situation with interrupts, the CPU *can* respond immediately, since its internal state is not changed during DMA cycles; there is no need to push (or pull) any information onto the stack (indeed this would defeat the purpose of DMA).

Once the DMAC takes control of the bus, it places the memory start address of the desired block in the address register, acknowledges the peripheral controller's request, then requests the data from the peripheral. The peripheral controller then inverts the Read/Write line (since a *read from* disk corresponds to a *write to* memory), and places the data on the bus. The data is latched into memory, after which the DMAC acknowledges the transfer to the disk.

The peripheral controller negates the Transfer Request line, and waits for the next byte to become available from disk (there can be quite a mismatch in speed between the peripheral, peripheral controller and DMAC). The DMAC relinquishes the bus, increments the start address register and

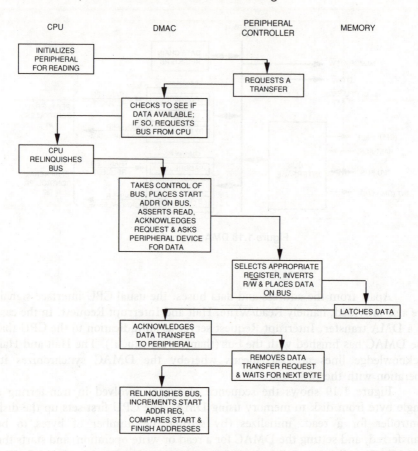

Figure 1.19 DMA handshake protocol.

compares the start and finish addresses. If they are equal, the DMA transfer is terminated and the DMAC interrupts the CPU (DMA end). If they are not equal, the DMAC waits for the next transfer request from the disk controller. Thus, the DMAC keeps a record of how many bytes have been transferred, how many bytes are still left to transfer and the starting addresses in both memory and disk.

The characteristics of some representative DMACs are summarized in Table 1.2. All support at least two independent DMA channels, with each channel having its own dedicated address, command and byte count registers. A data chain register is often also provided, which supports the repeated transfer of the same block of data. Maximum data transfer rates range from 1.6 to 32 Mbyte/second.

The MC6844 DMAC is designed to work with a synchronous CPU (one that can supply an E-clock). Apart from address, byte count, control, interrupt and data chain registers, each channel has associated with it a

Table 1.2 Representative DMACs.

DMAC	HOST CPU	MAX TRANSFER RATE (MBytes/sec)	ADDRESSING CAPABILITY	DATA CHAINING	NO. OF CHANNELS
MC6844	MC6800	2	16 bits	yes	4
MC68440	MC60000	5	24	no	2
MC68450	MC60000	5	24	yes	4
i8237	i8086	1.6	16	yes	4
i82258	i80286	8	24	yes	4
i82380	i80386	32	32	yes	8

priority control register. The register is used to enable the desired DMA channel, as well as to select which priority scheme is to be used; either rotating or fixed priorities are possible (channel 0 having the highest and channel 3 the lowest priority in the case of the latter).

The MC68440 and MC68450 DMACs can be used with explicit processors (MC68000) or implicitly with hosts employing either two or three handshake protocol (Request, Acknowledge and Ready in the case of the latter). There are 17 registers associated with each channel of the MC68440(450), together with an (8-bit) general control register. DMA requests can be generated either externally by the peripheral device or internally by the DMAC itself. Autorequests can be generated at rates varying from 100% down to one-sixteenth of the available time (the channel always has a request pending at the maximum rate).

The MC68440(450) can support both continue and reload operating modes. In the former, multiple non-contiguous block transfers are possible, whereas the latter allows block transfers to be restarted.

Each channel has three I/O lines associated with it, namely $\overline{\text{Request}}$ and Peripheral Control Line (PCL) (both inputs), and $\overline{\text{Acknowledge}}$ (output). The PCLs are general-purpose lines which can be programmed to act as ready, abort, reload, status or interrupt inputs. There are two device control lines: Data Transfer Complete is an output which indicates a successful transfer, whereas $\overline{\text{Done}}$ is a bidirectional line asserted either by the peripheral device or the MC68440 to indicate that the data currently being transferrred is the last item in the block.

Three different transfer modes are possible with the MC68450 DMAC, namely single block, array chain and linked array chain (chaining is not supported on the MC68440). In transferring single blocks, the programmer must initialize the memory and device address registers as well as the count register. Repeated transfers are possible using continue mode, where the memory address and count registers are automatically loaded from internal registers following completion of each block transfer.

In transferring non-contiguous blocks of data, a record needs to be kept of the starting addresses and lengths of each successive block. This is done in the form of a lookup table in memory. The programmer still needs to load the device and base starting addresses, as well as the base transfer count initially. Blocks cease to be transferred when the base transfer count decrements to zero.

In linked array chaining mode, the programmer only needs to supply the device and base addresses, but not the count. The starting addresses and lengths of each block reside in (non-contiguous) memory; a third entry for each block provides a link to the next block (and a null link serves as a terminator).

Apart from using a separate, dedicated DMAC chip, an alternative approach is to use a processor with inbuilt support for DMA. Such is the case with the Philips SCC68070. This CPU is an enhanced version of Motorola's original MC68000. It incorporates a 68000 CPU, an on-chip MMU, two DMA channels, a serial bus interface (I^2C bus), an RS232c interface and a 16-bit timer. The two independent DMA channels have a fixed priority, and the maximum transfer rate is 1.6 Mbyte(word)/second, in either cycle-steal or burst mode. Transfers can take place either from memory to memory using channel 2, or simultaneously from memory to peripheral on channel 1 and from peripheral to memory on channel 1. The transfer format can be either byte or word. DMA signals are compatible with the MC68440(450); each channel has a $\overline{\text{Request}}$ input and an $\overline{\text{Acknowledge}}$ output. Other DMA handshake signals include a $\overline{\text{Device Ready}}$ input, a $\overline{\text{Device Transfer Complete}}$ output, and $\overline{\text{Done}}$, which indicates the last item in a block transfer.

There are five registers for each channel, as well as seven general registers in the Intel i8237DMAC. Each channel has a base address, base word count, current address and current word count register (all 16-bit), together with a mode register. One of the following four modes can be selected: single transfer, block transfer, demand transfer or cascade mode. (In demand mode, the peripheral device is allowed to 'catch up' with the DMAC following temporary exhaustion of available data, by reasserting the DMA Request input.)

The handshake signals between an i8237 and the host CPU are Hold Request (HRQ) and Hold Acknowledge (HLDA), and between the i8237 and peripheral device they are DMA Request (DREQ) and DMA Acknowledge (DACK). When cascading DMACs, the HRQ and HLDA of the second tier i8237s are connected to the DREQ and DACK lines of the first tier i8237 DMAC.

When a channel is running in autoinitialize mode, an $\overline{\text{End of Process}}$ input will cause the base address and base word count registers to be automatically reinitialized without needing assistance from the CPU, such that a further DMA transfer can proceed as soon as the next DREQ is detected. A choice of channel priorities is available on the i8237, namely fixed (channel 0 having highest priority), and rotating.

Like the SCC68070, the i8089 dedicated I/O processor incorporates two DMA channels, and is designed to expand the instruction set of an i8086(88) host logically. It can address 1 Mbyte of memory, and can support any combination of 8- or 16-bit buses. It is capable of transfer rates of up to 1.25 Mbyte/second. Internally, the i8089 is a dedicated CPU, tailored specifically for I/O transfers. The i8089 is capable of operating in either local or remote mode. In local mode, the i8089 and host CPU share the same bus and system buffers, whereas in remote mode its bus is physically separate from the system bus. The i8089 I/O processor communicates with its host CPU via shared memory locations.

Intelligent DMA functions such as translation, search and word assembly (and disassembly) are supported within the i8089 instruction set. Flexible termination conditions are also possible, ranging from single transfer, mask compare, byte count expired to external termination.

Separate registers are provided for each DMA channel, in order to control their respective transfers, and to process their own instruction stream (there being four 20-bit registers and four 16-bit registers per channel).

The 16-bit i82258 Advanced DMA Controller is designed to operate with an i80286 CPU rather than an i8086. Each of its four channels has three I/O pins associated with it: DMA Request, DMA Acknowledge and End Of DMA. Channel 3 can be programmed to act as a multiplexer channel, for connecting up to 32 slow peripherals (up to 30 kbaud). Each channel has 11 associated registers, and there are five general registers. The i82258 supports both command and data chaining. Command chaining, together with inbuilt data manipulation capability (such as compare, verify and translate), allows simple I/O programs to be executed without referring back to the CPU. Moreover, *conditional* command chaining is also supported.

Data chaining allows for the linking of scattered data blocks into a single block (and vice versa). Data blocks can be included, removed or altered in sequence *dynamically*, thus allowing the host i80286 to manipulate link pointers.

Automatic assembly of bytes into words (and disassembly of words into bytes) allows the i82258 to interface to both 8- and 16-bit peripheral devices.

The i82258 does all of its processing on blocks resident in memory. Following initialization by the CPU, it fetches its own code from memory, thus enabling the i82258 to work *concurrently* with its host CPU.

The i82380 DMAC includes other system support functions besides DMA; an interrupt controller, timers, wait state generator, DRAM refresh controller and reset logic are also included. The interrupt controller can support 15 external devices, as well as generating five internal interrupts. Each interrupt source has its own unique programmable interrupt vector. There are four 16-bit timers. Each channel of the i82380 can transfer data between devices of different path widths, and can be programmed to operate in several different operating modes.

In practice, manufacturers do not always use standard off-the-shelf DMACs in their systems. Apple, for example, used a proprietary DMAC in their Macintosh computer, built from PALs (programmable logic devices are covered in more depth in Chapter 2). DMA is used for updating the bit-mapped Macintosh screen, generating sounds and controlling the disk motor speed. DMA is not employed for disk accesses, which explains the comparatively slow transfer rates of the Macintosh.

The NeXT computer likewise uses a custom VLSI DMAC. *Twelve* DMA channels are provided, namely two Ethernet (one transmitter, one receiver), two disk (one SCSI hard disk and one magneto/optical), two sound (one input and one output) and one each for video, serial I/O, digital signal processor (onboard Motorola DSP56001), printer, memory-to-DMA register and DMA register-to-memory.

1.7   SOFTWARE I/O DRIVERS

One function of a computer's Operating System (OS) is to provide a set of high-level routines for interfacing the various I/O devices to the CPU. These I/O routines relieve applications programmers from having to concern themselves with the low-level (hardware) details of the peripheral devices in question. These I/O routines together constitute the software driver.

Each peripheral device has associated with it, within the software driver, a Device Control Block (DCB). Entries in this DCB describe the particular device characteristics, such as the number of read/write heads, number of cylinders and number of tracks per cylinder in the case of a multiplatter disk drive. The DCB also keeps track of useful information (such as at which track and cylinder its head(s) is (are) currently located, whether it was moving in or out), as well as cumulative statistics (such as the number of seeks, number of reads/writes, error checking, and so on).

The software driver can utilize this information in order to optimize disk I/O (in terms of speed). For example, rather than handle all disk accesses as they arrive at random, they can be queued such that all requests inwards from the current position are handled in increasing order (followed by all similar requests outwards from the current position). In this manner it is possible to optimize head movement, and hence system throughput. (Disk drives are covered in more detail in Chapter 10.)

An applications programmer does not want to be bothered with such details; in fact it is the job of the software driver to mask such low-level information from the application at hand. Apart from such shielding, another important characteristic of a software driver is device independence. As far as the application software is concerned, a disk drive is a disk drive (and similarly for printers, terminals, and so on)!

Differences between various I/O devices of the same type are handled by the software driver, which performs all logical-to-physical device mapping (translation). For example, a particular OS may expect data to be handled in 512 byte blocks from disk, despite the fact that the CPU actually handles the data in 256 byte blocks.

A common interface for *all* I/O devices, irrespective of type, would be preferable from the point of view of the applications programmer, and this is indeed provided by some software drivers (such as UNIX and OS9).

Apart from device independence and masking the low-level details from the user, a software driver has to queue I/O requests and return data to the various applications running in a multitasking environment. Such a queue and system interface resides at the high end of the software driver. The middle portion will typically comprise all the logic required for protocol translation, while the interrupt handler and dispatcher will be located at the low end.

Interrupt handling was discussed earlier in Section 1.6.2; suffice it to say here that the software driver handles all of the task switching detail necessary for handling interrupts (such as fetching the interrupt vector, saving the current context on the stack, and so on). Buffering likewise is masked from the application.

The functions of the low-level dispatcher are twofold: queue management (pushing and popping from the FIFO queue) and dispatching of the various I/O requests (operations) residing therein. Inherent in this is the ability to lock and unlock the system until the current request has been serviced (which is facilitated by the Test-and-Set instruction).

Quite often I/O transfers are required to take place either at a particular instant in time (or as soon as possible thereafter), or alternatively at regular intervals within a given time period. Thus, the peripheral device and the software driver need to be synchronized. This can be achieved by connecting an external pulse generator of known and constant frequency to the Interrupt Request input of the CPU. A simple yet effective clock such as this can be derived from the AC mains supply, interrupting the CPU 50 (60) times every second (hence the name line frequency clock). Hardware watchdog timers are also often used to provide timeouts for the software driver; otherwise the system could hang indefinitely, due to some malfunction of the peripheral device (programmable timers and real-time considerations are covered in Chapter 8).

SUMMARY

In our discussion of microcomputer architecture, we saw that the predominant architecture is still Von Neumann. The three main component parts of the computer were introduced, namely the Central Processing Unit (CPU), Arithmetic Logic Unit (ALU) and register set.

The stored program concept was mentioned, and the fundamental instruction fetch–decode–execute cycle examined. Macroinstructions were seen to break down into a number of more primitive microinstructions within the CPU. Microcoding was discussed, as were different techniques for speeding up a processor's throughput, such as internal concurrency, pipelining and instruction prefetch queue.

The storage of instructions and data within memory was treated, as well as the interface signals between a CPU and memory array. Here we met the concepts of byte swapping and alignment of words in memory.

Next we dealt with the interfacing of Input/Output (I/O) devices to a CPU. This was seen to be facilitated by the use of user-programmable peripheral support chips. Such peripheral chips are connected to the CPU in master–slave configuration, with their onboard command and status registers accessible via the system bus. More recent peripheral support chips comprise dedicated I/O processors, some of which employ a coprocessor philosophy, which leads to concurrent operation of the peripheral chip and the CPU.

Memory-mapped and ported I/O schemes were compared and contrasted, and the advantages and disadvantages of each mentioned.

The need for both hardware and software buffering between CPU and peripheral device was highlighted – the former for matching electrical signal levels, and the latter for the temporary storage of data until the CPU (and/or peripheral) can deal with it.

The basic I/O techniques of software polling, interrupts and Direct Memory Address (DMA) were introduced, and their respective advantages and disadvantages pointed out.

Finally, the basic concepts of software I/O drivers within a computer's Operating System were introduced.

REVIEW QUESTIONS

1.1 What characterizes a Von Neumann architecture?

1.2 Explain the difference between a microinstruction and a macroinstruction.

1.3 The control unit within a CPU can be either hardwired or microprogrammed. Explain.

1.4 Discuss the instruction fetch–decode–execute cycle. How can this be speeded up?

1.5 The i8086 uses little-endian addressing, whereas the MC68000 uses big-endian addressing. Which one leads to byte swapping in memory?

1.6 Discuss the advantages and disadvantages of memory-mapped versus ported I/O.

1.7 Why is buffering important between a CPU and a peripheral device?

1.8 Give an example of where both double buffering and circular buffering would be useful.

1.9   With respect to interfacing generally, what is meant by the term handshaking?

1.10   Discuss the advantages and disadvantages of polling, interrupts and DMA.

1.11   In relation to interrupts, what is meant by the term autovectoring?

1.12   What does chaining refer to in a DMAC?

1.13   What functions does a software driver perform in a computer's operating system?

2

Hardware Building Blocks

OBJECTIVES

In this chapter we concentrate on the electronic building blocks that are used to construct digital computers. We start by considering the fundamental building block, the transistor switch. We then turn our attention to firstly combinational logic, then sequential.

The importance of such functional units as buffer/latches, registers, decoders, adders and timer/counters are also discussed. The concept of programmable hardware units is also introduced.

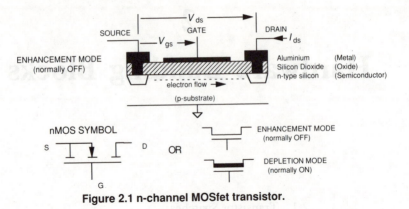

Figure 2.1 n-channel MOSfet transistor.

2.1 TRANSISTOR SWITCHES

At their most fundamental level, computers consist of nothing more than thousands (perhaps millions) of miniature transistor switches, which can only ever be in one of two binary states: either ON (TRUE) or OFF (FALSE). The binary state the switch is in at any particular time depends on the voltage (or current) applied to its input or control terminal.

Figure 2.1 shows the internal construction of a basic transistor switch. It consists of alternate layers of aluminium, silicon dioxide and silicon, grown on a semiconductor substrate, hence its name Metal Oxide Semiconductor (MOS). (Semiconductors are materials that ordinarily do not conduct electrical current, but when doped with certain impurities can be made to conduct. There are two types of semiconductors: n-type, which has an excess of electrons, and p-type, which has a depletion of electrons.)

There will be no current flow through the MOS transistor unless a positive voltage is applied to the gate (or control) input. When this occurs, electrons are attracted towards the positive charge on the gate, and thus form a connecting link along the channel between the two n-type wells located under the source and drain terminals. Electrons can then flow from the external source terminal through the transistor channel and out to the drain terminal, thus constituting a conventional current flow from drain to source.

The insulating silicon dioxide layer between the two conductors (metal and n-type silicon) results in the gate of this type of transistor behaving very much as a parallel plate capacitor. With two such devices connected together, the output voltage of the first transistor will charge up the input 'capacitor' of the second.

Figure 2.1 also shows the n-channel or nMOS transistor symbol (pMOS transistors can also be fabricated, and when both nMOS and pMOS are used in the same device, it is referred to as CMOS or Complementary Metal Oxide Semiconductor).

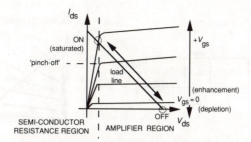

Figure 2.2 nMOS transistor characteristic.

The nMOS transistor characteristic – the plot of output current versus output voltage for various values of control voltage – is illustrated in Figure 2.2. Each member of this family of curves exhibits the same basic behaviour: for small applied output voltage V_{ds}, the device acts as a semiconductor resistor (with the current varying linearly with voltage). For increasing V_{ds}, the curve levels off, with the channel becoming 'pinched off' around the knee of the curve, such that any further increase in V_{ds} results in no further increase in I_{ds}. Increasing the control voltage V_{gs} enhances current flow through the channel, whereas making V_{gs} negative results in a depletion of electrons.

Small changes of V_{gs} result in much larger changes in V_{ds}, and it is this property which enables a transistor to be used as an amplifier. When used as an amplifier, the transistor's operating point varies up and down the load line as indicated. When used as a semiconductor switch, only the two extreme points of the transistor load line are used, namely ON (or saturated) and OFF, and the voltage applied to the gate is used to switch between these two extremes.

Besides the MOS transistor, there is another type which depends for its operation on the *current* applied to its input or control terminal, rather than the voltage. This type of transistor is the bipolar type, formed by connecting three regions of doped silicon together, resulting in either an npn or a pnp transistor. The three regions thus formed are referred to as the base, emitter and collector, as illustrated in Figure 2.3.

Applying a positive voltage to the base will cause a current to flow into the base of the transistor, which in turn will cause a much larger current to flow between collector and emitter. As with the MOS transistor, the bipolar type is used as a switch rather than as an amplifier within a digital computer, and is made to switch between its two extreme operating points – saturation (ON) and cutoff (OFF).

Figure 2.4 shows the use of a bipolar transistor as a logic inverter. The base constitutes the input terminal, the collector the output terminal, and the emitter is connected to ground and serves as the common reference point for both input and output. The DC supply voltage is used to bias the transistor at the required operating point on its output characteristic (the output load line).

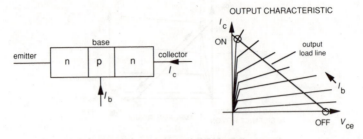

Figure 2.3 Bipolar junction transistor.

Since we are working with a binary system, the voltage levels that can appear at the inputs and outputs of this circuit are +5 V (ON, HI or TRUE) or 0 V (OFF, LO or FALSE) only. Injecting a current into the base input (by applying +5 V at point A) will turn the transistor on, and effectively present a short-circuit connection between collector and emitter. This will cause current to flow from the DC supply, through the load resistor into the collector, and thence through the transistor to ground. Little voltage will be dropped across the transistor itself, so that 0 V will appear at the collector or output terminal. (Note that any device connected to the output terminal will be able to send current back *into* the output terminal of the transistor to ground. Thus bipolar transistors are said to be able to 'sink' current in this state.)

Applying 0 V to the base will cause no current to flow into the input terminal; the transistor will be turned off, and will present an open circuit between its collector and emitter terminals. The only path left for current to flow is then from the DC supply through the load resistor and into the next device connected in series. Assuming little voltage is dropped across the load R_C, then almost all of the +5 V will appear at the output. (Note that in this state the transistor is *sourcing* rather than sinking current.)

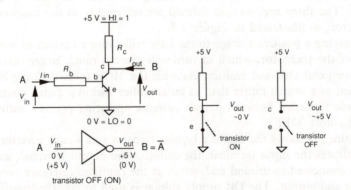

Figure 2.4 Bipolar inverter action.

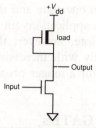

Figure 2.5 nMOS inverter.

The basic action of such a bipolar transistor inverter is to change the logic level at point A to its inverse at point B; +5 V becomes 0 V and vice versa. A similar inverter action occurs in the nMOS transistor shown in Figure 2.5: $+V_{dd}$ applied to the input will turn the nMOS transistor on, thus presenting 0 V at the output; conversely 0 V applied to the input will turn the transistor off, resulting in $+V_{dd}$ appearing at the output. Note that in this circuit a (3-terminal) load transistor is being used in place of a (2-terminal) discrete load resistor, since it is easy to manufacture such a device in IC form.

Whenever the inverters of Figures 2.4 and 2.5 are in their ON state, current will be passing from the DC supply through the transistor to ground. Thus, so long as the transistor is switched on, there will be a certain current drain from the DC supply, which could be derived from the AC mains supply or from batteries.

The CMOS inverter of Figure 2.6 avoids this constant current drain by employing both nMOS and pMOS transistors within the same device. A positive voltage on the gate (with respect to the source) is required in order to turn the lower (nMOS) transistor on; conversely, a negative voltage (0 V) relative to its source is required to turn the upper (pMOS) transistor on. In the former case, the lower transistor will be turned on and the upper transistor off, presenting 0 V at the output terminal. In the latter case, the lower transistor will be off, and the upper transistor on, which results in $+V_{dd}$ appearing at the output. The only time there is a current drain on the DC supply is when the

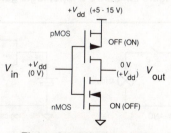

Figure 2.6 CMOS inverter.

transistor is switching between one state and the other. This is why CMOS is the family chosen for portable applications (in other words, where battery life is a critical consideration). Note, however, that the power consumption of CMOS increases rather rapidly with increasing switching speed (since both transistors will be turned on for a longer proportion of time).

2.2 BOOLEAN LOGIC GATES

Besides the inverter already discussed, transistors can be used to fabricate other basic boolean logic gates. Figure 2.7 shows the internal construction of CMOS 2-input NAND- and NOR-gates, which are straightforward extensions of the CMOS inverter of Figure 2.6.

Consider firstly the NAND-gate. The only input combination for which both nMOS transistors are turned on (and both pMOS transistors off) is when $+V_{dd}$ is applied to inputs A and B simultaneously; ground potential then appears at the output terminal. For all other input combinations, either or both of the lower transistors is/are turned off (and at least one pMOS transistor turned on), such that $+V_{dd}$ appears at Y.

In the 2-input NOR-gate, applying $+V_{dd}$ to either or both input(s) will turn one of the nMOS transistors on, so that 0 V appears at Y. The only input combination which causes both nMOS transistors to turn off (and both pMOS to turn on) is when 0 V is applied simultaneously to A and B.

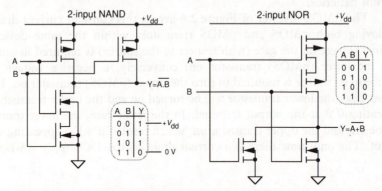

Figure 2.7 CMOS 2-input logic gates.

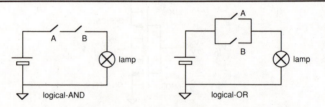

Figure 2.8 Electrical analogies of boolean logic functions.

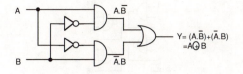

Figure 2.9 Exclusive-OR gate.

Table 2.1 Boolean logic truth tables.

INPUTS		OUTPUTS						
A	B	$\bar{A}$	A.B	$\overline{(A.B)}$	A+B	$\overline{(A+B)}$	A⊕B	$\overline{(A⊕B)}$
0	0	1	0	1	0	1	0	1 ---------HI
0	1	1	0	1	1	0	1	0
1	0	0	1	0	1	0	1	0 ---------LO
1	1	0	1	0	1	0	0	1

FUNCTION	NOT	AND	NAND	OR	NOR	EXOR	EXNOR

SYMBOLS:
Math   ¬   ∧   v   ∀
C-language !   & | ~

CIRCUIT SYMBOL

Electrical analogies of these basic 2-input logic functions are shown in Figure 2.8. In the case of the AND circuit, electrical current will only flow from the battery to the lamp if *both* switches are operated. In the OR circuit, *either* (or both) switch(es) will cause the lamp to light.

These basic logic gates can be used to realize another useful building block, and this is the EXclusive-OR (or EXOR), which is illustrated in Figure 2.9. Its output is true whenever A and B are different (A ≠ B).

Table 2.1 summarizes the fundamental 2-input logic functions, in terms of their individual truth tables (which show the outputs corresponding to all possible input combinations). The standard boolean operators and logic symbols for each gate are also shown.

2.3 INTEGRATED CIRCUITS

We have already seen how a logic gate can be formed from several transistors. Now, rather than fabricate such gates from discrete transistors (as was done in the early 1960s), it is also possible to realize them in integrated form. In an Integrated Circuit (IC), several transistors are formed on the same slice of silicon. All functional units within the logic gate are formed out of transistors,

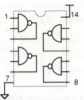

Figure 2.10 7400 quad 2-input NAND.

whether they be used as the switching elements themselves, as load transistors, or as diodes (two-terminal devices which only allow current flow in one direction); hence the term Transistor-Transistor Logic (TTL) – at least where bipolar transistors are employed.

The manufacture of ICs consists of first growing a pure silicon (cylindrical) crystal, then taking a thin slice of this crystal on which the various layers are to be grown. The silicon slice is repeatedly exposed to ultraviolet (UV) light, followed by etching in an acid bath. By placing different masks over the silicon during successive UV exposures, different layers can be formed below the silicon surface, thus allowing transistors to be gradually built up. The (metal) interconnections between these various transistors can also be formed as part of this fabrication process.

The silicon slice is subdivided into a number of square elements (typically $10\,mm^2$). Finally, the slice is tested, then cut up, and the individual dies thus formed are soldered into place inside individual IC packages. The IC package serves two purposes: firstly, it provides a means of interconnection to the outside world, and secondly, it assists in the dissipation of heat generated onboard the chip during normal operation. The package also prevents UV light from impinging on the chip, since this has an adverse effect on the chip's operation. The schematic of a typical IC package is shown in Figure 2.10, which indicates how four 2-input NAND-gates are fabricated within a 14-pin dual-in-line chip carrier.

2.3.1 Scale of Integration

The scale of integration refers to the number of transistors which can be fabricated on a single silicon chip. Developments in miniaturization have continued unabated since the development of the first IC in the late 1950s. Table 2.2 shows the increased miniaturization which has taken place during the last couple of decades, both in terms of the number of transistors and the number of logic gates per device.

By the mid 1980s, it became possible to fabricate hundreds of thousands of transistors on a single chip. Nowadays, high-speed CMOS is the preferred fabrication process; it rivals TTL in speed, but at much lower levels of power dissipation and with a far superior packing density.

Table 2.2 Scale of integration.

SCALE	SSI	MSI	LSI	VLSI
number of gates/chip	1-8	10-100	1000s	10000s
number of transistors	10-20	100-1000	10000s	100000s
first introduced	early 60s	late 60s	early 70s	late 70s

time

Small-scale integrated circuits (SSI) typically consist of one to eight logic gates, each of which consists of half a dozen or so transistors (a typical example is the quad 2-input NAND of Figure 2.10). Medium-scale ICs (MSI) shrink several SSI functions onto a single chip. The adders, decoders, counters and latches discussed later in this chapter fall into this category.

Large-scale integrated circuits effectively shrink several MSI functions onto a single chip, with the physical dimensions of the transistors and interconnecting tracks becoming smaller and smaller. Small-sized memory chips are examples of LSI (a memory chip can be conceived of as an array of data latches – themselves MSI devices). Very Large Scale Integrated (VLSI) circuits are able to incorporate even more functionality, to the point where an entire CPU – comprising registers, ALU and control unit – can be fabricated onto a single chip.

2.4   COMBINATIONAL LOGIC BUILDING BLOCKS

The fundamental logic gates presented in Section 2.2 can be used to provide a great variety of boolean logic functions, simply by interconnecting various types and numbers of gates together. Typical functions are enable gates, comparators, adders, decoders and encoders.

Figure 2.11 shows the use of an AND-gate which performs the enable function. The signal appearing at input A will only be passed through to the output A' if the enable input is HI; applying a 0 will disable the gate, whereas applying a 1 will enable it. The signal on the EN input thus provides a 'window' on the signal appearing on the A (or data) input. If the signal applied to the EN input is derived from a system clock, then the A input is said to be strobed (sampled or steered through the AND-gate) during the time that EN

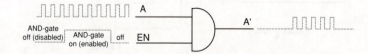

Figure 2.11 AND-gate enable (strobe).

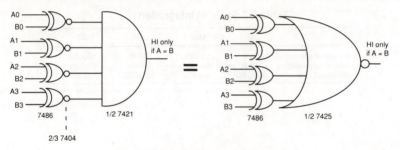

Figure 2.12 EXOR comparator.

is HI. This configuration, where one input is data and the other a control signal, is very commonly encountered in practical circuits.

A different use of an AND-gate is shown in Figure 2.12. Here two 4-bit binary numbers are being compared, bit by bit. Each bit is compared using an EXNOR-gate (you will recall that the basic EXNOR property is one of equivalence – whether or not both bits are the same). In this circuit, a HI input is presented to the AND-gate only if the respective bits of A and B are both 1s or both 0s. Moreover, all four inputs must be HI together in order for a HI to be produced at the AND-gate output. Both circuits shown in Figure 2.12 are equivalent; the one on the right results from realizing that an inverted input AND-gate can be replaced by a NOR-gate. (This is known as De Morgan's Theorem, and can be readily verified by constructing the truth tables for each.)

Apart from boolean functions, combinational logic gates can also be used to form arithmetic circuits. The circuit of Figure 2.13 shows a binary half adder, which can be derived by inspection of the desired truth table on the left (the sum and carry outputs correspond to standard logic gates, as indicated). A full adder requires a third input, to allow for a carry from a previous computation. It is a straightforward matter to construct a full adder from two half adders, and this is illustrated in Figure 2.14. Moreover, full adders can be cascaded to form n-bit binary adders.

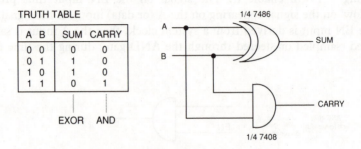

A B	SUM	CARRY
0 0	0	0
0 1	1	0
1 0	1	0
1 1	0	1

TRUTH TABLE

EXOR   AND

Figure 2.13 Binary half adder.

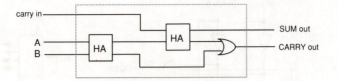

Figure 2.14 Full adder.

Another important combinational building block is the decoder, where n inputs are used to select 1-of-2^n outputs. This is used extensively in address decoding, in order to access unique memory locations (we shall return to this in our discussion of memories in Section 2.6). In the 1-of-2 decoder, outputs CS0 and CS1 are asserted (HI) by applying a 0 and 1 respectively to the A0 select input.

In the 1-of-4 decoder, the binary pattern appearing on the A0 and A1 inputs determine which of the four outputs are asserted (selected), as indicated. This can be readily extended to a 1-of-8 decoder, which would require three select inputs, a 1-of-16 decoder (4 select inputs), and so on.

Apart from the binary decoder of Figure 2.15, another commonly encountered decoder is the Binary Coded Decimal (BCD)-to-7 segment decoder, used in seven-segment LED displays (which are covered in more detail in Chapter 4).

The decoder of Figure 2.15 is readily extended into a demultiplexer, where a single data input is switched through to one of several outputs, depending on the setting of the select (control) inputs. A 1-of-4 demultiplexer is shown in Figure 2.16, based on the decoder circuit of Figure 2.15, but using 3-input AND-gates rather than 2-input ones.

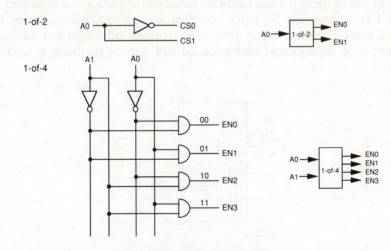

Figure 2.15 Address decoders.

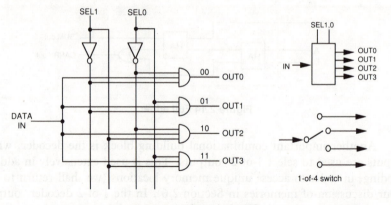

Figure 2.16 Demultiplexer.

The complementary function to demultiplexing is multiplexing, just as encoding is to decoding (another name for multiplexing is switching). Thus, a multiplexer switches 1-of-2^n inputs through to a single output, depending on the setting of the n control inputs.

Figure 2.17 shows a decimal-to-BCD encoder, which consists of 10 inputs and 4 outputs. Depending on which input is asserted at any particular time, the corresponding output lines will be asserted (for example outputs 8 and 1 will be asserted when input 9 is activated). OR-gates replace the AND-gates that we had previously in the decoder.

The simple adder of Figure 2.14 can be easily extended into a parallel adder; eight such adders would be used in a system employing an 8-bit architecture. The four fundamental arithmetic functions required within a computer are addition, subtraction, multiplication and division. All four functions can be derived using hardware based on the basic adder presented in Figure 2.14 (subtraction by two's complement and add, multiplication by repeated shifts left and add, and division by repeated shifts right and subtract. Actually, more sophisticated multiplication and division hardware is used in practice).

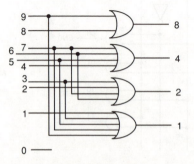

Figure 2.17 Decimal-to-(8421)BCD encoder.

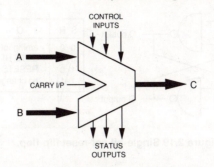

Figure 2.18 Arithmetic and logic unit (ALU).

The ALU of Figure 2.18 would incorporate multiple-bit addition, subtraction, multiplication and division, as well as the fundamental boolean operations of inversion, AND, NAND, OR, NOR and EXOR; the control inputs would be used to select which particular function would be invoked at any particular time. Moreover, status outputs would indicate whether a carry was generated during the last calculation, whether the result was negative, whether it was zero, and so on. A carry input would also enable adds both with and without carry, as well as subtracts with and without borrow.

Such an ALU is available in discrete form (such as the 74LS181 4-bit ALU), but is more likely to be encountered in practice in integrated form, as the ALU within a microprocessor chip. Such ALUs are usually restricted to integer arithmetic, with perhaps double as well as single precision accuracy (and perhaps BCD); floating-point arithmetic is usually handled by a coprocessor chip, such as the MC68881(2) Floating Point Unit or the i8087 Numeric coprocessor. The MC88000 family, by way of contrast, has inbuilt support for both integer and floating-point arithmetic. (The MC88000 is a Reduced Instruction Set Computer (RISC), and is not source code compatible with MC68000 family processors.)

2.5   SEQUENTIAL LOGIC BUILDING BLOCKS

The set-reset latch of Figure 2.19 differs from the combinational circuits we have considered up to now inasmuch as its outputs are fed back to its inputs. Thus its output state depends not only on its current input state (as with combinational logic), but also on its previous output state. Care has to be taken in such circuits however, in order to prevent the outputs chasing the inputs (like a cat chasing its own tail!). A full analysis is beyond the scope of the present text; suffice it to say that this device has two stable states only: SET ($Q = 1$; $\overline{Q} = 0$) and RESET ($Q = 0$; $\overline{Q} = 1$). The behaviour of this circuit is summarized in the truth table of Figure 2.19.

The device is seen to have active LO inputs, such that a LO pulse

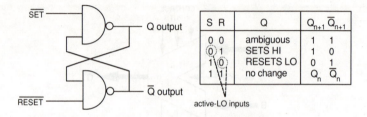

S R	Q	Q_{n+1}	$\overline{Q}_{n+1}$
0 0	ambiguous	1	1
0 1	SETS HI	1	0
1 0	RESETS LO	0	1
1 1	no change	Q_n	$\overline{Q}_n$

active-LO inputs

Figure 2.19 Single-bit set-reset flip-flop.

applied to the $\overline{\text{SET}}$ input (with the $\overline{\text{RESET}}$ input held HI) will set Q HI; conversely, a 0 applied to the $\overline{\text{RESET}}$ input will clear Q to 0. Applying LOs to both the $\overline{\text{SET}}$ and $\overline{\text{RESET}}$ inputs together will cause the Q and $\overline{Q}$ outputs to both go HI together, which represents an ambiguous state. Taking both inputs HI again results in unpredictable behaviour (actually, the device will settle in either its set or reset state, depending on which of the two NAND-gates is the faster). Applying HIs simultaneously to both inputs will affect no change in this circuit, since it has active-LO inputs.

As it stands, this device is found quite often in practical circuits. A typical application is as a reset switch, where earth potential applied momentarily to the $\overline{\text{RESET}}$ input will produce a clean negative pulse output from Q, irrespective of the number of spurious inputs caused by mechanical bounce of the switch contacts (the question of contact bounce will be considered again in Chapter 4).

If steering gates are inserted in between the inputs and the set–reset latch, an active HI device is formed, which has a third (enable or control) input, as well as SET and RESET as before. If this enable input is connected to a system clock, then a clocked set–reset latch is formed.

The set–reset latch of Figure 2.20 would respond to a positive level triggered clock, since it has active HI inputs. Other clocking possibilities are shown in Figure 2.21, where we see that clocks can be either level or edge

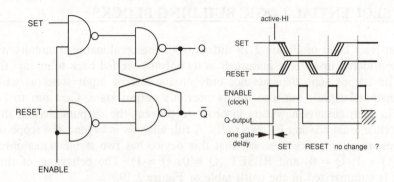

Figure 2.20 Set-reset latch (active-HI inputs).

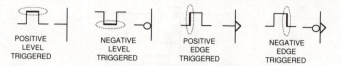

POSITIVE LEVEL TRIGGERED

NEGATIVE LEVEL TRIGGERED

POSITIVE EDGE TRIGGERED

NEGATIVE EDGE TRIGGERED

Figure 2.21 Clocking conventions.

sensitive. Edge triggered devices are usually preferred over level triggered ones, since this leads to more accurate synchronization (edges are only present for very short periods of time).

A further clocking convention is the master–slave one, where two such latches are cascaded together, such that the first acts as a master and the second acts as a slave device. The master device is made to clock on one edge (say, positive) and the slave on the other (say, negative). In this manner the outputs of the master device (which are connected to the inputs of the slave) have time to stabilize (settle) before the slave device is activated. This results in safe, reliable, guaranteed transfer of data within a system. Such a two-phase clocking scheme is used extensively in VLSI circuits.

One way of avoiding the indeterminate state of the set–reset latch is to insert an inverter between the two inputs, such that only half of the possible set–reset truth table is used, as shown in Figure 2.22. The addition of this inverter converts the set–reset latch into a data or D-type latch; the datum present on the D input is passed through to the Q output on the arrival of the next negative clock edge. For n such D-type latches cascaded together, there would be a delay of n clock cycles before data is shifted through the n latches. Thus this type of latch is often used to provide delays in computer circuits.

Figure 2.23 shows the use of four clocked D-type latches in forming a 4-bit latch. The data present on D0–D3 is latched on the rising edge of the $\emptyset$ clock. This data then becomes available on outputs D0'–D3' whenever $\overline{OE}$ (Output Enable) is LO, or until the next rising edge of $\emptyset$, when it is overwritten with new data.

Such latches are used extensively in situations where the incoming (or outgoing) data may only be present for a very short time; latching the data ensures that it will still be available when needed at some later time (either by

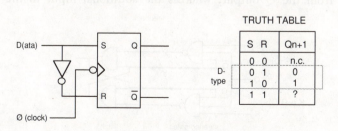

TRUTH TABLE

	S R	Qn+1
	0 0	n.c.
D-type	0 1	0
	1 0	1
	1 1	?

D(ata)

S   Q

R   Q̄

Ø (clock)

Figure 2.22 D-type latch.

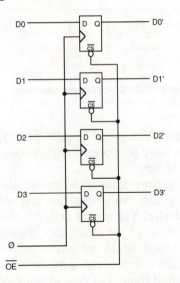

Figure 2.23 Clocked 4-bit data latch.

the CPU or by the peripheral device in question). They are commonly encountered in microcomputer bus interfaces, for example.

Thus it can be seen that an important function of D-type latches is their storage capability. Another use of latches is to hold data temporarily until it can be read into (or written out from) the CPU, under the control of the system clock (synchronized).

The flip-flop is so called because its outputs can be made to 'flip' and 'flop' between its two stable states (Q = 1 and Q = 0), depending on the binary pattern applied to its inputs. We have seen how one way of ensuring that the indeterminate state of the set–reset flip-flop could never occur is to reduce the number of inputs from two to one, thereby using only half of the set–reset truth table.

An alternative method is to add feedback between the outputs and inputs, as indicated in Figure 2.24. The steering gates of the flip-flop now have three inputs instead of two; the additional input to the upper NAND-gate comes from the $\overline{Q}$ output, whereas the additional input to the lower

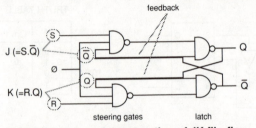

Figure 2.24 Internal construction of JK flip-flop.

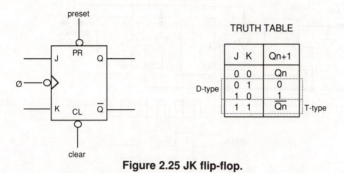

Figure 2.25 JK flip-flop.

NAND-gate is connected to the Q output. This results in two new inputs, J and K (where $J = S \text{ AND } \overline{Q}$, and $K = R \text{ AND } Q$).

The resulting truth table of the new flip-flop thus formed is shown in Figure 2.25, along with its symbol. We see that the JK flip-flop can be made to behave as a D-type flip-flop, simply by connecting an inverter between the J and K inputs, as we did previously with the set–reset latch.

Rather than making the J and K inputs opposite to each other, we can make them the same. If J and K are both taken LO, then the Q output will remain unchanged following the arrival of the next clock pulse. However, if J and K are taken HI together, then the Q output will change to the opposite of whatever it was prior to the arrival of the next clock pulse (in other words it will 'toggle').

Thus we see that it is possible to use a JK flip-flop as either a D-type or a T(oggle)-type flip-flop, simply by connecting the J and K inputs to the appropriate logic levels.

Figure 2.26 shows the use of JK flip-flop in order to form a clocked 3-bit data latch. The datum appearing at the input of the first D-type flip-flop in the chain is transferred to its output following the arrival of the next clock pulse (the next negative edge to be precise). Now, since the output from the first flip-flop is hardwired to the input of the next flip-flop, then at the arrival of the next clock edge, the datum at the input of the second flip-flop will be transferred to its output, simultaneously with the shifting of the second datum from the input of the first flip-flop to its output. The third clock edge will cause the third datum to appear at Q1, the second datum at Q2 and the third datum at Q3, as illustrated in the timing diagram of Figure 2.26. Thus, it has taken three clock cycles for the 3-bit data to be shifted into this latch. Hence another name for this circuit is a shift register. Once the data has been stored within the shift register, it can be clocked out in either parallel or serial form; the former would take one clock pulse, whereas the latter would take three further clock cycles to shift the data out one bit at a time.

The shift register of Figure 2.26 can be used to perform conversion of data from serial to parallel form (and, with minor variations, parallel-to-serial

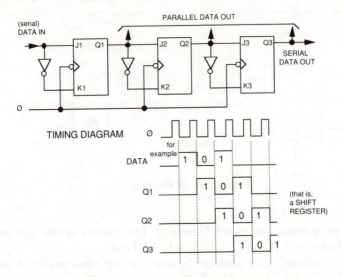

Figure 2.26 Use of a JK as a D-type flip-flop (J = *K).

conversion as well, using the same basic shift register building block). Figure 2.27 shows an application which uses both serial-to-parallel and parallel-to-serial converters in order to transmit 8-bit parallel data from a transmitter to a remote receiver via a serial data communications link. The synchronization of transmitter and receiver in such a system is critical; the clock has to be derived in some manner at the distant receiver (this will be elaborated upon in Chapter 5).

We have seen how D-type latches can be cascaded together to form multiple-bit shift registers. The programmable registers within a CPU are identical to these clocked D-type latches. Figure 2.28 shows three typical CPU registers: an 8-bit data register, an 8-bit stack pointer, and a 16-bit address register (the convention used here is that the most significant bit (msb) is shown on the left-hand side, whereas the logic circuits considered up to now show the least significant bit (lsb) on the left-hand side of the figure). Moreover, the bit numbering convention adopted throughout this book is bit 0 for the lsb, up to bit n for the msb.

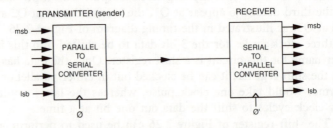

Figure 2.27 Serial data communications link.

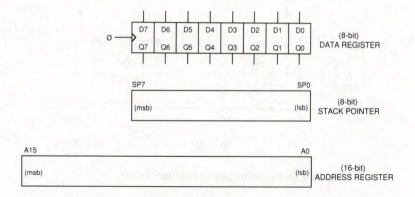

Figure 2.28 CPU registers.

Rather than connect the JK flip-flops as D-types, in Figure 2.29 they are connected as T-type flip-flops. Moreover, the output from each preceding flip-flop is connected as the clock for the succeeding flip-flop. Thus negative going edges of ∅ will cause Q1 to toggle (change from LO to HI), negative going edges on Q1 will toggle Q2, and negative going edges on Q2 will cause Q3 to change state. The Q outputs will change state as indicated in the timing diagram of Figure 2.29.

Notice that Q2 will only change half as often as Q1, likewise Q3 will only toggle half as often as Q2. Thus there is a divide-by-2 action as the count 'ripples through' each successive flip-flop. Notice also that there will be a certain delay experienced in moving from left to right down the flip-flop chain, increasing the further we travel down the chain (normally this delay is an order of magnitude smaller than the clock period, and so is not significant for a small number of flip-flops).

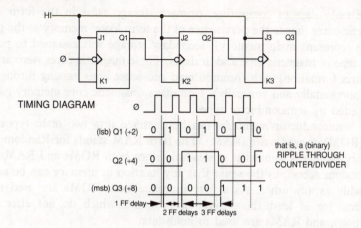

Figure 2.29 Use of a JK as a T-type flip-flop (J = K = HI).

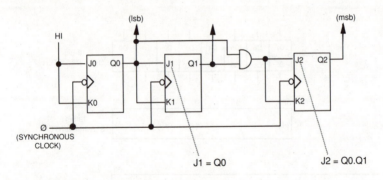

Figure 2.30 Synchronous ÷8 counter/divider.

The ripple counter of Figure 2.29 counts up from 000_2 to 111_2, then resets automatically to 000_2 again; thus this type of counter has a total of eight count states (and for n flip-flops, there will be 2^n count states).

In practice, rather than have the count ripple through from the least significant flip-flop to the most significant one, it is preferable to have the outputs of all flip-flops change state simultaneously. In other words, synchronous counters are preferred to the asynchronous type illustrated in Figure 2.29. Figure 2.30 shows such a synchronous counter. The additional AND-gate is required to set up the J2 input in readiness for the change from the 011_2 state to 100_2.

2.6 SEMICONDUCTOR MEMORIES

In the early days of computing, primary storage came in the form of tiny magnetic cores (hence the persistence of the term 'core' memory to the present day to represent main memory); secondary storage was assigned to punched paper tape or magnetic tape and/or disks. These magnetic cores were arranged in matrix formation, with common read and sense lines passing through each core (horizontally and vertically). Nowadays, magnetic core memory has been superseded by semiconductor types.

Semiconductor memories can be classified into two main types: read-only (ROM) or read/write (RAM). The term RAM stands for Random Access Memory, which is somewhat misleading, since both ROMs and RAMs are in fact random access, in the sense that any location in memory can be accessed as readily as any other. As a first approximation, ROMs are used to hold programs (or at least those parts of programs which do not alter during execution), and RAMs are used to hold data.

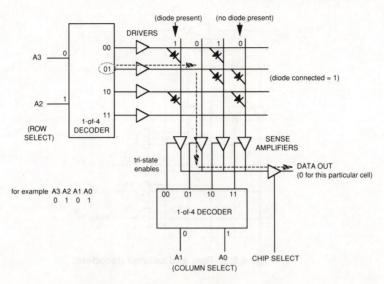

Figure 2.31 Internal construction of a ROM.

2.6.1 Read Only Memories (ROMs)

Figure 2.31 shows the internal construction of a semiconductor ROM. During manufacture, a diode is fabricated at each node of the matrix; the presence of a diode allows the passage of electrical current through it, and constitutes a logic 1 (HI) (conversely the absence of a diode constitutes a logic 0 (LO)). The desired pattern of HIs and LOs is set either during manufacture, in the case of a mask-programmed ROM, or by the user in the case of a field-programmable, fusible-link Programmable ROM (PROM). In the latter type of ROM, fusible links are fabricated in series with the diodes, such that a sufficiently large current can be applied to remove these links (and hence effectively the diodes) from the matrix where so desired (in order to add 0s; the ROM contents being initially all 1s). These types of PROM can only be programmed once.

Another type of programmable ROM is the EPROM or (UV light-) Erasable (electrically-) Programmable Read Only Memory. Such devices are re-programmable; they can be reprogrammed in the event of an incorrect bit pattern being set the first time. (Mask-programmed ROMs and fusible-link PROMs are not so 'forgiving'; once the pattern has been set, that is it!). Electrically Erasable PROMs (EEROMs) have also become popular in recent times; they have the advantage over EPROMs in that they can be reprogrammed *in situ* (they do not need to be removed from the PCB and exposed to a UV light source).

Apart from the basic diode matrix, a ROM also comprises row and column decoders for locating a particular location in memory, as well as

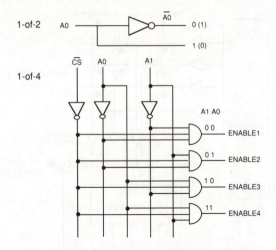

Figure 2.32 Row and column decoders.

drivers and sense amplifiers (the latter boosts the current output). In the example shown in Figure 2.31, an address of 0101_2 selects the second driver from the top coming from the output of the row decoder, together with the second sense amplifier from the left connected to the output of the column decoder. This has the overall effect of selecting the memory cell at row 2, column 2, at which we see that there is no diode connected. Thus when current is supplied from the driver, it cannot pass through to the sense amplifier, with the result that a LO is registered at the output (that is, providing Chip Select has been asserted). In other words, that particular memory location has a 0 stored within it.

Figure 2.32 shows the internal construction of two simple decoders, as used in the ROM of Figure 2.31. In the 1-of-4 decoder, the assertion of lines A0 and A1 together would select the lowest AND-gate only. This latter circuit is readily extended into a 1-of-8 decoder, which comprises three inverters and eight 3-input AND-gates.

ROMs have a very simple and regular structure, and moreover can be packed quite densely into the available area of silicon within an IC. Typical

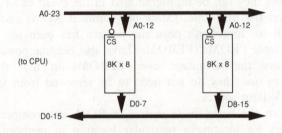

Figure 2.33 8K x 16 ROM array.

capacities are 64K, 128K, 256K, 512K and 1M × 8 bits. Figure 2.33 shows how two smaller PROMs can be configured within a microcomputer. In this example, two 8K × 8-bit ROMs are configured to provide a total of 8K × 16-bit words of system 'firmware' (firmware because the primitive operating system or monitor is fixed in hardware; a new version of the monitor would require burning a new pair of ROMs).

2.6.2 Read/Write Memories (RAMs)

We have already seen how a recirculating shift register constitutes a basic memory cell; the single-bit data latch can store one datum of information indefinitely, or at least as long as power is connected to the circuit. As soon as power is disconnected, the contents of the memory cell are lost. Thus the D-type latch is said to be volatile. The contents of a ROM, by way of contrast, are non-volatile; their contents are burnt in and do not depend on the power being applied.

There are two basic types of semiconductor RAM, namely static and dynamic. The basic static RAM cell is shown in Figure 2.34. It comprises a pair of cross-coupled transistors, together with their respective load transistors, and two enable transistors connected to the Word Select line. Activating the Word-line will transfer the stored digit (either a 1 or a 0) onto the Digit line (simultaneously with its inverse being transferred to the $\overline{\text{Digit}}$ line). This cross-coupled configuration is reminiscent of the cross-coupled NAND-gate discussed previously in Section 2.5.

It is possible to reduce the number of components required in this basic Static RAM (SRAM) cell to an absolute bare minimum, by utilizing the inherent capacitance within a MOS transistor. In fact this capacitance can become the storage element, rather than the transistor itself. Figure 2.35 shows how the original six-transistor RAM cell can be reduced to a three-transistor cell by utilizing this gate capacitance. This three-transistor cell can

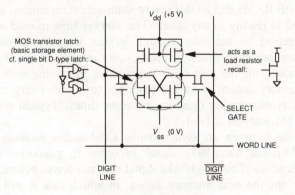

Figure 2.34 Static RAM.

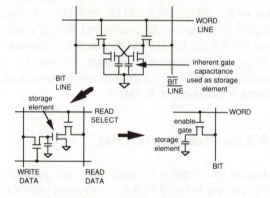

Figure 2.35 Dynamic RAM.

be further reduced to a one-transistor cell, as indicated. In its ultimate form, the RAM cell requires only a capacitive storage element and an enable gate.

Proceeding in this manner, it is possible to pack more memory cells into the same area of silicon. However, the penalty paid for such an improvement is that a periodic refreshing of the cell is required. This is because the basic storage element has now become a capacitor, which means that its charge will gradually leak away unless it is recharged at regular intervals. Hence the reason for calling this type of memory cell Dynamic RAM (DRAM). Refreshing is usually required of the order of every few milliseconds, whereas the time taken to access a specific memory location (memory cycle time) will be of the order of tens or possibly hundreds of nanoseconds.

Because of their regular structure and high packing density, DRAMs tend to lead the push forward into newer fabrication technologies. The highest integration occurs firstly with DRAMs, followed a year or so later by SRAMs (CPUs have nowhere near the regular structure of memories). Larger systems tend to use disk-based operating systems, rather than ROM-based, hence the emphasis on read/write rather than read-only memory in this regard.

Since both RAMs and ROMs are random access memories, any location can be accessed as readily as any other. The average time to read or write any location is referred to naturally enough as the memory access time (or alternatively memory cycle time). Typical cycle times are of the order of 50 to 500 nanoseconds, with the cost of memory chips increasing with decreasing cycle time. Memory capacities have a tendency to double every two or three years, with an accompanying decrease in access times. Typical capacities are 256K, 512K, 1M and 4M × 1-bit.

Interfacing between an asynchronous CPU and a memory array will require an additional handshake signal in order to guarantee secure and reliable data transfers. This handshake signal may not arrive before the CPU is ready to carry out the next memory access, in which case it will insert wait states until this occurs. Memory speeds usually lag somewhat behind CPU

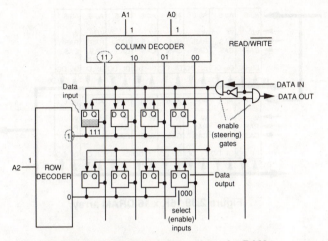

Figure 2.36 Internal construction of a RAM.

speeds, and this speed mismatch is usually described in terms of the memory's ability to keep up with the CPU, namely as 'zero wait state', '1 wait state', '2 wait state' and so on.

Figure 2.36 shows the internal construction of the RAM within a typical microcomputer system. The memory consists of an array of single-bit data latches, row and column decoders, and the associated read and write enable circuitry. The external address lines are converted into the corresponding row and column enable inputs to the individual D-type latches. This figure does not specify whether the D-type latches are static or dynamic. We have already seen that DRAMs have higher packing densities than SRAMs; they also have faster access times. However they suffer the disadvantage that they require additional external logic in order to refresh their contents. Let us take a closer look now at this refreshing circuitry.

A typical DRAM refresh controller is shown in Figure 2.37. Refreshing involves first reading each memory location, then immediately writing the contents back into each cell, and is usually done an entire row (or column) at a time. A refresh counter is needed in order to cycle through all memory locations. The multiplexer is needed to provide access to the DRAM array for

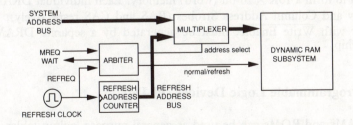

Figure 2.37 Dynamic RAM refresh controller.

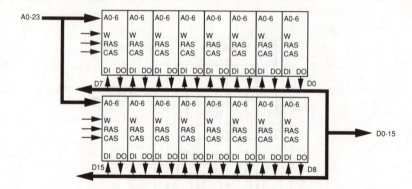

Figure 2.38 16K x 16 DRAM array.

both ordinary memory read and write operations, and for refreshing. Obviously refreshing cannot proceed while a memory read (write) operation is in progress, so some form of arbitration must be provided.

The refresh algorithm is as follows:

```
/* DRAM refresh */
while (!mem_read || !mem_write)
{
    read_memory ();
    write_memory ();
    memory = (memory + 1) % mem_size; /* modulo memory size */
}
```

The Wait signal is a handshake signal from the arbiter to the CPU, and indicates that the DRAM is temporarily unavailable. The refresh controller is driven by its own independent clock, which you will recall has a much lower operating frequency compared with the system clock. Some processors, such as the Zilog Z80, incorporate built-in support for refreshing DRAMs, which cuts down on the external logic required.

RAMs can be fabricated as either single-bit or multi-bit devices. Figure 2.38 gives an example of the former, where 4116 16K × 1-bit DRAMs are used to form a 16K × 16-bit (word) memory. Each individual DRAM chip has Row and Column Address Strobes (RAS and CAS respectively), which, together with $\overline{\text{Write Enable}}$, must be generated by a separate DRAM controller chip.

2.6.3 Programmable Logic Devices (PLDs)

Both RAMs and ROMs can be used as general-purpose lookup tables, where the memory addresses are used to index into the table in order to access the

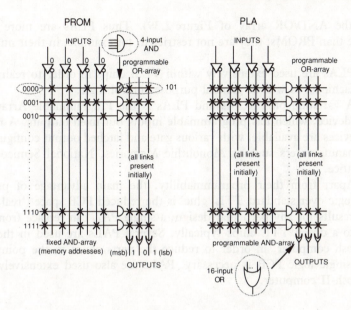

Figure 2.39 Programmable Logic Array (PLA).

various table entries. In a PROM, the contents are not fixed at the time of manufacture, but can be altered as desired by the user, using a PROM programmer. PROM programmers can either be stand-alone devices that interface to a host computer (usually via RS232c), or integrated within a more sophisticated Microcomputer Development System.

A PROM can be considered as an array of AND- and OR-gates, as shown in Figure 2.39. A shorthand representation is used for these multiple-input gates, in order to simplify the figure. Inverted and non-inverted versions of each external address line are formed internally and used to select one of the sixteen 4-input AND-gates. The contents of this particular memory location (three bits in this particular example) are then presented to the inputs of the three 16-input OR-gates at the bottom of the figure.

Every memory location is set initially to 111_2, by virtue of an internal link. The PROM programmer supplies a high voltage to the bit locations where a 0 is desired rather than a 1, in order to fuse the link which was present initially (this 'burn-in voltage' is typically around $+12\,\text{V}$, as compared with the $+5\,\text{V}$ supply voltage).

It is now possible to produce a device which is similar to the PROM, but where not only the OR-array is programmable, but also the AND-array. The resulting device is known as a Programmable Logic Array (PLA). The inputs to the PLA no longer correspond to memory addresses as such, but rather to general-purpose combinatorial inputs. It is possible to show that any combinatorial logic expression can be realized in so-called sum-of-products form (the AND/OR array of Figure 2.39). Thus PLAs are more general purpose than PROMs; they are not restricted, for example, in their number of inputs.

PLAs are used extensively within VLSI chips in order to realize finite state machines, as well as general-purpose control logic.

A variation on PROMs and PLAs is the Programmable Array Logic (PAL) device, which has programmable inputs but fixed outputs. A range of such devices are available, with various gate and latched output configurations, from manufacturers such as Monolithic Memories, National Semiconductor and Lattice.

Apart from their programmability, the main advantage of programmable logic over standard TTL 'glue' is the reduced PCB space ('real estate') which results for any particular design; a single PAL can replace from half a dozen to a dozen TTL chips typically. Several PALs are used in the Apple Macintosh computer, in order to reduce the parts count to the point where only a single logic PCB is necessary. PALs are also used extensively in the Macintosh-II computer.

2.7 PROGRAMMABLE ICs

So far we have considered basic building blocks such as latches, decoders, adders and counters. Such MSI devices themselves consist internally of several (or even dozens of) SSI functional building blocks (namely gates and flip-flops). These devices have had their functions fixed at the time of manufacture.

The step up in circuit complexity during the early 1970s from MSI to LSI, saw the introduction of software-programmable ICs. This enabled the chip functionality to be defined by the user as required from a predefined set of alternatives. Thus the flexibility of designing with such building blocks was greatly enhanced.

By fabricating LSI devices in MOS transistors rather than TTL, much higher packing densities were possible; several thousand logic gates (corresponding to tens of thousands of transistors) could be fabricated on a single silicon chip, representing an order of magnitude increase over what had been achieved previously using bipolar techniques. More importantly, this increased complexity allowed the incorporation of user-accessible software-programmable registers onboard the chip. These registers could be used to alter the chip functionality dynamically.

Some of the first LSI devices developed were microprocessor chips, which arose from the need to provide rudimentary programming capability within desktop calculators. For the first time, digital circuit designers had at their disposal a *programmable* electronic building block, incorporating similar component parts to that of a digital computer's CPU, but in miniature scaled-down form. These devices comprised an ALU, a small number of programmable registers and a control unit.

In Chapter 1, we saw how the function of the control unit was to fetch commands (instructions) from external memory, decode these instructions and then respond to these commands in a predefined manner. Small programs, consisting of sequences of such instructions, are stored in external (semiconductor) memory, and loaded into the microprocessor for execution when required. Indeed, several such programs can be stored in this manner.

It did not take long for manufacturers and users alike to realize the power and versatility inherent in such a programmable electronic device. More powerful microprocessor chips were developed during the ensuing years, to the point where in the next quantum leap in circuit complexity – VLSI, towards the end of the 1970s – microprocessor chips were beginning to rival their 'elder brother' minicomputers in terms of processing power.

What follows is an historical introduction to the development of microcomputer chips, from the development of the transistor in the 1950s to the appearance of 32-bit microprocessors in the mid 1980s.

2.8 HISTORY OF INTEGRATED CIRCUITS

The bipolar transistor originated at Bell Telephone Laboratories in 1947 from research conducted by Shockley, Bardeen and Brattain (and the name transistor was first coined by Pierce, also of Bell Laboratories). Transistors were first used commercially in the early 1950s as amplifiers in hearing aids. Shockley subsequently left Bell Laboratories in 1954 to found his own company in Palo Alto California, which in turn spawned the entire Silicon Valley semiconductor industry (via such companies as Fairchild Semiconductor).

The Field Effect Transistor (FET) dates from RCA Laboratories during the late 1950s. The metal oxide semiconductor (MOSfet) was subsequently developed around 1962.

The first IC – the fabrication of more than one transistor on a single slice or chip of silicon – was achieved by Kilby at Texas Instruments in 1958. The first flip-flop was released commercially (by Fairchild) in 1961. By the mid 1960s more than 25 companies were producing ICs, the leader of which was Fairchild (who were concentrating on analog or linear ICs rather than digital at that time).

The US Government's space program of the 1960s and 70s provided the impetus for developments in the electronics field, and the race was on for greater and greater miniaturization. Computers received an enormous boost as a (natural) flow-on from developments in the semiconductor industry.

In 1967, Fairchild introduced the first ROM. During that same year a large proportion of Fairchild's staff left to form other electronics companies, such as National Semiconductor and Intel (just as staff from Intel were to later leave to start up Zilog).

Intel's Gordon Moore and Robert Noyce were responsible for the microprocessor – the fabrication of a computer's entire CPU on a single chip – with the development of the i4004 in 1969. This device had been created in response to a request from the Busicom Corporation for some 'programming capability' in a family of calculator chips. It was released commercially in 1971. At around the same time, the Datapoint Corporation contracted with Intel to integrate the registers and push-down stack of one of their intelligent terminals onto a chip. This device was subsequently released as the i8008 in 1972. Both the i4004 and i8008 were marketed as programmable electronic building blocks.

The evolution of microprocessor chips, from 1971 to the mid 1980s, is summarized in Figure 2.40.

Intel revamped the pMOS i8008 as the nMOS i8080 in 1973. The i8080 was the microprocessor which really caught on in the marketplace, aided considerably by Kildall's CP/M operating system and Altair's S-100 computer bus. Moreover, the i8080 ended up being second-sourced by numerous other semiconductor manufacturers.

By the mid 1970s, close to 40 different microprocessors were available commercially.

Motorola released their upgrade of the i8080 in the form of the MC6800 in 1974. The MC6800 only required a single $+5$ V supply, whereas the i8080 also required $+12$ V and -5 V supplies.

In 1975, Mos Technology released their competitor to the MC6800, in the form of the 6502, which in terms of cost was far cheaper than either Intel's or Motorola's 8-bit processors. This CPU was immediately incorporated into several home/hobby computers, such as the Apple II, Atari and Commodore. Peripheral support chips could be interchanged between the MC6800 and 6502 families of processors.

Intel released their upgrade of the i8080 – the i8085 – in 1976, but this was overshadowed by the Z80, developed around the same time by a group of expatriate Intel employees who had left to form Zilog. The i8085 was totally software compatible with its predecessor, but only required a single $+5$ V supply. The Z80 expanded the i8080 instruction set considerably, ensuring however that i8080 code could run as a subset on it, thus enabling Zilog to tap into the considerable software base already existing for the i8080. Most CP/M systems subsequently developed were Z80 based (even though the CPU was only being utilized in its '8080-subset' mode!). The devices discussed to date have all been 8-bit processors; instructions and data are handled both internally within the CPU and externally to and from the outside world in units of 8-bit bytes. The development of more powerful microprocessor chips witnessed a preference for firstly 16-bit and subsequently 32-bit processors. One of the first 16-bit processors which appeared in the marketplace was the Texas Instruments TMS9900, which was followed shortly thereafter by Intel's i8086.

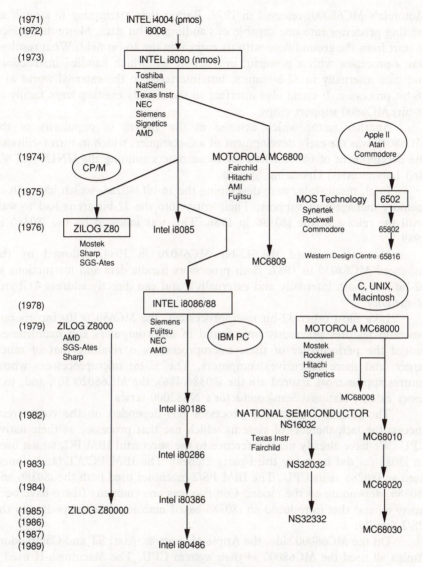

Figure 2.40 Evolution of microprocessors.

8-bit microprocessors, whilst handling data and instructions in byte lots, were usually equipped with 16 address lines, which allowed the processor to access 2^{16} or 64K different memory locations. The i8086 had 20 address lines, thus expanding its addressing capability to 1 Mbyte (albeit in 64K segments). A variation on the i8086 was the i8088, which while being a 16-bit processor internally, interfaced to the outside world via an 8-bit data bus. The future of this family of procesors became assured when IBM selected it as the CPU for its extremely successful IBM Personal Computer.

The first 16-bit microprocessor to really make an impact, however, was

Motorola's MC68000, released in 1979. Rather than attempting to stretch an existing processor into one capable of handling 16-bit data, Motorola decided to start from the ground floor with its entry into the 16-bit field. What resulted was a processor with a powerful instruction set, which handled instructions and data internally in 32-bit units, but interfaced to the external world as a 16-bit processor. It could also interface to the already existing large family of (8-bit) MC6800 support chips.

Another factor which assisted in the growth of popularity of the MC68000 was the early development of a C-compiler, which in turn facilitated the development of 68000-based microcomputers running the UNIX (AT&T Bell Laboratories) Operating System.

Intel, meanwhile, were developing the 16-bit i80286, which has built-in memory management support. Their entry into the 32-bit arena had to wait until the release of the i80386 in 1986. This was followed by the i80486 in 1989.

Motorola released the 32-bit MC68020 in 1984, followed by the enhanced MC68030 in 1987. Both processors handle data and instructions in 32-bit lots (both internally and externally), and can directly address 4 Gbytes of memory.

Like most other 32-bit microprocessors, the MC68020(30) incorporate powerful features previously only found in minicomputers and mainframes; indeed the performance of these microprocessors is rivalling that of much larger (and more expensive) computers. The 32-bit microprocessors whose futures appear most assured are the i80386(486), the MC68020(30), and, to a lesser extent, National Semiconductor's NS32000 series.

The fate of a particular processor has depended on the commercial success (or lack thereof) of systems which use that processor as their native CPU. We have already made reference to the successful IBM PC, which used an i8088 (as did its many third-party clones). The IBM PC/AT (and clones) used an i80286 as its CPU. The IBM PS/2 machines used both the i80286 and i80386, depending on the model. Compaq was one company (there have been many others) that introduced an i80386-based machine as a competitor to the PS/2 familly.

On the MC68000 side, the Apple Macintosh, Atari ST and Commodore Amiga all used the MC68000 as their system CPU. The Macintosh-II used a MC68020, as did Sun and Apollo in their engineering workstations. The MC68030 was chosen as the CPU for the Macintosh-SE/30, Macintosh-IIx and . NeXT computers.

SUMMARY

In this chapter we have looked at the various electronic building blocks which together can be used to build a microcomputer. We saw how transistors (both bipolar and MOS) could be used as electronic switches, and how several such transistor switches could be used to fabricate the basic boolean logic functions in IC form.

Examples of both combinatorial and sequential logic circuits were presented, most attention being devoted to shift registers and counter/dividers. From the discussion of sequential circuits, the concept of a system clock was introduced. We discovered that more complex logic functions are available in MSI form, and that programmable LSI and VLSI devices can be used to form the basis of complete computer systems.

In terms of hardware, computers consist of a number of PCBs, connected together by a system bus, powered by a central power supply and housed together within a cabinet (or several cabinets). Each PCB usually contains most or all of the electronic building blocks mentioned above, in varying quantities.

At the heart of the computer will be the programmable LSI and VLSI chips referred to earlier. Most boards will also contain SSI and MSI ICs (as well as discrete components) in order to connect the various functional components of the computer together. Used in this sense such chips are sometimes referred to as TTL 'glue'.

REVIEW QUESTIONS

2.1 Computers are really very simple devices; they consist of nothing more than simple binary switches. Comment.

2.2 What is the difference between a MOS and a bipolar switch?

2.3 Sketch the internal construction of a 3-input CMOS NOR-gate.

2.4 De Morgan's Theorem states that an inverted-input AND-gate is equivalent to a NOR-gate. Use a truth table to prove this for the 2 input case.

2.5 Sketch the internal construction of the MSI 3-to-8 decoder/demultiplexer in Figure 2.41, in terms of standard logic gates:

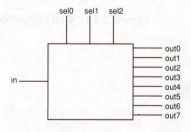

Figure 2.41   3-to-8 decoder/demultiplexer.

2.6 Reduce Figure 2.42 to a single standard 2 input logic gate (that is, Z = A?B):

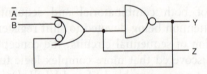

Figure 2.42 Boolean logic gate.

2.7 Starting with the SR flip-flop in one of its two stable states, investigate what happens when the set input is taken LO (then HI again). Repeat for the reset input. Repeat for both inputs together. Repeat this entire process for the SR flip-flop starting in its other stable state. Hence verify the SR flip-flop truth table.

2.8 What is the advantage of master-slave clocking over edge- or level-triggered?

2.9 Why is the JK flip-flop preferred in practice to the SR?

2.10 Show how a JK flip-flop can be used as either a D-type latch or a T-type flip-flop.

2.11 Explain the operation of the 4-bit buffer/latch in Figure 2.43:

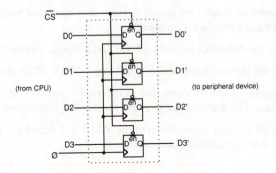

Figure 2.43 4-bit buffer/latch.

2.12   Explain the operation of the sequential logic circuit shown in Figure 2.44:

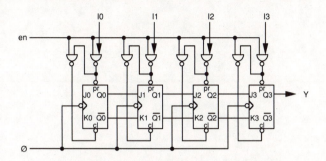

Figure 2.44   Sequential logic circuit.

2.13   What is the counting modulus of the counter/divider in Figure 2.45? Is this counter a synchronous or an asynchronous counter?

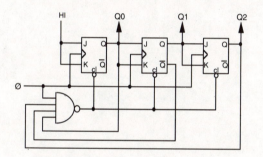

Figure 2.45   Counter/divider.

3

Microcomputer Bus Structure

OBJECTIVES

This chapter discusses microcomputer buses – the interconnecting highways which connect the various constituent parts of a microcomputer together.

Bus timing is covered, as well as the protocols necessary to synchronize the different operations which take place within the computer. We also see how bus arbitration is necessary in systems where there is more than one potential bus master. System expansion via standard buses is also covered.

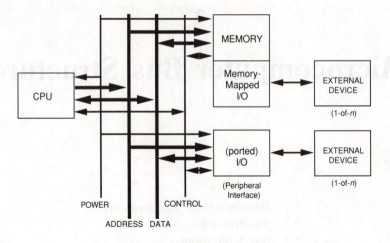

Figure 3.1 Bus structure.

3.1 MICROCOMPUTER BUS STRUCTURE

The component parts of a microcomputer are connected by a number of different wires, which usually appear in the form of tracks on a Printed Circuit Board (PCB). These wires can be classified into four functional groups: power, address, data and control.

The physically largest PCB tracks are the power rails, since they have to carry the largest electrical currents. These days the voltage levels are usually +5 V and ground; in the early days of microcomputers, ±12 V supply lines were often required as well (early MOS memories, and indeed processors, were not TTL compatible). Other power supply lines may be required on occasion, depending on the particular application of the microcomputer in question, particularly if it has to interface to analog (linear) circuitry.

The address bus consists of a number of parallel lines which travel between CPU, memory and I/O chips. Information on the address bus enables the various memory and I/O devices to be accessed. Local address decoding circuitry is necessaray for the memory (I/O device) to recognize the address as its own. The number of address lines varies with the particular microcomputer concerned, but is typically 16 for systems which use an 8-bit CPU, 24 for 16-bit CPUs, and 32 for 32-bit processors. It should be noted that the external address bus is not necessarily the same width as the address bus used *internally* within the CPU.

The data bus likewise consists of a number of parallel lines, and is either 8, 16 or 32 bits wide. Both instructions and data travel along the data bus.

The control lines do not constitute a bus as such, but rather are a collection of individual lines or wires. Typical control lines are read, write, interrupt request and reset.

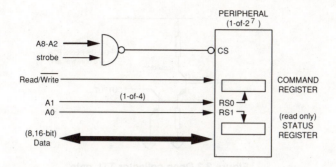

Figure 3.2 Chip and register selection with a peripheral chip.

Figure 3.1 shows this bus structure, where both ported and memory-mapped I/O are used. Each external device connects to the microcomputer system via its own dedicated peripheral support chip. These chips are controlled using on-chip programmable registers. In the memory-mapped chip of Figure 3.2, the middle order address lines are used to select the peripheral device shown from 127 other devices. The low order address lines are used to select one of four on-chip registers, only two of which are shown in Figure 3.2 (the other two could be data registers). At the very least, a peripheral chip will contain a control register and a status register, as indicated. By writing various bit patterns to the control register, the chip can be made to perform its various functions. Similarly, by reading the bit patterns in the status register and responding accordingly, the CPU can effectively interact with the external world.

Controlling a peripheral device can thus be described as 'bit twiddling', which is why it is best done at the assembler level (time-critical I/O routines in high-level language programs will usually need to be written in assembly code).

Because computer buses on a PCB consist of many parallel wires separated by an insulating fibreglass layer, they behave electrically as a long capacitor. Any circuit, such as a CPU which is attempting to drive such a bus, must therefore be capable of driving a capacitive load. TTL circuits are well suited to this task, but MOS circuits have limited drive capability.

The bipolar (TTL) transistor was described in Section 2.1. If the collector (or load) resistor is removed, and made external to the gate, as indicated in Figure 3.3 then it becomes an Open Collector (OC) gate. ICs can incorporate such OC outputs, thus necessitating the connection of an external resistor in order to operate correctly. A typical device is shown in Figure 3.4, and this is the OC bus driver. An external resistor needs to be connected (at either the far distant or near ends) as indicated. Maximum electrical power (the product of voltage and current) is transmitted down the line when the terminating resistor (near or far end) is chosen to match the characteristic

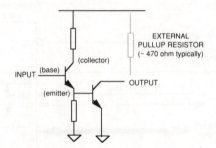

Figure 3.3 Open collector TTL gate.

impedance of the miniature transmission line formed from the copper track and the insulating fibreglass of the PCB (this characteristic impedance, Z_0, depends on the distributed resistance, capacitance and inductance along the PCB track, which is typically around 100 ohms).

Several such OC drivers are needed in order to send data from a CPU to a peripheral support chip located some distance away on the same PCB. Thus bus drivers will be required at the transmitter end, and bus receivers at the receiver end in such a system. Figure 3.5 shows the internal construction of a typical 4-bit bus transceiver (which incorporates four transmitters and four receivers within one IC package).

Figure 3.6 shows a complete microcomputer system in block diagram form. Memory-mapped I/O is assumed. Bus drivers and transceivers are shown, as well as the address decoders and latches. The drivers on the address and control buses are needed in order to boost the electrical outputs from the nMOS (CMOS) CPU, to a level sufficient to travel to the distant peripheral chip without significant degradation. The chips in question would be located some distance away from the CPU.

Bidirectional bus transceivers are required on the data bus, since data can travel not only from the CPU to the peripheral device, but also in the opposite direction. Transceivers are required at both the CPU and peripheral device ends, and can be likened to terminators at either end of a long transmission line (in this case the transmission line is formed from the

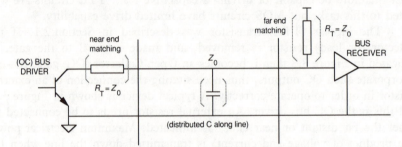

Figure 3.4 Bus driver and receiver.

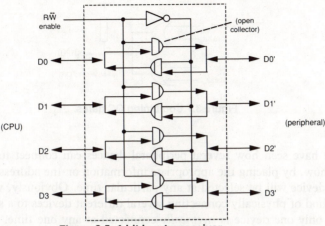

Figure 3.5 4-bit bus transceiver.

interconnecting tracks on the PCB and the insulating fibreglass on which the tracks have been etched).

Address decoders compare the information present on the address bus at any time with the device's own unique identification (ID) address; when both addresses are identical, the output of the decoder is latched in order to form a Chip Select signal for the peripheral chip in question. In this way only 1-of-2^n devices is selected at any particular time, assuming n address lines are used for decoding.

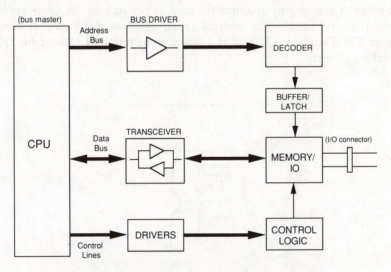

Figure 3.6 Bus drivers and (bidirectional) transceivers.

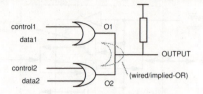

Figure 3.7 Combining OC gates.

We have seen how several peripheral devices can connect to the same bus, and how, by placing the appropriate information on the address bus, only one such device will be selected at any particular time. Obviously, we require some method of physically connecting several different devices to a single bus, such that only one device is *electrically* connected at any one time. There are two widely used methods of achieving this in practice, namely OC and Three State (TS).

Since OC devices require the connection of an external load resistor in order to function, this means that several such gates can utilize the same external resistor, without them interacting (which is what happens with ordinary TTL gates). Such an OC connection is shown in Figure 3.7. The external resistor will pull the outputs of all gates HI, unless one such gate is being driven LO internally. Thus an implied or 'wired-' OR function results at the common output point, as indicated. It is up to the CPU to ensure that only one such OC device is enabled at any time. OC gates were commonly used in minicomputer buses during the 1970s, but have since been superseded by TS bus drivers/transceivers, owing to the high power consumption of the former.

TS gates consist internally of an additional output transistor which has the effect of enabling or disabling the gate, depending on the signal applied to a third control input. The internal construction of a TS gate is shown in Figure 3.8. Transistor Q2 acts as a (semiconductor) load resistor for Q1, the switching element.

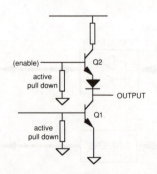

Figure 3.8 Three-state TTL gate.

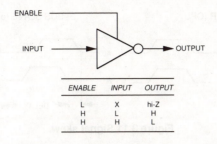

ENABLE	INPUT	OUTPUT
L	X	hi-Z
H	L	H
H	H	L

Figure 3.9 TS gate operation.

The truth table for a TS inverter is shown in Figure 3.9. If a LO is applied to the control input, then the gate is disabled; applying logic levels at the inverter input will produce neither a LO nor a HI at the output. Under these conditions the output is said to be floating, or in its high impedance state; the device output is effectively disconnected. Applying a HI to the control input enables the inverter, such that the usual truth table applies, as indicated.

Figure 3.10 shows how two different devices can be made to share a common bus; one method uses OC bus drivers, and the other uses TS drivers. Depending on whether a HI or a LO is applied to the select input, then either the upper or lower eight lines respectively are connected through to the common bus. In this manner, 8-bit data can be transferred from either of the two sources indicated.

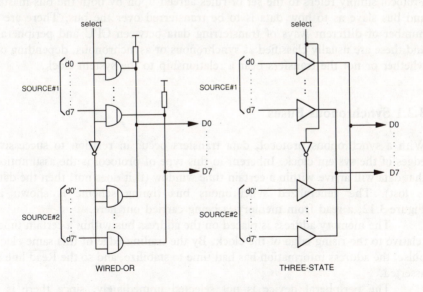

Figure 3.10 Multiplexing of common bus between two sources.

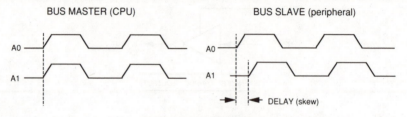

Figure 3.11 Signal skew.

The individual PCB tracks which constitute a bus will not always be exactly the same physical length. This is not so critical at low speeds (1 or 2 MHz), but becomes increasingly more significant as the system clock is increased (the more recent 32-bit processors are capable of operating at speeds in excess of 25 MHz).

These minor differences in distance travelled across the surface of a PCB manifest as differences in the time it takes the different bits of data to travel from the CPU to the peripheral chip(s). A phase difference between adjacent signals is experienced at the distant receiver (or slave) end, when compared with what was transmitted by the bus master. This delay or skew is illustrated in Figure 3.11.

3.2 BUS PROTOCOLS

Protocol simply refers to the set of rules agreed upon by both the bus master and bus slave as to how data is to be transferred over the bus. There are a number of different ways of transferring data between CPU and peripheral, and these are usually classified as synchronous or asynchronous, depending on whether or not the transfers bear a relationship to the system clock.

3.2.1 Synchronous Buses

With a synchronous protocol, data transfers occur in relation to successive edges of the system clock. Inherent in this type of protocol is the assumption that data will arrive within a certain time window (if it does not, then the data is lost). The generalized synchronous bus timing scheme is shown in Figure 3.12; a read from memory is being carried out here.

The memory address is placed on the address bus within a certain time, relative to the rising edge of the clock. By the trailing edge of this same clock pulse, the address information has had time to stabilize, and so the Read line is asserted.

The peripheral device is not selected immediately, since there is a certain delay experienced in decoding the particular address in question at the

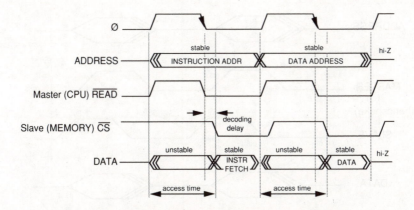

Figure 3.12 Synchronous bus timing (memory read).

distant peripheral chip. Thus Chip Select becomes asserted a short time later. Once the chip has been selected, then the memory can place the contents of the specified location on the data bus. Again, there is a certain delay experienced during which the signals on the individual lines stabilize. This information remains stable until the arrival of the next rising edge of the clock, so the CPU has sufficient time to read this data into its internal register.

A typical synchronous processor is the Motorola MC6800 8-bit CPU, which actually uses a two-phase non-overlapping clock, a common clocking technique used for guaranteed transfers in VLSI circuitry (recall the master–slave clocking scheme of Section 2.5). Transfers are set up on the rising edges of the $\varnothing1$-clock, but not actually latched until the trailing edge of the following $\varnothing2$-clock. Thus the $\varnothing2$-clock is also referred to as the system E-clock (and any MC6800 interface chip must be capable of supporting such a clocking scheme).

3.2.2 Asynchronous Buses

Asynchronous bus transfers bear no particular timing relation to the system clock; transfers can take place at any time. Additional handshake lines are required in order to guarantee data transfers between master and slave. Synchronous bus transfers, by way of contrast, only depend on the system clock (the protocol being built into the system).

Asynchronous buses are useful when matching the different speeds of the CPU and peripheral chips. For example, a processor can interface to both slow and fast semiconductor memories using an asynchronous protocol.

Figure 3.13 shows a write and read cycle for a fully interlocked asynchronous bus, such as the one used on the Digital Equipment Corporation

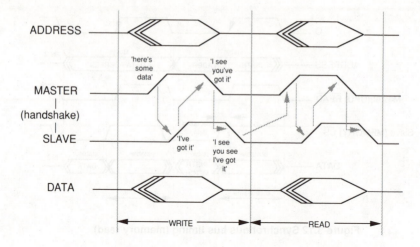

Figure 3.13 Asynchronous bus handshaking.

PDP-11 minicomputer (after Stone (1982), reprinted by permission of Addison-Wesley). For a write operation, the protocol involves the bus master advising the slave that it has some data ready to send. The slave advises the master upon receipt of the data. The master then sends a message back to the slave acknowledging advice of the successful transfer. Finally, the slave responds to this acknowledgement from the master; a read operation follows a similar protocol. As with the synchronous bus, there will be delays due to address decoding, setup times and skew.

3.2.3 Semi-synchronous Buses

A compromise between the two previous bus protocols is found in the semi-synchronous bus, which approaches the speed of synchronous buses, but allows for interfacing to peripheral devices of varying speeds. The semi-synchronous bus operates essentially as an asynchronous bus until the peripheral device is ready for a transfer, after which the bus becomes synchronous for the duration of the transfer.

A semi-synchronous bus is illustrated in Figure 3.14. Four separate cycles are shown here. The first write (from master to slave) occurs during a single clock cycle, as does the first read (from slave to master). The next two cycles involve the assertion of the wait handshake line by the slave, because it cannot keep up with the speed of the master. Whenever the CPU detects the wait line as being asserted, it inserts additional clock cycles or 'wait states'

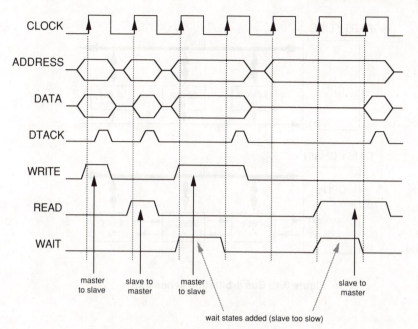

CLOCK

ADDRESS

DATA

DTACK

WRITE

READ

WAIT

master
to slave

slave to
master

master
to slave

slave to
master

wait states added (slave too slow)

Figure 3.14 Semisynchronous protocol.

until the peripheral device becomes ready. Thus the CPU effectively executes 'no operation' (no-op) instructions until the wait line becomes negated.

The MC68000(20) and i80286(386) processors both employ semi-synchronous buses. Computer systems are often described in terms of the number of wait states inserted by the CPU in interfacing to the particular memory used in the system. Thus it is possible for a 10 MHz 0-wait state machine to outperform a 12 MHz 2-wait state machine, for example. (Memory speeds continued to lag behind CPU speeds during the 1980s.)

3.3 BUS ARBITRATION

In the discussion of DMA in Section 1.6.3, it was mentioned that the DMAC and CPU share the common bus. In applications where more than one potential bus master can request control of the bus, there needs to be some method of arbitrating between them.

The simplest arbitration scheme consists of having all potential bus masters connected to a common Interrupt Request line. This is referred to as a party line scheme, and is illustrated in Figure 3.15. Devices are serviced on a 'first come, first served' basis, since all potential bus masters effectively have

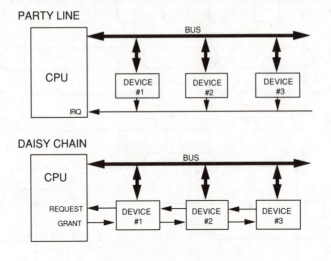

Figure 3.15 Bus arbitration schemes.

the same priority. Some priority could be imposed by polling the devices in a specific order, or else circular polling could be used.

The alternative arbitration scheme shown in Figure 3.15 is daisy chaining. This scheme requires two handshake lines rather than one, as with the party line scheme. Daisy chaining works as follows: a device asserts its request line, which is passed through the devices further up the chain to the CPU. The grant signal is passed through to the device that requested the bus, but only if devices further up the chain do not require it themselves. There is thus an inbuilt priority scheme with daisy chaining, namely that a device's priority decreases the further down the chain from the CPU we travel.

Figure 3.16 shows a typical timing diagram for the daisy chain arbitration scheme. The four signal lines shown relate to stage n of the chain. Three separate transactions are shown in this diagram. The first transaction involves a request from the module itself; no request signal comes in from further down the chain, and hence the grant signal is not passed on.

The second transaction illustrates the case where stage n does not want the bus itself, but simply acts as a relay station, passing a request from further down the chain to the CPU, and subsequently returning bus grant down the chain.

In the third example, stage n itself asserts a bus request, and shortly thereafter receives a request from further down the chain. When bus grant is received back at stage n, it is not passed on, but that stage becomes the bus master for however long its transaction requires. Only after stage n has finished with the bus is bus grant passed further down the line.

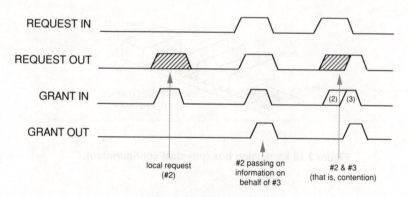

local request
(#2)

#2 passing on
information on
behalf of #3

#2 & #3
(that is, contention)

Figure 3.16 Daisy chain timing.

3.4 SYSTEM EXPANSION

A microcomputer system can be extended by expanding its bus, as indicated in Figure 3.17. Such expanded systems are more complex than the original system, since there is often more than one processor connected to the expanded bus. Bus arbitration obviously becomes critical in such a multiprocessor system. Indeed, each processor could have its own system resources connected to its own local bus, as well as having access to global facilities connected to the common bus.

The physical construction of a typical expanded system is shown in Figure 3.18. There will usually be some form of backplane or motherboard on which resides the larger capacity power supply, as well as several slots into which various (daughter) boards can be plugged. In this manner, large systems can be built up out of an arrangement of smaller, standard boards. Particular attention has to be paid however to the total power supply requirements in such a system.

One of the earliest commercially available buses was the S100, so called because it has 50 pins on either side of its edge connector. It has 16 address and 16 data lines (8 in and 8 out), and was originally designed around the i8080 processor. It was very popular with hobbyists during the late 1970s, and

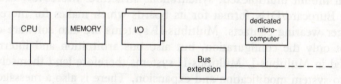

Figure 3.17 System expansion (multiprocessing).

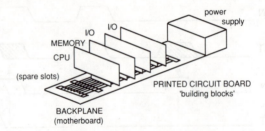

Figure 3.18 Expansion bus (physical configuration).

formed the foundation of many CP/M microcomputer systems. It was restricted to 2 MHz operation, and was subject to noise problems due to the close proximity of some of its control lines. Another popular 8-bit bus is the STD bus, which uses a 56-pin edge connector.

We shall devote our attention here to the Multibus, VME, IBM-PC, Nubus and IEEE488 bus standards. Another parallel bus, the SCSI standard, is commonly used to interface disk drives and tape backup units to microcomputer systems.

3.4.1 Multibus

Neither the S100 nor STD buses could support the 16-bit processors when these began to emerge during the early 1980s. Intel responded by developing Multibus-I, which was designed around the i8086 processor. It has been since formalized as IEEE standard 796.

Multibus boards use two different edge connectors, P1 and P2, as indicated in Figure 3.19. The 60-pin P2 is an optional connector, and is used primarily for power failure detection and handling (such as loss of the AC mains supply). Connector P1 has 86 pins, of which 20 are address lines, and 16 data. The remainder are command and handshake (13), bus access control (6) and utility lines (power and timing). The 20 address lines restrict Multibus-I to a 1 Mbyte addressing range. Full 32-bit addressing is, however, supported by the updated Multibus-II, released in 1986.

Whereas Multibus-I is a non-multiplexed, asynchronous bus, Multibus-II has an inbuilt multiplexed, synchronous structure. Moreover, Multibus-II uses the Eurocard/DIN format for its boards which makes for more positive and longer wearing contacts. Multibus-II systems are also software configurable; not only the configuration, but also bus arbitration and interrupts are hardwired in Multibus-I. Multibus-II systems therefore lend themselves more readily to system modification and expansion. There is also a message passing communication protocol built into Multibus-II.

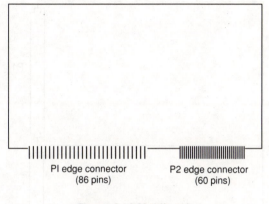

PI edge connector
(86 pins)

P2 edge connector
(60 pins)

Figure 3.19 Multibus-I.

3.4.2 VMEbus

VMEbus was co-developed by Motorola, Philips/Signetics and Mostek during the early 1980s. It is an adaptation of the earlier Versabus, which Motorola used in some of its early EXORmac systems, however VME uses different PCB dimensions, connectors and bus timing. It was designed around Motorola's MC68000 processor. VME boards follow the Eurocard format, as illustrated in Figure 3.20. All lines are TTL-compatible, with parallel termination networks providing pullup for OC (TS) lines, as well as reducing signal reflections.

The DIN pin-and-socket combination prevents long term contact problems and is more resistant to vibration. Single and double height cards are provided for, since only one plug (J1)/socket (P1) is required for a basic system. Sockets P1 and P2 contain 48 pins each, arranged in three lines of 16, as indicated in Figure 3.20. J1/P1 is the primary connector, and contains 16 data, 23 address (plus 2 data strobes), bus arbitration, priority interrupt control and diagnostic signals. J2/P2 extends the system to 32-bit data and addresses, as well as providing user I/O lines (of up to 20 Mbyte/second transfer rates).

VMEbus has a built-in asynchronous, non-multiplexed protocol, with seven levels of priority interrupt and four levels of bus arbitration (for multiprocessing applications). Support for local buses is provided via VMXbus (just as iLBX-II is used for local bus support in Multibus systems).

However, while Multibus was developed around Intel processors, and VME around Motorola, systems based on either standard are not restricted to the corresponding family processor. For example, there are several MC68000-based Multibus boards available in the marketplace.

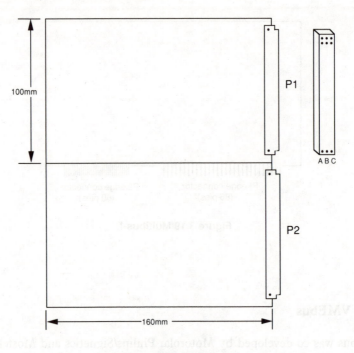

Figure 3.20 VMEbus.

3.4.3 IBM-PC bus

Apart from the standard buses already mentioned, several buses have become *de facto* standards simply by virtue of the large number of boards developed by third-party vendors for particular microcomputers. Two notable examples of such *de facto* bus standards are the Apple/IIe and IBM-PC expansion buses. Both computers allow the user to expand the basic system beyond its original capabilities, simply by adding plug-in boards into its onboard expansion slots. There are numerous boards available for both the Apple-II and IBM-PC computers, in fact many plug-in boards far exceed the host microcomputer in terms of power and sophistication. A typical example is the National Semiconductor SYS/32 UNIX plug-in board for the IBM-PC.

The original PC could not support hard disks, which led to the subsequent development of the PC-XT. The IBM-PC is controlled by an i8088 CPU, and thus only requires an 8-bit data bus; the IBM-PC/AT, on the other hand, is controlled by an i80286 processor, and thus requires a 16-bit data bus (and like the XT, the AT also has built-in hard disk support). This explains why two expansion sockets are required on AT boards, as opposed to one on the PC, as indicated in Figure 3.21. All IBM PCs have a 62-pin basic expansion slot; the AT has an additional 36-pin one.

Apart from the usual address and data lines, control lines such as clock,

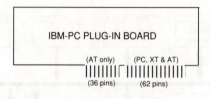

Figure 3.21 J1/P1 pin assignments.

reset, read, write and refresh signals are also provided. Power, interrupt request, DMA request (and acknowledge) lines are also brought out. Pin D1 indicates a 16-bit transfer, and pin D18 discriminates between an XT and an AT.

The Micro Channel Architecture (MCA) is the bus used on the newer PS/2 line of IBM microcomputers. MCA is neither mechanically nor electrically compatible with the earlier PC and AT buses. It is capable of higher speed data and I/O transfers, and supports both resource sharing and multiprocessing. MCA is an asynchronous, non-multiplexed bus. The PS/2 models 50 and 60 use a 16-bit extension of the MCA, while the model 80 uses a 32-bit extension. Channel slots accept 11 ½ inch × 3 inch plug-in cards. A user configurable MCA interface chip is available from Altera Corporation which replaces the 14 or so TTL and PLD ICs needed to interface plug-in boards to MCA.

One of the reasons for the success of both the Apple-IIe and IBM-PC computers has been their ready expandability using plug-in boards connected to the system bus. MCA, by way of contrast, is an IBM proprietary bus. This was a significant factor in an alternative 'standard' being developed for i80386-based machines. The Extended Industry System Architecture (EISA) is supported by, among others, Compaq, Hewlett-Packard, NEC, Olivetti, AT&T, DEC, Unisys and Wang. The EISA bus, unlike MCA, is compatible with the IBM PC/AT bus; alongside and parallel to the two AT connectors, there is a third connector. Thus plug-in EISA boards occupy two slots on an AT machine.

3.4.4 Nubus

The original Apple Macintosh was developed as a closed system; it was basically not designed to be expanded. The Macintosh-SE and Macintosh-II, by way of contrast, have slots included for system expansion (one on the SE and six on the Mac-II). These additions were largely prompted by the huge success in the marketplace of the IBM-PC, and the ready availability of third-party plug-in boards.

The Macintosh-SE is powered by an MC68000 CPU, and thus is

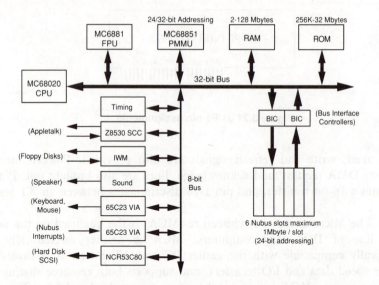

Figure 3.22 Macintosh-II (Nubus)(courtesy of Apple Computer Inc.).

restricted to 16 bits of data. The Macintosh-II, by way of contrast, is controlled by an MC68020 CPU, and thus supports a 32-bit data bus.

The Texas Instruments Nubus has been incorporated into the Mac-II, in order to provide an 'open architecture' (in other words, for system expandability). Nubus is a synchronous, 10 MHz, multiplexed bus. The architecture is completely memory mapped which fits in well with the MC68020 CPU. All objects on the bus, whether they be memory locations *per se*, I/O commands or interrupts, are treated as memory locations. Direct addressing of 4 Gbytes is supported (full 32-bit addressing), as well as data transfers of 8-, 16- and 32-bits.

Each Nubus slot is hardwired with a unique 4-bit address, which is passed on in turn to any card plugged into that slot. One megabyte of memory is dedicated to each slot. Any plug-in board can become the master, and the system configured to start up from that board. The Macintosh-II internal architecture is shown in Figure 3.22.

More recently, Nubus has been included in the NeXT computer. Four 32-bit Nubus slots are provided, each of which connects to the backplane bus via a Eurocard type-C connector. A CMOS implementation is used, which results in twice the data rate of standard Nubus.

3.4.5 IEEE488 Bus

Apart from the standard system expansion buses already mentioned, there are also a couple of (parallel) instrumentation buses in existence. CAMAC was

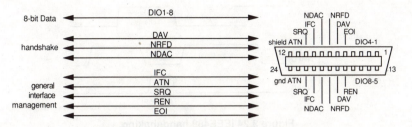

Figure 3.23 IEEE488 bus connector and signals.

developed during the early 1970s by the European Standards on Nuclear Electronics, and has been widely used in nuclear instrumentation since that time. The IEEE488 standard is a formalization of the earlier Hewlett-Packard Interface Bus (HPIB), developed during the mid 1970s.

The 16 parallel lines that constitute the IEEE488 instrumentation bus comprise eight data, three handshake and five general interface management, as shown in Figure 3.23. These latter five lines are used to connect the various instruments together. Each instrument connected to the bus can be in one of four different states: it can be idle, acting as a talker, acting as a listener, or controlling communication between talkers and listeners.

The bus itself is passive; all talking, listening and controlling circuitry is contained within the instruments connected to the bus (not every instrument needs all three types of circuitry though). All lines are TTL compatible (LO $\leq$ 0.8 V; HI $\geq$ 2.4 V), but the negative logic convention is assumed (LO = true; HI = false). The bus can extend up to 20 metres in length, and support data transfer rates of up to 500 Kbit/second (or up to 1 Mbit/second for 10m).

The three handshake lines comprise Data Valid (DAV), Not Ready For Data (NRFD) and Data Not Accepted (NDAC). Initially a listener's NRFD and NDAC lines would be LO. A talker about to transmit data to a listener would set DAV HI, indicating that data is being changed, but is not yet ready for transmission. In response to DAV being set HI, a listener sets NRFD HI, indicating that it is aware that data is being changed, and that it will be ready to accept this data as soon as DAV is sent LO. In the case where there are multiple listeners, NRFD will only be set HI if *all* listeners set their respective NRFD outputs HI. NRFD and NDAC both being set HI together indicates an error condition.

When the talker detects that NRFD has been set HI, it indicates valid data on the bus by setting DAV LO. The first listener to accept the data byte sets NRFD LO and releases NDAC. NDAC goes HI only after *all* listeners have accepted the data. The talker then sets DAV HI again to indicate that more data is being prepared for transmission. This handshaking is illustrated in Figure 3.24.

The general interface management lines are used primarily by the

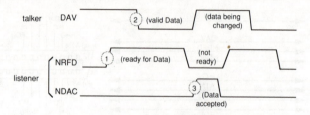

Figure 3.24 IEEE488 handshaking.

instrument acting as controller. These signals are designated as Interface Clear (IFC), Attention (ATN), Service Request (SRQ), Remote Enable (REN) and End or Identify (EOI).

IFC is used by the controller to initialize all instruments to an idle state, where there are no listeners or talkers, and all instruments simply monitor the bus. It is an active LO signal. ATN defines the eight data lines as being either in data mode (ATN = HI) or command mode (ATN = LO). The controller changing ATN from LO to HI will gain the attention of all instruments connected to the bus.

The active LO SRQ line serves as an interrupt to the controller which allows an instrument to request access to the bus. REN going LO indicates that the controller is disabling an instrument's front panel and placing it in remote control mode. EOI can be used by a talker to indicate the end of a data transmission. EOI can also be used together with ATN to implement a parallel poll of all instruments which can support such an operation. For example, by assigning each of the eight data lines to a different instrument, it can determine which instrument asserted the SRQ line.

Figure 3.25 shows a typical transaction over the IEEE488 bus, involving device#3 sending data to device#5 (after Stone (1982), reprinted by permission of Addison-Wesley).

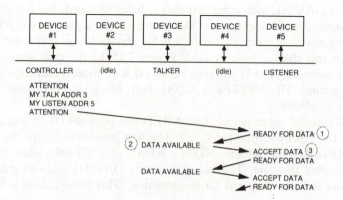

Figure 3.25 Typical IEEE488 transaction.

Whilst the IEEE488 bus is primarily an instrumentation bus, it is nevertheless encountered in many microcomputer applications. Its 8-bit parallel nature and TTL compatability make it readily accessible to many microcomputer applications. An IEEE488 interface was incorporated into the Commodore PET microcomputer, for example.

3.4.6 Small Computer Systems Interface (SCSI)

The SCSI (ANSI X3T9.2) was developed from the Shugart Associates System Interface for interfacing hard disk and streaming tape units to a host computer, however it has since become a more general-purpose standard. Unlike RS232c and the Centronics parallel printer interfaces, SCSI can support multiple processors and multiple peripheral devices (up to eight devices in total). Moreover, unlike the IEEE-488 bus, it is not restricted to a *single* host processor. A common use of SCSI is to interface mass storage devices to microcomputers (hence its relevance in this chapter). For example, the Macintosh plus. Macintosh-II and NeXT computers both have built-in SCSI interfaces.

Figure 3.26 shows the SCSI bus signals. There are nine data lines (eight data plus parity), and nine handshake signals which coordinate the transfer of data between SCSI bus host and controller. A 50-way connector is standard. Data transfers can take place up to 4 Mbyte/second in synchronous mode; in asynchronous mode, this drops to 1.5 Mbyte/second.

SCSI data transfers consist of three main phases, namely arbitration, selection and information. The initiating processor first checks to see if the bus is free, and if so, then attempts to take control of it. If no higher priority processor also bids for it, the initiator captures the bus. During the selection phase, the initiator flags the target device (peripheral) with which it desires to

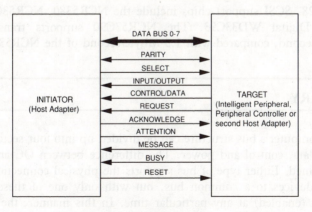

Figure 3.26 SCSI I/O bus.

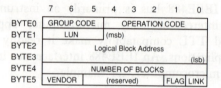

	7	6	5	4	3	2	1	0
BYTE0	GROUP CODE			OPERATION CODE				
BYTE1	LUN			(msb)				
BYTE2	Logical Block Address							
BYTE3								(lsb)
BYTE4	NUMBER OF BLOCKS							
BYTE5	VENDOR		(reserved)				FLAG	LINK

Figure 3.27 SCSI command packet.

```
GROUP 0

        00 TEST UNIT READY              13 VERIFY
        01 REZERO UNIT                  14 RECOVER BUFFERED DATA
        03 REQUEST SENSE                15 MODE SELECT
        04 FORMAT UNIT                  16 RESERVED UNIT
        05 READ BLOCK LIMITS            17 RELEASE UNIT
        07 REASSIGN BLOCKS              18 COPY
        08 READ                         19 ERASE
        0A WRITE (print)                1A MODE SENSE
        0B SEEK (select track or slew)  1B START/STOP (load/unload)
        0F READ REVERSE                 1C RECEIVE DIAGNOSTIC
        10 WRITE FILE MARK (flush buffer) 1D SEND DIAGNOSTIC
        11 SPACE                        1E PREVENT/ALLOW MEDIA REMOVAL
        12 INQUIRY

GROUP 1

        25 READ CAPACITY                30 SEARCH DATA HIGH
        28 EXTEND ADDRESS READ          31 SEARCH DATA EQUAL
        2A EXTENDED ADDRESS WRITE       32 SEARCH DATA LOW
        2E WRITE & VERIFY               33 SET LIMITS
        2F VERIFY                       39 COMPARE
                                        3A COPY & VERIFY
```

Figure 3.28 SCSI commands.

communicate. The target device then responds with the type of transfer in which it is prepared to engage: data in/out, command request, status acknowledgement or message in/out.

Initiators and target devices communicate via a set of high-level command description bytes, transmitted in packets. The SCSI command packet is shown in Figure 3.27, and the commands are summarized in Figure 3.28. SCSI support chips include the NCR5380, NCR53C90 and the Western Digital WD33C93. The NCR53C90 supports transfers up to 4 Mbyte/second, compared with 1.5 Mbyte/second of the NCR5380.

SUMMARY

A microcomputer's bus structure can be divided up into four sections, namely address, data, control and power. The difference between OC and TS buses was explained. Either type of bus supports the physical connection of several different devices to a common bus, but with only one of these electrically connected (enabled) at any particular time. In this manner, the bus can be shared or multiplexed between many different devices.

Synchronous, asynchronous and semi-synchronous bus protocols were discussed. Synchronous buses support the highest data transfer rates. Asynchronous buses provide for more secure transfers, through the use of handshaking, and also allow devices of varying speeds to be connected. The role of wait states in semi-synchronous buses was also covered.

System expansion is often accomplished using plug-in boards which connect to the system bus. Several standard buses – both industry standard and *de facto* – were discussed in this regard. We looked briefly at Multibus, VMEbus, IBM-PC and Nubus. The IEEE488 instrumentation bus and SCSI were also introduced.

REVIEW QUESTIONS

3.1   What is the significance of open-collector and three-state devices in relation to microcomputer buses?

3.2   Compare and contrast the ability of TTL and MOS ICs to drive capacitive PCB tracks.

3.3   Explain the terms signal skew, and bus master (slave) in relation to microcomputer buses.

3.4   The i8086 uses a multiplexed bus. Explain.

3.5   What is meant by the term handshaking in relation to microcomputer buses?

3.6   What is meant by the term protocol in a microcomputer bus context?

3.7   Discuss the advantages and disadvantages of synchronous versus asynchronous buses.

3.8   What is the role of wait states in a semisynchronous bus?

3.9   Why are bus arbitration lines usually provided on a microprocessor IC?

3.10 In connecting several processors and peripheral devices onto a common backplane, bus bandwidth becomes a limiting factor. Explain.

3.11 Explain the term daisy chaining. What priority scheme is inherent in daisy chaining?

3.12 Compare and contrast Multibus, Multibus-II, VMEbus, IBM-PC bus and Nubus.

3.13 There are so many third-party plug-in boards available nowadays for the IBM-PC (and PC/AT) that the future of this particular computer is assured. Comment.

3.14 Is it possible for a plug-in board not to use the host CPU in a system which has expansion slots?

3.15 How many host processors can reside on an IEEE488 bus? Repeat for SCSI.

3.16 Name a typical application of both IEEE488 and SCSI.

4

Parallel Input/Output

OBJECTIVES

Basic I/O devices are introduced in this chapter. Simple output devices include lamps, light emitting diodes and 7-segment LED and LCD displays. The input devices covered are mechanical switches, multiple position switches and keyboards. The problems of contact bounce and ghosting are discussed.

The keyboard reversal technique of keyboard encoding is introduced and discussed in relation to typical parallel interface chips, such as the MC6821 PIA and i8255 PPI.

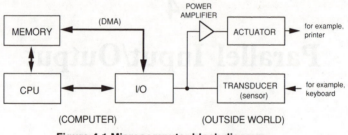

Figure 4.1 Microcomputer block diagram.

4.1 OUTPUT DEVICES

As discussed in Chapter 1, a computer communicates to the external world through its Input/Output (I/O) section. Output transducers convert the digital signals produced by the computer into other energy forms, such as light, sound, heat and motion.

Physical movement of external devices is achieved using some form of power actuator, such as an electromagnetic solenoid or stepper motor. Often the digital output from the computer needs to be first converted into analog form, and then given a power boost sufficient to move the external device physically (this could require a much larger power supply than that required to drive the computer itself). This arrangement is shown in block diagram form in Figure 4.1.

Typical optical transducers include lamps, Light Emitting Diodes (LEDs), LED and Liquid Crystal Displays (LCDs), and Cathode Ray Tube (CRT) displays. Lamps and LEDs are typically used as visual indicators (such as ON/OFF power indicators), with LEDs being preferred these days owing to their lower power consumption. LEDs require series resistors to limit the current passing through them, as illustrated in Figure 4.2. Seven-segment displays come in either common anode or common cathode form, the latter being illustrated in Figure 4.3. Optical lenses are provided within the 7-segment package in order to magnify the emitted light from each rectangular LED segment. Besides 7-segment LED and LCD displays, 16-segment displays such as the one shown in Figure 4.4 are also available, which allow for the display of true alphanumeric characters; 7-segment displays are only suitable for displaying decimal (or at most hexadecimal) digits.

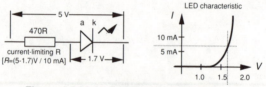

Figure 4.2 Light Emitting Diode (LED) .

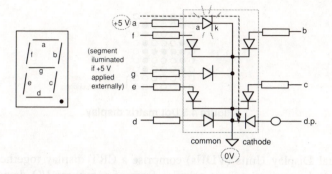

Figure 4.3 7-segment display.

The information as to what character is to be displayed at any particular time will be output on the computer's bus in Binary Coded Decimal (BCD) form. An MSI BCD-to-7 segment decoder chip is usually employed to carry out this conversion (and to provide the current boost necessary to drive the 7-segment display as well).

Dot matrix displays consist of a matrix of individual dots (either LED or LCD), arranged as rows and columns (typically 9 × 7), as shown in Figure 4.5. These displays are capable of higher resolution than the 16-segment types, and thereby result in characters that are more pleasing to the eye. However, they require more complicated external circuitry to drive them; the information as to which dots are to be lit up in any partiuclar row (column information, in ASCII) must be continuously updated as the output on the computer's data bus is repeatedly switched (multiplexed) between each row in turn.

Multiple 16-segment or dot matrix displays can be used to form a multicharacter alphanumeric display, as is done in flat panel LCD or plasma displays. Such flat panel displays are used in portable (laptop) computers, where the more conventional CRT displays would lead to prohibitive size, weight and battery power drain. However, the number of characters per line and the number of lines per screen page are both limited by comparison with CRT displays.

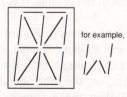 for example,

Figure 4.4 16-segment alphanumeric display.

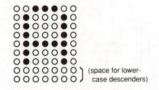

Figure 4.5 Dot matrix display.

Visual Display Units (VDUs) comprise a CRT display together with a keyboard, and remain the most popular form of computer I/O device. CRT displays comprise a number of lines (typically 24), each of which consists of a number of character cell blocks (typically 80). Characters are formed in the same manner as they are on a dot matrix display, namely as a 7×9 two-dimensional array. The display starts at the top leftmost corner, traces out each horizontal line from left to right, finishing at the bottom rightmost corner, with the entire display being repeated at a fast enough rate that it appears steady to the human eye. (CRT displays are discussed in more depth in Chapter 6.)

4.2 INPUT DEVICES

The simplest form of computer input device is a switch. Switches can be mechanical, membrane, capacitive or Hall effect in construction. In the mechanical type, two metal contacts are brought together in order to complete an electrical circuit. In the membrane type, a plastic or rubber membrane presses one conductor onto another. The advantage of this type of switch is that it can be made very thin, and as a sealed unit. Capacitive switches internally comprise two plates of a parallel plate capacitor; pressing the key cap thus effectively increases the capacitance between the two plates. Special circuitry is needed in order to detect this change in capacitance, but the advantage of this type of switch is that it uses no mechanical contacts (which can become dirty or corroded over time). There is similarly no mechanical contact in a Hall Effect keyswitch; instead, motion of a crystal perpendicular to the magnetic flux lines of a permanent magnet is detected as a voltage appearing between the two faces of the crystal. It is this voltage which registers a switch closure.

These four switch types are shown in Figure 4.6. Both pushbutton and toggle mechanical switches are shown. Toggle switches have two stable positions, one where the electrical connection is made, and the other where it is broken. Pushbutton switches, on the other hand, have only one stable or rest position; when operated they make (break) the electrical connection momentarily, for however long finger pressure is applied to it.

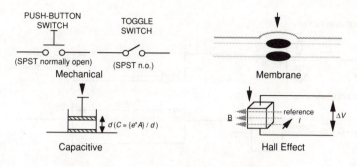

Figure 4.6 Switch types.

The toggle switch shown in Figure 4.6 is a Single-Pole Single-Throw (SPST) type. It is also possible to obtain switches which have a third (central) position (referred to as double-throw), as well as having multiple switch contacts (called *n*-pole). Moreover, switches are referred to as being either normally open (n.o.), where the switch contacts are disconnected, or normally closed (n.c.), where the contacts are connected. A normally open SPST switch could be used where a fixed input (say +5 V or ground) needs to be connected from time to time to the computer. A normally closed switch could be used as an emergency OFF switch to disconnect power to the entire computer system, for example.

There is a problem which exists in mechanical switches, due to their construction, and this is 'contact bounce'. Rather than obtaining a *single* clean pulse output, a series of pulses results due to the switch contacts not coming to rest immediately. As shown in Figure 4.7, a single physical push of the button results in multiple electrical signals being generated and sent to the $\overline{\text{RESET}}$ input of the CPU (this $\overline{\text{RESET}}$ input will be pulled HI without any signal connected to it. Its normal or rest state is to rise to the +5 V supply rail; it is an active LO signal input). The response time of the switch is several orders of magnitude slower than that of the computer (tens of milliseconds, rather than microseconds), so that the computer could read the single switch closure many times over during the time the switch is operated, interpreting each LO signal as a new input whereas in fact it is the same one all the time.

Contact bounce can be overcome in practice either by one of the techniques illustrated in Figure 4.8, by synchronizing the switch to the system clock, or by using software debouncing. The RC time constant of the integrator (smoothing filter) determines the rate at which the capacitor charges

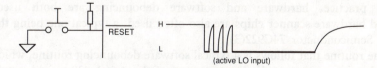

Figure 4.7 Contact bounce.

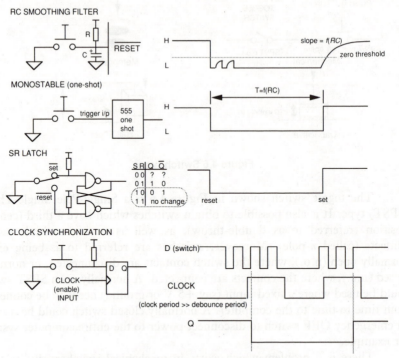

Figure 4.8 Remedies for overcoming contact bounce.

up towards the supply voltage once the earth connection via the switch has been removed. So long as the capacitor voltage does not exceed the zero threshold value, then the $\overline{\text{RESET}}$ input will continue to recognize a logic 0.

A monostable or one-shot is a dedicated hardware timer chip which produces a fixed pulse width output in response to the *first* LO signal applied to its input; it ignores all subsquent LO inputs from the switch until it has finished producing its own pulse output. (One-shots are discussed in more detail in Chapter 8.)

Like the one-shot, the SR latch only responds to the first LO signal applied to its Reset input, and ignores all subsequent (spurious) LOs applied to it.

Synchronizing the switch input requires the use of an external D-type latch, and results in additional software overhead, in order to sample or poll the switch after it has had time to come to rest.

In practice, hardware and software debouncing are both used. Dedicated hardware scanner chips are also often used, a typical one being the National Semiconductor 74C922(3).

The routine that follows is a typical software debouncing routine, which uses a delay appropriate to the time constant of the switch (20 ms). A single SPST switch is connected to the lsb of port number 10H in an i8086 system:

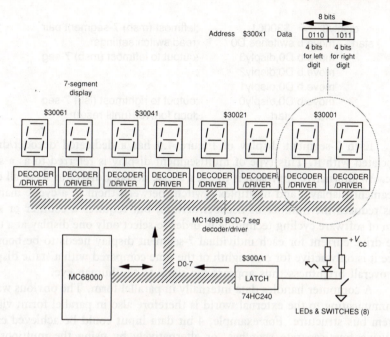

Figure 4.9 Multiple 7-segment LED display.

```
PRESS?:  mov   DL,10H      ;switch → lsb of port#10H
         in    AL,DL       ;read in from port
         and   AL,10H      ;mask off msbs
         mov   CX,2DF5H    ;load loop count (assuming a 10 MHz
DBNCE:   loop  DBNCE       ;clock) each LOOP takes 17 cycles
         in    AL,DL       ;read a second time
         and   AL,10H      ;if still pressed, proceed
         cmp   AL,01H      ;if not, wait for a keypress
         je    PRESS?      ;
ACTION:        :           ;proceed with appropriate action
               :           ;
```

As a simple example of interfacing multiple switches and seven-segment LED displays to a microcomputer, consider Figure 4.9. It shows the connection of a bank of SPST switches to an 8-digit seven-segment LED display, via the data bus of an MC68000-based front display panel. A simple routine to read the 8-bit input from these switches and output it to the display would be as follows:

```
switches = $300A1
disply0  = $30001          ;rightmost (lsb) 7segment pair
disply1  = $30021          ;
disply2  = $30041          ;
```

```
        disply3  = $30061        ;leftmost (msb) 7-segment pair
start:  move.b switches,D0       ;read switch settings
        move.b D0,disply3        ;output to leftmost (msb) 7-seg
        move.b D0,disply2        ;
        move.b D0,disply1        ;
        move.b D0,disply0        ;output to rightmost (lsb) 7-seg
        bra    start             ;loop forever (until reset)
```

Each 7-segment display of Figure 4.9 has a dedicated decoder/driver associated with it. This type of multisegment display is referred to as a static type. An alternative approach is to use a single decoder/driver to serve all eight 7-segment displays, and multiplex (switch) between them in a cyclic manner. This reduces the number of decoder/drivers, but requires a counter or some form of software cycling technique in order to select only one display at a time. The drive current for each individual 7-segment display needs to be boosted, since it is only active for one eighth of the time compared with a static display; the overall brightness thus appears the same to the human eye.

A computer handles data internally in parallel form. The obvious way of communicating to the external world is therefore also in parallel form, via the system bus structure. For example, 4-bit data input could be achieved either by using four separate switches, or alternatively by using the multiposition switch shown in Figure 4.10. Each of the four positions of the switch could be tested in turn by the CPU, to ascertain which had 0 V connected to it (the other inputs would be pulled HI by the resistors, as discussed earlier). In this scheme, a buffer/latch is required in order to hold the data until the CPU is ready to use it. The computer first enables the latch's $\overline{\text{Chip Select}}$ $(\overline{\text{CS}})$ control input, and then transfers the data stored in the latch onto its own data bus, to be subsequently read into its registers or memory. The inbuilt buffer isolates the data from the bus until it is required. Pull-up resistors are used to ensure that the latch inputs return to the +5 V supply rail when the earth connection is removed.

The software required to determine switch positions in a multiposition switch becomes inefficient as the number of switch positions increases; each

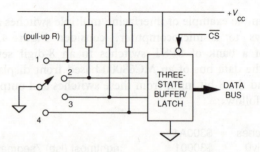

Figure 4.10 Multiposition switches.

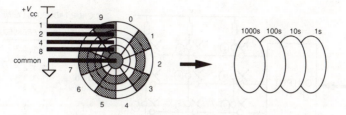

Figure 4.11 Thumbwheel (BCD) switches.

switch has its own dedicated input line, and must be polled by the CPU in turn to see if it has 0 V connected to it. By using external hardware to firstly encode the switches, not only does this result in less expensive hardware, but more efficient software can also be written in order to determine switch closures. In the BCD thumbwheel style switch shown in Figure 4.11, each switch represents a different power of ten (thousands, hundreds, tens and units, from left to right). Thus instead of having one thousand individual switches, each connected to a dedicated input line, the four switches shown only require four I/O lines. The computer can recognize the BCD data by inspection; no polling of the individual lines is required. Encoded switches are preferred to multiposition switches in practice.

For large numbers of switch positions, an array of pushbutton switches provides a much more efficient solution than either dedicated or multiposition switches. A keyboard is nothing more than an array of switches, in the form of an m-row $\times$ n-column matrix. Only $m + n$ physical wires need connect to the computer's data bus, however $m \times n$ discrete switch positions are catered for in the matrix itself. Additional software overhead is required in order to resolve individual switch closures though, as we shall see shortly.

In the 3-row $\times$ 3-column keyboard matrix shown in Figure 4.12, the computer's data bus is divided in two, with three lines permanently connected to the rows, and another three to the columns. In the row–scan technique of keyboard encoding, each row has a zero written to it in turn, with the columns being read immediately after each write. Whenever a zero is detected in a column, this indicates that a key has been pressed; a lookup table then needs to be consulted to determine which key was in fact pressed. There are eight possibilities for each row; 000_2 indicates that all three keys are pressed, 001_2 keys 1 and 2, and so on down to 111_2 (indicating no key pressed). However, this software decoding technique is memory intensive, assuming all possibilities need to be catered for ($8 \times 3 = 24$ in this simple example). This may or may not be a significant penalty, with memory capacities increasing (and cost per bit decreasing) as rapidly as they have been in recent years. Often only single keypresses would be of interest; multiple keypresses would be treated as miskeying on the part of the operator.

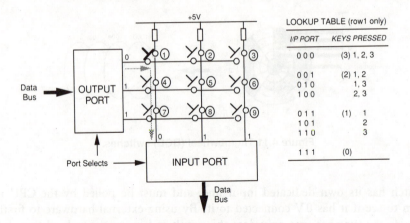

Figure 4.12 3 x 3 Keyboard matrix (array).

A problem can exist with such keyboards however, and this is 'ghosting'. Consider the 3×3 matrix shown in Figure 4.13: with the three switches closed as indicated and a zero written to row #2, a zero appears on the middle column output as expected, but an unexpected zero also appears on the right-hand column output (due to the alternate current path shown). The simple remedy for ghosting is to place diodes in the columns as indicated, to ensure that currents cannot flow back through one of the top two switches, forcing another row LO.

Practical keyboards range in size from 4×4 hexadecimal keypads to full computer keyboards comprising 115 or more keys (moreover, a shift key can add duplicate functions to some of these keys, so that the standard ASCII character set can be supported).

The program which follows illustrates the interfacing of a simple 6-row $\times$ 4-column keyboard matrix to the MC68000-based system shown in

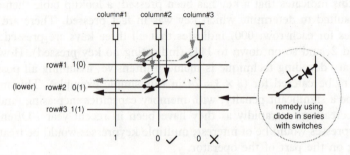

Figure 4.13 Ghosting.

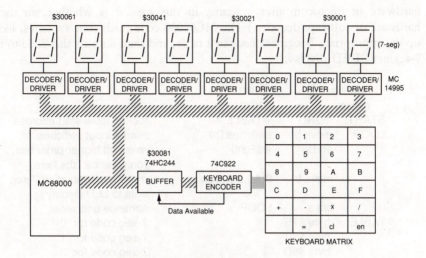

Figure 4.14 Front panel keyboard.

Figure 4.14. The program outputs whatever key has been pressed to the rightmost 7-segment LED display. The 74C922 keyboard encoder outputs scanning information on its column outputs, and reads in key information via its row inputs. Whenever any key is pressed, the Data Available output of the 74C922 becomes asserted, and is latched through onto the system data bus (as the msb) to flag the fact that a key has been pressed. Information as to what key has been pressed is read in from the data bus.

```
    keypad  = $30081
    disply0 = $30001
    disply1 = $30021
    disply2 = $30041
    disply3 = $30061
INIT:   move.b #0,disply3    ;set all displays to zero
        move.b #0,disply2    ;
        move.b #0,disply1    ;
        move.b #0,disply0    ;
START:  move.b keypad,D1     ;read keypad
        bpl    START         ;bit-7 HI indicates a keypress
        and.w  #$1F,D1       ;mask off msbs
        move.b D1,disply0    ;output to leftmost (lsb) display
        bra    START         ;look for further keypresses
```

The following program segment ilustrates the additional software overhead required in displaying this same information to an undecoded 7-segment LED display. (There will often be a tradeoff between software and hardware in microcomputer systems; in this case it is whether we use a hardware or software decoder.) The MC68000 code reads four switches, looks up the appropriate 7-segment code in a table, and then outputs this code to the 7-segment LED display:

```
        switches   =    $30601
        display    =    $30701
START:  move.l     #TABLE,A0          ;lookup table start address
LOOP:   move.b     switches,D0        ;read 4 input switches
        and.w      #$F,D0             ;mask off higher-order bits
                                      ;(only want 8 lsbs here)
        move.b     0(A0,D0),display   ;move corresponding 7-seg
                                      ;data to LED display
        bra.s      LOOP               ;continue until reset
TABLE:  .byte $7E                     ;7-seg code for '0'
        .byte $30                     ;7-seg code for '1'
        .byte $6D                     ;7-seg code for '2'
        .byte $79                     ;7-seg code for '3'
        .byte $33                     ;7-seg code for '4'
        .byte $5B                     ;7-seg code for '5'
        .byte $5F                     ;7-seg code for '6'
        .byte $70                     ;7-seg code for '7'
        .byte $7F                     ;7-seg code for '8'
        .byte $7B                     ;7-seg code for '9'
        .byte $77                     ;7-seg code for 'A'
        .byte $1F                     ;7-seg code for 'B'
        .byte $4E                     ;7-seg code for 'C'
        .byte $3D                     ;7-seg code for 'D'
        .byte $4F                     ;7-seg code for 'E'
        .byte $47                     ;7-seg code for 'F'
                                      ;(active HI 7-seg displays)
```

Line reversal is an alternative keyboard encoding technique. This technique relies on the dynamic characteristics of a dedicated I/O support chip (and will be elaborated upon in Section 5.3.1). In the example shown in Figure 4.15, a Peripheral Interface Adapter (PIA) is connected to an 8×8 switch matrix. The two 8-bit ports on the PIA can be programmed by the CPU to act as either inputs or outputs. The CA1 control input is used to interrupt the CPU to flag the fact that a key has been pressed; a zero out from the keyboard matrix will appear as a one at the active HI CA1 input. Port A is first selected as an output port and port B as an input port. Zeroes are then written out to all eight rows simultaneously, and the columns read (a zero indicates a keypress). The ports are then reversed, zeroes written out to the columns and the rows read (again a zero indicating a keypress). A lookup table is then consulted to determine which key(s) have been pressed.

Since this technique involves simultaneous or parallel reads and writes, it is inherently more efficient than the row-scan technique mentioned earlier

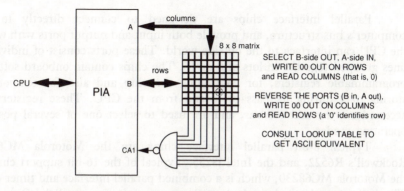

Figure 4.15 Line reversal technique of keyboard encoding.

(which reads the rows one at a time, and thus takes considerably longer to execute).

Keyboard rollover refers to the simultaneous pressing of more than one key (which could result from a typist's finger rolling over from one key to the next, with the second key becoming pressed before the first is released).

Two-key rollover is what is most commonly provided in practice, but some keyboard encoders are capable of handling n-key rollover ($n > 2$). N-key rollover can be catered for by using a fast strobe to store the key sequence in a buffer, and subsequently reading this information out at some later time. The other extreme is n-key lockout, where only one key is recognized, either the first pressed or the last released, irrespective of how many have in fact been pressed. This can slow down typing to unacceptably slow rates however.

LSI keyboard encoder chips usually incorporate row outputs and column inputs, debouncing, diodes (to prevent ghosting), conversion from parallel to serial form and subsequent conversion to ASCII (for transmission back to the CPU), n-key rollover and generation of interrupts to the host CPU. Typical of such chips are the National Semiconductor 74C922, Intel i8279, and dedicated single-chip microcomputers, such as the Intel i8021 used in the Apple Macintosh computer.

4.3   PARALLEL INTERFACE CHIPS

The use of dedicated LSI support chips greatly facilitates the interfacing of external devices to a computer. By incorporating into hardware functions otherwise required in software, the CPU can be freed to carry out other tasks. Thus, peripheral chips during the last decade have become more and more 'intelligent', and in some cases rival the CPU itself in terms of processing power. This trend has culminated in the introduction in recent times of coprocessor chips, which can be used to extend logically the functionality of the main CPU.

Parallel interface chips are designed to connect directly to the computer's bus structure, and provide both input and output ports with which the CPU can interface to the outside world. These ports consist of individual lines grouped together in lots of 8 or 16. The chips contain onboard software programmable registers, for controlling the chip and also for temporarily storing data during its passage to and from the CPU. These registers are accessed via the address bus, and are used to select one of several possible operating modes.

Typical 8-bit parallel interface chips are the Motorola MC6821, Rockwell's R6522, and the Intel i8255. Typical of the 16-bit support chips is the Motorola MC68230, which is a combined parallel interface and timer chip. We shall now take a closer look at these representative parallel I/O support chips.

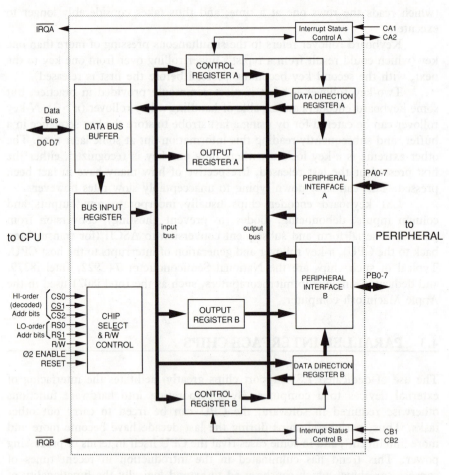

Figure 4.16 Motorola MC6821 Peripheral Interface Adapter (PIA) (courtesy of Motorola Inc.).

4.3.1 Motorola MC6821 PIA

The MC6821 PIA shown in Figure 4.16 was originally designed to interface to the synchronous 8-bit MC6800 family of processors; however it can interface to the 16/32-bit MC68000 family as well. The MC6821 has two bidirectional doubly-buffered 8-bit ports, as indicated in Figure 4.17. Each line is capable of acting as either input or output, either individually or in groups of up to 8. Two control lines are provided, one of which can be used as either input or output, the other one being restricted to input only. Interrupts can be generated independently from either port.

Three chip select lines are provided, which reduces external decoding in systems employing multiple support chips. The two register select lines are used to access the onboard user-programmable registers (recall that the MC68000 uses memory-mapped I/O, so that I/O addresses are accessed in exactly the same manner as memory). Control lines are also provided to interface to the MC68000, namely $\overline{\text{RESET}}$, R/$\overline{\text{W}}$ and the synchronizing E-clock signal.

There are three user-programmable registers in the MC6821 for each of port A and port B: data register, Data Direction Register (DDR) and control register. However, only two register select lines have been provided: RS0 and RS1. Six unique addresses are derived for these registers by utilizing bit 2 of the control register, as shown in Figure 4.18. The data register and DDR share the same address; which one is selected at any time depends on whether bit 2 is HI or LO. Since the MC68000 uses memory-mapped I/O, RS0 is usually connected to address line 1 and RS1 to A2.

Depending on whether the individual bits in the DDR are set HI or LO, the corresponding port lines are selected as input or output lines respectively. The Interrupt flags IRQ1 and IRQ2 reflect the appropriate signal transition on the external CA1 and CA2 lines respectively. They can be cleared either by reading the appropriate data register, or by a $\overline{\text{RESET}}$.

As shown in Figure 4.19, the two least significant bits of the control register are used to control the CA(B)1 input line, bit 0 enabling/disabling interrupts from the MC6821 to the CPU, and bit 1 determining whether to expect a HI→LO or LO→HI transition on that line. Since CA(B)2 can be

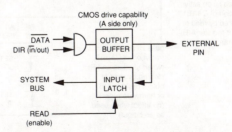

Figure 4.17 MC6821 PIA bidirectional port structure.

	A2	A1			
			bit 2 of		
	RS1	*RS0*	*CONTROL REG*	*SELECTED REGISTER*	
shared ⎰	0	0	0	DATA DIRECTION REG A	$30001
address ⎱	0	0	1	DATA REGISTER A	$30001
	0	1	X	CONTROL REGISTER A	$30003
shared ⎰	1	0	0	DATA DIRECTION REG B	$30005
address ⎱	1	0	1	DATA REGISTER B	$30005
	1	1	X	CONTROL REGISTER B	$30007

Figure 4.18 MC6821 PIA addressing (courtesy of Motorola Inc.).

used as either an input or an output, it requires an additional bit in the control register (bit 5 set indicates output, while bit 5 cleared indicates input). Bit 3 enables (disables) interrupts, while bit 4 determines the type of transition (negative or positive), as previously. Figure 4.20 describes the options available on CA(B)2 in more detail. A typical use of CA(B)2 would be as a read/write strobe for an external device.

The following code shows how to program an MC6821, in this particular case with port A as an output port and port B as a combined I/O port (4 lines each). The base address for the PIA is assumed to be $30001:

```
move.b  #$00,$30003        ;select DDR A
move.b  #$FF,$30001        ;select all 8 lines as outputs
move.b  #$04,$30003        ;select data register A
move.b  #$xx,$30001        ;write data to data reg.A
move.b  #$00,$30007        ;select DDR B
move.b  #$0F,$30005        ;select 4 msb lines as i/p, 4 lsb as o/p
move.b  #$04,$30007        ;select data register B
move.b  #$yy,$30005        ;write data (only affects bits 0–3)
move.b  $30005,D0          ;read data from data reg.B
and.b   #$F0,DO            ;have to mask off bits 0–3
```

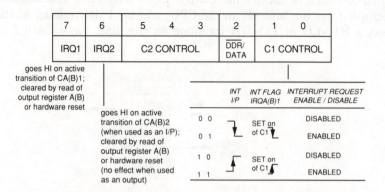

Figure 4.19 MC6821 PIA control register (courtesy of Motorola Inc.).

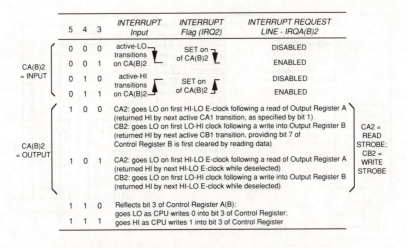

	5	4	3	INTERRUPT Input	INTERRUPT Flag (IRQ2)	INTERRUPT REQUEST LINE - IRQA(B)2	
	0	0	0	active-LO transitions on CA(B)2	SET on of CA(B)2	DISABLED	
CA(B)2 = INPUT	0	0	1			ENABLED	
	0	1	0	active-HI transitions on CA(B)2	SET on of CA(B)2	DISABLED	
	0	1	1			ENABLED	
CA(B)2 = OUTPUT	1	0	0	CA2: goes LO on first HI-LO E-clock following a read of Output Register A (returned HI by next active CA1 transition, as specified by bit 1) CB2: goes LO on first LO-HI clock following a write into Output Register B (returned HI by next active CB1 transition, providing bit 7 of Control Register B is first cleared by reading data)			CA2 = READ STROBE; CB2 = WRITE STROBE
	1	0	1	CA2: goes LO on first HI-LO E-clock following a read of Output Register A (returned HI by next HI-LO E-clock while deselected) CB2: goes LO on first LO-HI clock following a write into Output Register B (returned HI by next HI-LO E-clock while deselected)			
	1	1	0	Reflects bit 3 of Control Register A(B): goes LO as CPU writes 0 into bit 3 of Control Register:			
	1	1	1	goes HI as CPU writes 1 into bit 3 of Control Register			

Figure 4.20 MC6821 PIA CA(B)2 control (courtesy of Motorola Inc.).

Figure 4.21 shows the interconnection of a turtle robot and an MC68000 CPU via an MC6821 PIA. Port A of the MC6821 is used to provide output signals to control the movement of the turtle, while port B senses feedback information from the turtle's touch sensors. The turtle is fitted with two independent drive motors – left and right – a horn, two LED 'eyes' and a solenoid which raises and lowers a pen mounted in the centre of its body. The following portions of MC68000 code illustrate how the MC6821 is programmed in order to control the turtle via an ASCII keyboard:

```
INIT:     move.b  #$00,$30303     ;set up port A as 8 output lines
          move.b  #$FF,$30301     ;(base address of MC6821 = $30301)
          move.b  #$34,$30303     ;select data register A
                                  ;CA2 reflects bit 3 (0→LO; 1→HI)
          move.b  #$00,$30307     ;set up port B as 8 input lines
          move.b  #$00,$30305     ;(only PB0–3 actually used)
          move.b  #$04,$30307     ;select data register B
                 :
CMND:            :                ;keyboard input routine
                 :                ;(not included here) –
                 :                ;command passed via D0
                 :                ;
          cmp.b   #$74,D0         ;ASCII for 't(urn)'
          beq     TURN            ;
          cmp.b   #$..,D0         ;(for other commands)
          jmp     CMND            ;await next valid keyboard command
                 :
                 :
```

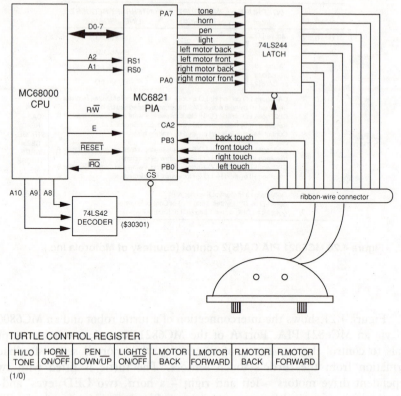

TURTLE CONTROL REGISTER

HI/LO TONE (1/0)	HORN ON/OFF	PEN DOWN/UP	LIGHTS ON/OFF	L.MOTOR BACK	L.MOTOR FORWARD	R.MOTOR BACK	R.MOTOR FORWARD

TOUCH SENSOR REGISTER

		BACK TOUCH	FRONT TOUCH	RIGHT TOUCH	LEFT TOUCH

(active LO)

Figure 4.21 Interfacing a turtle robot to an MC68000 system.

```
TURN:     move.b   #$06,$30303    ;turn clockwise – drive left motor
                                  ;forwards & right motor backwards.
          jsr      OPUT           ;VDU output routine (not shown)
          jmp      CMND           ;await next valid keyboard command
          :
          :
SENS:     btst     #$00,$30307    ;if bit 0 of data reg.B is set,
          bne      LEFTSW         ;left bumper switch is activated
          :
          :
LEFTSW:   move.b   #$06,$30303    ;turn clockwise to back away
          jmp      CMD            ;await next valid keyboard command
          :
```

Peripheral support chips within the Motorola MC6800 and Rockwell R6502 ranges can be used with processors in the other family, since both assume memory-mapped I/O, and depend for their operation on a synchronizing E-clock. The equivalent 6502 interface chip to the MC6821 PIA is the 6522 Versatile Interface Adapter (VIA). Apart from providing two bidirectional 8-bit ports, the 6522 also includes two 16-bit programmable timers. The VIA has two Chip Select pins rather than three, as on the MC6821, whereas twice the number of register select lines are provided, in order to access the sixteen onboard registers of the 6522. (The R6522 VIA will be discussed again in Chapter 8 in relation to timers.)

4.3.2 Intel i8255 PPI

Whereas Motorola and Rockwell processors use memory-mapped I/O, Intel and Zilog use ported I/O. The Intel i8255 Programmable Peripheral Interface (PPI) is a typical ported I/O peripheral chip. It comprises three 8-bit ports; ports A and B can be programmed as either input or output, port A can be alternatively programmed as bidirectional, and port C as either input, output or a pair of 4-bit bidirectional control ports (one for A and one for B). Furthermore, port C lines can be individually set or reset in order to generate strobe signals for controlling external devices. The internal organization of the i8255 is shown in Figure 4.22.

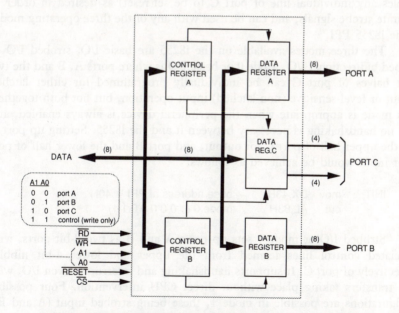

Figure 4.22 Intel i8255 Programmable Peripheral Interface (PPI) (courtesy of Intel Corp.).

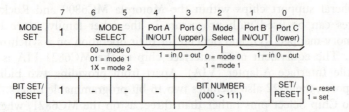

Figure 4.23 i8255 PPI control register (courtesy of Intel Corp.).

Commands, data and status information are all transferred between the i8086 CPU and the i8255 PPI over the 8-bit bidirectional data bus during an I/O bus cycle. Address lines A0 and A1 connect directly to the register select inputs, and are used together with $\overline{\text{Read}}$ ($\overline{\text{RD}}$), $\overline{\text{Write}}$ ($\overline{\text{WR}}$) and $\overline{\text{Chip Select}}$ ($\overline{\text{CS}}$) to specify the type of transfer, as shown. As can be seen from this diagram, the base address of the i8255 must be divisible by four. $\overline{\text{RESET}}$ initializes the i8255 such that all three I/O ports are configured as input ports.

The i8255 PPI control register is shown in Figure 4.23. It is accessed by writing data to port number [base + 3H], where base is the base port address of the PPI. The msb set in the control register indicates that the operating mode of the i8255 is being selected; the i8255 PPI can be programmed in one of three different modes, as illustrated in Figure 4.24. A zero in the msb of the control register means that the bit set/reset facility has been invoked, which enables any individual line of port C to be set(reset) as desired in order to generate strobe signals, and can be used with any of the three operating modes of the i8255 PPI.

The three modes available on the i8255 are basic I/O, strobed I/O or strobed bidirectional I/O. Mode 0 or basic I/O is where ports A, B and the two 4-bit halves of port C can be individually programmed for either latched output or level-sensitive (non-latched) input operation, but not both together. This mode is appropriate when the peripheral device is always enabled, and thus no handshaking is necessary between it and the i8255. Setting up port A and the upper half of port C for output, and port B and the lower half of port C for input would be achieved as follows:

```
INIT:   mov   DX,43H      ;base address of PPI = 40H
        out   AL,83H      ;mode 0 (1 0 0 0 0 0 1 1)
```

Strobed I/O or mode 1 sets up ports A and B as two 8-bit ports, with associated control lines formed from the upper and lower 4-bit nibbles respectively of port C. It supports handshaking and interrupt-driven I/O, with data transfers taking place without direct CPU intervention. Four possible configurations are possible in mode 1, these being strobed input (A and B), strobed output (A and B) and strobed I/O (either A as input and B as output, or A as output and B as input).

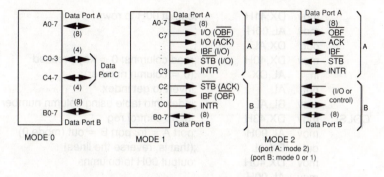

Figure 4.24 i8255 PPI modes (courtesy of Intel Corp.).

When port A acts as an input port, bit 3 of port C serves as an Interrupt Request (INTR) input, bit 4 becomes a $\overline{\text{Strobe}}$ ($\overline{\text{STB}}$) input, relying on external hardware to generate this signal. Bit 5 becomes an Input Buffer Full (IBF) signal. Bits 6 and 7 are undefined, and may be used as either control signals to, or status signals from, the external device. For port B as an input port, bit 0 of port C becomes INTR, bit 1 IBF and bit 2 ($\overline{\text{STB}}$). Bit set(reset) operations can be used in mode 1 (and 2) to mask off interrupts.

For port A as an output port, bit 3 of port C again acts as INTR, bits 4 and 5 are for general-purpose control(status) functions, bit 6 acts as an $\overline{\text{Acknowledge}}$ ($\overline{\text{ACK}}$) handshake line, and bit 7 becomes an $\overline{\text{Output Buffer Full}}$ ($\overline{\text{OBF}}$) status line. For port B as an output port, bit 0 again acts as INTR, bit 1 becomes $\overline{\text{OBF}}$ and bit 2 $\overline{\text{ACK}}$. It is also possible to set up one port for mode 0 operation, and the other for mode 1, in which case two more lines become freed in port C for I/O.

Mode 2 operation is where port A becomes a strobed, bidirectional I/O port, with port B operating in either mode 0 or mode 1. Thus four configurations are possible in mode 2, since port B can be used for either input or output. Bit 3 becomes INTR, bit 4 $\overline{\text{STB}}$, bit 5 IBF, bit 6 $\overline{\text{ACK}}$ and bit 7 $\overline{\text{OBF}}$. (Note that there is only a single interrupt line available to the user in mode 2.) Moreover, interrupts can be masked using a bit set(reset) operation (as in mode 1). Bits 0 to 2 of port C are used in conjunction with port B, as indicated in Figure 4.24.

The following i8086 code illustrates how an i8255 PPI could be programmed in a keyboard decoder application. This routine uses the line reversal technique discussed previously, and relates to the hardware configuration of Figure 4.15. A port base address of 40H is assumed:

```
INIT:     lea    BX,TABLE    ;start address of key lookup table
ROWS:     mov    DX,43H      ;i8255 control reg (A1A0 = 1 1)
          mov    AL,82H      ;port A = out; port B = in (mode 0)
          out    DX,AL       ;(base address = 40H)
```

```
            mov   DX,41H        ;output 00H to rows
            mov   AL,00H        ;
            out   DX,AL         ;
            mov   DX,40H        ;read columns; 0 = key pressed
            in    AL,DX         ;(0 = column number)
            not   AL            ;invert to get index
            mov   BL,AL         ;index into table using column number
  COLS:     mov   DX,43H        ;i8255 control reg
            mov   AL,90H        ;port A = in; port B = out (mode 0)
            out   DX,AL         ;(that is, reverse the lines)
            mov   DX,40H        ;output 00H to columns
            mov   AL,00H        ;
            out   DX,AL         ;
            mov   DX,41H        ;read rows; 0 = key pressed
            in    AL,DX         ;(0 = row number)
            not   AL            ;invert to get index
            xlat                ;(BX + AL) index into lookup table
             :
             :
  TABLE:    DW    ...           ;lookup table of key numbers
                                ;row-m (1–8); column-n (1–8)
                                ;(assuming only one key pressed)
```

Up to now we have only considered the interfacing of an i8255 PPI to an 8-bit data bus. It is also possible to connect multiple i8255 PPIs to a 16-bit bus. Two i8205 address decoders would be required, one for even addresses, and another for odd addresses. The upper address decoder would be selected whenever the i8086 CPU asserts $\overline{\text{BHE}}$, in which case I/O transfers would take place over data lines D8 through D15. The lower address decoder would be selected whenever address line A0 becomes asserted, in which case I/O transfers would take place over D0–7.

4.3.3 Motorola MC68230 PI/T

The 48-pin MC68230 Programmable Interface/Timer (PI/T) chip is an asynchronous support chip designed for interfacing to the 16/32-bit family of MC68000 processors. It incorporates two 8-bit ports and a 24-bit timer, the latter incorporating a 5-bit prescaler for generating longer time intervals. The parallel interface section comprises port A, port B, four handshake lines (H1–4), two general I/O lines and six dual-function lines. The dual-function pins can be used to provide either a third port (port C) or alternative functions related to port A (B) or the timer. The MC68230 is shown in block diagram form in Figure 4.25.

The MC68230 PI/T is a doubly-buffered chip, which is useful in situations where a peripheral device is capable of transferring data at roughly the same speed as the CPU. Data fetch operations at the transmitter can be

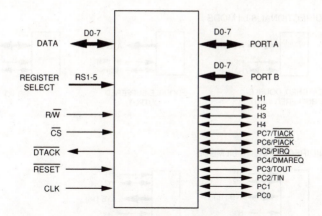

Figure 4.25 Motorola MC68230 Parallel Interface/Timer (PI/T) (courtesy of Motorola Inc.).

overlapped with data stores at the receiver, which results in greater throughput. No penalty ensues however where a significant mismatch exists between the transfer rates of the two devices.

Interfacing to a MC68000 is achieved by using the 8-bit data bus D0–7, Register Select ($\overline{\text{RS1–5}}$), Chip Select ($\overline{\text{CS}}$), R/$\overline{\text{W}}$, $\overline{\text{RESET}}$, $\overline{\text{DTACK}}$ and Port Interrupt Acknowledge ($\overline{\text{PIACK}}$). Five register select lines are necessary since 25 registers are accessible to the user, as indicated in Figure 4.26. Moreover, the MC68230 registers can support the MOVEP instruction, which enables the transfer of word (longword) data between a MC68000 and *alternate* bytes of memory.

```
base address +  $1  PORT GENERAL CONTROL REGISTER (PGCR)
                $3  PORT SERVICE REQUEST REGISTER (PSRR)
                $5  PORT A DATA DIRECTION REGISTER (PADDR)
                $7  PORT B DATA DIRECTION REGISTER (PBDDR)
                $9  PORT C DATA DIRECTION REGISTER (PCDDR)
                $B  PORT INTERRUPT VECTOR REGISTER (PIVR)
                $D  PORT A CONTROL REGISTER (PACR)
                $F  PORT B CONTROL REGISTER (PBCR)
               $11  PORT A DATA REGISTER (PADR)
               $13  PORT B DATA REGISTER (PBDR)
               $15  PORT A ALTERNATE REGISTER (PAAR)
               $17  PORT B ALTERNATE REGISTER (PBAR)
               $19  PORT C DATA REGISTER (PCDR)
               $1B  PORT STATUS REGISTER (PSR)
                :
               $21  TIMER CONTROL REGISTER (TCR)
               $23  TIMER INTERRUPT VECTOR REGISTER (TIVR)
                :
               $27  COUNTER PRELOAD REGISTER - high (CPRH)
               $29  COUNTER PRELOAD REGISTER - middle (CPRM)
               $2B  COUNTER PRELOAD REGISTER - low (CPRL)
                :
               $2F  COUNTER REGISTER - high (CNTRH)
               $31  COUNTER REGISTER - middle (CNTRM)
               $33  COUNTER REGISTER - low (CNTRL)
               $35  TIMER STATUS REGISTER (TSR)
```

Figure 4.26 MC68230 PI/T registers (courtesy of Motorola Inc.).

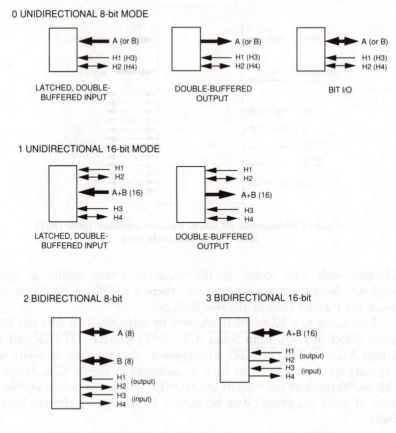

Figure 4.27 MC68230 PI/T port options (courtesy of Motorola Inc.).

The parallel interfaces can operate in either unidirectional or bidirectional modes, with data paths of either 8- or 16-bits. In unidirectional mode an associated DDR determines whether the pins are used as output or input. In bidirectional mode the DDRs are ignored and the direction is determined dynamically by the state of the four handshake pins; H1–4 are programmable, and thus provide for flexible connection to a wide variety of low-, medium- or high-speed peripherals.

Both vectored and autovectored interrupts are possible on the MC68230, and a DMA Request pin is provided for connection to DMAC chips, such as the MC68440(50).

Each Port General Control Register (PGCR) contains a 2-bit field which specifies one of the four operational modes shown in Figure 4.27. This can be further specified within the PGCR: for example, the dual unidirectional 8-bit mode can be implemented as either latched, doubly-buffered input, doubly-buffered output or as bit I/O (that is, individual I/O lines).

SUMMARY

In this chapter we have considered the interfacing of peripheral devices to a microcomputer in parallel form. Typical output devices such as LEDs and 7-segment LED displays were introduced. More complex output devices were not included in our discussion (CRT displays are covered in Chapter 6, while printers are covered in Chapter 7). Nevertheless, the output devices considered were sufficient to illustrate the need for both latching output data and also decoding it (from binary to some other code) before applying it to the peripheral device in question.

Our discussion of typical input devices began with simple switches and progressed through switch matrices (keypads) to ASCII keyboards. The practical problems of contact bounce and ghosting were raised, and appropriate solutions described. The row-scan and line-reversal techniques of keyboard encoding were discussed. We also discovered the need for buffering input data, until the computer is ready to read it, for example with n-key rollover.

Short example programs illustrated some of the principles mentioned above. Sample programs were also given to illustrate the use of dedicated LSI and VLSI peripheral support chips. These programs concentrated on initializing parallel interface chips ready for use in each particular application. The actual transfer of data between peripheral devices and the CPU could be achieved in practice using either polling, interrupts or DMA, as discussed in Chapter 1.

The advantage of parallel interfacing is speed; all eight bits of an 8-bit data byte can be transferred simultaneously. The disadvantage of parallel interfacing is space; 8 (16 or 32) parallel wires running across the surface of a PCB constitutes a significant percentage of the available board real estate (cabling to external devices even more so). Serial interfacing is much more economical in terms of board space, but the tradeoff is much lower data transfer rates. Serial interfacing is the topic for discussion in the next chapter.

REVIEW QUESTIONS

4.1 With reference to mechanical switches, what is contact bounce, and how can it be overcome?

4.2 What is meant by ghosting in relation to a keyboard switch matrix, and how can it be overcome?

4.3 We made mention of n-key rollover in Section 4.2, but what is meant by the term n-key lockout?

4.4 Describe the line reversal technique of keyboard encoding. Can this technique handle n-key rollover?

4.5 An example of the classic hardware–software tradeoff in microcomputer systems is interfacing unencoded versus encoded 7-segment LED displays. Explain.

4.6 Explain how the RS0,1 inputs on an MC6821 PIA are used to access its six onboard programmable registers.

4.7 Write a short MC68000 routine for initializing both ports of an MC6821 ready for reading data in and writing data out, as follows:

      PORT A   lines 0 through 3 as inputs,
                        lines 4 through 7 as outputs
      PORT B   all 8 lines as inputs

(the base address of the PIA is $10001).
Do not assume that the MC6821 is necessarily reset beforehand.

4.8 Write a short i8086 routine which initializes an i8255 PPI for strobed I/O (mode 1), with port A set up as an input port and port B as an output port. Repeat for mode 2 operation.

4.9 Explain how the bit set(reset) ability of the i8255 PPI can be used to mask interrupts.

5

Serial Input/Output

OBJECTIVES

The focus of attention in this chapter on serial I/O is on data communications. The conversion of data into a form suitable for sending from a transmitter to a distant receiver is discussed first. Modulation techniques are examined, along with the devices which perform this function – modems.

Both asynchronous and synchronous communication protocols are discussed, with particular attention paid to the RS232c asynchronous standard. The MC6850, R6551 and i8252 serial support chips are covered.

Networks are introduced, with particular mention made of Local Area Networks (LANs).

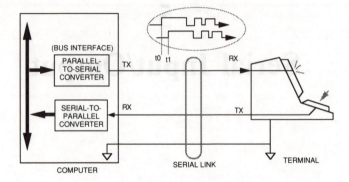

Figure 5.1 Serial data communications.

5.1 INTRODUCTION

The previous chapter dealt with the interfacing of a microcomputer to parallel peripheral devices. Our concern in this chapter is with *serial* interfacing. The advantage of parallel interfacing is speed; all data bits are transferred simultaneously via the system bus (or an extension of this bus). In serial I/O, the data bits are sent one at a time across a *single* line. The advantage of serial I/O is lower cost (in terms of the number of wires connecting the microcomputer to the peripheral device), while the disadvantage is slower speed.

Since communications within a microcomputer take place over the system bus in parallel form, there is obviously a need for parallel-to-serial (and serial-to-parallel) conversion when interfacing to serial I/O devices. Such parallel-to-serial and serial-to-parallel converters were discussed in Chapter 2. These devices are essentially shift registers (which themselves are formed from D-type single-bit data latches).

Figure 5.1 shows a typical serial I/O application, in this case a data communications link between a terminal and a microcomputer. Data is converted from parallel to serial form in the bus interface, and transmitted one bit at a time along the line. The electrical signal that travels down the wire is illustrated in Figure 5.1; a fixed point along the line 'sees' different voltage (or current) levels at different times. The signals travel down the line at a speed of around 3 nanoseconds per metre (they do not travel at the speed of light, but only a fraction thereof).

Depending on the length of this line, the data could be corrupted by noise and/or electromagnetic interference during the course of its travel. Thus there could be a need for some form of error correction at the receiver end. This length could vary anywhere between a few centimetres in the case of the CRT display of a desktop microcomputer, to thousands of kilometres in the case of transmission via satellite to a receiver on the opposite side of the earth.

This incoming serial information is converted back into parallel form and stored in the terminal's screen refresh memory. Updating the display screen involves the conversion of this parallel information back into serial form in order to fire the CRT electron gun, which turns individual pixels on or off. (CRT displays will be discussed in more detail in Chapter 6.)

Pressing the keyboard selects the encoded binary representation of that particular key from a lookup table, then converts this parallel information into serial form for transmission to the microcomputer. This serial information is transmitted back down the line, then converted into parallel form in the bus interface for communication over the system bus.

5.2 DATA COMMUNICATIONS

The basic data communications link is shown in Figure 5.2. A terminal (computer) at one end of the link communicates with a computer (terminal) at the opposite end. The communications link proper consists of a Data Termination Equipment (DTE) and its associated modem at either end (modems are described in more detail later in this section).

There are two main types of data link configurations, namely point-to-point and multidrop, as indicated in Figure 5.3. In the former, the two end stations communicate as peers, whilst in the latter, one device is designated as the master (primary), and the others designated as slaves (secondaries). Each station has its own unique address, with the primary station controlling all data transfers over the link (such addressing is unnecessary in point-to-point links).

The physical data communication link can consist of either two or four wires, as illustrated in Figure 5.4. A two-wire link provides a signal line and ground, whereas a four-wire link provides two such communication paths, each with its associated ground wire.

The logical data communication link is illustrated in Figure 5.5. In the simplex facility, the line is dedicated either for transmission or reception, but not both. In the half duplex facility, transmission can occur in either direction, but only in one direction at any particular time. In a full duplex link, transmission and reception can occur simultaneously in both directions. It

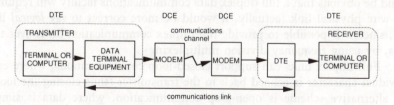

Figure 5.2 Data communications system.

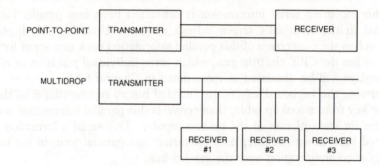

Figure 5.3 Point-to-point and multidrop systems.

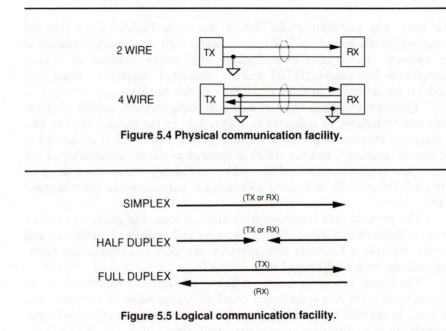

Figure 5.4 Physical communication facility.

Figure 5.5 Logical communication facility.

should be obvious that a full duplex data communications facility will require a four-wire physical link (actually, it would be more correct to say *logical* link here, since it is possible to provide full duplex communication links over two wires, by using frequency division multiplexing).

Full duplex links can support closed-loop communications, where each individual character is echoed back to the transmitter (thus closing the loop). The alternative scheme is open-loop communication, where data is simply assumed to reach its distant destination. Obviously closed loop communication is preferable, since characters will be echoed at the transmitter.

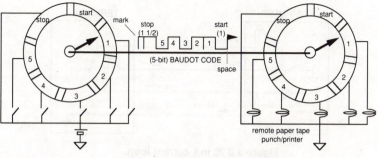

Figure 5.6 Teletypewriter (TTY).

5.2.1 Modulation techniques

In order to send information between a transmitter and a receiver station, the basic logic signals must first be converted into a form suitable for transmission over the relevant communications channel. Several different techniques are available to perform this function. In the older style electromechanical Teletypewriter (TTY) shown in Figure 5.6, the information is encoded as a train of unipolar DC pulses (marks and spaces).

By way of contrast, *bipolar* pulses are used in the RS232c standard shown in Figure 5.7; any signal greater than $+3$ V is considered as a mark, and any signal less than -3 V is considered as a space (typical signals lie in the range ±5–15 V). We shall return to consider RS232c in more detail shortly.

An older data communications standard is the 20 mA current loop. It stems from the days of electromechanical teletypewriters and, generally speaking, requires fewer interconnecting wires than RS232c. The four wires are transmit$+$, transmit$-$, receive$+$ and receive$-$, and are shown in Figure 5.8. Voltage is applied at one end, and current travels to the far end, passes through the load resistor there, then returns to the transmitting end. Two such current loops are provided, resulting in a full duplex link. HIs and LOs are sensed by the presence or absence of the 20 mA current. In the original teletypewriter machines, the current loop was made and broken by rotating

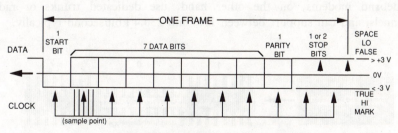

Figure 5.7 RS232c voltage levels.

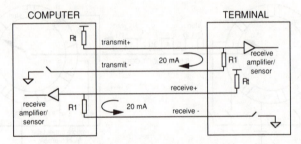

Figure 5.8 20 mA current loop.

switch contacts at the transmitter (as illustrated previously in Figure 5.6). At the receiver, this current loop drove a print solenoid.

Other encoding schemes involve varying a fixed radio frequency carrier signal in some manner or other. In the scheme shown in Figure 5.9, the amplitude of the carrier signal is varied to indicate either a HI or a LO, as indicated. This modulation technique is used in Radio Teletype (RTTY).

Instead of modulating the amplitude of the carrier, we can instead modulate its frequency. The resulting Frequency Shift Keying (FSK) technique is shown in Figure 5.10; LOs are encoded as one frequency, and HIs as twice that frequency. For example, in the Kansas City Standard used in cassette recorders, a 0 is encoded as 1200 Hz and a 1 as 2400 Hz.

A third modulation technique involves varying the *phase* of the carrier wave, and is illustrated in Figure 5.11 (and incidentally is used in many 4800 and 9600 bit/second modems).

The devices which modulate binary signals into a form suited to reliable and relatively error-free transmission over a communications channel, and back again into digital form, are known as modems (*mo*dulator/*dem*odulator). There are basically three types of modem, namely short-haul, voice-grade and wideband. Short-haul modems, as the name suggests, involve communication between a transmitter and receiver placed in relatively close proximity to each other, where it is not necessary to utilize the public telephone carrier network. Voice-grade modems utilize the public telephone network, and thus are restricted to the frequency range (bandwidth) of 300–3000 Hz. The maximum data transfer rate with this type of modem is around 9600 bit/second. Wideband modems, on the other hand, use dedicated trunks or radio channels, and can support between 19.2 and 230.4 kbit/second typically.

Figure 5.9 RadioTeletype (RTTY).

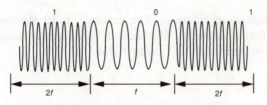

Figure 5.10 Frequency Shift Keying (FSK).

Earlier forms of modem generated voice frequency signals suitable for transmission over a telephone network. They came fitted with acoustic pads which fitted over the mouthpiece and earpiece of a telephone handset. The binary information was first converted into acoustic signals, then coupled onto the telephone line via the handset; hence the name acoustic coupler.

More recent modems are of the direct connect type, which are more efficient, reliable and less error prone compared with acoustic couplers, since the signals do not pass through an intermediate acoustic phase. Such direct connect modems employ one of the modulation techniques described above. A typical example of a direct connect modem is the Hayes 2400 Smartmodem, which became a *de facto* industry standard during the mid 1980s.

Up to now we have assumed that the entire frequency capacity (or bandwidth) of the communications channel has been available for the transmission of suitably encoded digital information, by modulating a carrier signal in some manner or other. In such a baseband scheme, different communications devices can utilize the capabilities of the channel at different times, using a technique known as Time Division Multiplexing (TDM).

An alternative approach is to employ a medium which has a much higher bandwidth – a broadband system – and instead of utilizing *all* of the available frequency band, to split this up into several smaller sized bands, each of which can be utilized all of the time by different communications devices. This is referred to as Frequency Division Multiplexing (FDM), and is often used in coaxial cable, optical fibre and satellite (broadband) systems. It necessitates the use of a Radio Frequency (RF) modem, since the carrier frequency is much higher than with baseband systems.

Thus broadband media can be used in either of two ways; TDM can be used for high-speed transmission, or FDM can be used to provide several

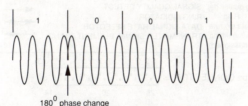

180^0 phase change

Figure 5.11 Phase modulation.

lower speed transmission channels. For example, a 10 Mbit/second channel could support either a single 10 Mbit/second TDM transmission, or just over one thousand 9600 baud channels using FDM.

5.2.2 RS232c

Control over a modem's operation is specified in the RS232c standard. The Electrical Industries Association of America (EIA) established the RS232 interface standard for interfacing between a computer and a modem in 1960. It was revised into the RS232c version in 1969.

The international communications body, CCITT, has a standard which closely resembles RS232c, namely V.24. It is important to note that these standards refer to the interfacing of DTE to DCE, and were never intended to be used for interfacing peripheral devices to a computer (a point to which we shall return shortly).

The RS232c signals are illustrated in Figure 5.12; the numbering refers to the 25-pin D-type connector, as shown. It should be readily apparent that RS232c can support full duplex communication; separate lines (2 and 3) are provided for transmission and reception. These are referred to as TxD and RxD in the RS232c standard (or BA and BB in V.24).

PIN NO.	CCITT	EIA	DESCRIPTION	DIRECTION (DTE<->DCE)
1	AA	ground		
2	BA	TxD	TRANSMIT DATA	→
3	BB	RxD	RECEIVE DATA	←
4	CA	RTS	REQUEST TO SEND	→
5	CB	CTS	CLEAR TO SEND	←
6	CC	DSR	DATA SET READY	←
7	AB	signal gnd		
8	CF	DCD	DATA CARRIER DETECT	←
9	-	(test)		←
10	-	(test)		←
11	-	(unassigned)		←
12	SCF	sec DCD	SECONDARY DCD	→
13	SCB	sec CTS		←
14	SBA	sec TxD		
15	DB	Tx sig timing	TRANSMITTER SIGNAL ELEMENT TIMING	←
16	SBB	sec RxD		←
17	DD	Rx sig timing	RECEIVER SIGNAL ELEMENT TIMING	→
18	-	(unassigned)		→
19	SCA	sec RTS		→
20	CD	DTR	DATA TERMINAL READY	→
21	CG	sig quality det	SIGNAL QUALITY DETECT	←
22	CE	Ring	RING INDICATOR	←
23	CH(CI)	Data sig rate	DATA SIGNAL RATE SELECTOR	←→
24	DA	Tx sig timing	TRANSMITTER SIGNAL ELEMENT TIMING	→
25	-	(unassigned)		

D-type CONNECTOR

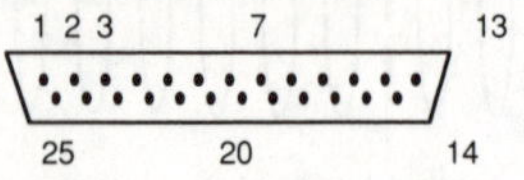

Figure 5.12 The (EIA) RS232C standard.

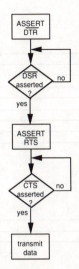

Figure 5.13 Modem control.

Request To Send (RTS) (CA) is sent from the DTE (computer or terminal) to the DCE (modem) in order to prepare the DCE for transmission. It is also used to indicate the direction of the transmission for half duplex communication channels. It is asserted whenever the DTE has a character ready to send. Clear To Send (CTS) (CB) is generated by the DCE to indicate to the DTE that transmission can begin whenever it is ready. For full duplex lines, RTS and CTS are simply tied together.

Data Set Ready (DSR) (CC) is used to indicate the status of the local DCE. A mark indicates that it is 'off the hook' and ready for use; it is neither disconnected from the telephone line nor in test mode. Data Terminal Ready (DTR) (CD) is used to control switching of the DCE to the communications channel. These two lines are often simply connected to the power supplies of the DCE and DTE respectively, to indicate that each is switched on and ready to go.

A mark on the Ring indicator (CE) indicates that ring tone is currently present on the telephone line. It is used to initiate a connection to the caller.

A mark received on Data Carrier Detect (DCD) (CF) indicates that a signal which meets the modem's specifications is being received by the DCE. It is alternatively known as Receive Line Signal Detector. In the OFF condition, it indicates either that no signal is being received, or that the signal being received is unsuitable for demodulation by the DCE. DCD indicates that the remote connection is active; if connection should be lost, an interrupt is flagged to the computer.

The interaction between DSR, DTR, RTS and CTS is illustrated in Figure 5.13.

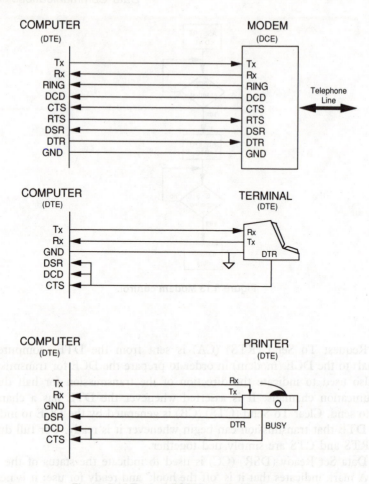

Figure 5.14 Typical RS232 applications.

As already mentioned, RS232c was originally designed for the inter-connection of computers or computer terminal equipment to modems; it was never intended for connecting computers to peripheral equipment. Neverthe-less, it is probably in this latter application that most use has been made of RS232c. Unfortunately, manufacturers rarely agree on which device is designated as the DTE and which as the DCE. Accordingly, RS232c is perhaps the most *unstandard* 'standard' in use in the computer industry.

Figure 5.14 shows some typical uses of RS232c. The topmost example shows the interconnection between a computer and a modem, which is the type of application for which RS232c was originally designed. Each control line connects through to its counterpart on the other device.

The other two examples in Figure 5.14 illustrate non-standard yet typical uses of RS232c. The first shows the connection of a computer to a

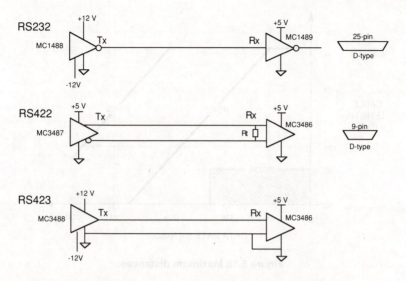

Figure 5.15 Comparison of current loop, RS232 and RS422(3).

terminal, where a single control line is all that is required at the terminal end. DSR, DCD and CTS are joined at the computer, so that transmission is enabled so long as power is applied to the terminal.

The second non-standard use of RS232c illustrated in Figure 5.14 involves the connection of a printer to a computer. An additional control signal is required, besides DTR, and this is BUSY, which connects to DCD and CTS at the computer end. This latter signal is required in order to stop further transmissions once the printer's buffer becomes full.

The problem with connecting computers to peripherals using 'RS232c' connectors is that different manufacturers interpret the control lines differently. For example, either the computer or peripheral could be regarded as the DTE or DCE, depending on the manufacturer.

Extreme care has to be exercised in connecting such devices; there are numerous specially built RS232c patch cables in existence!

RS232c first appeared in 1969. In the intervening years it has found difficulty in meeting demands placed on it by data communications equipment. Longer links, less susceptibility to noise and higher transmission rates have led to the development of other more suitable standards, such as the RS422 and RS423 illustrated in Figure 5.15.

RS423 allows for higher data rates (up to 100 kbaud), and longer lines (up to 1.2 km), but is still susceptible to noise. Like RS232, RS423 is an unbalanced system; it utilizes a single signal path only (with respect to ground).

RS422, on the other hand, is a balanced system, which means that the *difference* signal between the two lines carries the information. Any noise or

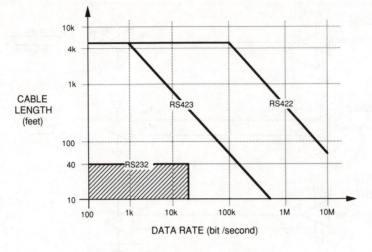

Figure 5.16 Maximum distances.

interference signal common to both lines will not appear at the (differential) line receiver input (this is referred to as common mode rejection). With the problem of ground loops removed, the threshold levels can be reduced considerably; the difference between a mark and a space in RS232c is 6 V ($\geq +3$ V for a mark; ≤ -3 V for a space), whereas with RS422, this margin drops to 0.4 V ($\geq +0.2$ V for a mark; ≤ -0.2 V for a space). Thus a ± 5 V supply is sufficient for generating the appropriate signals; no separate ± 12 V supply is necessary, as with RS232c (recall that a $+5$ V supply will be already be present in order to power any TTL/CMOS circuitry).

Whereas both electrical and functional specifications are contained within RS232c, in the newer standards, these have been separated out into RS422(3) (electrical) and RS449 (functional). RS449 also includes mechanical specifications (plugs and sockets). Signals are divided between 37-pin and 9-pin connectors, with ground and common handled separately for each connector. The 9-pin connector is intended for interfaces where the device at one end of the DTE/DCE connection is RS232c compatible, while the device at the other end is RS449 compatible, and split (or reverse) channel operation is required. RS449 has not been widely adopted in the marketplace; the Apple Macintosh, for example, uses a single 9-pin connector for its RS422 interface.

In terms of functionality, minor enhancements over RS232c have been made in terms of automatic modem testing and provision of a standby channel, but outward dialling is still not supported.

A comparison of the maximum transmission rates and line lengths possible using the three standards is shown in Figure 5.16.

5.3   ASYNCHRONOUS DATA COMMUNICATION

In transmitting data over a serial data communications link, synchronization between transmitter and receiver is of paramount importance. Data can be received either synchronously, with reference to a system clock, or asynchronously. With asynchronous transmission, data arrives in short bursts or frames, at irregular, unpredictable intervals. A single such frame was shown previously in Figure 5.7.

The first bit transmitted is a fixed bit to indicate the start of the frame. The receiver clock must lock onto the incoming bit stream for the next 10 cycles, but thereafter synchronization is not critical (the receiver clock has to *re*synchronize at the start of the *next* character).

The data is encoded in 7-bit form, and follows immediately after the start bit, which means that 128 discrete characters can be discriminated. Following the seven data bits is the parity check bit, which provides a rudimentary error detection facility, on a character-by-character basis. If parity is not maintained at the receiver end, retransmission can be requested by the receiver. One or two stop bits terminate the transmission.

Several different parity schemes are encountered in practice, namely odd, even, mark and space. With odd (even) parity, the msb is cleared if the total number of 1s in the character is odd (even). With mark (space) parity, the msb is always set (cleared).

The rate at which bits travel down the line is referred to as the baud rate (but this is strictly true only if each bit occupies a single clock cycle). Typical baud rates are 110, 300, 1200, 2400, 4800, 9600 and 19 200 bit/second.

The receiver clock can be made equal to the baud rate, however this means that the clock must be very accurate in order to sample the incoming bit stream in the *centre* of its cycle. The actual variation from the centre of the bit cell is referred to as the ratchet error. If the clock is made 16 times the baud rate, then the ratchet error can be relaxed from $\pm 1\%$ to $\pm 5\%$ (which relaxes further to $\pm 25\%$ for 64 times the baud rate). In other words, the sample point need not be *exactly* in the centre of the bit cell for reliable data recovery. Furthermore, a clock of 16 times the baud rate can tolerate a difference of around 5% in the clocks at the transmitter and receiver. Baud rate generator ICs are readily available, for use in data communication circuitry.

Characters can be encoded using either the Extended Binary Coded Decimal Interchange Code (EBCDIC) or ASCII standards, using either seven or eight bits. EBCDIC is used by IBM, whereas most other computer manufacturers use the ASCII (American Standard Code for Information Interchange) standard. Table 5.1 shows the encoding of characters in ASCII, EBCDIC and the older Baudot code.

Much longer frames, comprising up to 80 characters typically, are used in synchronous data communication links. Figure 5.17 illustrates the difference between asynchronous and synchronous frame formats; in the asynchron-

Table 5.1 ASCII, EBCDIC and Baudot character sets.

CHARACTER (control)				ASCII (space parity)				EBCDIC				BAUDOT (letters/figure shift + char)		
nul	space	@		00	20	40	60	00	40	7C	79	04		
soh	!	A	a	01	21	41	61	01	5A	C1	81			1F 03
stx	"	B	b	02	22	42	62	02	7F	C2	82		1B 11	1F 19
etx	#	C	c	03	23	43	63	03	7B	C3	83			1F 0E
eot	$	D	d	04	24	44	64	04	5B	C4	84		1B 0D	1F 09
enq	%	E	e	05	25	45	65	05	6C	C5	85			1F 01
ack	&	F	f	06	26	46	66	06	50	C6	86		1B 1A	1F 0D
bel	'	G	g	07	27	47	67	07	7D	C7	87	1B 0B	1B 05	1F 1A
bs	(	H	h	08	28	48	68	08	4D	C8	88		1B 0F	1F 14
ht	)	I	i	09	29	49	69	09	5D	C9	89		1B 12	1F 06
lf	*	J	j	0A	2A	4A	6A	25	5C	D1	91	02		1F 0B
vt	+	K	k	0B	2B	4B	6B	0B	4E	D2	92		1B 09	1F 0F
ff	,	L	l	0C	2C	4C	6C	0C	6B	D3	93		1B 0C	1F 12
cr	-	M	m	0D	2D	4D	6D	0D	60	D4	94	08	1B 03	1F 1C
so	.	N	n	0E	2E	4E	6E	0E	4B	D5	95		1B 1C	1F 0C
si	/	O	o	0F	2F	4F	6F	0F	61	D6	96		1B 1D	1F 18
dle	0	P	p	10	30	50	70	10	F0	D7	97		1B 16	1F 16
dc1	1	Q	q	11	31	51	71	11	F1	D8	98		1B 17	1F 17
dc2	2	R	r	12	32	52	72	12	F2	D9	99		1B 13	1F 0A
dc3	3	S	s	13	33	53	73	13	F3	E2	A2		1B 01	1F 05
dc4	4	T	t	14	34	54	74		F4	E3	A3		1B 10	1F 10
nak	5	U	u	15	35	55	75	3D	F5	E4	A4		1B 10	1F 07
syn	6	V	v	16	36	56	76	32	F6	E5	A5		1B 15	1F 1E
etb	7	W	w	17	37	57	77	26	F7	E6	A6		1B 07	1F 13
can	8	X	x	18	38	58	78	18	F8	E7	A7		1B 06	1F 1D
em	9	Y	y	19	39	59	79	19	F9	E8	A8		1B 18	1F 15
sub	:	Z	z	1A	3A	5A	7A	3F	7A	E9	A9		1B 0E	1F 11
esc	;	[	{	1B	3B	5B	7B	27	5E		C0		1B 1E	
fs	<	\	|	1C	3C	5C	7C	1C	4C	E0	6A			
gs	=	]	}	1D	3D	5D	7D	1D	7E		D0			
rs	>	^	~	1E	3E	5E	7E	1E	6E		A1			
us	?	_	del	1F	3F	5F	7F	1F	6F	6D	07		1B 19	

ous case, there is a variable delay between the start of each character 'frame', whereas in the synchronous case, the frames follow continuously one after the other. Thus synchronous links are inherently faster than asynchronous ones, and make more efficient use of the available bandwidth of the link or channel.

Some form of buffering will usually be required in communicating between transmitter and receiver, since they may not necessarily be using the same baud rate. Most asynchronous links use a flow control protocol to oversee data transmission. Three common protocols are X-on/X-off, Lead Control and ENQ/ACK.

In the X-on/X-off protocol, when the receiver buffer reaches its buffer capacity, it sends an ASCII 'DC3' (X-off) to the transmitter requesting it to stop sending data. When the receiver buffer becomes sufficiently empty again, it sends an ASCII 'DC1' (X-on) back to the transmitter, requesting it to start sending data again.

Lead control involves asserting one RS232c (typically DTR or CTS) line HI to enable data flow, or LO to stop communication. ENQ/ACK is a block-oriented handshake protocol, in which a fixed size block of characters is transmitted each time. The transmitter sends ENQ to the receiver, and waits for an ACK to be returned before starting transmission.

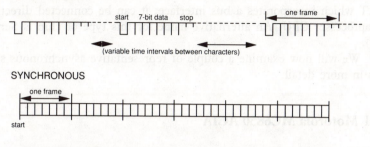

ASYNCHRONOUS

start 7-bit data stop

one frame

(variable time intervals between characters)

SYNCHRONOUS

one frame

start

Figure 5.17 Asynchronous vs synchronous transmission.

5.4 SERIAL SUPPORT CHIPS

We have already seen how RS232c signals are different from the TTL levels encountered within a microcomputer (±3–12 V, compared with 0 V and +5 V). Thus in interfacing serial I/O devices to a microcomputer, we will need some form of voltage level translation or buffering (in fact with short-haul modems, this is *all* that is required). Two such widely used line drivers (receivers) are the Motorola MC1488(9), shown in Figure 5.18. The function of the MC1488 is to convert TTL inputs into bipolar RS232c outputs, and thus it requires a ±12 V supply. The MC1489 only requires a +5 V supply however, since it produces TTL outputs. Corresponding RS422 and RS423 line driver (receiver) support chips are the MC3487(6) and MC3488(6) respectively.

The fundamental operation performed by a serial I/O device is parallel-to-serial and serial-to-parallel conversion. These conversions can be performed by MSI shift registers, but in data communications circuitry it is more usual to find specialized support chips to carry out these functions.

A Universal Asynchronous Receiver/Transmitter (UART) not only contains a parallel-to-serial and serial-to-parallel converter pair, but also their associated control circuitry and error-checking logic. Synchronous chips are also available, in the form of USRTs.

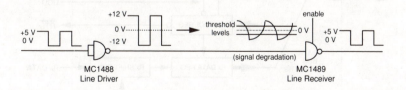

+12 V
0 V
+5 V
0 V
-12 V

threshold
levels

enable

0 V

+5 V
0 V

(signal degradation)

MC1488
Line Driver

MC1489
Line Receiver

Figure 5.18 MC1488/9 Line driver/receiver.

An Asynchronous Communications Interface Adapter (ACIA) is a UART which incorporates a bus interface; it can be connected directly to a microprocessor CPU. An alternative name for this type of chip is Serial I/O (SIO).

We will now examine a couple of representative asynchronous support chips in more detail.

5.4.1 Motorola MC6850 ACIA

The MC6850 is a serial support chip designed to operate with the MC6800 family of 8-bit processors. It can also be used with the MC68000, since this CPU has the ability to interface to synchronous peripheral devices as well as asynchronous ones. The MC6850 is shown in block diagram form in Figure 5.19.

It has two 8-bit data registers, one each for receive and transmit. It also has a programmable control register, and a (read only) status register. The functional configuration of the ACIA is set during initialization by writing the appropriate 8-bit binary pattern to the control register.

There are three Chip Select inputs, two active HI and one active LO, which reduces the amount of external decoding circuitry needed in systems which employ several such devices. It has a single Register Select input, which usually connects to address line 0 in MC6800 systems.

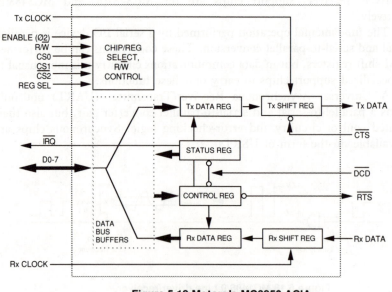

**Figure 5.19 Motorola MC6850 ACIA
(courtesy of Motorola Inc.).**

Table 5.2 MC6850 Registers.

RS (A0)	R/W̄	REGISTER
1	0	Tx DATA REGISTER
1	1	Rx DATA REGISTER
0	0	CONTROL REGISTER
0	1	STATUS REGISTER

The MC6850 provides three control lines for modem operation, namely CTS, DCD and RTS. Separate clock inputs are provided for transmitter and receiver, with an external programmable baud rate generator required to provide the basic clock signal.

Doubly-buffered serial I/O is built into the MC6850, with both 8- and 9-bit transmission being catered for.

Table 5.2 illustrates the use of the Register Select input together with the Read/W̄rite line for selecting one of the four on-chip registers.

The (write-only) MC6850 control register is selected whenever both Register Select and R/W̄ are LO together. It controls the function of receiver and transmitter, enables interrupts, and controls the Request To Send modem control output.

The two least significant bits determine the divide ratio to be used in conjunction with the external clock; the higher ratios allow for more accurate clocking of receiver and transmitter, as mentioned previously. A 11_2 written into these bit positions acts as a master reset for the ACIA chip.

Bits 2–4 select the word length, parity and the number of stop bits, as indicated in Figure 5.20. Bits 5 and 6 serve as transmitter control bits. They allow for interrupts following the Transmit Data Register Empty condition as well as controlling the Request To Send output. A 11_2 will set RTS LO, disable transmit interrupts, and then transmit a continuous break (or space) level on the Transmit Data Ouput line.

The msb of this 8-bit register is used to enable interrupts in the event of

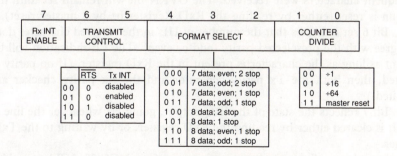

Figure 5.20 (Write-only) MC6850 control register(courtesy of Motorola Inc.).

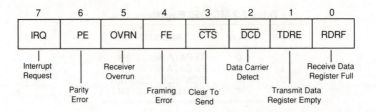

Figure 5.21 MC6850 (read-only) status register(courtesy of Motorola Inc.).

one of the following conditions: Receive Data Register Empty, Receiver Overrun, or a LO-to-HI transition on the DCD input line.

The (read-only) MC6850 status register is selected whenever RS is LO and R/$\overline{\text{W}}$ is HI. It is illustrated in Figure 5.21. Bit 0 set indicates that data has been transferred to the receive data register. RDRF is cleared either by the CPU reading the RxD register, or by a master reset. A HI condition on the DCD line also causes RDRF to indicate empty.

Bit 1 set indicates the contents of the TxD register have been transferred and that new data can be entered. Bit 1 cleared indicates that the TxD register is full and that transmission of a new character has not commenced since the last write command.

Bit 2 will be set whenever the DCD input from the modem goes HI, indicating that the carrier has been lost. This in turn will generate an Interrupt Request, provided the Receiver Interrupt Enable has been set previously.

Bit 3 reflects the CTS input from the modem; a HI signal on the line will inhibit the TDRE bit and set the CTS bit (Master reset does not affect the CTS status bit).

A Framing Error results either from improper synchronization, faulty transmission or a break condition on the line. It is detected by the absence of the first stop bit, and is only set while the associated character is present.

Bit 5 set indicates that one or more characters in the data stream were lost; a character was received but not read from the RxD register before subsequent characters were received. The OVRN bit will remain set until the overrun is reset (either by reading the RxD Register or by a master reset).

Bit 6 set indicates that the number of HIs in the received character does not agree with the preselected parity (odd or even). The PE indication will be present as long as the character is present in the RxD register. (If no parity is selected, then both the Tx parity generator and the Rx parity checker are inhibited.)

Bit 7 reflects the state of the $\overline{\text{IRQ}}$ output, going HI whenever the line is LO. It is cleared either by reading the RxD register, or by writing to the TxD register.

In order to illustrate the programming of an MC6850 ACIA, consider the hardware configuration of Figure 5.22. A dedicated MC68000-based

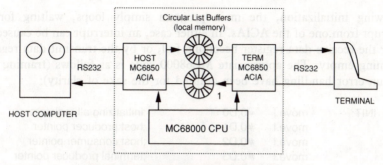

Figure 5.22 Transparent link hardware.

microcomputer acts as a transparent link between a host minicomputer and a terminal. The microcomputer has two ACIAs, one each for the host and terminal. Local RAM has addresses in the range $1000 to $3FFF, whereas the range $30000 to $3FFFF is allocated to MC6800-type peripheral devices.

The data structure employed in this transparent link is a circular list; MC68000 data registers are used to point to the producer and consumer of each circular buffer. 1200 baud RS232c links are used throughout.

The algorithm used in this transparent link is shown in Figure 5.23.

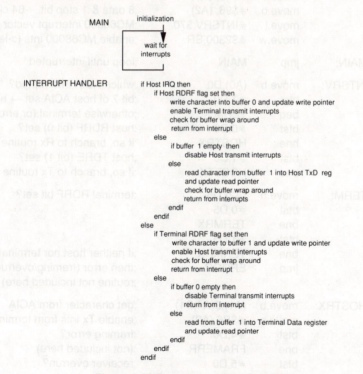

Figure 5.23 Transparent link algorithm.

Following initialization, the main program simply loops, waiting for an interrupt from one of the ACIAs. In either case, an interrupt can be caused by either the receive data register becoming full, or by the transmit data register becoming empty. The appropriate MC68000 code is as follows (framing and overrun error handling have been omitted for the sake of clarity):

```
INIT:     move.l    #0,D0              ;initializing all registers
          move.l    #0,D1              ;host producer pointer
          move.l    #0,D2              ;host consumer pointer
          move.l    #0.D3              ;terminal producer pointer
          move.l    #0,D4              ;terminal consumer pointer
          move.l    #0,D5
          move.l    #0,D6
          move.l    #$30801,A0         ;host ACIA control/status reg
          move.l    #$30803,A1         ;host ACIA data register
          move.l    #$30805,A2         ;terminal ACIA control/status reg
          move.l    #$30807,A3         ;terminal ACIA data register
          move.l    #$2000,A4          ;host circular buffer start addr
          move.l    #$2100,A5          ;terminal circular buffer address
          move.b    #3, (A0)           ;master reset of host ACIA
          move.b    #3, (A2)           ;master reset of terminal ACIA
          move.b    #$96, (A0)         ;enable Rx ints, RTS disabled,
          move.b    #$96, (A2)         ;8 data & 1 stop bit, ÷64 clock
          move.l    #INTSRV,$70        ;MC68000 interrupt vector
          move.w    #$2300,SR          ;enable MC68000 ints (>lev3)

MAIN:     jmp       MAIN               ;loop until interrupted

INTSRV:   move.b    (A0),D0            ;which ACIA interrupted?
          btst      #7,D0              ;bit 7 of host ACIA set → host
          beq       TERM               ;otherwise terminal (or error)
          btst      #0,D0              :host RDRF (bit 0) set?
          bne       HOSTRX             ;if so, branch to Rx routine
          btst      #1,D0              ;host TDRE (bit 1) set?
          bne       HOSTTX             :if so, branch to Tx routine

TERM:     move.b    (A2),D5            ;terminal RDRF bit set?
          btst      #0,D5
          bne       TERMRX
          btst      #1,D5
          bne       TERMRX             ;if neither host nor terminal,
          jmp       ERROR              ;then error (framing/overrun –
                                       ;routine not included here)

HOSTRX:   move.b    (A1),0(A4,D1)      ;get character from ACIA
          move.b    #$B6,(A2)          ;enable Tx ints from terminal
          btst      #4,D0              ;framing error?
          bne       FRAMERR            ;(not included here)
          btst      #5,D0              ;receiver overrun?
```

```
          bne      OVERUN            ;(not included here)
          add.b    #1,D1             ;buffer full?
          cmp.b    D1,D2
          beq      HBFULL            ;(not included here)
          cmp.b    #$50,D1           ;reset buffer pointer if
          beq      RESBUFF           ;necessary
          jmp      RETURN
RESBUFF:  clr.l    D1
          jmp      RETURN

HOSTTX:   cmp.b    D3,D4             ;is buffer empty?
          beq      SEND1             ;if so, send another character
          move.b   #$96, (A0)        ;enable Rx ints from host
SEND1:    move.b   0 (A5,D4), (A1)   ;char from buffer → ACIA
          add.b    #1,D4
          cmp.b    #$50,D4           ;reset buffer pointer if
          beq      RES2              ;necessary
          jmp      RETURN
RES2:     clr.l    D4
          jmp      RETURN

TERMRX:   move.b   (A3),0 (A5,D3)    ;char from buffer → ACIA
          btst     #4,D5             ;framing error?
          bne      FRAMERR           ;(not included here)
          btst     #5,D5             ;receiver overrun?
          bne      OVERUN            ;(not included here)
          cmp.b    #$90,(A3)         ;Data Link Escape character?
          jmp      LOCAL             ;if so, leave transparent link
                                     ;& return to local
                                     ;(stand alone) mode
          move.b   #$B6, (A0)        ;enable transmit ints from host
          add.b    #1,D3             ;buffer full?
          cmp.b    #$50,D3           ;reset buffer pointer if
          beq      RES3              ;necessary
          bra      RETURN
RES3:     clr.l    D3
          bra      RETURN

TERMTX:   cmp.b    D1,D2             ;is buffer empty?
          beq      SEND2             ;if so, send another character
          move.b   #$96, (A2)        ;enable Rx ints from terminal
SEND2:    move.b   0(A4,D2), (A3)    ;char buffer → ACIA data reg
          add.b    #1,D2
          cmp.b    #$50,D2           ;reset buffer pointer if necessary
          beq      RES4
          bra      RETURN
RES4:     clr.l    D2
          bra      RETURN
RETURN:   rte                        ;return to main
```

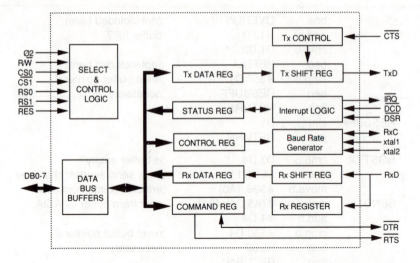

Figure 5.24 Rockwell R6551 ACIA (courtesy of Rockwell International).

5.4.2 Rockwell R6551 ACIA

The Rockwell R6551 ACIA is designed to interface to the MC6800 and R6502 families of 8-bit synchronous processors. It is an enhanced version of the earlier MC6850, in the sense that it does not require an external baud rate generator; only an external crystal is needed in order to generate one of 15 different baud rates, in the range 50–19 200 baud. Moreover, the receiver baud rate can be selected to be either the same as the transmitter baud rate, or 1/16 of the external clock rate.

The R6551 ACIA is shown in block diagram form in Figure 5.24. Now whereas the MC6850 has a single Register Select line, the R6551 has two, which means that a total of four addresses can be discriminated, although these are actually shared between *five* registers, as indicated in Figure 5.25.

Control of the R6551 is spread between the command and control registers (recall that the MC6850 has a single control register only). The four least significant bits of the R6551 control register are used to select the baud rate. Bit 4 is used to select the receiver clock source (either the internal baud rate generator or an external clock source). Bits 5 and 6 select the word length, either 5,6,7 or 8. The most significant bit determines the number of stop bits, either 1 or 2 (or 1½ for a word length of 5 and no parity).

Bit 0 of the R6551 command register controls the DTR output, whereas bit 1 enables interrupts. Bits 2 and 3 serve as the transmit control bits, in a similar fashion to bits 5 and 6 of the MC6850 control register. Bit 4 selects normal or echo mode operation; in receiver echo mode, the transmitter returns each transmission received by the receiver, but delayed in time by half a bit.

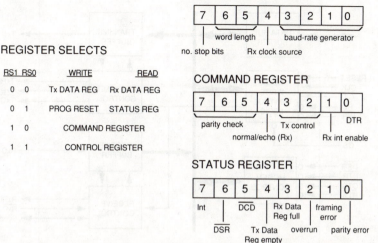

CONTROL REGISTER

| 7 | 6 | 5 | 4 | 3 | 2 | 1 | 0 |

word length   baud-rate generator

no. stop bits   Rx clock source

REGISTER SELECTS

RS1	RS0	WRITE	READ
0	0	Tx DATA REG	Rx DATA REG
0	1	PROG RESET	STATUS REG
1	0	COMMAND REGISTER	
1	1	CONTROL REGISTER	

COMMAND REGISTER

| 7 | 6 | 5 | 4 | 3 | 2 | 1 | 0 |

parity check   Tx control   DTR

normal/echo (Rx)   Rx int enable

STATUS REGISTER

| 7 | 6 | 5 | 4 | 3 | 2 | 1 | 0 |

Int   DCD   Rx Data Reg full   framing error

DSR   Tx Data Reg empty   overrun   parity error

Figure 5.25 R6551 registers (courtesy of Rockwell International Corp.).

The three most significant bits of the command register select and enable parity.

The R6551 status register is functionally very similar to the MC6850 status register, with some of the bit positions interchanged (for example, RDRF and TDRE are in positions 3 and 4, rather than 0 and 1 as in the MC6850). It should also be noted that attempts to write to the R6551 status register function as a software reset, as indicated in Figure 5.25.

5.4.3 Intel i8251 USART

The Intel i8251 Programmable Communications Interface is shown in block diagram form in Figure 5.26. It is capable of being programmed for either synchronous or asynchronous operation, hence it is alternatively referred to as a Universal Synchronous/Asynchronous Receiver/Transmitter (USART). Data paths are doubly buffered, with separate registers for control, status, received and transmitted data. This simplifies control, minimizes CPU overhead and allows for full duplex operation. Five to 8-bit characters are supported, at transmission rates of up to 19.2 kbaud (asynchronous) and 64 kbaud (synchronous). In asynchronous mode, support is provided for false start bit detection, as well as for handling automatic break detection. In synchronous mode, both internal and external character synchronization modes are supported.

Address line 0 connects to the Control/Data input of the i8251, resulting in two port addresses being allocated to the device. Table 5.3 shows how the

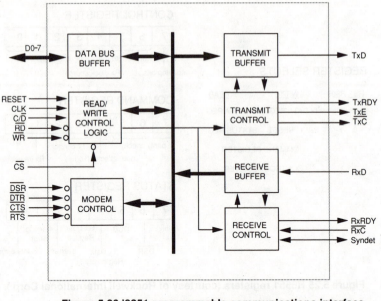

**Figure 5.26 i8251 programmable communications interface
(courtesy of Intel Corp.).**

Read and Write lines, together with C/D̄, select the appropriate data operation. The selection of the mode, control or sync character registers in the case of a control write depends on the accessing sequence used.

Figure 5.27 shows the i8251 mode, control and status registers. The following sequence must be followed in programming an i8251: the mode must be specified immediately following a reset. Further writes will then affect the control register rather than the mode register. If synchronous operation has been selected, either one or two sync characters will then be expected, followed by a control bit pattern (these sync characters are obviously not required in asynchronous mode however). The mode register can be subsequently selected by setting the master reset bit (bit 6) of the control register, with sync and control characters following the mode character, as previously.

Clearing bits 0 and 1 of the mode register selects synchronous operation.

Table 5.3 i8251 addressing (courtesy of Intel Corp.).

C/D(A0)	R̄D̄	W̄R̄	FUNCTION
0	0	0	DATA INPUT FROM DATA_IN BUFFER
0	1	0	DATA OUTPUT TO DATA_OUT BUFFER
1	0	1	STATUS REGISTER -> DATA BUS
1	1	1	DATA BUS -> MODE, CONTROL or SYNC CHAR REG

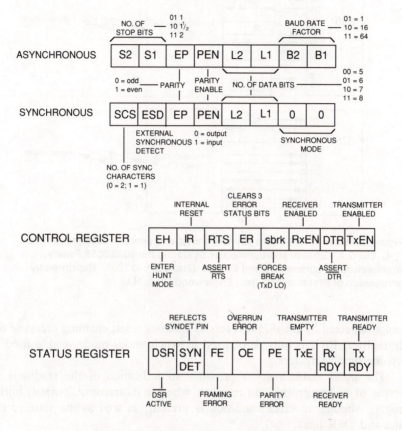

Figure 5.27 i8251 registers (courtesy of Intel Corp.).

Alternatively, a non-zero pattern selects the baud rate factor for asynchronous operation, either the same as the external clock, 1/16 or 1/64 of this rate. Bits 2–5 of the mode register are identical for both synchronous or asynchronous operation: bits 2 and 3 determine the number of data bits (in the range 5–8), bit 4 enables parity, while bit 5 selects either odd or even parity. In asynchronous mode, bits 6 and 7 select the number of stop bits, either 1, 1½ or 2. In synchronous mode, these bits serve the following functions: bit 6 selects the Syndet line as either an input or an output, while bit 7 selects the number of sync characters (either 1 or 2).

The i8251 control register enables transmit and receive interrupts and asserts the modem lines DTR and RTS, as indicated in Table 5.3. Asserting bit 3 will force the TxD line LO, which results in break characters being sent indefinitely. Bit 4 is used to reset an error condition, due to parity, overflow or framing. Bit 6 has already been mentioned in relation to the initialization

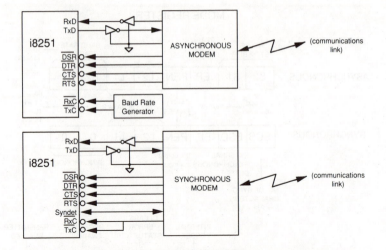

Figure 5.28 Use of i8251 with asynchronous and synchronous modems.
(Y-C. Liu/G.A. Gibson, Microcomputer Systems: the 8086/8088 Family,
Architecture, Programming and Design, (2nd edn). © 1986. Reprinted by
permission of Prentice-Hall, Inc., Englewood Cliffs NJ.)

sequence expected by the i8251; it acts as a master reset, enabling access of the mode register. Bit 7 is only recognized in synchronous mode, and is used to search for sync characters.

The i8251 status register provides an indication of the readiness or otherwise of its transmitter and receiver, whether its transmit (output) buffer is empty, whether an error condition is present, as well as the state of the Syndet and DSR lines.

Interfacing an i8251 to both an asynchronous and a synchronous modem is illustrated in Figure 5.28 (after Liu and Gibson, reprinted by permission of Prentice-Hall). The major difference is that whereas the $\overline{RxC}$ and $\overline{TxC}$ clock lines are connected to an external baud rate generator in the asynchronous case, they are connected through to the transmitter signal element timing (DCE) or DB (pin 15) line of the modem. The Syndet line of the i8251 is also connected through.

Figure 5.29 shows a system where a local terminal connects through to a remote terminal using a dedicated i8086-based microcomputer. Each terminal is connected to its own i8251 USART via RS232c lines. (7-bit ASCII) characters typed on either keyboard are passed through to the other terminal, as well as being echoed back to the corresponding terminal. The following routine illustrates how the i8251 would be programmed for this particular application (Y-C. Liu/G.A. Gibson, *Microcomputer Systems: the 8086/8088 Family, Architecture, Programming, and Design,* (2nd edn). © 1986. Reprinted by permission of Prentice-Hall, Inc., Englewood Cliffs N.J.):

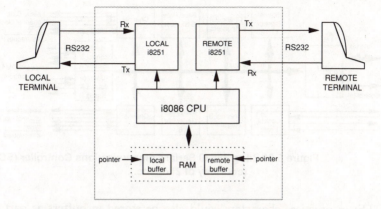

Figure 5.29 Communication between two terminals.

```
LOCDAT        equ  80H        ;local terminal i8251 data
LOCAL         equ  81H        ;local i8251 control/status
REMDAT        equ  90H        ;remote terminal i8251 data
REMOTE        equ  91H        ;remote i8251 control/status
INIT:    mov  AL,CAH          ;asynchronous mode, 7 data bits,
         out  LOCAL,AL        ;2 stop bits, no parity, ÷16 clock
         mov  AL,15H          ;(clear errors) and enable Tx and Rx
         mov  AL,CAH          ;initialize remote terminal
         out  REMOTE,AL       ;(same as local terminal)
LOCTERM: in   AL,LOCAL        ;poll local terminal
         mov  AL,BL           ;check for errors
         and  38H,BL          ;
         jmp  ERROR           ;(error handler not shown here)
         and  2H,AL           ;receiver ready (with a character)?
         jnz  LOCCHAR         ;if so, send to both terminals
REMTERM: in   AL,REMOTE       ;poll remote terminal
         mov  AL,BL           ;check for errors
         and  38H,BL          ;
         jmp  ERROR           ;(error handler not shown here)
         and  2H,AL           ;receiver ready (with a character)?
         jnz  REMCHAR         ;if so, send to both terminals
         jmp  LOCTERM         ;else keep polling each in turn
LOCCHAR: in   AL,LOCDAT       ;input character from local terminal
         and  7FH,AL          ;strip off parity
         out  AL,LOCDAT       ;echo to local screen (via local i8251)
         out  AL,REMDAT       ;send to remote screen (via rem i8251)
         jmp  LOOP            ;return to poll for more characters
REMCHAR: in   AL,REMDAT       ;input character from remote terminal
         and  7FH,AL          ;strip off parity
         out  AL,REMDAT       ;echo to remote screen (via rem i8251)
         out  AL,LOCDAT       ;send to local screen (via local i8251)
         jmp  LOOP            ;return to poll for more characters
```

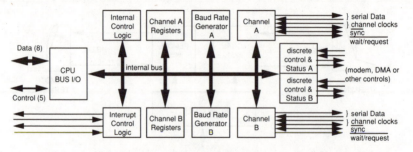

Figure 5.30 Zilog Z8530 Serial Communications Controller (SCC) (courtesy of Zilog Inc.).

(NOTE: in practice, characters could also be stored in buffers as part of the LOCCHAR and REMCHAR loops, as illustrated in Figure 5.29. This would be necessary for implementing a message passing communication system, for example.)

5.4.4 Zilog Z8530 SCC

Like the i8251 USART, the Zilog Z8530 Serial Communications Controller (SCC) supports both asynchronous and synchronous communications. It has two independent full duplex channels, each with its own crystal oscillator, baud rate generator and digital phase-locked loop. Transfer rates of up to 1 Mbit/second are supported. The Z8530 can be programmed for several different protocols, such as bipolar Non-Return to Zero, (NRZ) and Frequency Modulation (FM). Specific support for the bisync and SDLC/ HDLC synchronous standards is also included in the chip (these synchronous standards are discussed in Section 5.5). Local loopback and auto echo modes are also supported.

The Z8530 can be used either as a data communications support chip, or as a general-purpose serial peripheral, offering such features as vectored interrupts, polling and simple handshake capability. Figure 5.30 shows the Z8530 SCC internal architecture.

From what has already been said about the Z8530, it should be obvious that it is a more sophisticated chip than either the MC6850 or the i8251 (which reflects its more recent arrival into the marketplace). Each channel has nine read registers and 14 write registers associated with it.

Read register #2 contains the interrupt vector, while read register #4 contains the Interrupt Pending (IP) flag. Read registers 0, 1, 10 and 15 supply status information, while registers 12 and 13 contain the baud rate generator time constant.

The write registers are programmed to set the particular configuration of either channel. Two registers, 2 and 9, are shared between the two channels; number 2 contains the interrupt vector for both channels, while number 9 specifies the interrupt control bits.

The Z8530 is used in the Apple Macintosh and NeXT computers to control serial I/O via their RS422 ports.

5.5 SYNCHRONOUS DATA COMMUNICATION

In a synchronous data communications link, a well-defined protocol (or set of rules) is necessary in order to initialize stations, to establish and terminate conversations between two stations, to identify the sender and receiver and to acknowledge received information.

Synchronous serial I/O is usually required for high-speed (several Mbytes/second typically) data communication links (recall that asynchronous transmission rates are limited to around 19.2 kbaud). By using a synchronizing clock, the need for start and stop bits is eliminated, resulting in more efficient use of the available system bandwidth. The tradeoff, however, is in maintaining the integrity of this system clock; recall that the receiver and transmitter in an asynchronous system only have to be synchronized for the duration of a single character (typically 10 bits).

Synchronous protocols are block oriented rather than character oriented, which means that the clocks have to remain synchronized for much longer periods. However, a block-oriented protocol provides for more control and error checking than a character protocol.

Figure 5.31 shows the typical structure of a synchronous serial I/O port, which bears a close resemblance to the asynchronous devices considered earlier in this chapter; input and output shift registers provide the necessary serial-to-parallel and parallel-to-serial conversions respectively. However, instead of the single transmit and receive buffers of the asynchronous I/O port, the synchronous port utilizes First In First Out (FIFO) buffers, sufficient to hold several characters at a time.

The actual electrical signals transmitted along the communications line will consist of data and clock mixed together. At the receiver end, this clock information has to be separated out from the incoming bit stream. Instead of using start and stop bits, special synchronizing bit patterns at the start of each block are used by the receiver for establishing both character-by-character and block-by-block synchronization. The clock extractor and synchronization detector are shown in Figure 5.31.

There are a number of synchronous protocols in existence, two of the more common ones being Bisync and HDLC. Binary Synchronous Communication (Bisync) is an IBM protocol for synchronous transmission of binary coded data between stations in a data communications system. Two successive sync characters are used to establish both character and block synchronization. Half duplex communication is assumed, with handshaking between the two transmitters used to confirm that synchronization has been established; synchronization is maintained thereafter by the protocol itself.

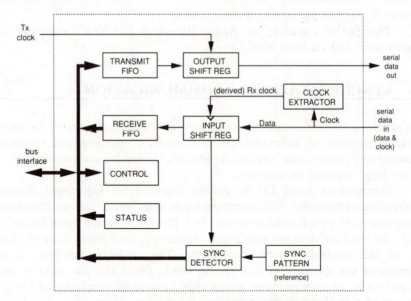

Figure 5.31 Structure of a synchronous I/O port.

Immediately following these sync characters is the Start Of Header (SOH) block. The SOH block consists of ASCII control characters, and contains source and destination addresses, together with a message sequence number (all of which are required in the event of a retransmission being requested).

A Start of Transmission (STX) block precedes the data block, which is followed in turn by an End of Transmission (ETX). Redundant check bits allow for error checking of the block as a whole; parity bits within each ASCII character allow for error checking at the individual character level as well. The Bisync protocol uses the Data Link Escape (DLE) character to signify that the next character should be interpreted as data rather than as a control character. This data transparency is an inherent feature of Bisync. Figure 5.32 shows this Bisync block structure.

Bisync originally only supported point-to-point communications; in the event of simultaneous bids from two different devices desiring to transmit to a third, precedence was granted to one or the other. Bisync has since been extended to support multidrop configurations.

The block-oriented Bisync protocol has been largely superseded in recent times by bit-oriented protocols such as the High level Data Link Control (HDLC). HDLC defined by the International Standards Organization (ISO) is an outgrowth of the earlier IBM Synchronous Data Link Control (SDLC) and Advanced Data Communications Control Procedure (ADCCP) protocols.

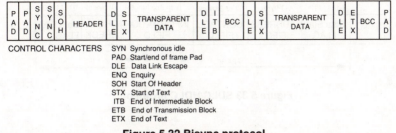

P A D	P A D	S Y N C	S Y N C	S O H	HEADER	D L E	S T X	TRANSPARENT DATA	D L E	I T B	BCC	D L E	S T X	TRANSPARENT DATA	D L E	E T X	BCC	P A D

CONTROL CHARACTERS

SYN Synchronous idle
PAD Start/end of frame Pad
DLE Data Link Escape
ENQ Enquiry
SOH Start Of Header
STX Start of Text
ITB End of Intermediate Block
ETB End of Transmission Block
ETX End of Text

Figure 5.32 Bisync protocol.

In the HDLC protocol, a unique bit pattern – 01111110 – is used to maintain character synchronization, as indicated in Figure 5.33. In order to prevent the sync character being transmitted as data, the HDLC protocol ensures that no more than five 1s are transmitted in succession; an additional zero bit is inserted at the transmitter and removed automatically at the receiver. Full duplex operation is implied with bit-oriented protocols such as HDLC. Moreover, fewer handshake sequences, synchronizing characters and interblock gaps are required, which altogether leads to roughly twice the throughput compared with Bisync.

With SDLC/HDLC, the primary or controlling station has responsibility for the data link, and repeatedly polls the secondary or controlled (responding) stations. SDLC/HDLC frames fall into one of three categories: non-sequenced, supervisory or information. Non-sequenced or management frames convey (primary) commands and (secondary) responses; they are used for controlling secondary nodes and indicating transmission errors. Supervisory frames are used for acknowledgement, indicating busy condition, requesting retransmission and so on. Data is actually transmitted within an information frame.

There is abundant support for synchronous data communications by way of microprocessor peripheral support chips. Apart from the i8251 USART mentioned in the previous section, other Intel support chips include the i8273 HDLC/SDLC Protocol Controller, i8274 Multi Protocol Serial Controller (asynchronous, Bisync and HDLC/SDLC), and i82530 (dual channel) Serial Communications Controller. Intel also manufacture the i83C152 Universal Communications Controller, which is a dedicated i8051 microcontroller incorporating inbuilt support for both the SDLC/HDLC and CSMA/CD protocols (CSMA/CD will be discussed in Section 5.7.3 in relation to Ethernet). Data transfer rates of up to 2.5 Mbit/second (SDLC/HDLC) and 1.5 Mbit/second (CSMA/CD) are supported. 256 bytes of RAM and 8 Kbytes of ROM are provided on chip, as well as two DMA channels, two 16-bit timers, five 8-bit I/O ports, a boolean processor and two hardware interrupts.

We have already discussed the Zilog Z8530 Serial Communications Controller; it too has inbuilt support for the SDLC/HDLC protocol.

Motorola produce a wide range of 8- and 16-bit serial support chips, ranging from the MC6852 Synchronous Serial Adapter and MC6854 Advanced

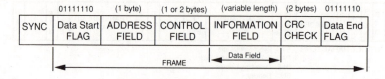

Figure 5.33 SDLC/HDLC protocol.

Data Link Controller, to the more recent MC68661 Enhanced Programmable Communications Controller, MC68652 Multi Protocol Communications Controller and MC68564 Serial I/O. The MC68652 MPCC chip, for example, can support synchronous byte- and bit-oriented protocols at data rates up to 2 MHz, in either full or half duplex operation. Programmable error control is provided, and the device can interface to either 8- or 16-bit bus systems.

Rockwell offer the R65560 Multi Protocol Communications Controller, which supports both bit- and character-oriented protocols, for both R6502 and MC6800 processors.

Another type of serial support chip which became prominent during the mid 1980s was the 'modem-on-a-chip'. A typical example is the Advanced Micro Devices Am7910 FSK Modem World-Chip. It incorporates all digital signal processing, digital filtering and A/D (D/A) conversion on-chip. Auto answer and local copy/test modes are supported. It satisfies the CCITT V.21 and V.23 modem specifications, supporting up to 2400 bit/second full duplex (4-wire) communication. CCITT V.24 (RS232c) handshake signals are also supported.

5.6   NETWORKS

Communications between a computer in one location and another in some remote location will often take place via some form of network. There are a number of different networks in existence, most of which are incompatible with each other. We will look briefly at Systems Network Architecture before moving on to consider the general area of local area networks.

5.6.1 Systems Network Architecture

Systems Network Architecture (SNA) was developed by IBM during the mid 1970s. It was originally designed as a single host-based networking system, but has since evolved into a sophisticated architecture allowing communication between the various network elements, including multiple hosts. It is currently one of the world's most widely used data communications standards.

In SNA there are four types of nodes: type 1 are terminals, type 2 are terminal controllers, type 4 are front-end processors, and type 5 are hosts (there are no type 3 nodes). SNA supports a two-level hierarchical architecture, with type 4 and type 5 (subarea) nodes forming a distributed backbone. Subarea nodes form a tree, whose root is the controlling subarea node. Type 1 and type 2 nodes are peripheral nodes, and each attaches to a specific type 4 (5) node.

Under SNA, the specification of explicit routes, the mapping of virtual routes onto these, and the ordering of these virtual routes is carried out at system definition time. Routes are specified end-to-end for each session.

SNA consists of the following layers: data link control, path control, transmission control, data flow control and function management. The data link control layer oversees local communications, ensuring that data travelling beyond it conforms to wider SNA protocols. SDLC is the protocol used at this level. The path control layer determines the routeing of data within SNA, between the various Network Addressable Units (NAUs). The transmission control layer handles data routeing, regulates data flow, and performs encryption and decryption. The data flow control layer regulates the transmission and reception of data, including error correction and the synchronization of packets within the network. The function management layer incorporates network services such as configuration, maintenance, measurement and network management facilities. Each SNA layer has its own protocol associated with it.

5.7 LOCAL AREA NETWORKS

Experience shows that communication between different computers takes place within the same building in 60% of cases. A further 20% take place within 80 kilometres, and only 10% venture further than 800 km. Thus, most of the communication between computers tends to be localized. Such local networks should be distinguished from wide area networks, which utilize the public telephone facilities, and extend across the country and indeed between different countries.

Local networks can be classified into three different groups, namely Local Area Networks (LANs), high-speed local computer networks (machine-to-machine links), and computerized branch exchanges (PABXs). We shall only concern ourselves with the first type here.

The advantages of LANs are resource sharing, increased reliability, distributed processing capability, easier system evolution and the potential to connect devices from different manufacturers. The increased complexity which results from using LANs leads to a number of disadvantages, namely loss of control in distributed systems, difficulty in maintenance, creeping escalation of the LAN system and the incompatibility of the different equipment which connects to the LAN (different formats, for example).

The ISO has developed the Open Systems Interconnection (OSI) 7-layer

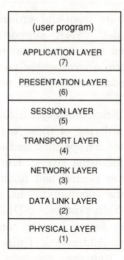

Figure 5.34 ISO/OSI (7-layer) reference model.

model for intersystem communications. It should be emphasized however, that LANs did not come of age until long after the OSI 7-layer model was defined. This 7-layer model is illustrated in Figure 5.34.

Associated with each layer is a different protocol. Layer 1 is concerned with the encoding (decoding) and transmission of electrical signals between adjacent nodes. The next level (data link) is concerned with synchronization and errors on the physical layer. The network layer performs the message routeing and switching functions for data transfers involving non-adjacent nodes. Layer 4 uses the three lower layers to provide transparent, reliable data transfer from end node to end node. The session layer manages address translation and access security. It controls the establishment and termination of transport connections. Layer 6 restructures data to and from the standardized format used within the network; both data formatting and code conversion can be involved here. Layer 7 provides all the services directly comprehensible to application programs. The users' application programs sit on top of this layer, and are not part of the OSI model.

The 7-layer OSI-ISO model overlaps somewhat with other network models, as illustrated in Figure 5.35. In this figure the OSI, TCP/IP, SNA, X.25 and IEEE802 models are compared.

X.25 is a packet switching network standard. In packet switching networks, messages are decomposed into much smaller segments and transmitted over a common communications channel, which is only occupied for the duration of a packet. Messages from several end stations are multiplexed over a single channel. Moreover, in the event of a node failure, an *alternate* route will be found through the network. In other words, the routeing is dynamic, being determined *during* rather than prior to the packet transfer. ·

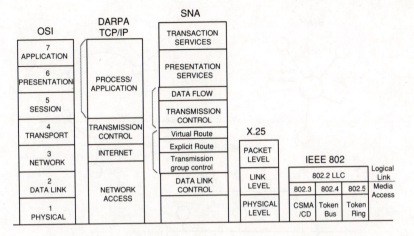

Figure 5.35 Comparison of OSI, TCP/IP, SNA, X.25 and IEEE802.

TCP/IP, developed by the US Department of Defense Advanced Research Project Agency (DARPA), treats all end users and application specific software as processes. The Internet Protocol (IP) handles network routeing so that processes can communicate over different networks, and is similar to OSI layer 4. The transmission protocol layer enables processes to communicate with each other. There are no application-oriented layers; these need to be written into user processes. Nevertheless, several specific application service elements are available, such as a file transfer protocol, virtual terminal (Telnet), a remote job entry process and simple mail transfer protocol.

There is some overlap between the different standards, but generally speaking they are not very compatible. Some of the standards only define the lower levels of such an interconnection; the IEEE802 standard, for example, really only defines two: the logical link and media access levels.

Figure 5.36 shows the various LAN topologies. The star topology has a centralized switching element, and is more usually found in PABXs rather than LANs. The ring consists of a number of nodes connected to repeaters which relay circulating data packets around the ring. In the tree topology, transfers take place in parallel rather than serial form. Terminations are required in order to prevent reflections from the branch ends (a bus LAN is a single-branch tree).

Access to the transmission medium can be achieved either synchronously, as in the case of a PABX, or asynchronously, as with most LANs. Medium access can be either random or controlled. Random access techniques include Carrier Sense Multiple Access (CSMA), register insertion and slotted ring. Controlled access techniques include token bus, token ring and collision avoidance. We shall examine some of these techniques in more detail in our discussion of specific LANs.

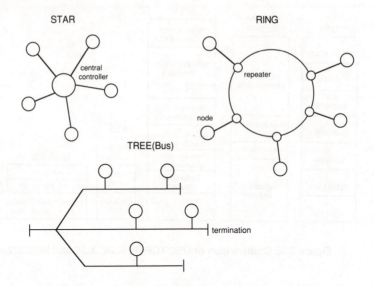

Figure 5.36 LAN topologies.

The transmission media used to implement LANs ranges from telephone grade twisted-pair cable, through coaxial cable to optical fibre. (The advantage of fibres is that, unlike metal cables, they are not susceptible to electromagnetic interference. They are also difficult for eavesdroppers to tap into.) The maximum data rates for each medium are of the order of 1 Mbit/second, 50–500 Mbit/second, and 1 Gbit/second, respectively. Maximum ranges are tens of metres, tens of kilometres and hundreds of kilometres, respectively. The cost per metre of twisted pair is much lower than either coaxial or optical cables however.

Both baseband and broadband techniques can be used with coaxial cable (and optical fibre) LANs. In our discussion of modulation techniques in Section 5.2.1, we saw how the usable frequency range (bandwidth) available on a communications channel can be shared (multiplexed) in terms of either time of frequency. Moreover, the actual modulation technique can be either digital or analog. Baseband and broadband signalling on LANs is contrasted in Figure 5.37.

Digital modulation is used for baseband signalling, but is limited due to the rapid attenuation of signals along the line. Analog modulation is necessary with broadband signalling, which increases the maximum usable distance of the LAN.

In baseband signalling, digital information is transmitted as discrete changes in the voltage level travelling down the line. Two common baseband encoding techniques are Manchester Encoding (in which a 1 is encoded as a LO–HI transition, and a 0 as a HI–LO transition), and bipolar or FM (where 0s are encoded as bipolar signals of twice the frequency used to encode 1s). In

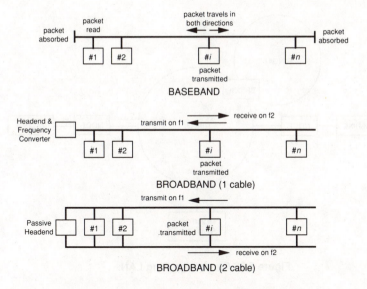

Figure 5.37 Baseband vs broadband transmission.

broadband signalling, the digital information is modulated using a carrier frequency (into different bands).

Baseband cables can support bidirectional, simplex transmission, with signals broadcast simultaneously towards both ends of the cable. Broadband, by way of contrast, is a unidirectional medium, but can support full duplex transmission. Two types of broadband system are used in industry, these being one- and two-cable systems, as shown in Figure 5.37. In the one-wire system, a frequency converter is necessary to convert incoming (transmitted) frequencies to outgoing (received) frequencies. Since separate cables are used in the two-wire system, stations can transmit and receive on the *same* frequency, hence the head end only acts as a passive repeater, retransmitting incoming signals on the same frequency.

5.7.1 Cambridge Ring LAN

Ring LANs exhibit a number of common characteristics. Their main advantage is that since they support serial transmission, the interconnecting cables are few in number and can often be low grade telephone-type cable. Their main disadvantage is that the failure of just one node (repeater) disables the entire network. The Cambridge Ring is a representative type of ring LAN, and is shown in Figure 5.38.

Physically, it consists of up to 256 nodes (stations) spaced at regular intervals (but not exceeding 100 metres between nodes), and connected by a 2-

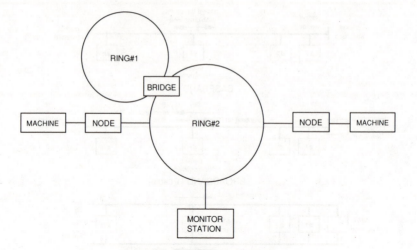

Figure 5.38 Cambridge Ring LAN.

pair (twisted) cable. Each node consists of a repeater, a station and a node controller. One node, the monitor station, is unique; it is used to establish the slot structure during power up, to monitor traffic on the ring, to clear lost packets and to accumulate error statistics.

The Cambridge Ring supports full duplex transmission, at 10 Mbit/ second, with a minimum ring delay (one round trip) of around 5 microseconds. The operating frequency of the ring is adaptively controlled to ensure that the time delay around the network is equivalent to an integral number of cycles.

The Cambridge Ring works on the circulating empty slot principle: packets to be transmitted are placed in a shift register and clocked into the next empty slot that arrives at that particular node. The 40-bit minipacket structure is illustrated in Figure 5.39. The start bit is always HI, and is immediately followed by a bit which indicates whether the packet is full or empty. The third bit is a control bit used by the monitor station to detect (and clear) slots that have not been emptied; otherwise they would circulate indefinitely around the ring. The next two bytes contain the destination and source addresses respectively for the packet, and the following two bytes contain the data, Two control bits, two response bits and a parity bit make up the remaining five bits of the 40-bit minipacket.

The physical layer protocol is as follows: when a station is ready to transmit, it awaits the arrival of the next slot. It then reads the full/empty bit, whilst simultaneously writing a start bit out. If the minipacket is full, the attempted transmission is delayed until the arrival of the next slot. When an empty slot is found, the station transmits its prepackaged minipacket in place of the incoming slot. Whenever a station recognizes its own address in the

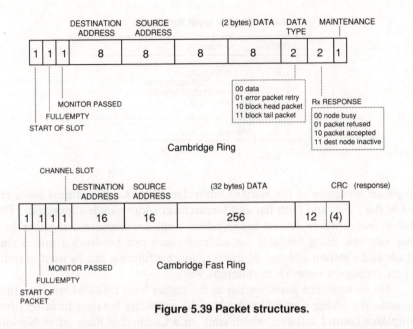

Figure 5.39 Packet structures.

destination field of an incoming minipacket, it reads the packet, sets the
control bits to indicate accepted, busy or rejected, and then retransmits the
packet. Each station knows the total number of slots circulating around the
ring, and can thus empty its own transmitted packet simply by counting the
number of packets that pass by, and then clearing the full/empty bit.

Higher level protocols can be overlayed onto this physical layer, in order
to support such functions as resource sharing amongst the various stations
connected to a single ring, as well as message passing between different
machines. Scheduling, priorities and error recovery would all be handled at
this higher level, with the physical layer remaining transparent to the user.

Support for the Cambridge Ring LAN is available via a chip set
developed by Acorn Computers of the UK, which boosts the speed of the Ring
to 60 Mbit/second. A two-chip set has also been developed to support the
Cambridge Fast Ring (CFR), a 100 Mbit/second (incompatible) upgrade of the
earlier Cambridge Ring.

The data length used in the CFR is 32 bytes, rather than 2 bytes as in
the Cambridge Ring minipacket. This results in maximization of the point-to-
point bandwidth, even for physically large rings (15 Mbit/second typically, in
comparison with around 2.5 Mbit/second on the Cambridge Ring). In the
CFR, an additional bit is added at the front of each slot, in order to control the
channel mode (necessary to handle the situation where a second, out-of-
sequence packet is retransmitted, despite the response to the first packet not
being accepted).

The CFR packet structure is shown in Figure 5.39, together with the

Table 5.4 Link layer functions.

FUNCTION	PURPOSE
0	(reserved)
1	ESTABLISH CIRCUIT
2	CIRCUIT CLOSE INDICATION
3	RESET PROTOCOL STATES
4	INACTIVITY POLL
5	STATE
6	DATA
7	(reserved)

minipacket structure of the earlier Cambridge Ring. Larger address fields are used in the CFR, and both flat and hierarchical addressing is supported. (The latter is useful where several independent rings are connected together in a larger network using bridges; the address space can be divided into a ring address and a station address. Moreover, address filtering can be used to route packets through a network in different ways.)

Let us now turn our attention to the higher level ISO/OSI layers as they map onto the earlier Cambridge LAN. The following is taken from terminal multiplexer control software which runs on a Cambridge Ring (after Nealon, 1985). (A terminal multiplexer allows many terminals to timeshare the limited number of serial ports available to connect to a host computer.) Communication between two stations connected to the ring takes place via a 'virtual circuit' (which is simply a logical link established for the duration of the transfer only). We shall restrict our attention to the link layer (OSI level 2), network layer (OSI level 3), and transport layer (OSI level 4) in this discussion.

Eight functions are supported in level 2 – the link layer protocol – as indicated in Table 5.4. Messages at this layer have the following C-code format:

```
struct   LinkHeader   {
         unsigned short      Function     :3;
         unsigned short      Originator   :1;
         unsigned short      CircuitId    :12;
         };
struct   LinkMessage {
         struct         LinkHeader  MessageHeader;
         char                       MessageData[ ];
         };
```

The originator bit and circuit ID are provided in the message header in order to uniquely identify each virtual circuit. Messages must be at least two bytes long, and have the following form:

Table 5.5 Recognized server names.

NAME	FUNCTION
LOGIN	INTERACTIVE TERMINAL SESSION
FILER	FILE TRANSFER
MAILER	MAIL TRANSFER
EXEC	BATCH EXECUTION
INFO	STATISTIC & INFORMATION
SPOOLER	PRINTER/NETWORK SPOOLING FUNCTIONS

```
struct   StateMessage     {
         short MaxIdleTime;
         short Free2ByteBuffers;
         short Free16ByteBuffers;
         short Free64ByteBuffers;
         short Free128ByteBuffers;
         short Free512ByteBuffers;
         short Free1024ByteBuffers;
         short Free2048ByteBuffers;
         short ReservedForLayer;
};
```

The first message to be sent establishes a circuit, the response to which is either state (success) or close (failure). The form of this establish circuit message is:

```
struct   Establish     {
         struct         LinkHeader       Header;
         struct         StateMessage     State;
         char                            ServerName[ ];
         }              EstablishCircuit =     {
                        {1,1,/*id*/},
                        {MessageActivity,/*buffer state*/},
};
```

An optional field follows the state message, which can be used to nominate the name of a logical process server which subsequently controls messages on the circuit. Allowable names are shown in Table 5.5.

At the next higher protocol layer – the network layer (OSI level 3) – the five message types of Table 5.6 can be exchanged. Messages will have the form:

```
struct   UserMessage {
         char  MessageType;
         char  MessageData[ ];
         };
```

Table 5.6 Message types (network layer).

TYPE	MESSAGE
1	USER DATA
2	USER END-OF-FILE
3	USER TRAP
4	USER CONTROL REQUEST
5	USER CONTROL REPLY

Table 5.7 User traps.

TRAP	MEANING
0	(reserved)
1	HANGUP
2	INTERRUPT
3	INTERRUPT WITH CORE IMAGE (abort)
4-63	(reserved)
64-255	USER DEFINED

Table 5.8 Packet types (transport layer).

TYPE	PURPOSE
0	(reserved)
1	SOFTWARE LOADER FORMAT
5	ACKNOWLEDGE PACKET
6	DATA BLOCK WITH INTEGRITY CHECK
7	DATA BLOCK WITHOUT INTEGRITY CHECK
8	SINGLE MINIPACKET
9	CAMBRIDGE PACKET

User data is passed directly to and from a user process without interpretation, with zero-length data being interpreted as 'end-of-file'. One data byte in 'message data' acts as a user trap, and can have any of the codes shown in Table 5.7. A trap will normally cause waiting data to be dumped, buffers to be flushed and generate a buffer save message.

The transport layer – OSI level 4 – guarantees delivery of packets, or alternatively indicates an I/O error on the vitual circuit. (A packet is a variable length data unit comprising up to 4095 bytes of data supplied by a higher layer protocol, and formed from the 40-bit minipackets described in Figure 5.42.) Seven different packet types are supported in this layer, as indicated in Table 5.8.

5.7.2 IBM Token Ring LAN

A token bus LAN is a bus LAN whose stations form a logical ring configuration. A token ring, on the other hand, is a physical ring. Both LAN types utilize a token-passing message protocol, which provides the access granting mechanism. Only one node can have control of the token at any one time, which thereby prevents data collisions.

The IBM Token Ring was developed for connecting IBM Personal Computers, and has since been formalized into IEEE standard 802.5. It has a

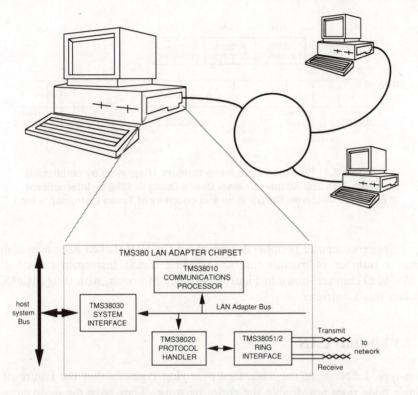

Figure 5.40 IBM Token Ring LAN. (Reprinted by permission from TMS 380 Adapter Chipset User's Guide © 1988 by International Business Machines Corporation and courtesy of Texas Instruments Inc.)

maximum data transfer rate of 4 Mbit/second, and uses unshielded twisted-pair cable. A maximum of 260 nodes can connect to the Ring. It is shown in diagrammatic form in Figure 5.40.

In the IBM Token Ring, the 24-bit token packet circulating around the ring is labelled as 'free' when all stations are idle. When a station wishes to transmit, it waits until it detects the token passing by, alters it from free to 'busy', then transmits a packet (frame) immediately following the busy token. A second station wishing to transmit must wait until a new free token appears.

The destination node copies the data and acknowledges receipt of the frame by setting the 'address recognised' and 'frame copied' bits. Each packet makes one round trip and is purged by the transmitting station, which then releases a free token. Figure 5.41 shows both the free token and frame formats used in the IBM Token Ring.

The deterministic approach of token ring LANs provides an orderly, collision-free access mechanism and load independent response times. Priority levels can also be assigned to tokens, which means that time-critical and synchronous traffic can be supported.

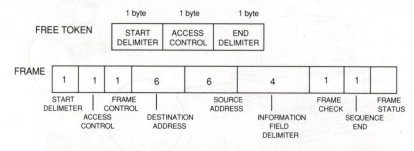

Figure 5.41 Free token and frame formats. (Reprinted by permission from TMS 380 Adapter Chipset User's Guide © 1988 by International Business Machines Corporation and courtesy of Texas Instruments Inc.)

Microcomputer peripheral support for the IBM Token Ring is available from a number of manufacturers, including Texas Instruments (with the TMS380x0 chip set shown in Figure 5.40), and Motorola, with their MC68824 Token Bus Controller.

5.7.3 Ethernet LAN

Bus-type LANs have the advantage over ring types in that the failure of a single node does not disable the entire network. They have the disadvantage that more expensive coaxial cable is required, which must be terminated at either end to avoid reflections that would otherwise destructively interfere with the wanted signals on the line.

Ethernet is perhaps the most widely known bus-type LAN, and was codeveloped by Intel, Digital Equipment Corporation and Xerox. It has been formalized into IEEE standard 802.3. Figure 5.42 shows the physical layout of Ethernet, including the physical distance constraints. It supports data rates up

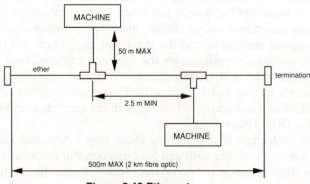

Figure 5.42 Ethernet.

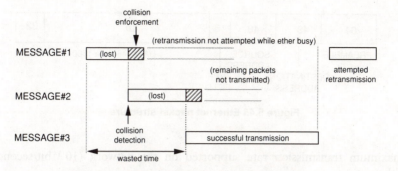

Figure 5.43 Listen-while-talk access mechanism.

to 10 Mbit/second, and uses baseband signalling. Theoretically, Ethernet can support 1024 stations, but the practical limit is around 100.

Ethernet uses the Carrier Sense Multiple Access with Collision Detection (CSMA/CD) protocol, otherwise known as 'listen-while-talk'. A station checks whether the network is busy before transmitting its own message. To transmit, a station keeps contending for the channel until it becomes free, by either backing off a random time and trying again, or by continuing to sense the medium until it becomes idle (or some combination of these two mechanisms).

If a collision is detected during transmission, the station immediately ceases transmitting the packet, then transmits a brief jamming signal to broadcast this fact to all other stations. The station then waits a random amount of time before attempting to retransmit, again using CSMA. This listen-while-talk access mechanism is illustrated in Figure 5.43. The worst-case collision scenario is when an attempted transmission from a station at one end of the network collides with a transmission from a station at the other end of the network, just as the first packet reaches its intended destination. Thus the worst-case time for collision detection is twice the propagation time from one end of the network to the other. This situation is illustrated in Figure 5.44.

The Ethernet packet structure is shown in Figure 5.45. The minimum packet size is 72 bytes, comprising 8 preamble, 14 header, 46 data and 4 CRC. Packet size is a compromise between distance and speed. On the one hand, it must be long enough so that the packet is still transmitting when its header reaches the far distant end of the network. This must be balanced with the

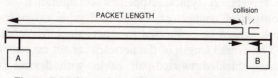

Figure 5.44 Worst case collision (baseband).

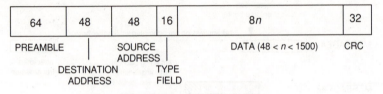

64	48	48	16	8*n*	32
PREAMBLE		SOURCE ADDRESS		DATA (48 < *n* < 1500)	CRC
	DESTINATION ADDRESS		TYPE FIELD		

Figure 5.45 Ethernet packet structure.

maximum transmission rate supported on the network (10 Mbit/second on Ethernet).

At first sight, the number of address bytes seems inordinately large. However, this was deliberately chosen, in order to provide a unique address for *each* computer in the world; 2^{48} provides over 280 *trillion* addresses! (Such an extreme assumption is reminiscent of an assertion from the early days of valve computers, but in the opposite direction, when it was estimated that around *six* computers, in total, would satisfy the world's computing needs forever more!)

The number of data bytes can range from 46 to 1500, thus the packet overhead is much higher than with the Cambridge Ring, say. This is the reason why Ethernet performs poorly in comparison with the Cambridge Ring in low-level applications such as terminal multiplexing. Where Ethernet shines though is in sustained high-speed data transfers between two computers.

Nevertheless, Ethernet has become the *de facto* industry standard LAN. Its popularity is reflected in the multitude of peripheral chip supports available for it. Intel offer the i82586 LAN coprocessor, i82501 Ethernet Serial Interface and i82588 single chip LAN controller. National Semiconductor produce the NS8390 Network Interface Controller, NS8391 Encoder/decoder Serial Network Interface and NS8392 Transceiver/driver. Advanced Micro Devices manufacture the AM7990 Controller, AM7991 Encoder/decoder and AM7995 Transceiver chip set. The AM7996 is used in the NeXT computer to provide a 10 Mbit/second Ethernet link. Motorola supports Ethernet via the MC68590 and MC68802 chip set.

5.7.4 Appletalk LAN

Appletalk is a low-cost multidrop bus LAN used for interconnecting Macintosh computers and providing access to shared facilities such as printer spoolers and file servers. A typical Appletalk configuration is shown in Figure 5.46. It consists of connectors, cables and cable extenders (the two ends of the network cannot be connected together, since Appletalk is a bus, not a ring LAN). The overall length of the network cannot exceed 300 metres.

Appletalk uses shielded twisted-pair cable, with devices (up to 32) connecting to this cable via passive taps. By using such transformer coupling

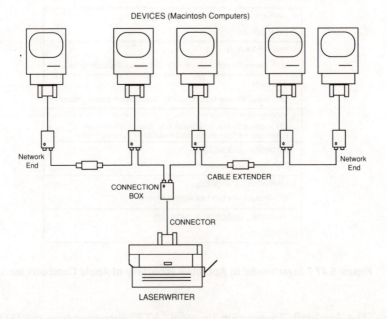

DEVICES (Macintosh Computers)

Network
End

CABLE EXTENDER

Network
End

CONNECTION
BOX

CONNECTOR

LASERWRITER

Figure 5.46 Typical Appletalk configuration (courtesy of Apple Computer Inc.).

(housed within each connector box), inactive devices do not affect other devices on the network. The maximum data transfer rate is around 230 kbit/second, and is controlled by Zilog Z8530 Serial Communication Controller chips inside the Macintoshes.

Figure 5.47 shows how the various Appletalk protocol levels map onto the ISO/OSI 7-layer model. The physical layer performs bit encoding (decoding), synchronization, bit transmission (reception) and carrier sensing. The Appletalk Bus Link Access Protocol (ATLAP) (data link layer) performs addressing, data encapsulation (decapsulation), data transmission (reception), access management and error detection. (Appletalk uses Carrier Sense Multiple Access, Collision Avoidance, rather than CSMA/CDetection, as used in Ethernet.) Each device assigns itself a network ID number each time it is powered up; these numbers are used to send messages between the different devices on the network. When a device wants to talk to another device, it broadcasts this information out onto the network. All devices are always listening to the network, and respond only when they hear information addressed to them.

The Datagram Delivery Protocol (DDP) level corresponds to layer 3 of the ISO/OSI model (network layer), and provides a socket-to-socket delivery of datagrams. Sockets are logical entities in the network nodes, identified by a unique socket number; datagrams are packets that are delivered as single, independent entities between sockets.

7. APPLICATION
(User Defined)

6. PRESENTATION
DCP Device Control Protocol; FSP File Server.Protocol (et al.)

5. SESSION
NBP Name Binding Protocol; DSAP Data Stream Access Protocol

4. TRANSPORT
ATP Applebus Transaction Protocol; DSP Data Stream Protocol; RTMP Routeing Table Maintenance Protocol; ZIP Zone ID Protocol

3. NETWORK (SOCKETS)
DDP Datagram Delivery Protocol

2. LINK ACCESS (NODES)
ATLAP Appletalk Bus Link Access Protocol

1. PHYSICAL (ELECTRICAL SIGNALS)
RS422

Figure 5.47 7-layer model of Appletalk (courtesy of Apple Computer Inc.).

The Appletalk Transaction Protocol (ATP) corresponds to the ISO/OSI transport layer (layer 4). The transactions supported are requests and responses, where socket clients request clients of other sockets to perform a higher level function and report the outcome back to the requester.

The Name Binding Protocol (NBP) performs conversions between node IDs, socket numbers and network numbers to network addresses. It allows a socket client to register (delete) the name and socket number of an entity in the node's table, and to determine the address (and confirm the existence of) an entity.

As with LANs in general, Appletalk provides file sharing, print spooling, intermachine communication and electronic mail. Moreover, Appletalk has been designed to allow its ready incorporation into large networks, through bridging devices.

5.8 WIDE AREA NETWORKS

Our discussion on networking has concentrated solely on local area rather than wide area networks. In Wide Area Networks (WANs), the communicating computers can reside in far distant locations within a country, or indeed in countries on opposite sides of the world. Communication takes place via public utility telecommunications networks. A particular data transfer could involve telephone cable, broadband coaxial, free space radio frequency (or micro-wave), fibre optic and/or satellite communication links.

The X.25 packet switching network was mentioned earlier, in Section 5.7, in our introductory remarks about LANs. Figure 5.48 shows a

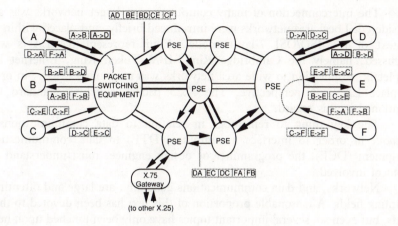

Figure 5.48 X.25 network.

typical X.25 network, which connects via an X.75 gateway to other networks (which could also be X.25). Gateways are required in order to interface two potentially incompatible protocols and/or signal levels with each other. They are usually capable of transferring data at much higher rates than the LANs themselves.

Typical services provided via WANs are file transfers and electronic mail (email).

SUMMARY

Speed considerations necessitate parallel data transfers within a micro-computer. However, for many interfacing applications, serial I/O is preferred. Serial I/O slows down communication, but greatly reduces wiring costs between the microcomputer and peripheral. This is especially significant for long distance communications.

Some common uses of serial I/O in microcomputer systems include data communications, CRT displays, and bar code readers. In this chapter we considered only the first of these applications, but many of the matters raised are common to serial I/O in general.

Data communications were discussed in general terms, specifically in relation to modulation techniques. Asynchronous and synchronous communications were compared and contrasted. Particular attention was devoted to the RS232c standard. The MC6850, R6551 and i8251 support chips were covered, and a couple of representative programs presented to illustrate the use of these devices. Protocols were discussed in relation to synchronous data communications, in particular Bisync and SDLC/HDLC.

The interconnection of many computers over larger networks was also considered. Local area networks were introduced briefly, and placed within the context of the ISO/OSI 7-layer model. Four representative LANs were discussed, namely the Cambridge Ring, IBM Token Ring, Ethernet and Appletalk. Connection to wide area networks was mentioned briefly, in order to place LANs in perspective. The X.25 packet switching standard was mentioned in this regard.

The key thing to remember in relation to data communications is *protocol*; in order to interface a computer (DTE) to data communications equipment (DCE), the programmer or design engineer must understand the protocol involved.

Networks, and data communications generally, are large and oftentimes daunting fields. A reasonable proportion of this text has been devoted to these fields, but even so, several important topics have only been touched upon here. The reader is referred to the reference lists for a more comprehensive coverage of data communications.

REVIEW QUESTIONS

5.1 What is meant by the term protocol in a data communications context?

5.2 Discuss two different types of modulation techniques commonly used in data communication links.

5.3 What are meant by the following terms: modem, USART, half duplex?

5.4 Describe the RS232c protocol. What baud rates can this protocol typically handle?

5.5 What are the minimum RS232c signals required for full duplex communication?

5.6 What is meant by the X-ON/X-OFF protocol?

5.7 What types of interrupts are possible on the MC6850 ACIA, and how can they be cleared?

5.8 The MC6850 ACIA can detect three types of errors. What are they, and what does each mean? Repeat for the i8251 USART.

5.9 What advantage does the R6551 ACIA have over the MC6850?

5.10 Explain the difference between synchronous and asynchronous data communication.

5.11 Write a short i8086 routine to program an i8251 USART for 7-bit asynchronous operation (even parity, 2 stop bits, ÷16 clock). Repeat for synchronous operation (7-bit data, even parity).

5.12 How does HDLC differ from BISYNC?

5.13 Comment on the compatability between OSI, SNA and X.25.

5.14 What characterises a local area network? How does a LAN differ from a wide area network?

5.15 A LAN must provide a mechanism whereby the various nodes obtain shared access to the common network resources. How is this achieved on Ethernet? Cambridge Ring? IBM Token Ring? Appletalk?

5.16 What functions are performed within each layer of the 7-layer ISO/OSI model?

6

Video Display Terminals

OBJECTIVES

In Chapter 5 we discussed serial interfacing in the context of data communications. In this chapter, we turn our attention to another type of serial interface, namely a video display terminal. Our discussion focuses on raster scan CRT displays, although LCD, plasma and electroluminescent displays are also mentioned. Colour graphics is also briefly discussed.

6.1   INTRODUCTION

Chapter 5 dealt with serial communications. One of the examples used to illustrate serial I/O was the communication of data between a CPU and a terminal (see Section 5.1). This chapter will deal in more detail with this common peripheral device, the terminal. A decade or two ago, computer terminals were electromechanical in nature, and consisted of a keyboard and (somewhat noisy) printer. The keyboard served as the input device, while the printer functioned as the output device. Electromechanical relays activated printer hammers which in turn impacted a print ribbon onto the surface of the paper. Typical of such electromechanical terminals was the ASR35 Tele-Typewriter (TTY; the abbreviation TTY is still sometimes used these days to denote a terminal device, irrespective of whether its internal construction is electromechanical or electronic).

It is more usual nowadays to find Video Display Terminals (VDTs), or Visual Display Units (VDUs), which consist of a keyboard and a CRT screen. Keyboards comprise a key matrix, some form of scanning this matrix and a decoder for converting from parallel to serial form for transmission over a single line to the CPU (see Section 4.2).

These days, terminal screens are usually of the CRT type, although LCDs (amongst others) have become popular in recent years; the predominant display however remains the CRT, particularly for colour graphics applications. The CRT display suffers from two main disadvantages, namely its physical size and the requirement for a high voltage (HV) supply for driving its electronic beam. Its main advantages are higher resolution, contrast and low cost (because of mass production).

6.2   CRT DISPLAYS

Figure 6.1 shows the construction of a typical CRT. The HV supply powers the heating filament, which heats the cathode, which in turn emits electrons into the vacuum inside the glass CRT tube. These electrons are attracted towards the positive anode, and actually pass by the anode to impinge on a phosphor-coated screen. Electrons striking this phosphor coating cause light to be emitted at that part of the screen. The combined emissions of light from the different parts of the screen give the impression to the human eye of a stationary rather than a flickering image (although in reality this image is constantly being refreshed 50 or 60 times every second). Some phosphor coatings persist or linger longer than others, and by so doing can compensate for flickering. However, if this persistence is *too* long, smearing can result, which is equally undesirable (smearing is the retention of previous screen images when the screen is updated, resulting in 'ghost' images remaining temporarily on the screen).

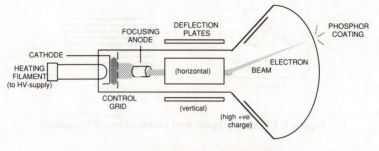

Figure 6.1 Cathode Ray Tube (CRT).

The intensity of the electron beam, and hence the resulting brightness on the screen, is varied by the control grid (and is directly proportional to the number of electrons emitted from the cathode). The focusing anode is used to form a sharp, convergent beam of electrons at the screen surface. One pair of deflection plates are positively charged, and thus attract electrons, while the other pair are negatively charged and thus repel them. Together they are used to deflect the electron beam horizontally and vertically to the desired screen position.

Colour CRT displays use three electron guns, one each to produce the Red, Green and Blue (RGB) primary components of the screen in question. Different colour phosphors are grouped in lots of three (triads) across the surface of the screen, with each gun directed to its corresponding colour-sensitive pixel. Additive mixing occurs at each group of RGB phosphors, such that equal intensities of red and green will produce yellow (likewise red and blue will produce magenta, and blue and green will produce cyan); equal proportions of all three colours will appear as either white or grey to the human eye. Figure 6.2 shows the formation of colour pixels on a CRT screen, together with an additive mixing chart.

There are two main methods of controlling the movement of the electron beam across the surface of the screen, and these are shown in Figure 6.3. In the vector graphic scheme, the electron beam can move to any location on the screen, under the control of the user, with the desired image being repeatedly traced out until a new image is required. In the raster scan scheme, the image is gradually built up from a series of horizontal lines traced across the screen, starting from the top left-hand corner, and working down to

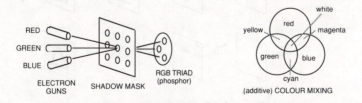

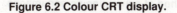

Figure 6.2 Colour CRT display.

Random Scan   Raster Scan

Figure 6.3 Vector graphic and raster scan CRT displays.

the bottom right. In this latter scheme the deflection of the electron beam is fixed, and is under the control of timebase circuitry (both horizontally and vertically), with the entire screen full of horizontal lines being repeated often enough to make the image appear stationary to the human eye.

In the raster scan CRT display, the entire screen is continuously retraced, even though much of it might remain in darkness for a particular image. Conversely, in the vector graphic CRT display, only those parts of the screen necessary to form the particular image in question are activated by the electron beam. This is illustrated in Figure 6.4. As its name might suggest, this latter type of display is more suited to graphics applications.

By far the most common form of CRT display is the raster scan type. Figure 6.5 shows a 625-line raster scan display, together with its associated timebase signals (625 lines corresponds to the European Phase Alternating Line television standard; 525 lines are used in the US NTSC standard). Note, however, that not all of these 625 lines are actually displayed on the screen. The horizontal timebase signal sweeps the electron beam across the screen from left to right (the more positive the voltage, the further to the right the beam is deflected). Similarly, the vertical timebase signal sweeps these horizontal traces down the screen from top to bottom, but at a much slower rate (the more positive the applied vertical voltage, the lower down on the screen the beam is deflected).

The CRT screen of 625 lines is retraced every 20 milliseconds, so that the entire frame appears stationary to the human eye, in much the same

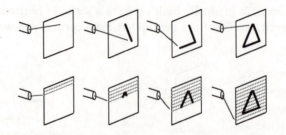

**Figure 6.4 Random scan vs raster scan
method of generating screen images.**

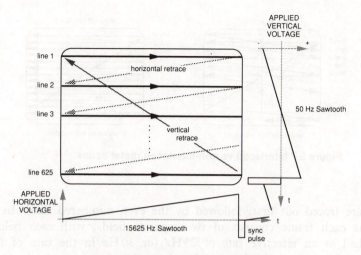

Figure 6.5 Raster scan CRT display.

manner that a motion picture film appears stationary when a shutter is placed in front of the moving film 24 times every second. Likewise it is the persistence of vision of the human eye which produces the illusion of moving pictures. (A 60 Hz refresh rate is used in NTSC, rather than 50 Hz as with Phase Alternating Line; in each case, the refresh rate turns out to be the same as the AC mains supply frequency).

The horizontal timebase signal traces out one horizontal line every 64 microseconds. The shape of both timebase signals is similar; each has a sawtooth shape, with a gradual buildup across (down) the screen, followed by a rather sharp return to the left-hand (topmost) position. Just prior to returning to the start position ready for the next trace, the waveform actually goes negative for a short time; such pulses are used for synchronization of the timebase (sweep) circuity. These synchronization pulses are illustrated in Figure 6.6. There are 625 (525) such horizontal sync(hronization) pulses, and one vertical sync pulse per frame traced out on the CRT screen.

Instead of tracing out all 625 (525) lines from top to bottom in order to form one frame, CRT displays often use interlacing, where the odd numbered

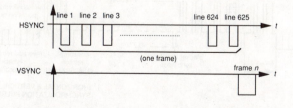

Figure 6.6 Horizontal and vertical synchronization pulses.

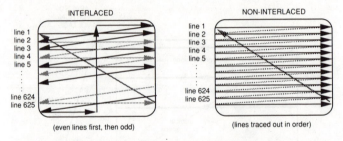

Figure 6.7 Interlaced vs non-interlaced raster scans.

lines are traced out first, followed by the even numbered lines. In such a scheme each frame consists of two separate fields, with each field being refreshed at an effective rate of 25 Hz (or 30 Hz in the case of NTSC). Figure 6.7 compares the interlaced and non-interlaced raster scan methods. Interlacing is commonly used in television-type monitors, but not in high resolution computer monitors.

The horizontal and vertical timebase signals are applied to the deflection plates, and thus determine the position of the electron beam on the screen surface at any particular time. The intensity of the individual dots or pixels on the CRT screen is determined by the voltage applied to the control grid; the more positive the voltage, the brighter the emission from the phosphor coating.

These CRT control signals – intensity and synchronization – are mixed together to form a composite video signal, as shown in Figure 6.8 (and are separated within the CRT display before being applied to the relevant electrodes/plates). In order to be detected as a synchronization pulse, and also to avoid the screen being lit up during either the horizontal or vertical retrace (flyback) periods, these pulses are made more negative than the blackest intensity level (0 V; +1 V corresponds to the whitest level). Thus, in order to use such a CRT display as a computer terminal, we need to be able to generate such composite video signals.

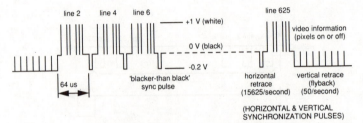

Figure 6.8 Composite video signal.

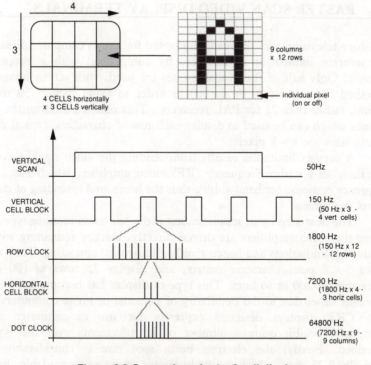

**Figure 6.9 Generation of a 4 x 3 cell display,
comprising 9 x 12 dot matrix characters.**

We have already seen how timing is critical for CRT displays. Figure 6.9 shows the generation of a character on a small CRT screen. The entire screen consists of only 12 cells, arranged in a 3-row × 4-column matrix. Each cell in turn consists of 108 pixels, arranged in 12-row 9-column matrix from. Thus only 12 characters in total could be displayed on such a screen.

The limiting timing constraint is the 50 Hz (60 Hz) refresh rate required for the screen image to appear stationary to the human eye. For three vertical cells (columns), this leads to a vertical cell block rate of 150 Hz, which is the rate at which horizontal lines are traced out on the screen. Now since there are 12 rows per cell, this results in a row clock rate of 1800 Hz. Thus horizontal cell blocks will be traced out at the rate of 7200 Hz. Now there are nine columns per cell, which results in a dot clock rate – the rate at which pixels are illuminated on the screen – of 64 800 Hz.

The purpose of this exercise is to illustrate that even for this ridiculously small screen size, the dot clock rate needs to be nearly 65 kHz! For a more realistic CRT display, say 24 rows × 80 columns, the required dot clock frequency becomes 13.5 MHz, as we shall see shortly.

6.3   RASTER SCAN VIDEO DISPLAY TERMINALS

Ordinary television receivers can be adapted for use as computer displays, but are severely limited in capabilities, by comparison with a proper VDT monitor. Only half of the available lines are used, with screen images being refreshed twice as often as normal in order to avoid flicker (50 times per second, rather than 25 for PAL receivers). This places a limit on the number of lines which can be used to display each row of characters (typical character matrix sizes are 8×8 pixels).

A further limitation results from sending the video signal through the television set's Radio Frequency (RF) video amplifier, which has a limited frequency response (or bandwidth); thus the horizontal spreading of characters across the screen.

The next step up in sophistication is the television monitor type display, where the video amplifiers are driven directly, thereby remaining within RF bandwidth limitations and hence avoiding horizontal spreading. They typically use a 5×7 pixel character matrix, and display 25 rows of (80 column) characters on 200 or so lines. This type of display has become quite common in recent times due to the popularity of personal or home computers.

CRT displays designed expressly for use as computer monitors (terminals) exhibit quite a number of improvements over the types just described. Firstly, the electron beam spot size is considerably smaller (typically 0.25 mm), which results in clearer, more easily readable characters. Secondly, larger character pixel matrices are used (9×16, with upper-case characters fitting in a 7×9 box within this window). Thirdly, they use special high bandwidth video circuitry, which results in even clearer, more legible characters, and moreover allows different font sets to be generated on the screen (although memory space for storing different fonts becomes a limiting factor here). In the case of colour monitors, separate signals are sent to the three electron guns, rather than the composite video signal described earlier – hence these types of displays are often referred to as RGB monitors. Fourthly, the number of lines displayed on the screen is much larger, typically 400 or more, which is roughly twice the number used in a television type monitor.

A recent innovation in CRT displays has been the introduction of multisync or multifrequency scanning capability. Instead of adhering to the fixed television frequencies of 15 625 Hz horizontally and 50 Hz vertically (PAL), multisync monitors allow these scan rates to be varied over a wide range (45–75 Hz vertically, for example). This leads to improved brightness (since the screen phosphors are being energized more often), faster screen updates and reduced flicker. Multisync also enables the same monitor to be connected to a range of different CRT adapter boards, such as CGA, EGA and VGA for the IBM PC (which have horizontal scan rates of 15.6, 21.8 and 31.5 kHz respectively).

Developments in computer terminals are driven largely by developments in television receivers, particularly in recent years with portable, pocket-sized televisions (and video Walkmans) at one end of the spectrum, and large-screen, high-definition television sets on the other.

Current trends in monitors include displaying characters as black-on-white, rather than the more conventional white-on-black, turning the screen through 90° in order to better represent a standard A4 written page, and increasing the resolution to around 1000×1000 pixels for graphics applications.

6.4   MAPPING BETWEEN MEMORY AND A RASTER SCAN DISPLAY

An entire screen display is stored within a computer's memory, with the screen being continually updated 50 or 60 times per second. The display appears stationary to the user, owing to the persistence of vision of the human eye. Thus new screens can be obtained by simply updating the area of memory designated to the CRT.

There are a number of factors to be taken into account in mapping from a computer's memory to a CRT display. The two devices differ markedly in several respects. Firstly, memory is organized as a matrix of rows and columns, and handles data in a parallel manner (although at the subsystem level, it is accessed as a serial device, in other words, one location at a time). A CRT display, by way of contrast, handles data in serial form (as a signal pulse train which drives the electron gun intensity as the beam sweeps out its horizontal and vertical trace on the screen surface). Secondly, a CRT screen needs to be refreshed at regular intervals, as previously indicated. Memory, on the other hand, will retain the current screen image, at least until a new screen image is loaded in.

Figure 6.10 shows the storage of a single character in a 12 row $\times$ 9 column memory array (which allows for lower-case descenders as well as spaces around each character both horizontally and vertically). Individual pixels are either activated (1) or left blank (0), with each row being stored as a 12-bit binary word in memory. This word is read out by selecting each row address in turn, and reading its contents out in parallel form. This parallel data is then converted into serial form before being sent to the video control circuitry.

For a screen comprising 24 lines of 80 characters, a total of 1920 memory locations would be required to store the video information. Figure 6.11 shows how a ROM can be used to look up the bit pattern corresponding to each character position (cell) on the screen.

The scan line (or row) clock selects one of 12 rows within the character cell currently seleted, and maintains this selection for a maximum of 80 cells across the row (thus the character addresses will be selected up to 80 times faster than the scan line clock). This procedure is repeated 12 times in order to

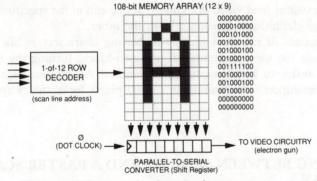

Figure 6.10 Storage of a character in memory.

build up successively a single character row (cell line) across the screen. Moreover, the scan line clock (cell counter) operates 24 times faster than the cell line counter, since there are a total of 24 cell lines displayed on the screen.

Figure 6.12 illustrates this mapping between memory and a raster scan CRT display. The character generator in this diagram is identical to that shown in Figure 6.11; it has three inputs (character select, scan line clock and dot clock), one output (serial video information), and comprises a ROM lookup, scan line counter and parallel-to-serial converter (shift register). An 80-character buffer has been added, sufficient for one complete line on the screen.

Note that changing fonts in such a scheme would necessitate the replacement of the character generator ROM, since the bit patterns for each character in the new font would be different.

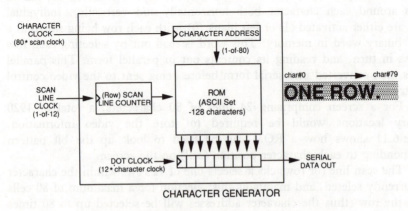

Figure 6.11 Storage of one row of characters.

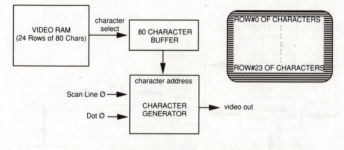

**Figure 6.12 Mapping from computer's memory
to raster scan display.**

6.4.1 VDT–Microcomputer Interface

Figure 6.13 shows the internal construction of a typical dumb computer terminal, which uses a screen comprising 24 lines × 80 columns. (An intelligent terminal, by way of contrast, would provide features such as local text editing, and indeed would usually incorporate a dedicated micro-controller.)

The number of lines generated within the CRT would typically be around 300. However, not all of these lines would be displayed on the screen; there would be around 10% more lines generated during the vertical retrace

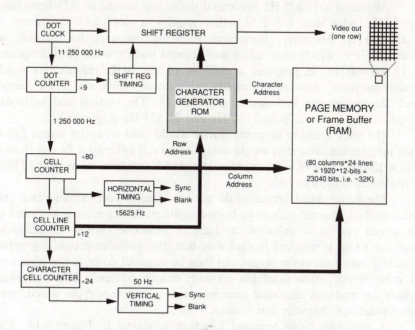

Figure 6.13 Video timing and control interface.

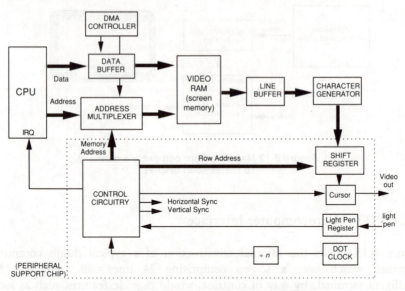

Figure 6.14 VDT-microcomputer interface.

period. For an 80 column cell line (one horizontal character row), and a 12 row × 9 column character cell, this translates to a 720 × 288 pixel screen (just over 207 000 pixels in all).

Assuming a 15 625 Hz horizontal deflection waveform (625 lines times the 50 Hz refreshing for PAL) this implies a dot clock frequency of 11 250 000 Hz. However, horizontal retracing accounts for roughly an additional 20%, which when taken into account leads to a dot clock frequency of 13 500 000 Hz (in practice, a multiple of the 50 Hz refresh rate would actually be used, in order to simplify the necessary division). These various clock frequencies are indicated in Figure 6.13. The vertical and horizontal refresh rates are also indicated (50 Hz and 15 625 Hz respectively).

The page memory or frame buffer would hold an entire screen full of pixel information, and thus would comprise 80 cell columns × 24 cell lines or 1920 × 12-bit words of video information (which translates to around 23 kbits of read/write memory).

The better dumb terminals do not use blank borders around each cell, which enables adjacent cells to be butted together. In this manner any pixel on the screen can be illuminated, at least in principle. When the character generator ROM is removed in such a system, this provides primitive graphics capability, since the entire screen can then be accessed down to the pixel level (in other words, each pixel has its own unique address). Some terminals replace the read-only character generator with a read/write type, which caters for user-defined character sets (fonts).

A complete video terminal interface is shown in Figure 6.14. This interface includes additional features such as cursor control, address

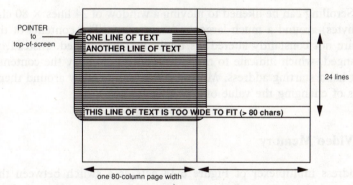

Figure 6.15 Horizontal and vertical scrolling.

multiplexing and DMA. Cursor control would comprise cursor type (underscore, a completely filled cell block etc.), cursor addressing (where to position the cursor on the screen) and blink rate (once or twice per second). The cursor simply indicates whereabouts the next character typed by the user will appear on the screen; it thus serves as a user prompt.

The light pen input indicates at what particular screen address the external light source is directed; it is sensed as the electron beam sweeps past it and the location stored within the light pen register. The user simply positions the light pen at the position(s) on the screen where the response is required.

In practice, all of the timing and control circuitry, the clock generator, shift register and cursor control would be contained within a single peripheral support chip, either a standard 'off-the-shelf' type or a custom CRT controller.

A terminal screen can be made to act as a window on a much larger document; only the part that is visible through the window is actually displayed on the screen. There is more to the document than what appears on the screen. Scrolling is the process whereby this window is moved, both horizontally and vertically around the document. Consider a word processing environment, for example: most documents will comprise more than 24 lines of characters, which you will recall was the maximum number we could display on a CRT screen at any one time.

Figure 6.15 illustrates both vertical and horizontal scrolling. Vertical scrolling can be likened to a typewriter, where the paper is physically wound forwards or backwards to get to the desired line. The example in Figure 6.15 is taken from a screen-based editor, which is not limited to the usual 80 columns across the screen. Horizontal scrolling is used to access text to the right of the currently displayed screen (ordinarily, if lines of text extend beyond 80 characters, the cursor would automatically move to the start of the next cell line; in other words it would 'wrap around'). Likewise, vertical scrolling is used to access the previous or subsequent page(s), using a single (different) control character in each case.

Scrolling can be likened to moving a window of 24 lines × 80 characters (1920 bytes) around a much larger memory array. The contents of the video RAM are not constantly altered, as might first be implied. Instead, pointers are changed, which indicate to the video control circuitry the contents of the top left-hand starting address. Moving the screen window around then simply consists of changing the value of a pointer (or two).

6.4.2 Video Memory

The address multiplexer of Figure 6.14 acts as a switch between the video memory and the computer's main memory; a certain portion of the address space will be dedicated to the VDT. Direct memory access is often employed to transfer the large amounts of data required to update an entire screen; doing so under processor control – a word at a time – would simply take too long. (Recall that the screen must be refreshed at least 50 times every second in order that the screen image appears stationary to the user.)

The screen can be addressed using either of two addressing schemes: linear and row/column addressing, as illustrated in Figure 6.16. With linear addressing, the top left-hand cell has address 0, and so on to the end of the first line (address 79). The next line commences with location 80, and finishes with location 159, and so on down to the 24th line, which starts with location 1840 and ends with location 1919. The advantage of linear addressing is that all 1920 cells are stored in sequential order in memory; there is no wasted memory space. The disadvantage is that accessing the different addresses is complicated by the fact that the number of characters per row is not a power of two.

Row and column addressing simplifies the addressing by ensuring that each line starting address is a multiple of 2, however gaps appear in memory as a result. Each cell can then be accessed using a 12-bit address, as indicated. (Note however that only 1920 of the possible 4096 addresses are actually used.)

In any VDT, the CPU and CRT Controller (CRTC) will share the common memory (RAM). Thus some means of resolving contention for memory needs to be incorporated. This can be achieved by a number of different means. An external DMA controller can be used to handle block transfers (typically one 80-character line at a time) between the CPU and screen memory, as well as from the screen memory to the CRTC. This is the approach taken by Intel with their i8275 CRTC, which includes two 80-character buffers in which to hold data transferred from the screen memory.

An alternative scheme is to have the CPU and CRTC share the memory (time division multiplexing). This is readily achieved in the MC6800 and 6502 8-bit processors, since they are driven by a two-phase clock; one clock phase can be devoted to the CPU, and the other to the CRTC. This is the approach taken by Motorola in their MC6845 CRTC.

A third alternative is to grant access to the CPU during horizontal and

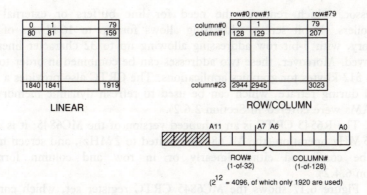

Figure 6.16 Screen memory addressing.

vertical retracing periods (namely when the CRTC is not writing information to the screen). In the Apple Macintosh computer, for example, accesses to RAM are interleaved between the CPU and custom video controller whenever the screen is being written to, but reverts exclusively to the CPU during non-display times. This results in the CPU having an overall RAM access rate of around 6 MHz: 3.92 MHz during display times, and 7.83 MHz during non-display times. (ROM access rate, by way of contrast is 7.83 MHz.)

6.5 CRT CONTROLLERS

CRT Controllers (CRTCs) often take the form of plug-in boards (cards or adapters). They utilize dedicated microcomputer peripheral support chips, such as the Motorola MC6845, Rockwell R6545, Intel i8275, National Semiconductor DP8350 and Advanced Micro Devices Am8052. Such CRTCs support both monochrome (black and white) and colour monitors, 50 Hz or 60 Hz refresh rate, cursor addressing, DMA, interlacing and light pen input.

6.5.1 Motorola MC6845 CRTC

The MC6845 CRTC was originally developed as an 8-bit support chip for the MC6800 processor, but such synchronous support is also provided on the 16-/32-bit MC68000. The MC6845 can be programmed for use with either interlaced or non-interlaced screens. It can be used in either alphanumeric or graphics mode, and with various screen formats (24 rows × 80 columns, 20 × 132 and so on). Hardware scrolling is provided, either by page, line or character. The cursor format and blink rate can be programmed by the user, and a light pen register is also provided.

Screen memory can be multiplexed between the CRTC and the host processor, which removes the need for line buffers or external DMA controllers. 14-bit screen addressing allows for up to 16 kbytes of screen memory, with 5-bit row addressing allowing up to 32 character lines to be displayed. Moreover, these two addresses can be combined in order to access up to 512 kbytes for graphics applications. The CRTC also provides a refresh signal during retrace, which can be used to refresh dynamic memory chips (DRAMs were covered in Section 2.6.2).

The R6545 CRTC is an enhanced version of the MC6845; it is capable of 2.5 MHz operation (the MC6845 is limited to 2 MHz), and screen memory can be configured either linearly or in row and column form (see Section 6.4.2).

Figure 6.17 shows the MC6845 CRTC register set, which comprises three main groups: timing, cursor control and miscellaneous. The timing registers allow the user to select horizontal screen width and vertical screen depth, both in terms of the total number of characters (rows), as well as the number actually displayed. Interlacing or non-interlacing is also selected via a timing register, as indicated. The cursor control registers allow the user to specify the cursor start and end addresses, its position on the screen (via R14,15), as well as the blink rate. Other registers are the start address register (which indicates the top left-hand position on the screen), and the light pen register.

Figure 6.18 shows a low resolution graphics display, based on a typical dumb computer terminal. A 4 MHz MC68000 is used as the host processor, with the CRTC being driven by its own 8 MHz clock. All 16 data lines are connected through to the video RAM, but only the lower eight bits (odd bytes) are connected through to the MC6845. Buffer latches are required in order to interface the asynchronous processor to the synchronous CRTC.

Address decoding is used to select one of four colour planes: luminance and three chrominance (red, green and blue), as indicated. The video RAM addressing is derived from the address lines and the refresh outputs of the MC6845, using multiplexers. 16K words of video (refresh) RAM is provided for each colour plane, organized as two 8-bit banks (odd and even bytes).

Memory cycles are alternated between the CPU and CRTC as indicated in Figure 6.19. The particular address decoding used here leads to the mapping scheme shown in Figure 6.20: the first eight rows are addressed as location 0, the next eight as address 1, and so on down to address 20 (only 21 of the 32 possible rows are actually displayed). Pixels are addressed in cells of eight, with the most significant byte corresponding to the leftmost pixel, and the least significant byte to the eighth pixel along the row. Pixel cells increase in sequential order starting from the top leftmost cell, down to the eighth row, then back up to the top row for the next eight, as indicated.

The 18 data registers of Figure 6.17 are accessed by a nineteenth register within the MC6845 – the address pointer. The appropriate CRTC initialization sequence for the application described above would be as follows:

TIMING REGISTERS

(Nht+1) + 1	R0 = HORIZONTAL TOTAL REGISTER
Nhd	R1 = HORIZONTAL DISPLAYED REGISTER
	R2 = HORIZONTAL SYNC POSITION REGISTER
	R3 = SYNC WIDTH REGISTER
Nvt+1	R4 = VERTICAL TOTAL REGISTER
Nadj	R5 = VERTICAL TOTAL ADJUST REGISTER
Nvd	R6 = VERTICAL DISPLAYED REGISTER
	R7 = VERTICAL SYNC POSITION REGISTER
	R8 = INTERFACE MODE & SKEW
Nr	R9 = MAXIMUM SCAN LINE ADDRESS REGISTER

bit 1 bit 0
0	0	normal sync mode
1	0	(non-interlace)
0	1	interlace sync mode
1	1	interlace sync & video mode

CURSOR CONTROL REGISTERS

R10 = CURSOR START REGISTER
R11 = CURSOR END REGISTER
R14,15 = CURSOR REGISTER

bit 6 bit 5
0	0	non-blink
0	1	cursor non-display
1	0	blink (1/16 field rate)
1	1	blink (1/32 field rate)

OTHER REGISTERS

R12,13 = START ADDRESS REGISTER
R16,17 = LIGHT PEN REGISTER

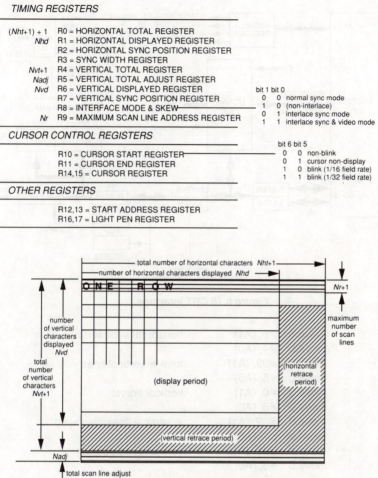

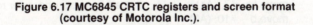

**Figure 6.17 MC6845 CRTC registers and screen format
(courtesy of Motorola Inc.).**

```
CRTC:   move.l  $30001, A0      ;CRTC base address (addr pointer)
        move.l  $30003, A1      ;MC6845 data register
        move.b  #0, (A0)        ;initialize address pointer
        move.b  #63, (A1)       ;total # horizontal lines − 1
        move.b  #1, (A0)        ;point to next MC6845 register
        move.b  #48, (A1)       ;# horizontal lines displayed
        move.b  #2, (A0)        ;
        move.b  #52, (A1)       ;horizontal sync delay
        move.b  #3, (A0)        ;
```

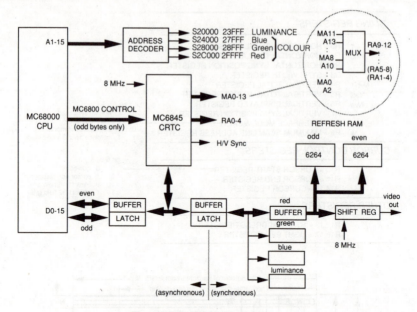

Figure 6.18 CRT interface.

```
move.b   #6, (A1)      ;horizontal sync width
move.b   #4, (A0)      ;
move.b   #39, (A1)     ;total # vertical lines − 1
move.b   #5, (A0)      ;
move.b   #0, (A1)      ;vertical adjust
move.b   #6, (A0)      ;
move.b   #32, (A1)     ;# vertical lines displayed
move.b   #7, (A0)      ;
move.b   #36, (A1)     ;vertical sync position
move.b   #8, (A0)      ;
move.b   #0, (1)       ;interlace mode control
move.b   #9, (A0)      ;(non-interlace here)
move.b   #7, (A1)      ;# scan lines per character row
move.b   #10, (A0)     ;
move.b   #0, (A1)      ;cursor start position (high)
move.b   #11, (A0)     ;
move.b   #0, (A1)      ;cursor start position (low)
move b.   #12, (A0)     ;
move.b   #0, (A1)      ;cursor end position (high)
move.b   #13, (A0)     ;
move.b   #0, (A1)      ;cursor end position (low)
move.b   #14, (A0)     ;
move.b   #0, (a1)      ;cursor position (high)
move.b   #15, (A0)     ;
move.b   #0, (A1)      ;cursor position (low)
;registers 16 & 17 not used here − no light pen
```

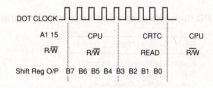

Figure 6.19 Timing.

The mapping between *x–y* positions on the screen and the refresh memory could be achieved using the following routine (the *x*-coordinate is entered via D1 and the *y*-coordinate via D2, while the outputs are screen address in A0 and pixel position in D0):

```
MAP:    move.l  D1,D0             ;x-coordinate
        not.b   D0
        and.l   #7,D0             ;pixel position
        and.l   #$FFFFFFF8,D1     ;x AND 7
        move.l  D2,D3             ;y-coordinate
        and.l   #7,D3             ;x AND 7
        and.l   #$FFFFFFF8,D2     ;x AND 7
        mulu    #48,D2            ;#horiz lines disp (x AND 7)
        add.l   D3,D2             ;hd (x AND 7) + (y AND 7)
        add.l   D2,D1             ;hd (x AND 7) + (y AND 7) +
                                  ;(x AND 7)
        add.l   $20000,D1         ; video RAM base address
        move.l  D1,A0             ;return screen address
        rts
```

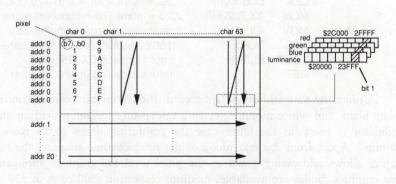

Figure 6.20 Mapping from memory to screen.

Table 6.1 IBM PC monochrome adapter character attributes.

Hex	ATTRIBUTE
00H	NOTHING DISPLAYED
01H	UNDERLINE
07H	WHITE-ON-BLACK
0FH	INTENSE white-on-black
70H	BLACK-ON-WHITE
80H	(additional) BLINKING

A Plot_Point primitive is readily constructed using a bit set instruction, as follows:

```
bset/clr   D0, (A0)      ;(D0)=8-bit pixel info; A0=pointer
```

Horizontal and vertical line drawing primitives could then be realized using Plot_Point and incrementing D0 as appropriate. Likewise, a Rectangle primitive could be constructed out of H_Line and V_Line primitives. (A diagonal line drawing primitive is rather more complicated, and will be referred to later in our discussion of graphics.)

The MC6845 was the CRTC chosen by IBM for their IBM Personal Computer, for both the monochrome and colour graphics plug-in adapter cards. The black and white adapter produces a 25-row × 80-column display. A 4 kbyte display buffer is provided on the adapter card, commencing at location B0000H. Characters are stored in successive words of memory: the even byte containing the ASCII character code, and the odd byte the character attribute. The various character attributes are shown in Table 6.1. The MC6845 CRTC address and data registers are connected to ports 3B4H and 3B5H respectively.

The following i8086 routine (D.J. Bradley, *Assembly Language Programming for the IBM Personal Computer*, © 1984. Reprinted by permission of Prentice-Hall, Inc., Englewood Cliffs NJ) shows how column *n* could be blanked out using the monochrome adapter card (this routine could itself be incorporated into a horizontal scrolling routine):

```
COLUMN: MOV    CX,25        ;25 rows displayed on the screen
        LEA    DI,B000nH    ;buffer start addr + n (0→79 columns)
        MOV    AX,7020H     ;20 = blank (70 = black-on-white)
BLANK:  MOV    (DI),AX      ;move blank into next buffer addr
        ADD    DI,A0H       ;160 bytes further on − 80* (char + attr)
        LOOP   BLANK        ;count index in CX (25 rows)
        RET                 ;return to calling (main) program
```

Unlike the monochrome adapter card, the colour card can be connected to *any* black and white monitor, or to a television receiver providing an RF modulator is used (in the latter case the resolution drops to 25 rows × 40 columns). Apart from the text mode of the monochrome adapter, the colour adapter allows addressing down to the pixel level for graphics applications. Two graphics modes are available, medium resolution (200 rows of 320 dots) and high resolution (200 rows of 640 dots). However, only black and white

IRGB	COLOUR
0000	BLACK
0001	BLUE
0010	GREEN
0011	CYAN
0100	RED
0101	MAGENTA
0110	BROWN
0111	LIGHT GREY
1000	DARK GREY
1001	LIGHT BLUE
1010	LIGHT GREEN
1011	LIGHT CYAN
1100	LIGHT RED
1101	LIGHT MAGENTA
1110	YELLOW
1111	WHITE

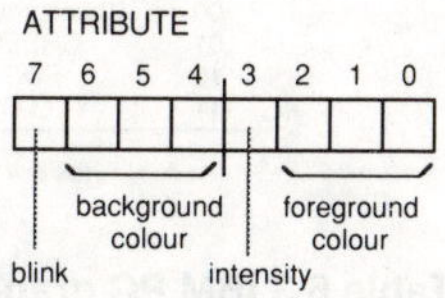

ATTRIBUTE

7 6 5 4 3 2 1 0

background colour | foreground colour

blink   intensity

Figure 6.21 Colour graphics adapter (text mode).

displays are possible in high resolution graphics mode.

Figure 6.21 shows the colours and character attributes possible with the colour graphics adapter. The display buffer commences at B8000H, while the MC6845 CRTC registers are connected to ports 3D4H and 3D5H. Altering the cursor from a blinking underline to a blinking block could be achieved using the following i8086 code segment (D.J. Bradley, *Assembly Language Programming for the IBM Personal Computer*, © 1984. Reprinted by permission of Prentice-Hall, Inc. Englewood Cliffs NJ)

```
CURSOR: MOV  DX,3D4H    ;MC6845 CRTC address pointer
        MOV  AL,#0AH    ;10 = cursor start address
        OUT  DX,AL      ;access cursor start address register
        INC  DX         ;MC6845 CRTC data register
        MOV  AL,#0       ;0 → 7 lines per character
        OUT  DX,AL      ;set cursor start line # (0→7 per char)
        DEC  DX         ;point back to 6845 address register
        MOV  AL,#0BH    ;11 = cursor end address register
        OUT  DX,AL      ;access cursor end address register
        INC  DX         ;MC6845 CRTC data register
        MOV  AL,#7       ;that is, block rather than underline
        OUT  DX,AL      ;set cursor end line number
        RET             ;return to main
;NOTE: could omit lines 7 through 12, since default values
;are R10 = 6 & R11 = 7 that is, underline rather than block
;(likewise a blinking cursor is the default attribute)
```

Table 6.2 shows the bit layout and colour palettes available when using the colour graphics adapter in medium resolution mode. Each pixel has two bits with which to specify one of four colours, as indicated (00 is the background colour). Bit 5 is the colour select register (3D9H) and determines which of the two colour palettes provided by IBM are in use at any time.

Table 6.2 IBM PC colour graphics adapter (medium resolution graphics mode).

COLOUR	PALETTE#0	PALETTE#1
00	(background)	(background)
01	GREEN	CYAN
10	RED	MAGENTA
11	YELLOW	WHITE
	(bit 5 = 0)	(bit 5 = 1)

Table 6.3 IBM PC graphics adapter standards.

STANDARD	# COLOURS	RESOLUTION (# pixels)	SIGNAL TYPE	HORIZONTAL SCAN RATES
CGA	4 of 16	320*200	digital	15.6 kHz
EGA	16 of 64	640*350	digital	21.8 kHz
VGA	256 of 256000	320*200	analog	31.5 kHz

A number of graphics adapter standards have been developed over the years for the IBM PC, and these are summarized in Table 6.3, together with their main characteristics (computer graphics will be covered more thoroughly in Section 6.7).

6.5.2 Intel i8275 CRTC

As previously seen, the i8275 CTRC is designed to work in conjunction with an i8257 DMAC in order to handle the block transfer of characters between screen (refresh) memory and the CPU (CRTC). The i8275 CRTC provides programmable screen and character formats, visual field and character attributes, cursor control, light pen support, dual row buffers and the ability to operate in DMA burst mode. It is shown in block diagram form in Figure 6.22. It is designed to handle character information in byte form, and thus employs an 8-bit bus interface.

The dual row buffers are 80 characters in length, which allows for updating of the screen on a line-by-line basis. Double buffering means that the second buffer can be filled while the first is simultaneously being displayed. Two FIFO buffers extend the length of these character buffers in transparent attribute mode.

The i8275 can be programmed to generate between 1 and 80 columns per row, and from 1 to 64 rows per screen (frame). It is also possible to blank alternate rows. The number of lines per character row is programmable in the range 1 to 16.

The i8275 CRTC has two programmable registers: the (read-only) command register and the (read/write) parameter register. A (write-only)

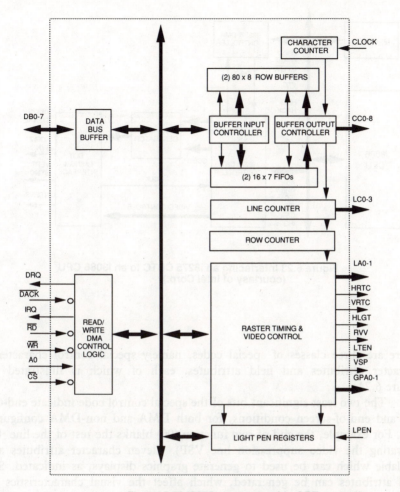

Figure 6.22 i8275 programmable CRT controller (courtesy of Intel Corp.).

status register shares the same address as the command register. The parameter register resides at the CRTC base address, while the command/status register is located at CRTC base address + 1.

The i8275 instruction set comprises the following commands: reset, start/stop display, read light pen, load cursor, enable/disable interrupts and preset counters.

Figure 6.23 shows the interconnection of an i8275 CRTC to an i8086 CPU, which incorporates video refresh RAM, an i8257 DMAC and character generator ROM. As already mentioned, the i8275 CRTC handles character information in byte form, however only the lower seven bits are used for accessing the character generator ROM; the most significant bit is used to distinguish between normal display characters and attribute/special codes.

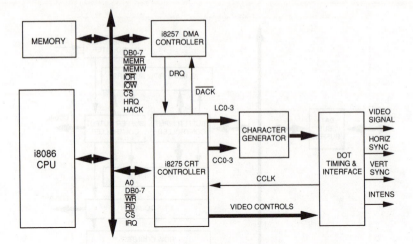

Figure 6.23 Interfacing an i8275 CRTC to an i8086 CPU (courtesy of Intel Corp.).

There are three classes of special codes, namely special control characters, character attributes and field attributes, each of which is illustrated in Figure 6.24.

The two least significant bits of the special control code indicate end-of-row and end-of-screen conditions, for both DMA and non-DMA configuration. For example, the end-of-row function (00) blanks the rest of the line (by activating the video suppression line VSP). Eleven character attributes are available which can be used to generate graphics displays, as indicated. Six field attributes can be generated, which affect the visual characteristics of characters from the following character up to the next field attribute code (or the next vertical retrace, which resets the field attributes). Highlighting, blinking, reverse video and underlining are all supported, or indeed any combination of these. Two user-programmable general-purpose attributes are also provided.

The following code segment shows how to initialize the i8275 cursor, assuming an i8275 CRTC base address of B000H:

```
CURSOR:  MOV   AL,#80H      ;80H = i8275 load cursor instruction
         OUT   B001H,AL     ;i8275 CRTC command register
         MOV   AL,#x        ;get cursor x-position (character #)
         OUT   B000H,AL     ;i8275 CRTC parameter register
         MOV   AL,#y        ;get cursor y-position (row #)
         OUT   B000H,AL     ;i8275 CRTC parameter register
         RET                ;return to calling program (main)
```

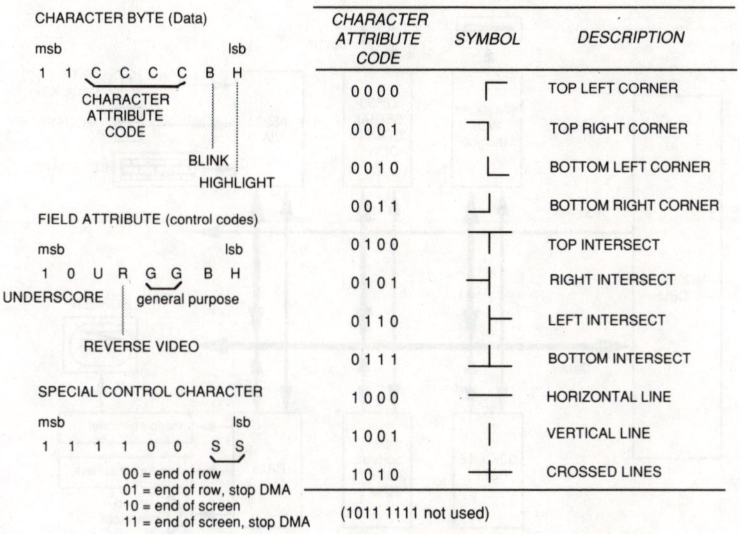

CHARACTER BYTE (Data)

msb   lsb

1   1   C   C   C   C   B   H

       CHARACTER
       ATTRIBUTE
       CODE

             BLINK
             HIGHLIGHT

FIELD ATTRIBUTE (control codes)

msb   lsb

1   0   U   R   G   G   B   H

UNDERSCORE | general purpose

     REVERSE VIDEO

SPECIAL CONTROL CHARACTER

msb   lsb

1   1   1   1   0   0   S   S

00 = end of row
01 = end of row, stop DMA
10 = end of screen
11 = end of screen, stop DMA

CHARACTER ATTRIBUTE CODE	SYMBOL	DESCRIPTION
0 0 0 0	⌐	TOP LEFT CORNER
0 0 0 1	¬	TOP RIGHT CORNER
0 0 1 0	L	BOTTOM LEFT CORNER
0 0 1 1	⌐	BOTTOM RIGHT CORNER
0 1 0 0	⊤	TOP INTERSECT
0 1 0 1	⊣	RIGHT INTERSECT
0 1 1 0	⊢	LEFT INTERSECT
0 1 1 1	⊥	BOTTOM INTERSECT
1 0 0 0	—	HORIZONTAL LINE
1 0 0 1	|	VERTICAL LINE
1 0 1 0	+	CROSSED LINES

(1011 1111 not used)

**Figure 6.24 i8275 character attributes (graphics)
(courtesy of Intel Corp.).**

6.5.3 Apple Macintosh CRTC

Rather than use an 'off-the-shelf' CRTC for their Macintosh computer, Apple produced their own custom controller, based on programmable hardware devices (PALs). Figure 6.25 shows the block diagram of the Apple Macintosh computer. It uses a 9 inch non-interlaced monitor, and employs a refresh rate of 60.15 Hz. The screen resolution is 80 pixels per inch, and the screen size is 512×342 pixels. (The NeXT computer uses a 17 inch monitor with 1120×832 resolution.)

    Pixel information resides in memory within a linear array, consisting of 10 944 (16-bit) words, with the msb of each word corresponding to the leftmost pixel. 32 words are required for each screen row, together with 12 words for horizontal blanking. A vertical retrace equivalent to 28 horizontal lines is used. The bits are shifted out using a 15.67 MHz clock.

    As previously seen, RAM accesses are shared between the MC68000 CPU and CRTC, with the CPU having an average access time of around 6 MHz (3.92 MHz during displays, and 7.83 MHz during retracing). It is worth noting that the Macintosh RAM is *triple* ported, which means that three different devices have access to it at different times, namely the CPU, CRTC and sound generation circuitry (the latter under DMA control).

    A user interface toolbox is provided in ROM which allows the applications programmer to access the mouse, windows, pull-down menus, dialogue boxes, desk accessories, text editor, fonts and so on. An inherent part

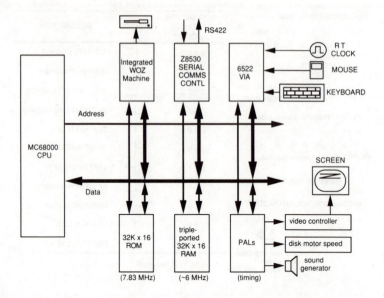

Figure 6.25 Apple Macintosh computer (courtesy of Apple Computer Inc.).

of the toolbox is the Quickdraw graphics package, which originated from the Macintosh's predecessor, the Lisa. Quickdraw can output over 7000 characters per second to the screen. It incorporates features such as fill (where any arbitrary shape can be filled with a preselected pattern) and clipping of an image to correspond to the boundaries of an arbitrary masking shape.

6.6 OTHER TYPES OF DISPLAYS

Despite its numerous drawbacks, the CRT type of VDT is still the predominant one used in computer systems, both large and small. There have been concerted efforts in the past to produce a display which overcomes the problems of bulk, weight and necessity for high voltage power supplies inherent in the classic CRT display. There have been several attempts at producing flat screen CRT displays, for example. One approach has been to turn the electron tube on its side, and fire the electrons at the phosphor coated screen 'around the corner', as was done by Sinclair in the UK during the mid 1980s.

The most notable developments, however, have been achieved using different technologies altogether. Of these alternate technologies, we will now turn our attention to liquid crystal, gas plasma and electroluminescent displays.

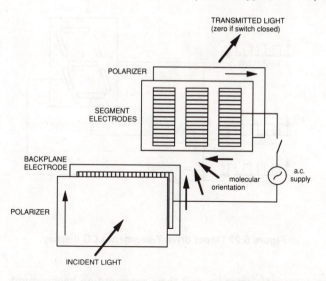

Figure 6.26 Construction of a Liquid Crystal Display (LCD).

6.6.1 Liquid Crystal Displays (LCDs)

Crystals are usually found in solids rather than liquid substances. However, there are certain organic fluids in which the constituent molecules are free to move around, yet at the same time gather together in an ordered manner. This gathering or aligning of the individual molecules affects the amount of incident light which is reflected, scattered and transmitted through the crystal. Moreover, the optical properties of such liquids vary with the application of an electric field across the liquid.

The internal construction of an LCD display is shown in Figure 6.26. It comprises two parallel glass plates separated by a few microns, in between which the liquid crystal resides. The inner surfaces of these plates are covered with a transparent conductive coating, which constitute the two electrodes. These electrodes are constructed in the shape of the characters or dots required; a typical example is the 7-segment display shown in Figure 6.27 (which can be likened to the 7-segment LED display presented previously in Section 4.1). Another type of LCD is the dot matrix type, which is better suited for alphanumeric displays.

In the 'twisted nematic' type of LCD display shown in Figure 6.26, there is a rotation of 90^0 in the polarization of the backplane electrode and that of the segment electrodes. Thus light will only pass through the liquid either side of the segment electrodes. Two polaroid filters are placed before and after the two electrodes, to assist in this alignment process. With the switch in the open position, the molecules will align as indicated, such that the incident light will pass right through the segments, with no discernible difference

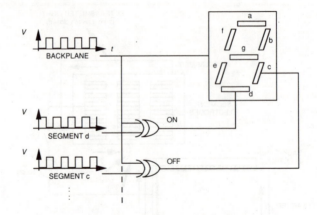

Figure 6.27 Direct drive 7-segment LCD display.

between the segment electrodes and their surrounding background. However, when the switch is closed and voltage is applied between the electrodes, the liquid molecules will align themselves *perpendicular* to the segment electrode, rather than parallel to it, as previously. Light will then be reflected back from the segment electrodes to the observer, and will only pass through the liquid on either side of the segment electrodes.

It is possible to utilize such an LCD in either reflective or transmissive mode. In reflective mode (the one illustrated in Figure 6.26), an ambient light source is required in order to produce legible characters. In transmissive mode, the LCD needs to be illuminated from the rear. This latter type of backlit display is required in situations where the ambient light is low, or indeed non-existent. The trend these days is away from the reflective type towards transmitting LCD displays. For a given applied voltage, the contrast of the display between the segments and their background varies markedly with viewing angle.

Square waves of at least 50 Hz (in order to avoid flicker) are used to drive LCDs, as indicated in Figure 6.27. LCDs require little drive current, and thus can be driven directly from CMOS devices, which makes them admirably suited to portable applications such as wristwatches, pocket calculators and laptop computers.

In the direct drive method employed in Figure 6.27, square wave pulse trains are applied to each individual segment either in phase or 180^0 out of phase with the pulse train applied to the backplane. Segments which have a net voltage applied between the two electrodes are turned on, whereas segments with zero net applied voltage are turned off.

For displays comprising more than three or four LCDs, a multiplex drive technique is usually preferred. This reduces the number of inter-connections to a more manageable number. In multiplexed displays, the desired segments are pulsed on at regular intervals, rather than continuously.

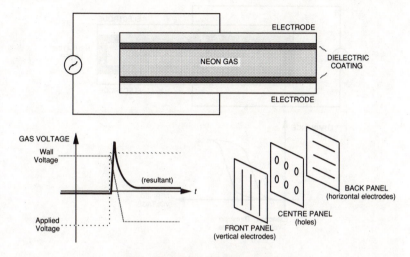

Figure 6.28 Gas plasma displays.

LCDs are limited in the refresh rate, since it takes a finite time for the liquid crystal to change its orientation as the voltage is applied or removed. This slowed development of LCD television screens for a number of years. The advent of portable laptop computers in the mid 1980s witnessed the wider acceptance of LCDs. Colour LCD flat panel screens have also become available in recent years.

LCD displays offer advantages of small size, removal of the need for a high voltage supply, flat screens and linearity (since each pixel can be addressed directly in terms of row and column information).

6.6.2 Gas Plasma Displays

One of the chief disadvantages of the LCD is the limited viewing angle. This is rectified in the gas plasma type of display illustrated in Figure 6.28. Gas plasma displays are essentially variations on the much older gas discharge or neon tube. Each pixel in the gas plasma display can be likened to a miniature neon tube; it consists of an anode and a cathode, with gas plasma in between (consisting of a charged mixture of neon and argon/xenon).

Applying a voltage between the two electrodes causes the gas to ionize, resulting in light being emitted. The voltage that produces ionization is actually a combination of the applied voltage and the wall voltage formed from positive ions migrating to the cathode. Normally, these two voltages will be of opposite polarity, but when the applied voltage is reversed, they combine to produce ionization. Two types of gas plasma display are available, namely DC and AC. The DC type is simpler in construction, but has a continuous glow due to its refresh voltage.

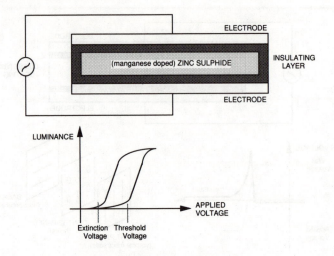

Figure 6.29 Electroluminescent displays.

As is common with most large displays, plasma panels incorporate all the necessary interfacing circuitry, so that they can be controlled directly by the standard RGB output from a video monitor. Orange-coloured gas plasma panels are perhaps the most commonly encountered type, although green panels are also available. In earlier displays, individual pixels could only be turned on or off. Nowadays, better control over pixel brightness means that grey scales (actually orange scales) can be generated.

Other advantages of gas plasma displays are their high brightness, absence of flicker and compactness (particularly in comparison with CRT displays). Their chief disadvantage is their high power consumption (they require a supply of around 200 V), which results in their poor showing against LCDs for portable applications.

6.6.3 Electroluminescent Displays

Both gas plasma and electroluminescent displays exhibit hysteresis, as illustrated in Figure 6.29; the pixels remain illuminated once they have been turned on. Electroluminescent displays are based on the property that some substances (such as doped zinc sulphide) emit light when subjected to high voltages. As with LCDs and gas plasma displays, it is a straightforward matter with electroluminescent displays to form a matrix of individual pixels, addressed by activating the appropriate row and column lines. Multiplexed drives are usually employed, and as with other large display panels, the power and interfacing circuitry is incorporated into a single module.

The advantages of electroluminescent displays are their ruggedness (owing to their completely solid state construction), brightness, high contrast ratio (compared to the background) and wide viewing angle. Their main disadvantage is their relatively high cost.

6.6.4 Support chips

Despite the continuing popularity of CRT displays, the alternate displays just described (particulalry LCD) continue to make inroads into the VDT market. This is reflected in the release of peripheral support chips such as the Yamaha Enhanced Panel Display Controller which supports IBM monochrome, CGA, EGA, NEC Multisync, (8 colour) LCD, EL and (grey scale) gas plasma displays, in five different pixel modes (namely 640×200, 400, 480 and 480×320, 200).

6.7   GRAPHICS DISPLAYS

The essential aim of graphics displays is to produce pictures on a screen, rather than alphanumeric characters. Some fundamental requirements are therefore high resolution (in terms of the total number of pixels or dots), number of available colours and screen update rate. Often monochrome displays are preferred to colour, due to their higher resolution (recall that only one phosphor is required for monochrome, whereas each pixel in a colour display requires three). Desktop publishing is a typical example of where monochrome displays are preferred.

Grey-scale monitors have been developed in recent years, prompted by developments with laser printers and desktop publishing. Conventional monochrome monitors use a technique called 'dithering' for simulating grey scales (with dithering, dots are clustered to give the illusion of shading). However, this technique sacrifices resolution, making it unsuitable for the kind of image manipulation required in desktop publishing. Grey-scale monitors offer between 16 and 256 shades of grey, thus enabling them to handle photographic image processing. For colour graphics, common screen resolutions are around 1000×1000 pixels, with the number of colours available at any one time being 256 from a palette of 65 536 (typically).

The high refresh rates demanded by such high resolution screens requires the use of fast DRAMs for the screen (video) memory (DRAMs were covered in Chapter 2). For example, refreshing a 1000×1000 pixel screen would require video memory with access times of less than 30 ns (assuming interlacing, a refresh rate of 25 Hz per field and recalling that each scan line takes around $64\,\mu s$ to trace out). These timing constraints also have repercussions regarding the bandwidths (frequency response) of the deflection circuitry and RF amplifiers inside the CRT.

It was mentioned in Section 6.2 that the vector graphic type of CRT

Table 6.4 Grey scale stored as intensity values in frame buffer.

INTENSITY	BINARY REPRESENTATION	GREY SCALE
0.0	00	black
0.33	01	dark grey
0.67	10	light grey
1.0	11	white

display was well suited to graphics applications, at least those involving line diagrams. The alternative type of CRT graphics display is the raster scan display, where the removal of the character generator ROM enables us to access down to the pixel level, as discussed in Section 6.4.1 (which is exactly what is required of course for graphics displays). The information describing each pixel is stored in a special-purpose RAM referred to as a 'bit plane'. This bit plane can be accessed either by x- and y-pointers, or by keeping a screen image in memory (which removes the need for pointers in the interface circuitry).

The simple graphics display presented in Section 6.5.1 allocated only a single bit per pixel; dots were either turned on or off. This is referred to as a digital type of monitor. Allocating two bits of memory to each pixel on the screen allows us to define one of four grey scales in a monochrome display (or alternatively one of four colours in a colour display), as indicated in Table 6.4.

Generally speaking, colour displays require more than two bits per pixel. A screen employing $m \times n$ pixels is shown in Figure 6.30. Eight bits per pixel are used, but the RGB guns are not driven directly. Instead, the 8-bit data is used as a pointer into a table in memory, each entry comprising 12 bits of colour information, four per primary colour.

Figure 6.31 shows how this 12-bit information is used to drive three 4-bit digital-to-analog converters (see Chapter 9), one for each colour gun within the CRT. Digital colour monitors can only reproduce a finite number of

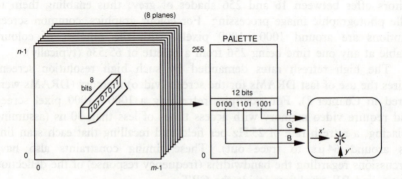

Figure 6.30 Video lookup table (pixel x'y').

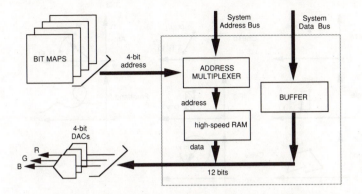

Figure 6.31 Colour palette using high-speed DACs.

colours, at discrete signal levels. Some typical examples are R(ed), G(reen), B(lue) and I(ntensity) in the IBM PC CGA standard, resulting in a total of 16 different colours. The EGA standard uses R, r, G, g, B and b, which yields 64 colours. The alternative to digital monitors are analog monitors, where the RGB signal levels are *continuous* rather than restricted to discrete levels. (In practice the number of levels is finite, due to the limited capacities of the graphics adapter. For example, in the VGA standard, 6 bits enable 2^{18} or 260 000 levels to be discriminated. VGA was originally developed for the IBM PC, but has since been incorporated into the IBM PS/2 models 50, 60 and 80. The PS/2 also supports the CGA compatible Multicolour Graphics Array (MCGA)).

In the Macintosh-II, 8 bits are sufficient to discriminate 2^{24} or 16 000 000 levels). The D/A converter inside the graphics adapter board provides the analog driving signals for the monitor's electron gun deflection circuitry.

In the system of Figure 6.31, one of 256 colours can be chosen from the palette currently selected. Changing to a palette of 256 *different* colours is achieved by simply moving the start address of the colour lookup table. Alternatively, individual entries could be changed in order to produce a custom colour set. Using such a system in a monochrome display would allow us to choose from 256 different shades of grey (grey scales).

A form of rudimentary animation can be achieved by assigning different areas of the screen to different table entries. If all entries are the same, then the screen will be the one colour throughout. Changing individual entries will highlight different regions of the display, which will produce the illusion of moving figures if each successive image differs only slightly from its predecessor.

A graphics display is not usually programmed at the bit level, but rather by using a set of graphics primitives or macros. Figure 6.32 shows some of the more fundamental graphics primitives. The ability to fill objects with

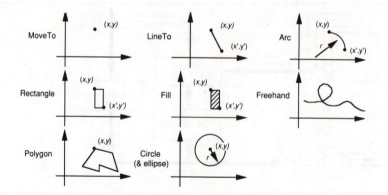

Figure 6.32 Graphics primitives.

different patterns (or colours) is also supported. Smoothing algorithms are often incorporated in order to convert freehand line drawings into smoother approximations of curves.

In Section 6.4 we looked at the mapping between video (refresh) memory and the *x-y* position of a pixel on the screen. Essentially this comprises the updating of a pointer in memory. Thus, the drawing of horizontal and vertical lines is straightforward; incrementing the horizontal position only for the former, and incrementing the vertical position by a constant amount for the latter. The drawing of lines at any angle of inclination requires a little more care however. Figure 6.33 shows the drawing of a diagonal line from point *x*1,*y*1 to *x*2,*y*2, where the line is constructed by simply incrementing the vertical coordinate by one for each new horizontal position. However, this is not a typical line; most diagonal lines will consist of *unequal* increments in the horizontal and vertical directions.

The pixel shape also plays a part in drawing such primitive shapes. The pixels of Figure 6.33 are oval shaped, whereas high resolution graphics displays utilize circular pixels. Objects mapped onto a raster scan display become distorted due to aliasing (sometimes referred to as 'jaggies'), which is caused by the rounding of coordinate points to discrete integer pixel positions in the raster (this effect can be likened to quantization in analog-to-digital conversion, discussed later, in Section 9.4). This can lead to lines having a jagged appearance. Line drawing algorithms can compensate for this effect by

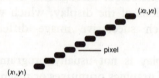

Figure 6.33 Staircase effect.

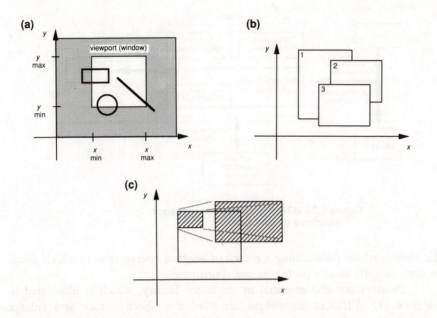

Figure 6.34 Graphics features (a) clipping (b) multiple windows (c) zoom.

incorporating anti-aliasing routines that smooth out jagged lines by adjusting pixel *intensities* along the length of the line.

Other graphics features include clipping, windowing and zoom. Clipping results from the graphics screen being of limited size, such that portion of the drawing of interest will not be displayed on the screen. The screen of Figure 6.34a displays only that area between x_{min} and x_{max} in the horizontal direction, and between y_{min} and y_{max} in vertical direction. Those portions of the rectangle, circle and line that lie outside this window are not displayed on the screen. The shaded region of the figure corresponds to the 'world view' of current interest, whereas the white portion represents the 'viewport' onto this world view. The entire world view would be stored in memory; displaying a different viewport would be achieved by simply changing the video refresh) memory pointers.

Multiple windowing is the ability of the graphics display to display simultaneously several different viewports on the same screen, one overlayed on the other. A typical example of this is the Macintosh 'desktop', where several windows are 'laid' on top of each other, just like laying several sheets of paper on a desktop. The background display and the current window form the background for the next window to be 'overlaid' onto the display, as illustrated in Figure 6.34b. Again, it is a relatively straightforward matter for the graphics control circuitry to alter pointers to display any desired window on

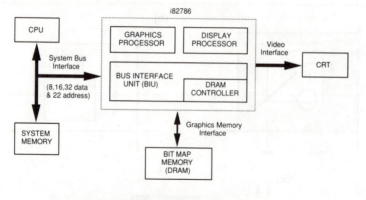

**Figure 6.35 i82786 graphics coprocessor
(courtesy of Intel Corp.).**

the screen, whilst maintaining a record of boolean operators as to which pixels to turn on (off) at any particular *x-y* coordinate.

Pointers are also essential in the zoom facility, which is illustrated in Figure 6.34c. Efficient algorithms are needed to both reduce and enlarge screen images, while simultaneously maintaining the original image in correct proportion.

6.7.1 Graphics Controller Chips

Sophisticated graphics controller chips first started to become available during the mid 1980s. Two of the first graphics controllers were the Hitachi HD63484 and the NECμ7220. Other manufacturers entered the market shortly thereafter, offering devices such as the Intel i82786, Texas Instruments TMS34010(20) and NCR7300. National Semiconductor produce a two-chip set, comprising the DP8500 raster graphics processor and DP8510 Bit-Block Logic Transfer processor (or BitBLT). AMD have incorporated BitBLT algorithms into their Am95C60 quad-pixel data flow manager. INMOS offer a range of colour lookup tables which incorporate D/A converters as well as a microprocessor interface.

The Intel i82786 graphics controller is designed as a coprocessor for the i80286/386 CPUs. Internally it consists of four separate units, as shown in Figure 6.35. The graphics processor executes instructions placed in RAM (up to 4 Mbytes) by the host CPU, producing bitmaps in the graphics memory. The display processor *simultaneously* converts these bitmaps into a form suitable for driving a raster scan CRT display. There is an inbuilt bus interface unit, and an on-chip dynamic memory controller.

The i82786 has built-in primitives such as point, line, polygon, rectangle, circle and arc, as well as clipped versions of all of these in clipping mode. It also supports more sophisticated commands such as bit-block

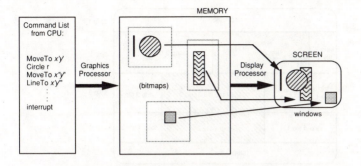

**Figure 6.36 Independent graphics and display modules
(courtesy of Intel Corp.).**

transfer, incremental point and fill (bit-block transfers allow for the quick duplication of images already resident in memory). The i82786 can perform block transfers at the rate of 24 Mbits per second, and can draw 25 000 characters per second in text mode, irrespective of font or orientation (fonts can be up to 16×16 pixels maximum, and multiple character sets can be supported simultaneously).

The i82786 can provide resolutions of 640×480 pixels (assuming 8 bits per pixel), or alternatively 1024×1024 pixels (for 2 bits). Screen updating is carried out every tenth of a second (which corresponds to around 400 ns per pixel). For a system clock of 10 MHz and a video clock of 25 MHz, the i82786 can draw lines at the rate of 2 500 000 pixels per second. The i82786 supports horizontal and vertical scrolling, as well as zoom (up to 64 times in both the horizontal and vertical directions). Its most notable feature, however, is its support for multiple windows, as shown in Figure 6.36. These windows are constructed in real time using a strip tile technique, as indicated in Figure 6.37. Up to 16 horizontal segments can be supported per scan line, while the number of vertical scan lines is only limited by the total number of scan lines displayed. Figure 6.37 shows how two windows could be formed using this multitasking technique.

Apart from the primitives already mentioned, the i82786 is designed to run applications written using the ANSI Video Device Interface, Graphics Kernel System and IBM Colour Graphics Adapter standards. Moreover, several such applications can be run *concurrently*, with each being displayed in its own window.

The Texas Instruments TMS34010 Graphics Systems Processor (GSP) is capable of burst instruction execution rates of around 6 MIPS (millions of instructions per second), using a 50 MHz clock. This performance is achieved by way of a 256-byte instruction cache, 30 general-purpose 32-bit registers (divided into two files, A and B), variable width ALUs, single-cycle instructions, a barrel shifter and mask/merge hardware. Moreover, inbuilt Video RAM (VRAM) interface and display control circuitry simplify interface

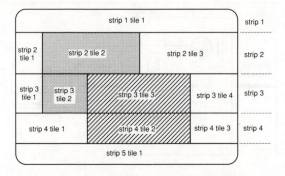

Figure 6.37 Use of strip tiles to create 'unlimited' windows (courtesy of Intel Corp.).

design (VRAMs comprise a DRAM and serial shift register/buffer internally). Separate interfaces are provided for the graphics display, host CPU and local memory bus. Five different pixel sizes can be selected (1, 2, 4, 8 or 16), and several pixels can be processed in parallel.

The TMS34010 instruction set supports floating-point arithmetic, graphics primitives and windows (with either pre- or post-clipping). The fundamental graphics instruction provided is Pixel Block Transfer (PixBLT), which is similar to Bit Block Transfer (BitBLT), but expanded to support both arithmetic and boolean operations on two-dimensional arrays. Preclipping is automatically applied to PixBLT and FILL operations.

The TMS34010 GSP uses the packed pixel format, in which all bits belonging to a pixel are contained in the same memory word. In planar pixel formatting, individual pixel bits are placed in *different* memory locations. The advantage of packed pixel memory organization is that an entire pixel can be accessed during a single bus cycle. Moreover, there is no need to extract and manipulate individual pixel bits from several memory locations prior to performing arithmetic functions on them. The planar and packed pixel formats are compared in Figure 6.38.

The TMS34020 GSP is an enhanced version of the earlier TMS34010. It has 32-bit buses both internally and externally (the TMS34010 only had a 16-bit external bus). The TMS34020 is between 5 and 50 times faster than its predecessor, and is rated as a 10 MIPS machine. It has a 512 byte instruction cache (compared with 256 byte in the TMS34010), and a coprocessor interface (for connection to a TMS34082 Floating Point Unit). Pixel- or bit-aligned block transfers of around 140 Mbit/second and FILLs of over 1 Gbit/second are supported (using 44C251 1-Mbit VRAMs).

The TMS34020 supports three-operand block transfers, which are useful, for example, in laser printers when dealing with large textured objects (texture referring to a specific surface pattern). Pitches (the distance between pixels on corresponding lines on the screen) are not restricted to multiples of 2^n, as with the TMS34010. Like its predecessor, varying field widths in

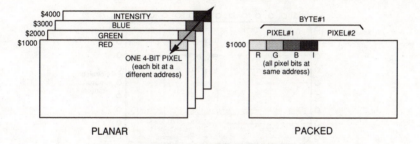

**Figure 6.38 Planar and packed pixel memory organization.
(courtesy of Texas Instruments Inc.)**

memory are catered for, which provide support for the packed array structure in the C language.

Both the TMS34010 and 34020 provide support for two-operand pixel block transfer instructions, enabling 16 binary and 6 arithmetic raster operations to be performed on a pair of two-dimensional pixel arrays. These are useful in manipulating and moving bounded objects and also with solid colour operations. A third operand – a binary mask – has been added to the TMS34020 PixBLT instruction.

'See through' pixels are supported in the TMS34000 family. The arithmetic pixel instructions allow maximum (minimum) calculation of source and destination pixels, which is useful in the orderly layering of planes of data, or in moving sprites around a screen without corrupting background (or foreground) images (recall the earlier comments regarding primitive animation).

6.8   INTERACTIVE GRAPHICS DISPLAYS

Interactive graphics displays allow the user to provide feedback information regarding the screen locations where objects are to be selected, moved from (to), deleted and so on. This information can be entered in a variety of ways, some of which we shall now consider briefly.

6.8.1 Light Pen

Light pens were mentioned previously in Sections 6.4.1 and 6.5.1. They come equipped with their own light source (activated by a button on their shaft), and connect to the CRT controller card via a roving cable. Special circuitry within the CRTC is able to detect the screen address corresponding to the position on the screen to which the pen points. Light pens can also be used to draw 'rubber bands' or polygons around objects in order to select that

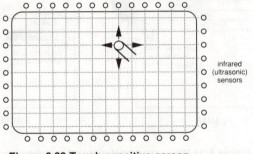

Figure 6.39 Touch-sensitive screen.

particular object(s), perhaps in order to zoom in on it (in other words, magnify it so that it fills the entire screen).

6.8.2 Touch-sensitive Screens

An alternative method by which a user can select specific items on the screen is by use of a special, touch-sensitive screen. There are basically two types of touch-sensitive screen, one which uses an additional transparent sheet mounted on the CRT screen, and the other which uses arrays of infrared or ultrasonic sensors mounted on the edges of the screen. This latter type is illustrated in Figure 6.39.

The transparent sheet types can be either resistive or capacitive. The resistive type actually uses *two* translucent sheets, one with embedded wires running horizontally, and the other with embedded wires running vertically. Pressing a particular point on the screen causes specific horizontal and vertical wires to make contact, thereby providing addressing information as to the user's finger position on the screen.

With the infrared (ultrasonic) sensor type of touch-sensitive screen, the user's finger disturbs light beams travelling across the screen and close to its surface, in order to register finger position.

6.8.3 Indirect Pointing Devices

Instead of pointing directly to the screen, an indirect method can be used, whereby physical motion of a controller is reflected on the CRT screen. Three commonly used devices are mice, joysticks and tracker balls. The mouse of Figure 6.40 uses optically-encoded disks mounted on its x- and y-shafts, and photodiodes (transistors) to detect the binary patterns corresponding to angular position of the shafts. Two-dimensional motion can alternatively be sensed by movement of potentiometers (variable resistors) connected to the x-

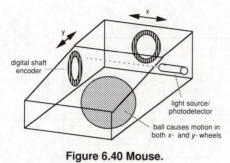

Figure 6.40 Mouse.

and y-shafts. Like the light pen, the mouse trails a long wire (tail) behind it, which connects to the CRT interface.

Tracker balls are similar to mice, in that they contain a spherical ball. However, instead of this ball moving indirectly as a result of the user moving the mouse, the user's hand moves the ball directly. The tracker ball can be likened to a mouse that has been flipped over onto its 'back', in order to allow the user's hand to make direct contact with the ball. Unlike the mouse, the tracker ball mounting cannot move around, but is rigidly mounted on the desk top.

Joysticks can be likened to miniature gear levers, where movements can be made either horizontally, vertically or diagonally. Springs are used to return the joystick to its 'neutral' position when released by the user. Unlike the mouse or the tracker ball, there are physical limits on the movements of the joystick in the x- and y-directions. (Mice and tracker balls can continue to rotate, however this motion is translated into $\pm360°$ by the controller hardware.)

6.8.4 Digitizing Pads

Digitizing pads or graphics tablets comprise a moveable pointer together with a sensitized pad of up to 1 m^2 in size, and with resolutions of around 1/1000th cm. The moveable pointer can either be in the form of an 'eyeglass', such as that depicted in Figure 6.41, or an electronic pen (similar to the light pen discussed earlier). The Wang Freestyle system uses an electronic pen, in order to mimic a user writing on an office desktop. The user can paste voice annotation (via a telephone handset) and handwriting (via the electronic pencil) into documents created in the usual manner on the IBM-PC compatible system.

The pointer of Figure 6.41 comprises a housing for a transparent eyeglass scribed with crosshairs, together with two buttons (one to four buttons are typical). Pressing these buttons in various combinations selects different functions, such as Select, MoveTo, Delete, Duplicate and so on.

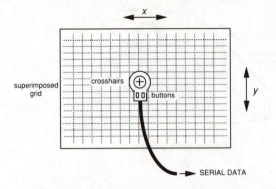

Figure 6.41 Digitizing pad (graphics tablet).

One common type of sensitized pad uses an electromagnetic grid, the x- and y-wires of which pick up a high frequency (or ultrasonic) signal transmitted by the pointer, hence allowing its position to be determined. Digitizing pads are higher resolution and more accurate devices than mice. They are used extensively in drafting and CAD environments.

6.8.5 x–y Scanners

Scanners scan an image (photographic, text or graphics) in a systematic manner, gradually building up a raster scan version of it, in a similar manner to a VDT building up an image on its CRT tube. Grey-scale data is transferred to the host computer in serial form as part of the scanning process. Obviously the resolution of such a device is critical, around 1000 dots per inch being typical (in one of 64 grey scales). An x–y scanner is shown in Figure 6.42.

One application area for scanners is with Optical Character Recognition (OCR). In fact OCR is touted by some as a possible replacement for keyboards in the computer terminals of the future.

Early OCRs were limited in the number of different fonts and font sizes (only two IBM typewriter golfball fonts being typical!). The technique used in these devices was matrix matching, where each typewritten letter was compared with 9×9 character images stored in lookup tables in local memory. More sophisticated techniques are used these days in order to recognize a wide variety of font types, sizes, slants and stylistic variations, in both regularly spaced (typewriter) and proportionally spaced (typesetter) type.

Modern-day scanners are also capable of scanning documents either vertically or horizontally. They also use the Tag Image File Format (TIFF) standard, which ensures that characters are produced in a form compatible with transmission over facsimile (FAX) networks.

Earlier OCRs were dedicated, expensive machines, performing all the necessary processing themselves, then feeding the decoded characters to a host

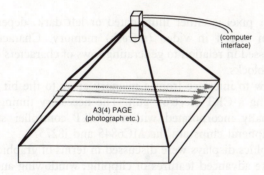

Figure 6.42 *x-y* **scanner.**

computer. These days, improvements in both memory capacity and speed allow processing tasks previously carried out by the OCR itself to be handled by a PC, thus enabling much less expensive, off-the-shelf scanners to be used.

6.8.6 Interactive Compact Disks (CDI)

CD-ROMs will be discussed in Chapter 10 in relation to mass storage devices. Essentially they are read-only storage media, capable of storing gigabytes of information (which corresponds to several thousand pages, sufficient to store an entire encyclopedia, or the complete works of Shakespeare, for example). *Interactive* CD-ROMs provide online access to a large database of still picture and text information, under user control and on a page-by-page basis.

SUMMARY

The most widely used computer peripheral is the Video Display Terminal (VDT). It comprises a (ASCII) keyboard as the input device and a CRT screen as the output device. In this chapter we concentrated on the raster scan type of CRT display, although LCD, gas plasma and electroluminescent displays were also mentioned. Nevertheless, the predominant display remains the CRT, despite its large size and requirement for a high voltage power supply.

We focussed our discussion on the raster scan type of CRT display, although the vector graphic type was also mentioned. In a raster scan type of CRT display, the screen image is built up gradually by an electron beam tracing out horizontal lines on a phosphor-coated screen, from top to bottom. Horizontal and vertical timebase circuitry controls the position of the electron beam on the screen at any particular time. Moreover, the entire screen needs to be refreshed at least 50 or 60 times every second, so that the image appears stationary to the human eye.

Each dot or pixel is either illuminated or left dark, depending on the binary bit pattern stored in video (refresh) memory. Character generator ROMs were discussed in relation to generating rows of characters on the screen using dot matrix blocks.

We saw how to interface from a memory array to the bit serial stream required for driving a CRT electron gun. The necessary timing and control functions are usually incorporated within a CRT controller support chip. Typical CRT peripheral chips are the MC6845 and i8275.

Colour graphics displays were discussed in terms of graphics primitives, as well as the more advanced features of clipping, windowing and zoom. The i82786 and TMS34010(20) graphics controller chips were introduced. In our coverage of interactive graphics displays, we considered such devices as light pens, touch-sensitive screens, mice, graphics tablets and scanners.

REVIEW QUESTIONS

6.1 Discuss the mapping from a computer's memory array to a VDU raster scan display.

6.2 What part does a character generator ROM play in a VDT?

6.3 In relation to a VDT, what is meant by the terms raster scan, scrolling, sync pulses, interlacing, retrace period, timebase and refreshing?

6.4 What functions are commonly performed by a CRTC peripheral support chip?

6.5 Discuss the advantages and disadvantages of the linear vs row-and-column screen (video) memory addressing schemes.

6.6 Explain how the 18 data registers are accessed on the MC6845 CRTC.

6.7 Discuss the advantages and disadvantages of the following display types as compared with VDTs: LCD, plasma, and electroluminescent.

6.8 Explain what is meant by the term graphics primitive.

6.9 What is meant by bit plane in relation to graphics displays?

6.10 Compare and contrast input devices for interactive graphics terminals.

7

Hard Copy Units

7.1 Introduction
7.2 Printers
7.3 Printer Interfacing
7.4 Laser Printers
7.5 *x–y* Plotters
SUMMARY
Review Questions

OBJECTIVES

Printers are discussed in terms of whether they use impact or non-impact methods to form characters on the page, whether characters are generated fully formed or as a dot matrix, and whether single characters or entire lines are printed at a time.

Connecting a printer to a microcomputer can involve either serial (RS232c) or parallel (Centronics) interfaces.

Laser printers and *x–y* plotters are also covered.

7.1 INTRODUCTION

Chapter 6 was devoted to CRT displays (and others). In this chapter we turn our attention to hard copy units, which are used to obtain more permanent records of the images stored temporarily on a CRT display, whether they be program listings (alphanumeric characters) or graphics. Most of our attention will be devoted to printers, however some mention will also be made of x–y plotters.

7.2 PRINTERS

There are many different types of printers used with computers, varying in sophistication from modified typewriters to phototypesetters. Irrespective of what type the printer is, it consists of three major parts: the printing mechanism itself, some means of moving the paper and the controlling electronics.

Printers can be distinguished by a number of different characteristics; they can be classified as impact or non-impact, fully formed or dot matrix, and line or character. With impact printers, the print mechanism presses the ribbon onto the paper. Their operation is much like a typewriter; indeed some printers use a golfball type of print mechanism. The paper rests against a platen, which can be either fixed or moveable (usually cylindrical in the case of the latter).

In non-impact printers there is no direct contact of a printhead onto the paper. In ink jet printers, for example, small electrostatically charged droplets of ink are fired at the paper surface as illustrated in Figure 7.1. Thermal printers use special sensitized paper, and depend on various voltages applied across the surface of the paper to 'burn off' where required in order to form the desired pattern(s).

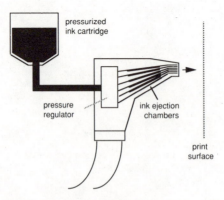

Figure 7.1 Ink jet printer.

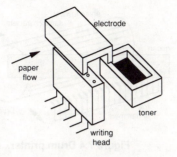

Figure 7.2 Electrosensitive printer.

Electrosensitive printers produce an electrostatic charge on the surface of the paper, to which toner adheres when the paper passes over the toner reservoir, as indicated in Figure 7.2. This is the same principle used in office photocopiers. Laser printers are another type of non-impact printer which also rely on this mechanism (they will be discussed in more detail in Section 7.4). Generally speaking, non-impact printers avoid the problem of mechanical wear on the printhead, but usually require the paper to be treated in some special manner.

Printers can also be distinguished in terms of whether the characters are printed in a fully formed manner, or whether they are built up gradually in dot matrix form. A common fully formed type of printer is the daisywheel, which is shown in Figure 7.3. Each fully formed character is attached at the end of one of the 'daisy's' stems. The desired character is brought into position in front of the hammer by rotating the daisywheel. The hammer is then activated, and the ribbon pressed onto the paper in order to print the character. The daisywheel printer has two main advantages: firstly, it produces letter quality output (in other words as good as a typewriter), and secondly, it

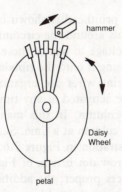

Figure 7.3 Daisywheel printer.

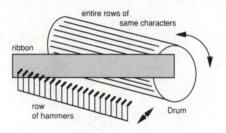

Figure 7.4 Drum printer.

is a simple matter to load in a different font set, by simply replacing the daisywheel. Dot matrix printers will be discussed in more detail later in this chapter.

Printers can also be classified in terms of whether they print a character at a time or an entire line. Figure 7.4 shows one type of line printer, a drum type (other types include band and comb). In the drum printer, entire rows of the *same* character appear across the surface of the drum, with the complete character set being distributed around the circumference. The drum is rotated through each character position in turn, with hammers activated wherever that particular character appears in the line. This results in much faster printing than with character printers (a thousand lines per minute of up to 132 characters per line, as opposed to several hundred characters per second), but line printers are usually more expensive than character printers. The ribbon is fed diagonally in order to ensure more even wear.

7.2.1 Dot Matrix Printers

Dot matrix printers are perhaps the most widely used hard copy computer peripheral devices. They are relatively inexpensive and yet perform their task quite effectively.

A typical dot matrix printhead is shown in Figure 7.5. Nine solenoids are spaced at regular intervals around the circumference of a circular housing. Applying the appropriate voltage to one of these solenoids activates the print wire associated with it, pressing it onto the ribbon, hence forming a dot on the paper surface. The nine print wires are organized in a vertical column, as shown. Which solenoids are activated at any time are determined by the dot pattern for that particular column. In this manner, characters are built up gradually across the page, a column at a time. Such a character (an upper-case A) is shown by way of illustration in Figure 7.6.

In the 7-column × 9-row dot matrix of Figure 7.6, only a 5 × 7 matrix is used to form the characters proper; the additional columns (and rows) are used for spacing between characters (and lower descenders or underline where necessary). In the cheaper type of dot matrix printer, the spacing of the dots is

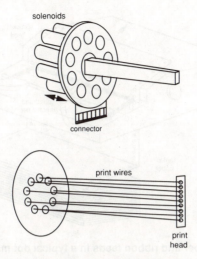

solenoids

connector

print wires

print head

Figure 7.5 Dot matrix printhead.

fixed. However, in higher quality dot matrix printers a choice of spacing is provided, which enables higher resolution characters to be formed. Moreover, the dots can be overlapped, so that only every second dot is needed to produce 'draft quality' printouts, or alternatively *every* dot can be used to produce 'letter quality' printing.

By having the printhead make several passes across a line (say once from left to right and again on the printhead's return from right to left), it is possible to support other fonts, such as *italics*, <u>underline</u> or **boldface**.

A typical dot matrix printer is illustrated in Figure 7.7. In this particular printer the paper feed mechanism is a sprocket one. Alternative feed mechanisms include friction and tractor feeds. Friction feeds are identical to those used in typewriters, and involve two rollers in contact with one another which pull the paper through between them. Tractor feeds can be likened to

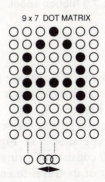

9 x 7 DOT MATRIX

Figure 7.6 Formation of characters using a dot matrix.

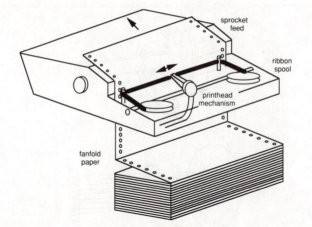

Figure 7.7 Paper and ribbon feeds in a typical dot matrix printer.

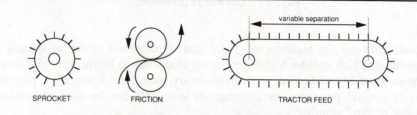

Figure 7.8 Paper feed mechanisms.

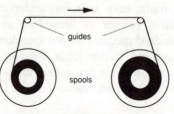

Figure 7.9 Ribbon spool.

an elongated pair of sprocket feeds, the distance between which can be varied, thereby providing a means of varying the paper tension. All three paper feed mechanisms are illustrated in Figure 7.8.

Ribbon feed mechanisms vary from the separate spool system shown in Figure 7.9, to the cartridge type shown in Figure 7.10. The moebius loop cartridge shown in Figure 7.10 consists of a single continuous loop of ribbon, with a single twist at one point of its travel to ensure that both the upper and lower halves of the ribbon are used equally.

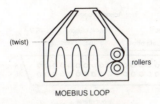

(twist)

rollers

MOEBIUS LOOP

Figure 7.10 Ribbon cartridge.

7.3   PRINTER INTERFACING

Interfacing a printer to a microcomputer can be achieved using either serial or parallel techniques. Perhaps the most commonly employed serial interface technique is RS232c, discussed previously in Section 5.3 in relation to asynchronous data communications. There it was noted that an additional signal was required, over and above the four basic signals (TxD, RxD, DTR and ground), this being Busy. This handshake line is used by the printer to flag the computer that its buffer has become full, so no more characters should be sent for a while (at least until the busy line becomes negated again). This onboard or local buffer is required in order to match the computer's speed of operation to the (much slower) speed of the printer.

Serial printer interfaces consist of the same component parts as the asynchronous data communications circuits described in Chapter 5, namely USARTs or ACIAs and line drivers/receivers. The basic tasks performed by a serial printer interface are parallel-to-serial (and serial-to-parallel) conversion, as well as synchronization with the CPU. The trend in recent years has been to incorporate more and more of the interfacing tasks into a local or dedicated processor, thus relieving the CPU of the responsibility of printer I/O. Typical of such printers is the Qume Sprint-5 daisywheel, which uses a Z80, the Apple Imagewriter, which uses an i8048 single chip microcomputer, and the Apple Laserwriter, which is controlled by a MC68000. The main RS232c interface signals relevant to interfacing to a printer are shown in Figure 7.11.

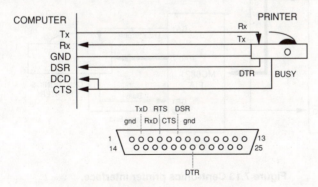

Figure 7.11 RS232c printer interface.

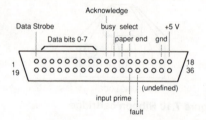

Figure 7.12 Centronics (parallel) printer interface.

An alternative means of interfacing a printer to a microcomputer involves using the Centronics parallel interface, illustrated in Figure 7.12. It uses a 36-pin connector (but with the pins arranged in parallel form, rather than staggered, as with RS232C and RS422 D-type connectors). It can handle byte-wide data (eight bits), under the control of a strobe pulse. Handshaking control is achieved by asserting (negating) either or both of the Acknowledge and Busy lines. Pins 12–15, 18, 31, 32 and 34–36 vary in function depending on the implementation; they are commonly used for auxiliary printer control and error handling. (Pins 16 and 17 are connected to ground.)

In the application shown in Figure 7.13, two MC6821 PIAs are used to

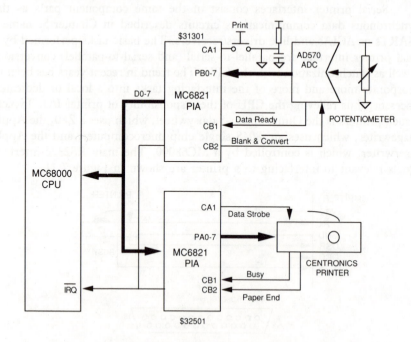

Figure 7.13 Centronics printer interface.

interface to a MC68000 CPU. A Centronics type printer connects to one of these PIAs, and an Analog-to-Digital Converter (ADC) to the other. A potentiometer is connected to the ADC. At the press of the pushbutton, a reading of the ADC is initiated, the setting on the potentiometer is stored in the computer's memory, and then printed on the printer. The following is an outline of the appropriate MC68000 driver software:

```
SWdat   = $31301        ;PIA Data Direction/Data Reg (A side)
SWctl   = $31303        ;PIA Control Register (A side)
ADCdat  = $31305        ;PIA Data Direction/Data Reg (B side)
ADCctl  = $31307        ;PIA Control Register (B side)
PRdat   = $32501        ;PIA DDR/Data Register (A side)
PRctl   = $32503        ;PIA Control Register (A side)
PRINd   = $32505        ;PIA DDR/Data Register (B side)
PRINc   = $32507        ;PIA Control Register (B side)

INIT:     move.l   #INTRUP,$70       ;set MC68000 interrupt vector
          move.b   #0,$31305         ;set up PIA port B as inputs
          move.b   #$FF,$32501       ;set up PIA port A as outputs
                    :
                    :
MAIN:     move.b   $31301,D6         ;clear any pending pb interrupts
          move.b   #$25,$31303       ;enable pushbutton interrupts
          move.w   $2300,SR          ;enable MC68000 interrupts > lev-3
                    :
                    :
INTRUP:   btst     #7,$31303         ;was it the 'PRINT' pushbutton?
          bne      PRINT
          btst     #7,$31307         ;was it the ADC, signalling
          bne      ADC               ;completion of a conversion?
          btst     #7,$32507         ;was it printer flagging 'BUSY'?
          bne      DELAY
          btst     #6,$32507         ;is the printer out of paper?
          bne      ERROR             ;(error routine not included here)
          rte

PRINT:    jsr      DELAY             ;wait in case printer busy
NEXT:     move.b   #$34,$32503       ;assert printer strobe
          move.b   (A5)+,$32501      ;output character to PIA Data Reg
          move.b   #$3C,$32503       ;negate printer strobe
          cmp      A5,A6             ;end of message?
          bne      NEXT              ;if not, get next character
          rts                        ;if so, return to main program

DELAY:    move.l   #$FF,D0           ;set delay value
WAIT:     sub      #1,D0
          bne      WAIT
          rts
```

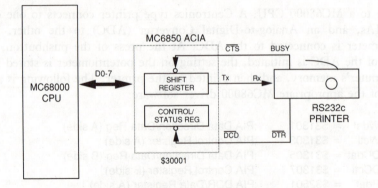

Figure 7.14 Serial printer interface.

```
SETUP:  movem.l DO–D1,–(SP)      ;save registers
        mulu    #5,D6            ;get index into digit table
        lea     TABLE,A0         ;start of digit lookup table
        add     D6,A0            ;calculate pointer to digit table
        move.l  #5,D0            ;5 chars to be printed (n.nnn)
MORE:   move.b  (A0)+,(A1)+      ;move first character
        sub     #1,D0            ;
        bne     MORE             ;5 characters sent yet?
        movem.l (SP)+,D0–D1      ;if so, restore registers
        rts                      ;& return to main program
                          :
                          :
TABLE:  .ascii  "0.0000.0390.078 .......... (etc) ......"
                "................ 9.9459.984              "
                                 ;resolution of ADC = 0.039V
```

Figure 7.14 shows an RS232c serial interface between an MC68000 CPU and a printer, which uses the MC6850 ACIA chip described earlier in Section 5.4.1. The $\overline{\text{DTR}}$ line is used to enable transmission of characters from the MC6850 to the printer; it is asserted whenever power is applied to the printer. The $\overline{\text{BUSY}}$ line is asserted whenever the printer's internal character buffer becomes full. The following MC68000 routine gives an idea of how the ACIA can be used to control the printing of characters:

```
INIT:   move.b   #3,$30001        ;master reset of MC6850 ACIA
        move.b   #$45,$30001      ;Rx interrupts disabled, 7 data,
                                  ;2 stop bits, odd parity, 1200
                                  ;Baud (÷16 external generator)
        movea.w  #STRING,A1       ;starting address of output string
LOOP:   jsr      OUTCH            ;output a character
        cmp.b    #$D,(A1)+        ;is next char a carriage return?
        bne      LOOP             ;if not, send next character
        rts                       ;if so, cease transmission
```

```
OUTCH:   btst.b   #1,$30001        ;transmit data register empty?
         beq      OUTCH            ;if not, check until it is
         move.b   (A1),$30003      ;send character (MC6850 data reg)
         rts
```

In practice, routines would also be included to test for interrupts due to loss of $\overline{DTR}$ (which corresponds to the printer being switched off), and the negation of $\overline{CTS}$ (caused by the printer buffer becoming full). In the case of the former, an error message would be sent to the user, and in the latter case the program would enter a wait loop until the printer buffer became free again.

Apart from the 'hardwired' configuration of Figure 7.4, it is also possible to use a simpler protocol, based on control characters transmitted over the serial link. This technique is referred to as X-ON/X-OFF, and is used where the printer is connected as a slave device to the controlling computer (master). Device control character DC1 (ASCII 11_{16}) turns the slave printer on, and device control character DC3 (ASCII 13_{16}) turns the printer back off again.

The following example is based on the IBM-PC Parallel Printer Adapter, which uses discrete logic rather than peripheral interface chips. This adapter has two output ports and one input (or status) port, at addresses 378H, 37AH and 379H respectively. The output port at location 378H is an 8-bit data port, while the output port at location 37AH comprises five control signals, including interrupt enable and strobe (bit 0). Bit 7 of the input (status) port indicates whether the printer is busy or not (if HI, the printer can accept another character for printing). The remaining four bits are used to flag error conditions such as 'out of paper'. The following routine shows how lines of characters would be sent from the IBM-PC to the printer (D. J. Bradley, *Assembly Language Programming for the IBM Personal Computer*, © 1984. Reprinted by permission of Prentice-Hall, Inc., Englewood Cliffs, NJ.):

```
BASE      equ    378H
MESSG     equ    'Message .......' '$'
START:    lea    BX,MESSG         ;BX = pointer to character string
PRLOOP:   mov    AL,CS:[BX]       ;get character string byte
          cmp    AL,'$'           ;end of character string?
          je     RETURN           ;if so, return
          call   PRINT            ;print the character
          inc    BX
          jmp    PRLOOP           ;onto the next character
RETURN:   ret
                  :
PRINT:    push   AX               ;save scratch register on stack
          mov    DX,BASE          ;data output port
          out    DX,AL            ;output character to O/P port
          inc    DX               ;Status port address = 37AH
          sub    AX,AX            ;clear AX
```

```
WAIT:   in      AL,DX           ;fetch status
        test    AL,80H          ;busy? (bit 7 = HI)
        jz      WAIT            ;loop if still busy
        inc     DX              ;point to Control port
        mov     AL,0DH          ;0DH sets print strobe HI
        out     DX,AL
        mov     AL,0CH          ;0CH sets print strobe LO
        out     DX,AL           ;(data shifted to printer by H→L
        pop     AX              ;    transition on strobe line)
        ret
```

Instead of the parallel printer interface just described, the i8086 can be readily interfaced to a serial type printer, in a similar manner to that described earlier in this section for the MC68000 CPU. Assuming an i8251 USART is used to control such a serial interface, it would be initialized as follows:

```
INIT:   mov   AL,DAH       ;asynchronous mode, 7 data bits,
        out   PRINT,AL      ;2 stop bits, odd parity, ÷16 clock
        mov   AL,15H        ;clear errors & enable Tx/Rx
```

7.4 LASER PRINTERS

Figure 7.15 shows the internal construction of a phototypesetter. It can be classified as a non-impact type of page printer. Projection of the characters is achieved using an inbuilt CRT tube, as indicated. The characters are projected onto photosensitive paper (or film), developed within the phototypesetter, and finally cut to size. The phototypeset copy is used to make the master plates for the printing of books, journals, newspapers etc. Fonts and font sizes are under computer control.

Laser printers have become commonplace in recent times. They offer a lower cost alternative to phototypesetters, but without the same resolution capabilities. Laser printers support printing speeds up to tens of thousands of lines per minute. Figure 7.16 shows the internal construction of a typical laser printer. The semiconductor laser directs a beam of infrared light onto the hexagonal scanner. This mirror reflects the beam onto a light sensitive drum, forming a raster scan as the drum rotates. The charging corona produces a positively charged dot on the drum, which is neutralized wherever the laser beam strikes the drum surface. The pattern of dots produced by the laser beam forms the complete image on the page. Toner adheres to the charged portions of the page as it passes by the toner cartridge, and is fused onto the paper under heat.

A typical laser printer is the Apple Laserwriter, which uses a Canon laser engine, and is controlled by a MC68000-based microcomputer with 1.5 MBytes of RAM and 500 kBytes of ROM. It is shown in diagrammatic

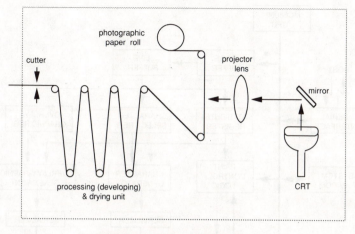

Figure 7.15 Phototypesetter.

form in Figure 7.17. Interfacing to the Laserwriter is via either 25-pin RS232c or 9-pin RS422 D-type connectors, at baud rates of either 1200 or 9600.

Pages to be printed on the Laserwriter are received in a format known as PostScript, converted into bitmaps and stored within the printer's RAM prior to being printed. The ROM is used to store the various fonts and PostScript definitions recognized by the printer. (PostScript is a simple interpretive programming language which incorporates graphics primitives,

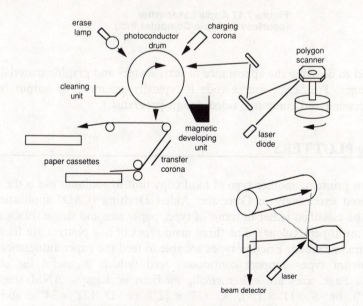

Figure 7.16 Laser printer printing mechanism.

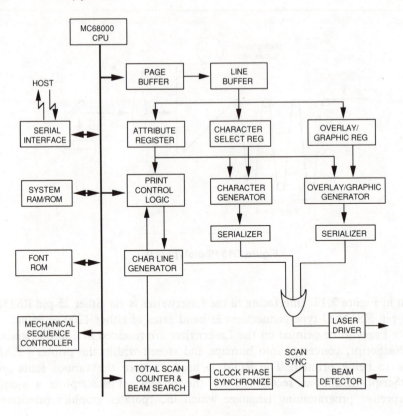

**Figure 7.17 Apple Laserwriter
(courtesy of Apple Computer Inc.).**

and is used to describe the appearance of text, images and graphic material on printed pages. PostScript source code is typically generated as output from word processing and computer aided design programs.)

7.5   *x–y* PLOTTERS

Apart from printers, another type of hard copy unit in common use is the *x–y* plotter, used extensively in Computer Aided Drafting (CAD) applications. They can be classified either in terms of type, paper size and single (black and white) or multi-pen (colour). The three main types of *x–y* plotters are friction roller, drum or flatbed. Friction types are able to feed the paper automatically, whereas drum types support continuous feed (which is useful for chart recorders). Page sizes are either small, medium or large – ANSI sizes A (8.5″ × 11″) or B (11″ × 17″), C (17″ × 22″) or D (22″ × 34″), and E (34″ × 44″) respectively. A typical flatbed plotter is illustrated in Figure 7.18.

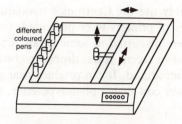

Figure 7.18 *x-y* plotter.

Separate motors drive the pen housing independently along both axes. These motors typically connect to the pen housing using a wire and pulley arrangement. Some means of raising and lowering the pen onto the page is also provided. For smaller sized plots, the paper usually remains fixed, using either mechanical or electrostatic means to hold the paper in position. For larger sized plots (A1 and A2 sheets), a friction roller or drum-type plotter is more appropriate. The paper is repeatedly moved backwards and forwards relative to the printhead in order to achieve coverage of the entire page.

The plotter illustrated in Figure 7.18 is a colour one; the pen-holding mechanism can be made to return to its home position, release the pen it currently holds, then pick up one of a different colour. It would take several passes over the entire page to produce colour hard copy, thus *x–y* plotters are typically much slower than printers.

Plot time and quality are the two important criteria for *x–y* plotters (together with pen changing time for multipen plotters). Pen response time (both velocity and acceleration) plays a significant part in the overall plot time. Pen velocity is more critical in drawing long straight lines and filling large areas. Pen acceleration is more critical in drawing tight curves and short unconnected lines.

SUMMARY

This chapter was devoted to hard copy units – devices which provide more permanent records of the screen outputs of video terminal displays. Our discussion concentrated on printers, but *x–y* plotters were also covered. It was seen that printers could be classified in a number of different ways, namely as impact or non-impact, fully formed or dot matrix, and character or line printers. Our discussion centred on perhaps the most common type of printer in use today, the dot matrix printer.

Interfacing to a printer can be achieved using either serial or parallel techniques. Serial interfacing involves the same asynchronous techniques as were discussed in Chapter 5. Most serial printers use RS232c connectors, although the more recent RS422 standard is becoming more commonplace.

Parallel printers invariably use the Centronics standard. Sample programs of interfacing to both types of printers were presented.

Laser printers were discussed in some detail, since this type of printer has become very popular in recent years, dropping considerably in price from when it was originally introduced. It can produce near phototypesetter quality output, but at much lower cost than a phototypesetter, and is used extensively in desktop publishing.

REVIEW QUESTIONS

7.1   Name two common printer interface standards.

7.2   Explain how characters are printed in a dot matrix printer.

7.3   Explain the need for buffering in a peripheral interface.

7.4   How is an entire row of characters printed simultaneously in a drum printer?

7.5   How is a laser printer similar to a photocopier?

7.6   There are three basic movements to be controlled by separate motors (solenoids) in an x–y plotter. What are they?

8

Timers/Counters

OBJECTIVES

In our consideration of timers, we shall first look at hardware timers before turning our attention to programmable timer interface chips. We shall see how to program such support chips to produce both single pulse and continuous waveform outputs. Besides producing waveforms, we will also see how programmable timer chips can be used to measure elapsed time intervals. Examples relating to computer music and bar code readers will be presented.

Real-time programming will also be discussed.

```
LOOP 1:    mov  AX,10H     4 clock cycles
           dec  AX         2 clocks
           mov  CX,0FH     4 clocks
LOOP 2:    dec  CX         2 clocks        INNER LOOP:      OUTER LOOP:
           jne  LOOP2      8 clocks        10 clocks*15 =   (154+10)*16
           jne  LOOP1      8 clocks        150 + 4 = 154    = 2624 + 4
                                                            = 2628 clocks
```

Figure 8.1 Software timing loops (i8086).

8.1   INTRODUCTION

Timing is a fundamental consideration in microcomputer systems. We saw in Chapter 1 how instructions are repeatedly fetched, decoded and executed in an ordered manner within a CPU, under the control of a Timing and Control Unit (TCU). The time reference scale of the CPU is in the nanosecond to microsecond range, whereas real world applications are more likely to be measured in units of seconds, minutes, hours or even days.

Precise time intervals therefore need to be generated in order to interface to the outside world. The CPU is controlled by a system clock which presents us with a simple method of generating accurate time intervals, by using software timing loops. A knowledge of the system clock frequency together with the execution times of the various instructions of the processor's instruction set enables us to generate accurate time intervals, as shown in Figure 8.1. Moreover, by building loops within loops of such timing routines, we can divide down the basic clock frequency from several million cycles per second to a timescale of milliseconds, seconds, minutes, hours and so on.

8.2   HARDWARE TIMERS

An alternative approach to generating precise timing intervals is to use a dedicated hardware timer chip, such as the Signetics NE555. The behaviour of such timer chips relies on the characteristics of the external components connected to them. Many different output waveforms are possible, chief among these being a single pulse or 'one shot', continuous pulse train output (either rectangular or square wave) and pulse width modulation, as indicated in Figure 8.2. The values of the external resistor(s) and capacitor determine waveshape characteristics such as period (and frequency, since $f = 1 / T$), and duty cycle or mark/space ratio (which give an indication as to the 'squareness' of the output wave).

The frequency range of the NE555 timer is limited to a few hundred kilohertz, so that in practice it is used primarily for audio applications. The NE555 is also limited in terms of accuracy and stability, both of which are determined by the accuracy and stability of the external resistors and capacitors used. For more accurate and stable clock sources, a mechanical

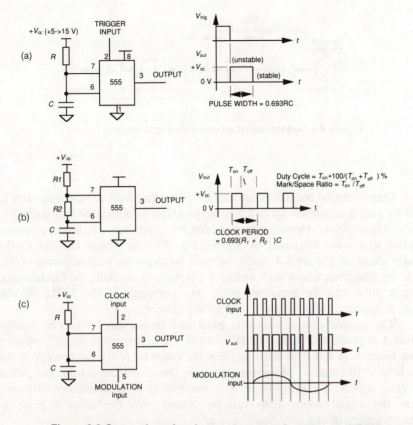

Figure 8.2 Generation of various output waveforms on an NE555
(a) single shot output (b) continuous (rectangular) output
(c) pulse width modulation.

crystal oscillator is usually preferred. Figure 8.3 shows the use of such a quartz crystal oscillator to produce a square wave output. The quartz crystal controls the frequency with which the outputs of the inverters change state, accurate to within a couple of parts per million. The output from the third inverter in the chain can then be used as a system clock.

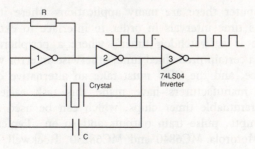

Figure 8.3 Crystal oscillator.

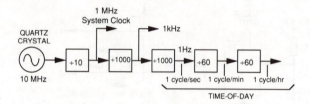

Figure 8.4 Generation of an accurate clock source.

Quartz crystal oscillators are also used together with counters/dividers to produce very accurate clocks of lower frequencies, as illustrated in Figure 8.4. The counter/divider elements in this divider chain are the same counters/dividers that were discussed in Section 2.5. The last three outputs in the divider chain of Figure 8.4 could be used to drive an accurate time-of-day clock. In situations where such accuracy amounts to overkill, the fundamental seconds pulse can be generated from zero crossings of the 50 Hz (60 Hz) mains frequency, followed by a $\div 50$ ($\div 60$) divider.

The simple counters/dividers presented in Section 2.5 can be readily extended to produce counters which count in a modulus other than 2^n, where n is the number of flip-flops used to form the counter. A typical counter is the decade or $\div 10$ counter. Moreover, by using the direct (asynchronous) preset and clear inputs of the flip-flops, it is possible to form *presettable* counters, where the initial count state can be loaded into the counter prior to commencement of the counting process.

Rather than *hardware* presettable counters, it is also possible to use *software* presettable counters, to which we shall turn our attention for the remainder of this chapter.

8.3 PROGRAMMABLE TIMER CHIPS

In a microcomputer there are many applications where it is necessary to generate various time intervals in order to interface to external devices. A typical example is a 'watchdog timer', where a peripheral device has to respond within a certain predefined time, otherwise an error will be deemed to have taken place, and the CPU must take an alternative course of action. Microprocessor manufacturers have made this task easier by producing (software) programmable timer chips, which can be used to produce time intervals, interrupts, pulse train outputs and so on. Typical of such timer chips are the Motorola MC6840 and MC68230, Rockwell R6522 and Intel i8254.

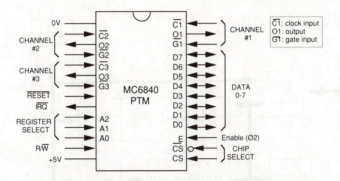

Figure 8.5 MC6840 PTM pinout (courtesy of Motorola Inc.).

8.3.1 Motorola MC6840 PTM

The Motorola MC6840 Programmable Timer Module (PTM) was originally designed as a support chip for the MC6800 family of 8-bit synchronous processors. However, since the MC68000 CPU incorporates a built-in MC6800-type interface, then the MC6840 can be used just as readily with either the MC6800 or MC68000.

Figure 8.5 shows the pinout of the MC6840, from which we see that the device has three separate channels, an 8-bit data bus interface, three register select inputs and two chip select inputs. The use of multiple chip select lines removes the need for external decoding logic when interfacing to several such timer chips (or other peripheral chips for that matter). The three register select lines are usually connected to the low order system address lines, and enable access to the onboard programmable registers.

Each timer channel consists of a clock input, a gate input (both active LO) and an output. The internal timer counts pulses appearing on the clock input, providing the corresponding gate input has been asserted.

The block diagram of the MC6840 PTM is shown in Figure 8.6. Internally, the MC6840 has three 16-bit timers, each with its own 8-bit control register. A single 8-bit status register is provided, together with 8-bit msb and lsb buffer registers. These buffer registers are necessary because the MC6840 only has an 8-bit data bus externally, whereas the timer registers must be loaded 16-bits at a time.

Figure 8.7 shows how 16-bit count values are loaded into the MC6840. The most significant byte is loaded first, and latched into the msb buffer. The least significant byte is then loaded directly into the lower byte of the counter, simultaneously with the contents of the msb register being loaded into the counter's upper byte. Transferring the data msb first is consistent with the order employed by MC6800 16-bit store instructions, as well as the MC68000 movep.w instruction.

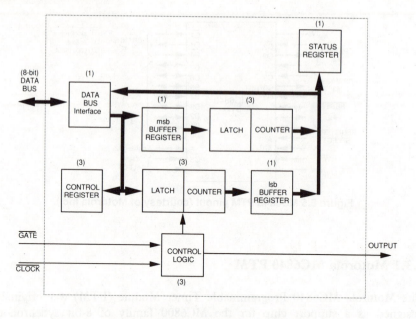

**Figure 8.6 MC6840 Programmable Timer Module (PTM)
(courtesy of Motorola Inc.).**

The MC6840 control register is shown in Figure 8.8. The topmost seven bits have the same effect on all three counters, however, the lsb has different functions, depending on which counter is being written to. In counter 1 it acts as an enable bit for all three counters. In counter 3 it is used to invoke the ÷8 prescaler (which is only available for counter 3). Bit 0 is not used in counter 2 for any function of its own, but simply to discriminate between the other two counters. This latter feature is used to access a greater number of registers than would be possible using the three register select lines; a similar technique is used in discriminating between the data registers and data direction registers in an MC6821 PIA (see Section 4.3.1).

Bit 1 is used to select either the system E-clock or an external clock as the source for the MC6840. Each 16-bit counter is capable of being used either as a single 16-bit counter, or as two separate 8-bit counters; bit 2 is used to

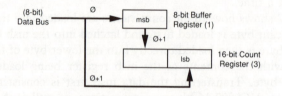

Figure 8.7 Simultaneous load of 16-bit count register.

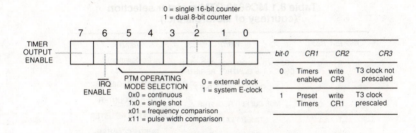

Figure 8.8 MC6840 control registers (one per counter) (courtesy of Motorola Inc.).

select which type. Bits 3–5 are used to select the operating mode of the PTM. Apart from producing standard single pulse and continuous pulse train outputs, the MC6840 can also be used to measure time intervals (frequency and pulse width comparison modes). Bit 6 is used to enable the MC6840 Interrupt Request output, and bit 7 is used to enable the respective output line.

The MC6840 PTM read-only status register is shown in Figure 8.9. Only four of the eight bits of this register are actually used. The three least signfiicant bits indicate that an interrupt has been generated by one of the three timers, as indicated. Bit 7 is used as an overall indicator that an interrupt has occurred, providing that the $\overline{\text{IRQ}}$ Enable bit of the corresponding control register has been previously set.

Table 8.1 indicates how the onboard registers are selected by the various bit patterns applied to the register select lines. Some of these registers are write only and some are read only, and thus are able to share the same address space, as indicated. Although there is only one msb buffer register, it has three unique addresses allocated to it. The lsb buffer register likewise has three images in the memory space. Writing data to the base address results in either control register 1 or control register 3 being written to, depending on whether bit 0 of control register 2 is set HI or LO.

As already mentioned, the 16-bit counters can be used as either dual 8-bit counters or alternatively as a single 16-bit one. Figure 8.10 shows the different output pulses which can be produced in either mode. Both continuous and single pulse outputs can be generated in either mode. Square wave outputs can be produced in either mode, however, variable duty cycle

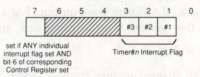

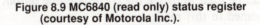

Figure 8.9 MC6840 (read only) status register (courtesy of Motorola Inc.).

Table 8.1 MC6840 PTM register selection
(courtesy of Motorola Inc.).

RS2	RS1	RS0	WRITE	READ
0	0	0	CR2-0 = 0 -> CONTROL REGISTER 3 CR2-0 = 1 -> CONTROL REGISTER-1	(no operation)
0	0	1	CONTROL REGISTER 2	STATUS REGISTER
0	1	0	MSB BUFFER REGISTER	TIMER 1 COUNTER
0	1	1	TIMER 1 LATCHES	LSB BUFFER REGISTER
1	0	0	MSB BUFFER REGISTER	TIMER 2 COUNTER
1	0	1	TIMER 2 LATCHES	LSB BUFFER REGISTER
1	1	0	MSB BUFFER REGISTER	TIMER 3 COUNTER
1	1	1	TIMER 3 LATCHES	LSB BUFFER REGISTER

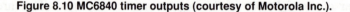

OPERATING MODE	TIMER MODE	OUTPUT	
SINGLE 16-bit counter	CONTINUOUS SINGLE-SHOT	SQUARE WAVE SINGLE PULSE	
DUAL 8-bit counter	CONTINUOUS SINGLE-SHOT	VARIABLE DUTY CYCLE PULSE	

Figure 8.10 MC6840 timer outputs (courtesy of Motorola Inc.).

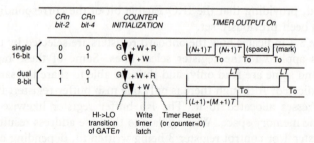

Figure 8.11 MC6840 continuous operating modes ($CRn\,3 = CRn\,5 = 0$).

pulse trains can only be produced in dual 8-bit mode. This is essentially because in 16-bit mode, only one parameter can be specified, whereas two parameters are required for duty cycles other than 50%. Figure 8.11 shows the generation of these two types of waveforms.

Consider the case of a square wave output. For a given clock source (T) and required pitch, this enables N to be calculated, since

$$1\,/\,\text{frequency} = 2(N + 1)T$$

When that particular channel counts from N down through zero (counter timeout), it can be used to toggle the corresponding output line. A duty cycle of 50% is assumed in this mode.

Now consider the case of a rectangular pulse train output. For a given clock source (*T*), desired pitch and specified duty cycle, then

1 / frequency = $(L + 1)(M + 1)T$ and
duty cycle   = $L / [M(L + 1)+1)]$

Hence appropriate values for *L* and *M* can be loaded into the two halves of the appropriate channel control register.

8.3.2 Computer Music

The fundamental parameters of interest in producing computer music are pitch, duration and tempo. Pitch is simply the number of cycles per second, or frequency. The relationships between piano keys, musical notation and frequency is illustrated in Figure 8.12. This figure also indicates the relationship between whole notes (breves), half notes (semibreves) and so on. Tempo is an absolute reference which determines the speed with which a musical piece is played. A typical value is 150 quarter notes (minims) per minute.

Figure 8.13 shows one method of using an MC6840 PTM to produce computer music. A fixed mark/variable space technique is used to produce music in this configuration. The advantage of this technique over that of a square wave output is that playing the same score in different octaves will produce different 'colouring'. In other words, the synthesized music will

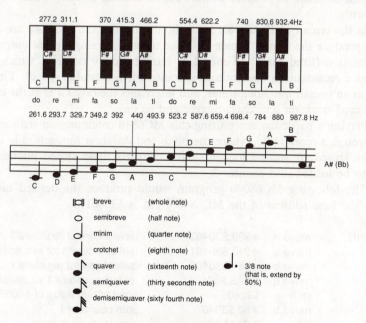

Figure 8.12 Musical notation.

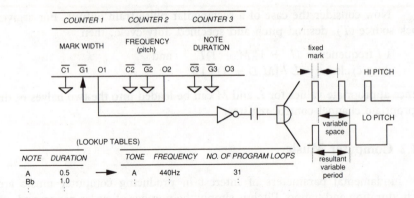

Figure 8.13 Using an MC6840 PTM to generate music.

appear to be generated by *different* musical instruments; a square wave technique for producing music will always produce sounds similar to an electronic organ.

It should be noted in passing that square waves comprise the fundamental frequency together with all the odd-numbered harmonics. By appropriate filtering and altering the magnitude of the various harmonics, many other basic sounds can be produced, such as sine wave (flute) and triangular wave. This ability to produce square wave outputs is the reason why organs can be made to produce sounds approximating to many other musical instruments.

In the circuit of Figure 8.13, all three timers of the MC6840 are being used to produce the music. Timer 1 is used to produce single pulse outputs of fixed duration (fixed mark). Timer 1 is retriggered by timer 2, which thus produces a rectangular pulse train of specified pitch (variable space). Timer 3 is used as an overall watchdog timer, and interrupts the host CPU at the end of each desired duration (crotchet, quaver and so on).

Playing a particular score using this MC6840 configuration reduces to a walk through a score table, where the pitch and duration for each note of the score are stored. A second look up table converts these stored pitches into values to be loaded into counter 2.

The following MC68000 program would produce the desired musical output (the base address of the MC6840 PTM is $30401):

```
INIT:   move.b   #$80,$30403      ;select control register#3
        move.b   #$43,$30401      ;set counter#3 for ints enab
        move.b   #$81,$30403      ;select control register#1
        move.b   #$A3,$30401      ;set up counter#1 as oneshot
        clr.b    $30405           ;load preset value of $0050
        move.b   #50,$30407       ;into counter#1
        lea      PITCH,A0         ;pointer to pitch table
```

```
              lea      SCORE,A1           ;pointer to score table
              move.w   #$2300,SR          ;allow interrupts > level 3
MAIN:         move.b   (A1)+,D1           ;get first note to be played
              jsr      PLAY               ;
              move.b   #$A2,$30401        ;start all 3 counters
WAIT:         bra      WAIT               ;loop until interrupted

INTSRV:       move.b   (A1)+,D1           ;get next note to be played
              cmp      #8,D1              ;dummy data to indicate end
              beq      EXIT               ;if end of score, return
              move.b   #1,$30403          ;disable counter#2 output
              move.l   #5000,D6           ;set up silence time
LOOP:         sub      #1,D6              ;
              bne      LOOP               ;time up yet?
EXIT:         clr.b    $30401             ;disable interrupts
              rte

PLAY:         mulu     #8,D1              ;pointer into pitch table
              move.b   0(A0,D1),$30409    ;msb of pitch → counter#2
              move.b   1(A0,D1),$3040B    ;lsb of pitch → counter#2
              move.b   #$81,$30403        ;play the note (enable o/p)
              move.b   (A1)+,D2           ;get note type from table
              asl      #1,D2              ;
              add      D2,D1              ;
              clr.l    D4                 ;
              move.b   0(A0,D1)           ;get note duration
              divu     D0,D4              ;Tempo (1→5)stored in D0
              move     D4,D5              ;set up for msb first,
              asr      #8,D4              ;followed by lsb
              move.b   D4,$3040F          ;msb of duration → count#3
              move.b   D5,$3040D          ;lsb of duration → count#3
              rts

PITCH:        DC.w     382                ;C   whole note (semibreve)
              DC.w     287                ;C   3/4 note (minim)
              DC.w     191                ;C   1/2 note (crotchet)
              DC.w     96                 ;C   1/4 note (quaver)
              DC.w     340                ;D   whole note
              DC.w     255                ;D   3/4 note
              DC.w     170                ;D   1/2 note
              DC.w     85                 ;D   1/4 note
                                          : (no sharps or flats here)
                                          :
SCORE:        DC.w     $203               ;E   1/4   ('Jingle Bells')
              DC.w     $203               ;E   1/4
              DC.w     $202               ;E   1/2
              DC.w     $203               ;E   1/4
              DC.w     $203               ;E   1/4
              DC.w     $202               ;E   1/2
```

```
        DC.w    $203        ;E  1/4
        DC.w    $403        ;G  1/4
        DC.w    $3          ;C  1/4
        DC.w    $103        ;D  1/4
        DC.w    $200        ;E  1
         :
         :
```

8.3.3 Rockwell R6522 VIA

We first met the R6522 Versatile Interface Adapter (VIA) in Section 4.3.2 during our discussion of parallel interface chips. The reason for its versatility is that it incorporates not only two 8-bit parallel ports, but also two 16-bit timers. The R6522 was originally designed as an 8-bit peripheral chip for the R6500 family of processors. However, since it incorporates a synchronizing E-clock, then it can be used just as readily with the MC6800 or MC68000 processors.

Like the MC6840 PTM, the R6522 needs to interface between 16-bit counters internally and an external 8-bit data bus. Thus internal buffering is again required. Four register select lines are provided on the R6522, and are used to access its various onboard registers. The auxiliary control register is the one that is used to select the various timer modes. Both 16-bit timers can be programmed to produce either continuous or one-shot outputs, and timer 2 can also be programmed to count the number of (negative edge) pulses appearing on one of the parallel data lines (PB6).

8.3.4 Motorola MC68230 PI/T

Like the R6522 VIA, the MC68230 Parallel Interface/Timer (PI/T) is a combined peripheral chip which incorporates both parallel ports and a timer. Two doubly buffered 8-bit ports are provided, along with eight general-purpose I/O pins which can be used either as a third port or for timer, interrupt or DMA functions. Figure 8.14 shows the MC68230 pinout, from which we see that PC2 can also serve as a timer input, PC3 as a timer output and PC7 as a timer interrupt acknowledge signal.

Unlike the MC6840 PTM and R6522 VIA, the MC68230 timer is a 24-bit one rather than 16-bit. Moreover a ÷32 prescaler can be invoked, which results in much longer time intervals being supported by the MC68230. The timer is in the form of a synchronous presettable-down counter, which is clocked either by the prescaler output or by an external timer. The prescaler in turn can be clocked either by the system clock or by the external timer input pin (PC2). The MC68230 can be used to generate periodic interrupts, square wave output, a single interrupt after a programmed time period (to measure

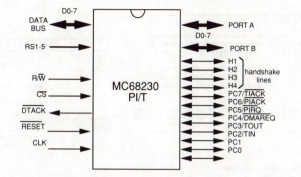

**Figure 8.14 MC68230 Parallel Interface/Timer (PI/T)
(courtesy of Motorola Inc.).**

elapsed time) or to act as a device watchdog. The MC68230 PI/T has 23 8-bit
registers, hence the need for the five register select lines in Figure 8.14. The
address space is divided equally between the port and timer functions.

Figure 8.15 shows the registers of interest when the MC68230 is being
used as a timer rather than as a parallel port. The timer control register
determines in what mode the MC68230 is operated, how it is to respond to the
zero count being reached, the clock source (including whether the ÷32
prescaler is invoked or not), as well as an overall enable control, as indicated.
A zero count is reflected in the lsb of the timer status register, so that it is
possible simply to poll this zero status bit rather than use interrupts, as
follows:

```
        clr.b    #0,$10021        ;disable timer (base addr=$10001)
        move.b   #12,$10027       ;load precount register msb first,
        move.b   #34,$10029       ;(24-bits)
        move.b   #56,$1002B       ;lsb last
        move.b   #1,$10021        ;initialize MC68230 & start count
LOOP:   move.b   $10035,D0        ;poll zero status bit
        beq      LOOP             ;loop until ZDS bit set
NEXT:   :                         ;(carry on with whatever),
        :                         ;(following delay of 123456*T/32)
        :                         ;(where T = system clock period)
```

The 24-bit count is loaded into the counter preload register (addresses
$10011 to $10101), while the counter register (locations $10111 to $11001)
reflects what the count has decremented to at any intermediate time during its
countdown.

Earlier timers like the MC6840 PTM and R6522 VIA are dumb by
comparison with the MC68230; they cannot supply an interrupt vector to their
host (master) CPU. Instead, they need to utilize the autovectoring capability of
a processor such as the MC68000 in order to determine where to jump in

REG SEL 5 4 3 2 1	MC68230 REGISTER
1 0 0 0 0	TIMER CONTROL REGISTER
1 0 0 0 1	TIMER INTERRUPT VECTOR
:	
1 0 0 1 1	COUNTER PRELOAD REG (hi)
1 0 1 0 0	COUNTER PRELOAD REG (mid)
1 0 1 0 1	COUNTER PRELOAD REG (lo)
:	
1 0 1 1 1	COUNTER REGISTER (hi)
1 1 0 0 0	COUNTER REGISTER (mid)
1 1 0 0 1	COUNTER REGISTER (lo)
1 1 0 1 0	TIMER STATUS REGISTER

7 6 5 4 3 2 1 0

Timeout/
Interrupt
control

Timer Enable
(1 = enable)

Zero
Detect
Control

Clock
control
(00=prescaler)

7 6 5 4 3 2 1 0

Zero Detect
Status

msb=0 -> parallel interface
=1 -> timer

Figure 8.15 MC68230 PI/T registers (courtesy of Motorola Inc.).

response to an interrupt. The MC68230 PI/T, by contrast, can define its own interrupt vector number which the MC68000 can use to determine the starting address of the appropriate interrupt service routine (by simply multiplying by four).

8.3.5 Intel i8254 PIT

The i8254 Programmable Interval Timer (PIT) has similar features to the MC6840 PTM described in Section 8.3.1. Figure 8.16 shows the internal construction of the i8254. The i8254 PIT has three onboard 16-bit counters, each of which has three associated pins; clock and gate inputs as well as an output.

Each counter or channel incorporates five internal registers, comprising an 8-bit (write-only) control register, an 8-bit (read-only) status register and three 16-bit count registers; the initial count value is loaded into the counter register, whereas the count is actually decremented in the counter element. This latter register remains transparent to the user, and needs to be loaded into the output latch in order to read its contents.

The control word registers are selected whenever the low order address lines are both HI. The counters are programmed by first writing the appropriate control word (which includes the counter number), and then loading the initial count value into the corresponding count register.

The i8254 PIT expects 16-bit data to be loaded into its count registers in a particular sequence, namely lsb first, followed by the msb (which is the exact reverse of the MC6840!). This former convention is also used in R6502 and Z80 peripheral support chips (little endian and big endian addressing was discussed in Section 1.4).

Table 8.2 shows the read and write operations selected by the various bit patterns applied to the low order address lines of the i8254 PIT.

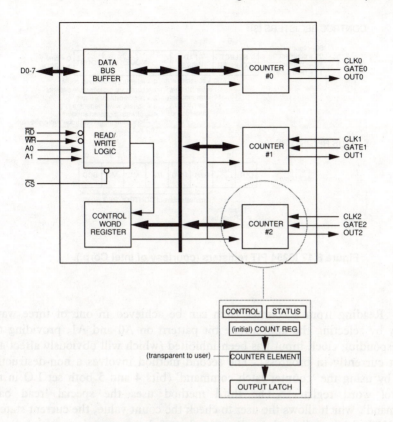

**Figure 8.16 i8254 Programmable Interval Timer (PIT)
(courtesy of Intel Corp.).**

The i8254 register set is illustrated in Figure 8.17. Consider firstly the
control word register. There are two conventions to be adopted in writing to
this register. The first is that the control word register must be loaded *before*
the initial count is loaded into the respective control register. The second is
that this initial count must conform to the format selected by bits 4 and 5 of
the control word register.

Table 8.2 i8254 addressing (courtesy of Intel Corp.).

RD	WR	A1	A0	OPERATION
1	0	0	0	Count Register#0
1	0	0	1	Count Register#1
1	0	1	0	Count Register#2
1	0	1	1	Control Reg#n / Command
0	1	0	0	Counter O/P Latch#0 / Status Reg
0	1	0	1	Counter O/P Latch#1 / Status Reg
0	1	1	0	Counter O/P Latch#2 / Status Reg
0	1	1	1	(no operation-tri-state)

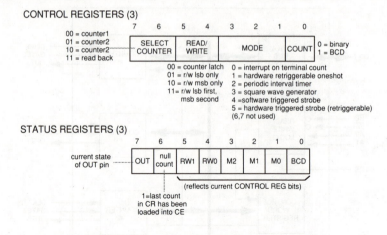

CONTROL REGISTERS (3)

STATUS REGISTERS (3)

Figure 8.17 i8254 PIT registers (courtesy of Intel Corp.).

Reading from a counter latch can be achieved in one of three ways: firstly by selecting the appropriate bit pattern on A0 and A1, providing the corresponding clock input has been inhibited (which will obviously affect any count currently in progress). The second method involves a non-destructive read by using the 'counter latch command' (bits 4 and 5 both set LO in the control word register). The third method uses the special 'read back command', which allows the user to check the count value, the current state of the OUT pin as well as the null count flag of the counter in question.

The i8254 PIT can be operated in one of five different operating modes, as set by the bit pattern in bits 1–3 of the control word register. Mode 0 or interrupt on terminal count mode is enabled by a HI pulse on the counter's gate and is typically used for event counting. Mode 1 or hardware retriggerable oneshot mode produces an active LO pulse on the OUT pin for the duration specified in the count register of that particular channel.

Mode 2 produces periodic time intervals, with the OUT pin making a HI to LO transition when the initial count value has decremented to one. Mode 3 is similar to mode 2, except that the OUT line makes the HI to LO transition at $N / 2$ rather than N, thus producing a square wave output.

Mode 4 is a software triggered strobe which produces an active LO pulse of one clock period duration when the count has been decremented to zero. Mode 5 is a retriggerable hardware triggered strobe mode which is similar in operation to mode 4, but which can be reinitialized at any time by a LO to HI transition on the GATE input at any subsequent time.

Bit 0 of each control register selects whether the maximum count is interpreted as 2^{16} or as 10^4.

The i8254 status registers each reflect the most recently specified mode, as contained in bits 0–5 of the corresponding control register. Bit 6 indicates

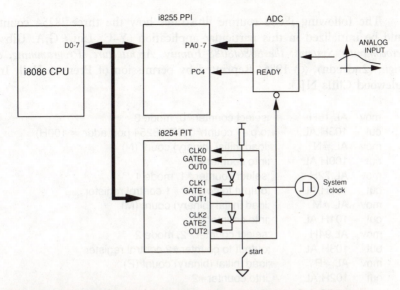

Figure 8.18 Use of an i8254 as an interval timer.(Y-C. Liu/ G.A.Gibson, Microcomputer Systems: the 8086/8088 Family, Architecture, Programming and Design, (2nd edn). © 1986. Reprinted by permission of Prentice-Hall, Inc., Englewood Cliffs NJ.)

when the contents of the count register are loaded into the counter element. The msb of the status register simply reflects the current state of the corresponding OUT pin.

Figure 8.18 shows a typical application using the i8254 PIT. In this system an Analog to Digital Converter (ADC) is interfaced to an i8086 CPU via an i8255 Programmable Peripheral Interface. Sampling and A/D conversion is under the control of the i8254 PIT. All three counters of the i8254 are used in this application, in order to produce a programmable sampling rate as well as being able to specify an overall sampling period. Counter 0 is used in mode 3 (square wave generator), counter 1 in mode 1 (retriggerable oneshot), and counter 2 in mode 2 (periodic interval timer).

Counter 0 is driven by the system clock, of period T. A continuous square wave output of period NT is generated on OUT0, which in turn is used as the clock source for counter 1 (after passing through an inverter, since the gate inputs respond to *rising* edges).

Counter 1 produces a negative-going pulse of length MNT. OUT1 is used as the gate input for counter 2, which in turn produces a negative-going pulse on OUT2 of duration PT. This negative-going pulse is used to initiate A/D conversions, the conversion being complete when PC4 of the i8255 becomes asserted. Note that the count P thus becomes limited by the conversion time of the ADC; A/D conversion will be discussed in more detail in Chapter 10. Thus there will be MN/P samples taken following closure of the switch.

The following i8086 routine illustrates how the three i8254 counters would be initialized in this particular application (Y–C. Liu / G.A. Gibson, *Microcomputer Systems: the 8086/8088 Family, Architecture, Programming, and Design*, (2nd edn), © 1986. Reprinted by permission of Prentice-Hall, Inc., Englewood Cliffs NJ.):

```
mov   AL,16H        ;select counter#0, mode 3
out   103H,AL       ;o/p → count#0 CR (i8254 port addr = 100H)
mov   AL,#N         ;load initial (binary) count (N)
out   100H,AL       ;into counter#0
mov   AL,72H        ;select counter#1, mode 1
out   103H,AL       ;output to counter#1 control register
mov   AL,#M         ;load initial (binary) count (M)
out   101H,AL       ;into counter#1
mov   AL,94H        ;select counter#2, mode 2
out   103H,AL       ;output to counter#2 control register
mov   AL,#P         ;load initial (binary) count (P)
out   102H,AL       ;into counter#2
```

8.4   BAR CODE READER

Let us turn our attention now to another timer application, this time in a bar code reader. Bar codes are the rectangular patterns of light and dark lines which appear on a wide range of consumer products, and are used to identify the manufacturer and product line. A printed version of the numeric code often appears alongside the bar code.

There are several bar code standards in common use; we shall restrict our discussion here to the Universal Product Code (UPC) standard shown in Figure 8.19. The UPC code consists of 30 dark and 30 light bars, together with a light margin on either side. Each module is nominally 0.033 cm wide, with each character being formed from two dark and two light bars, but of varying widths.

The bar codes are read either by holding the product stationary and passing a bar wand over the pattern, or alternatively by passing the product across an opening from which a light beam strikes the bar code. Figure 8.20 shows this latter type of scanner, in which several laser light sources are directed in the general direction of the product, at different orientations (typically a star pattern).

In this manner, *one* of the laser beams will usually strike the bar code pattern as an angle suitable for reading; if none of the laser beams strike the bar code at a suitable angle, then the product is passed by the opening again until a successful read occurs. There is a backup procedure, in that repeated failures can always be rectified by entering the numeric data manually.

The bar code reader (wand or fixed scanner) will produce an asynchronous waveform output of widely varying and *unknown* data rate, in

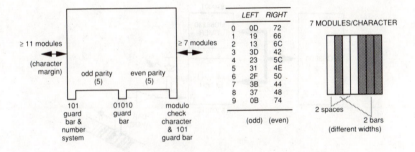

Figure 8.19 Universal Product Code (UPC).

the range 0.2–20 cm/second. A zero output could either be an unwanted noise spike, or the beginning of an authentic scan. If it represents the beginning of a scan, then the total scan time will lie in the range 3–300 milliseconds $(11 \star 0.033 \, \text{cm} / \text{scan rate})$.

Figure 8.21 shows a simple bar wand interface to an MC68000 CPU which uses a 74LS244 latch and an MC68230 PI/T. A programmable interface chip such as the MC6821 PIA could be used in place of the latch (or an i8255 if interfacing to an i8086 CPU); likewise an MC6840 PTM could be used in place of the MC68230 (i8254 PIT for a i8086 system).

At the commencement of the first LO to HI transition appearing on D0, a 'bar timing loop' is started, and at the next HI to LO transition, a 'space timing loop' is started. This procedure is repeated 30 times, until 60 time intervals have been recorded (30 bars and 30 spaces), as indicated in Figure 8.22. The appropriate algorithm is shown in Figure 8.23.

The following code segment illustrates the use of the MC68230 PI/T of

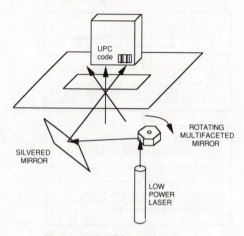

Figure 8.20 UPC scanner.

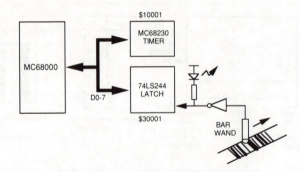

Figure 8.21 Bar code reader interface.

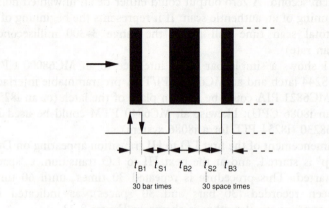

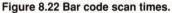

t_{B1} t_{S1} t_{B2} t_{S2} t_{B3}

30 bar times   30 space times

Figure 8.22 Bar code scan times.

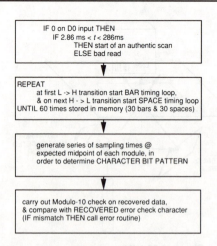

IF 0 on D0 input THEN
IF 2.86 ms < t < 286ms
THEN start of an authentic scan
ELSE bad read

REPEAT
at first L -> H transition start BAR timing loop,
& on next H -> L transition start SPACE timing loop
UNTIL 60 times stored in memory (30 bars & 30 spaces)

generate series of sampling times @
expected midpoint of each module, in
order to determine CHARACTER BIT PATTERN

carry out Modulo-10 check on recovered data,
& compare with RECOVERED error check character
(IF mismatch THEN call error routine)

Figure 8.23 Data recovery software.

Figure 8.21 (base address $10001) in counting the bar and space timing intervals:

```
START:    lea      TIMES,A0        ;pointer to TIMES table
          lea      $10001,A1       ;base address of MC68230 PI/T
          move.b   #59.,D1         ;60 times to be read in
READ:     move.b   $30001,D0       ;read bar wand input until HI
          btst     #0,D0           ;(possible valid scan for 0 →1,
          beq      READ            ;white → dark border)
          bsr      DEBOUNCE        ;delay routine to compensate for
                                   ;switch bounce (not included here)
FIRST:    move.b   $30001,D0       ;read bar wand input until LO
          btst     #0,D0           ;(first black bar)
          bne      FIRST           ;continue if still HI
          bsr      START           ;start the timer counting down
BARS:     move.b   15.(A1),D0      ;check ZDS-bit of status register
          btst     #0,D0           ;timeout indicates a bad read
          bne      BAD_READ        ;(routine not included here)
          move.b   $30001,D0       ;read bar wand input
          btst     #0,D0           ;end of black bar yet?
          beq      BARS            ;if not, continue until it is
          bsr      STOP            ;read the black bar width
          sub.b    #1,D1           ;decrement count
          beq      EXIT            ;read all the bars yet?
          bsr      START           ;restart the timer
SPACES:   move.b   15.(A1),D0      ;check ZDS-bit of status register
          btst     #0,D0           ;timeout indicates a bad read
          bne      BAD_READ        ;(routine not included here)
          move.b   $30001,D0       ;read bar wand input
          btst     #0,D0           ;end of white space yet?
          beq      SPACES          ;if not continue until it is
          bsr      STOP            ;read the white space width
          sub.b    #1,D1           ;decrement count
          beq      EXIT            ;read all the spaces yet?
          bsr      START           ;restart the timer
EXIT:     bra      READ            ;
START:    move.b   #0,0(A1)        ;disable timer ($10001=control reg)
          move.l   #$3FFFF,D0      ;load timer with max. 24-bit count
          movep.l  D0,5(A1)        ;$10005 = counter preload register
          move.b   #1,0(A1)        ;enable (start) timer
          rts
STOP:     move.b   #0,0(A1)        ;disable (stop) the timer (TCR)
          movep.l  D(A1),D0        ;read the count value
          not.w    D0              ;convert to an up count
          and.w    #$3FFFF,D0      ;mask off high order bits
          move.w   D0,(A0)+        ;store in TIMES table
          rts
TIMES:    ......
```

Once 60 times have been stored in the table, they need to be converted first to bar widths, and then to bit patterns (digit information). This digit information can then be used to look up prices corresponding to these product codes in an appropriate table.

The per character scan rate will be fairly constant, so that the average time per module (black or white) will be one seventh of the total character scan time (since each character is comprised of seven modules). The left, right and centre guard bands must be omitted from bar width calculations. The following routine shows the conversion firstly from times to widths, thence from widths to digits:

```
CONVERT:  move.l   #TIMES+6,A0    ;skip left hand guard (margin)
          bsr      WIDTH          ;convert first six times to widths
          add.l    #10.,A0        ;skip centre guard
          bsr      WIDTH          ;convert second six times to widths
          move.l   #TIMES+6,A0    ;addr of first digit after guard
          move.l   #DIGITS,A1     ;starting address of DIGITS table
          bsr      BITS           ;convert first six widths to digits
          add.l    #10.,A0        ;skip centre guard
          move.b   #':',(A1)+     ;colon separator used in table
          bsr      BITS           ;convert second six widths to digits
          rts
WIDTH:    move.b   #6,D4          ;six digits
LOOP:     move.w   0(A0),D0       ;sum the four bars
          add.w    2(A0),D0       ;
          add.w    4(A0),D0       ;
          add.w    6(A0),D0       ;
          and.l    #$FFFF,D0      ;mask off high order bits
          divu     #7,D0          ;time for a single bar
          move.w   D0,D1          ;
          lsr.w    #1,D1          ;halve bar time for rounding off
FOUR:     move.b   #4,D3          ;D3 = loop counter
          move.w   D1,D2          ;add half bar time to width time
          add.w    0(A0),D2       ;
          and.l    #$FFFF,D2      ;mask off high order bits
          cmp.w    #0,D0          ;divide-by-zero trap
          beq      ERROR          ;(note included here)
          divu     D0,D2          ;divide by single bar time,
          and.w    #$F,D2         ;to get bar width
          move.w   D2,(A0)+       ;replace bar time with bar width
          sub.b    #1,D3          ;decrement loop count
          bne      FOUR           ;continue unless = 0
          sub.b    #1,D4          ;
          bne      LOOP           ;continue until six digits converted
          rts
BITS:     move.b   #6,D5          ;six digits to be generated
AGAIN:    move.w   0(A0),D1       ;sum the four widths
          add.w    2(A0),D1       ;
```

```
add.w      4(A0),D1       ;
add.w      6(A0),D1       ;
cmp.w      #7,D1          ;restricted to seven bits
bne        ERROR          ;(not included here)
clr.w      D1             ;
bsr        BLK+WHT        ;two sets of black & white bars
bsr        BLK+WHT        ;per digit
move.l     #TIMES,A2      ;start address of TIMES table
move.b     0(A2,D1),D0    ;look up the digit
btst       #7,D0          ;bit 7 set means bar code
and.b      #$F,D0         ;mask off flag bits
move.b     D0,(A1)+       ;save in DIGITS list
sub.b      #1,D2          ;done all six yet?
bne        AGAIN          ;if not continue until you have
rts
```

The UPC bar code standard incorporates a modulo-10 error check character, which needs to be taken into account in the data recovery software. The modulo-10 algorithm is as follows:

starting at lhs (number system character), sum all characters in odd positions,

multiply the result by three,

starting at lhs, sum all characters in even positions,

add the product from step two to this sum,

the modulo-10 check character is then the smallest number which when added to the product yields a multiple of 10

8.5 REAL-TIME COMPUTING

It is appropriate in a chapter which deals with timers to introduce the concept of real time. As seen previously, a computer carries out its various operations under the control of a system clock; typically, it will be repeatedly fetching, decoding and executing instructions every few microseconds. The fundamental timing of the computer will not necessarily bear any relation to the time scale of the real world to which the computer must interface in some form or other.

The term 'real-time computing' covers a wide range of computer applications. What they all have in common, however, is a requirement to satisfy deadlines imposed by the real world. These deadlines vary considerably in time scale, from microseconds in the case of an airborne radar system, milliseconds in the case of a propellor shaft, seconds in the case of an automatic teller transaction, through to months and even years in the case of a seismic data logger. Data is absorbed by the computer at the actual time of its occurrence in the real world.

There is an inherent speed mismatch between the computer and the peripheral device, that needs to be rectified in the development of a Real Time

(RT) system. The commonly held yet erroneous view is that raw speed is required for *all* RT applications, however this is not always the case. For some applications, the CPU needs to be *slowed down* in order to match the speed of the external device.

An RT application can be defined as a system which controls its environment through interfaces subject to response time and throughput constraints. Response time is the time taken by the system to recognize and respond to an external event. Thus RT systems are inherently event-driven. Survival time is the time during which data remains present on the system inputs; it could remain valid for a short time only, in which case some form of buffering will be required. Alternatively, the data could remain valid long after a response was expected from the system.

Throughput is defined as the total number of external events to which the system can respond within a given time period. It is related to the response time by the following:

$$\text{Throughput} = 1/(\text{average Response Time} + \text{Recovery Time})$$

where recovery time is the time taken for the various 'housekeeping' functions required between one response and the next.

RT systems are sometimes classified as hard or soft, depending on the critical nature of the system timing contraints. Hard systems are those in which failure to respond immediately to external events could be catastrophic (for example, core meltdown in a nuclear reactor!). Soft RT systems are not as critical. A typical example would be a statistical multiplexer, used to share a limited number of serial ports on a host computer between a larger number of terminals; if one particular terminal cannot gain access at some time, it simply waits until a serial port is made available.

This brings us to another characteristic of RT systems, and that is the concept of 'average' and 'peak' loads on the system. Average loads are meaningless in RT systems; it is all very well to say that, *on average*, up to forty-eight 9600 baud lines can be supported on a particular system. However, there could well be periods when most of these 48 lines are idle (while their users think about what they are going to do next!). Then all of a sudden, all 48 users could send data to the host computer. In an RT system, it is the *maximum* load which is important, not the average. Indeed, RT system loads are often characterized by long periods of inactivity followed by bursts of peak load. Thus an RT system must be designed to handle such peak loads, *as if they were present all the time*. This would amount to considerable waste in a general-purpose, timesharing system, however it becomes necessary in RT systems.

Another common characteristic of RT systems is their dedicated, special- rather than general-purpose nature. There are usually only a few different functions to be performed, so that a lot of the different possibilities catered for in a general-purpose system are not necessary in an RT system. The system can then be pruned down to the bare essentials, so that it runs

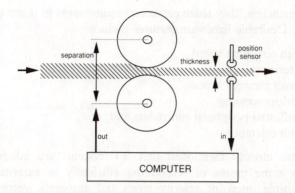

Figure 8.24 Hot slab mill.

faster and consumes less space in memory ('small is beautiful' in RT systems!).

Another important consideration in RT systems is the fallibility of the sensors providing information from the real world to the computer (sensors are covered in more detail in Chapter 9). Sensors can sometimes provide the wrong information, so RT software must be able to cater for this. If a position sensor on a railroad tells the system that the train has passed over sensor number n, missed sensor#$(n + 1)$, but all of a sudden appears at sensor#$(n + 2)$, then it is probably reasonable to conclude that the train did in fact travel along the straight section of track on which these sensors were fitted, but that sensor#$(n + 1)$ is malfunctioning. Conversely, it is possible for sensor#m to produce a system input when the train was nowhere near that section of track, due to faulty (yet different) operation.

The difference in time scales between the real world and the computer was referred to earlier. To illustrate this, consider the example of Figure 8.24. A hot slab mill in a steelworks produces steel slab of specified thickness. Position sensors mounted on either side of the steel plate feed information back to the controlling computer, from which the plate thickness can be derived, and the separation of the rollers adjusted accordingly. However, allowance must be made in such a system for lag time. The response time of the controlling computer will be in the microsecond range, whereas the response time of the rollers would be more like ½ to several minutes. Sufficient time must be allowed for the rollers to respond to the computer's control signals, otherwise we could have the situation where the computer is continually trying to adjust the roller separation before it has had a chance to respond to the previous setting! If left uncorrected, this would result in a plate of continually varying thickness, because the control software was too fast for the rollers. This is an example of where the computer needs to be slowed down relative to the real world.

We saw earlier how RT systems tend to be dedicated, specialized systems. Nevertheless, they share common requirements in terms of hardware and software. Desirable hardware features include:

(1) high operating speed,
(2) interrupts,
(3) direct memory access,
(4) multiprocessing,
(5) dedicated peripheral controllers and
(6) fault tolerance.

We have already mentioned that RT systems are inherently event driven. Thus some means of responding efficiently to external events is essential. Multiple interrupt priority levels and automatic vectoring to the appropriate interrupt service routine are desirable features to have in RT systems. It should be pointed out, however, that in some applications interrupts carry too much overhead, and polling is preferred. In general-purpose systems, polling represents wastage of system resources, since the computer cannot be doing other tasks while it is continually polling the status of a line on which there is little activity for long periods of time. However, in a dedicated RT system, where the computer is *only* concerned with the activity on a few I/O channels, then polling becomes the preferred alternative (since no context switching is needed in response to activity on the I/O channel, prior to responding to it).

Both DMA and multiprocessing can be useful in RT systems due to speed considerations. DMA is useful when high-speed transfers between an I/O device and memory (or vice versa) are required, since the CPU is bypassed altogether. Multiprocessing is useful in situations where dedicated peripheral controllers can better handle I/O transfers than the CPU; different processors can be assigned different tasks, on a one-to-one basis. Coprocessors can prove handy in this regard. Fundamental to the successful operation of a multiprocessing system is a bus capable of handling the increased system throughput (since we now have n processors connected into the system), as well as the associated bus arbitration between the processors.

Duplication of system power supplies is often necessary in RT systems; a steelworks furnace cannot be allowed to cool down every time the electricity supply in the area suffers an outage, for instance. Fault tolerance often needs to be extended into the computer system proper, in systems where downtime must be kept to an absolute minimum. A commonly used technique is to duplicate the critical system components, with backup components being switched in automatically following a component failure. In this manner, the failure of one particular component will not bring the system to its knees.

Software support for RT systems falls into two categories, namely operating system and language. Desirable RT operating system features include:

(1) task scheduling (and synchronization),

(2) task concurrency (multitasking),
(3) fast context switching (between one task and another),
(4) fast and reliable inter-task communication and
(5) fast and reliable bus protocols (in multiprocessor systems).

Support within the implementation language for concurrency is also desirable.

8.5.1 Real-Time Clocks

There are many applications where certain external events must occur at precise (and often regular) intervals during the course of the day. One such example is a time-of-day clock output, where the number of hours, minutes and seconds must be displayed at all times during the course of every 24-hour period. Such a system was illustrated in Figure 8.4. In order to use such a clock in an RT system, a backup power supply must be used, to cater for occasional loss of the mains supply. This is often provided in the form of a rechargeable nickel-cadmium battery (the Ni-Cd battery is charged up during normal operation, and provides the small amount of current needed to power the RT clock when the computer is switched off).

Typical functions provided by an RT clock include time-of-day, calendar (day, month and year), periodic system interrupts (every 100 ms, second and so on) and various 'wake up' (alarm) interrupts (at specific times during the day). The user also needs to be able to set and display the time (and date), as well as selection of the various interrupt modes available.

RT clock chips include the National Semiconductor MM58167 and Motorola MC14618A. They are self-contained LSI timer chips, only requiring an external crystal to control their operation. On-chip memory is often provided (64 bytes of RAM on the MC14618A; 14 bytes for the clock and the remaining 50 for the user). RT clocks are often low power CMOS chips, since low power drain is critical in battery-powered applications.

8.5.2 Real-Time Operating Systems (RTOS)

As we have seen, RT systems usually amount to dedicated controllers for specific applications, rather than general-purpose computers. For applications which exhibit concurrent internal operation, a multitasking operating system is normally required. Such an operating system is considered to be RT when the services it offers to its constituent applications enable each to meet its own individual timing and throughput constraints.

Typical commercial RT operating systems include Motorola's RMS68K, Intel's iRMX86, Zilog's ZRTS and National Semiconductor's EXEC (NS32000). Unfortunately, there is no industry standard RT Operating System (RTOS) like there is with general-purpose operating systems, which is understandable since most RT systems are unique to their respective applications (AT & T's UNIX and Microsoft's MS-DOS are examples of the latter). Every manufacturer tends to promote their own dedicated RTOS, since it usually relies heavily on the peculiarities of the host processor in order to meet the often stringent timing requirements. There has been some progress made in recent times with the Japanese Tron RTOS, which has proved more portable than most.

Let us consider a representative example of a commercial RTOS, the Intel iRMX86, which stands for Real Time Multitasking Executive for the i8086 family of processors. Figure 8.25 shows the iRMX86 in the form of an onion layer diagram. The iRMX86 consists of a collection of highly structured functional modules and utilities, with which the user builds their own *dedicated* RTOS to suit the particular application at hand. The only essential module is the nucleus (comparable to the kernel in a general-purpose OS like UNIX, for example). The next innermost layer is the basic I/O, which includes device drivers for disk, keyboard, CRT, printer and so on. The next layer provides extended I/O functions, which amount to higher level I/O routines, including buffering. The outer layer corresponds to the user interface, and is used to decode and execute user commands, such as disk file commands. (This outermost layer can be compared with the Bourne shell of UNIX.)

The three outermost layers of iRMX86 are optional; only the nucleus *has* to be used. Intel further provide a Universal Development Interface, which provides tools such as editors, assemblers, compilers, linkers and loaders, but the user does not have to make use of this development facility; instead, the users can build their own applications around the nucleus.

The basic building blocks in iRMX86 are referred to as objects, which are created using procedure calls to the nucleus. The various object types possible are tasks, jobs, segments, regions, mailboxes and semaphores. Tasks can be likened to processes in a general-purpose OS; they are the only active type of object, and are scheduled for execution on a preemptive, priority basis. Jobs are applications formed from several tasks. Segments are contiguous blocks of memory in the range 16–64 kbytes, whereas regions are areas in memory with different read/write/execute permissions. Mailboxes are used for passing objects from one task to another, while semaphores are single bit flags which indicate if a response is busy or not.

There are four possible states for any task within iRMX86, namely ready, running, suspended or asleep. A primary function of the RTOS is to schedule the various tasks and to switch between the various tasks in order to meet the imposed real-world time constraints.

RT systems are inherently event driven, therefore an efficient means of responding to external events is essential. Multiple interrupt priority levels and automatic vectoring to the appropriate interrupt service routine are processor features which assist in the development of an RTOS. The MC68000, for example, incorporates both these features, and also includes seven interrupt

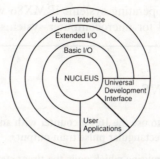

Figure 8.25 iRMX86 RTOS.

mask levels. The i80386 actually incorporates a task switch mechanism in hardware; it can save the entire state of the CPU (registers, address space and link to the previous task), load in a new execution state, perform protection checks, and commence execution of the new task in less than 20 microseconds (for a clock speed of 16 MHz).

DMA capability and bus arbitration logic also facilitate RTOS development, as mentioned previously.

SUMMARY

We have seen how the simplest method of producing time intervals within a microcomputer is to use software timing loops. This involves an intimate knowledge of the execution times of the various instructions in the processor's instruction set (as well as the system clock rate). This method has the advantage that no additional overhead is required; however, it ties up the CPU for the duration of the time period.

Hardware timers are capable of producing a wide range of outputs, depending on the resistor and capacitor values connected to their control inputs. However, it is not easy to change their outputs once they have been hardwired into a system in a specific configuration.

Programmable timer chips combine the flexibility of software timers with the power of hardware timers. They can be programmed to produce continuous pulse train outputs (both square and rectangular) or single pulse outputs, to count external events, interrupt the host CPU following precise time intervals and so on.

The timer chips we considered were the MC6840 PTM, MC68230 PI/T and the i8254 PIT. Programming examples were presented which used typical timers to produce computer music and a bar code scanner.

The concept of real time was introduced, followed by an introduction to real-time computing. Real-time clocks were discussed, as well as the requirements for a RT operating system. iRMX86 was briefly discussed as a typical RTOS developed for microcomputer systems.

REVIEW QUESTIONS

8.1 Why is it necessary to use the 16-bit counter with an MC6840 PTM in dual 8-bit mode to produce a rectangular pulse train output?

8.2 Write an MC68000 routine which polls the timer status register of an MC68230 PI/T in order to count a 1 ms time interval. Assume a 4 MHz system clock, and a base address of $10001. Repeat using interrupts rather than polling.

8.3 Write an i8086 routine which initializes an i8254 PIT for mode 2 operation. What other modes are possible on the i8254? Describe.

8.4 In relation to bar code scanners, what is a modulo-10 error check?

8.5 What characterizes a real-time system?

9

A/D and D/A Conversion

OBJECTIVES

This chapter begins with a discussion of transducers (sensors), devices which convert physical quantities of interest into electrical signals (and vice versa). Light, temperature, humidity, position, pressure, liquid level, optical, acoustic and power transducers are covered. The analog electrical signal has to be converted into digital form before data can be entered into a computer and subsequent calculations performed. Signal conditioning, sampling rate and quantization are all discussed in this context. The basic D/A conversion technique is presented first, followed by four different techniques for A/D conversion.

Typical errors encountered with both ADCs and DACs are discussed. MC68000 and i8086 routines for interfacing to a typical ADC are presented. Finally, the concept of A/D (D/A) subsystems is introduced.

9.1   INTRODUCTION

The essential element of a digital computer is a miniature electronic switch which can be turned either on or off. Thus a computer is inherently a binary processing device. In the real world, however, parameters can often take *any* value, not just HI or LO as in a computer. At other times, the real-world signal can be a simple on/off one (as is the case with a limit switch, for example), and hence corresponds more closely with the world of a digital computer. The interfacing between the real world and a computer involves the conversion of real-world quantities into digital form. Such conversion is referred to as Analog-to-Digital (A/D) conversion, since the quantity of interest is often a continuous rather than a binary signal. Conversion back from the domain of the computer to the real world is similarly referred to as Digital-to-Analog (D/A) conversion.

9.2   TRANSDUCERS

The first step in converting real-world (analog) quantities into digital form is to produce an electrical signal representation of that quantity. Transducers are the devices used to produce these electrical signals, converting other forms of energy into electrical energy (and vice versa). Input transducers are alternatively known as sensors. Output transducers which translate electrical energy into physical movement are referred to as actuators. Transducers which generate their own voltage (or current) are active transducers; passive transducers require an external power supply in order to produce an output.

Figure 9.1 shows a simple photographic light meter which senses the incident light level in the environment and converts this into electrical energy (using a Light-Dependent Resistor, LDR). This analog signal is then converted into digital form, prior to being processed within the CPU. A similar procedure occurs in reverse for outputting the processing information to the output transducer indicated.

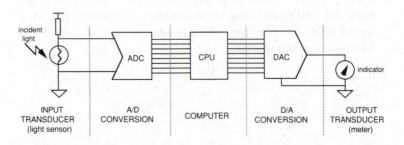

INPUT
TRANSDUCER
(light sensor)

A/D
CONVERSION

COMPUTER

D/A
CONVERSION

OUTPUT
TRANSDUCER
(meter)

Figure 9.1 Interfacing between the real world and a computer.

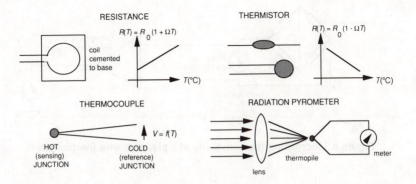

Figure 9.2 Temperature sensors.

Common transducer parameters include accuracy, repeatability, sensitivity, linearity, zero error, drift (as a function of time), variations due to temperature, pressure, acceleration, vibration and orientation, and strain (due to the mounting technique). Transducers can be classified into a number of different types, namely temperature, humidity, position, pressure, optical, acoustic and so on. The three most commonly measured quantities in industrial environments are temperature, pressure and flow rate.

9.2.1 Temperature

Temperature transducers are available in a number of different forms, as illustrated in Figure 9.2. Resistance Thermal Devices (RTDs) are usually constructed out of platinum, nickel or copper (or some alloy of these metals). Their temperature coefficient of resistance increases with increasing temperature. RTDs are highly repeatable and exhibit good linearity over wide ranges. Typical temperature coefficients and ranges are shown in Table 9.1, together with typical thermistor values, for comparison.

Thermistors (thermally sensitive resistors) exhibit *negative* temperature coefficients. They have fast response times (typically milliseconds) and exhibit the highest sensitivity amongst temperature transducers, but are inherently non-linear (exponential). Semiconductor temperature sensors also exhibit a negative temperature coefficient and require an excitation current or voltage. They are also non-linear, and require signal conditioning prior to entering

Table 9.1 Temperature ranges and coefficients.

MATERIAL	RANGE (°C)	SENSITIVITY (%/°C)
PLATINUM	-200 to +850	+ 0.39
NICKEL	-80 to +320	+ 0.67
COPPER	-200 to +260	+ 0.38
THERMISTOR	-80 to +150	- 4.0

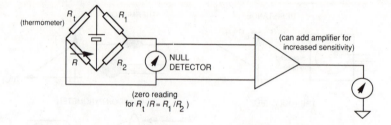

Figure 9.3 Increasing the sensitivity of a platinum wire thermometer.

readings into a measurement or control computer (to remove these non-linearities).

Figure 9.3 shows the amplification of the small variations emanating from a platinum RTD using a Wheatstone bridge (and amplifier if necessary). This is a simple form of signal conditioning, where the raw signal from the transducer is not in a form suitable for imputting to the ADC as is.

Thermocouples generate a small potential difference at the junction of two dissimilar metals, which increases (non-linearly) with temperature. This low output level usually needs some form of amplification, as well as referencing to a known temperature. There are several different types of thermocouple in common use, each with different temperature coefficients. Despite these limitations, the thermocouple remains the most widely used industrial temperature sensor today. Multiple thermocouples can be cascaded together in order to increase the voltage output. Such an arrangement is known as a thermopile, and forms the basis of radiation pyrometers.

9.2.2 Humidity

Humidity (or moisture) transducers can be constructed using either resistive, capacitive, mechanical, crystal or psychrometric elements, as indicated in Figure 9.4. Some electrical or mechanical property of the transducer varies as a function of the amount of moisture present in the air. In the case of the crystal sensor, its mechanical vibration varies as a function of the amount of water absorbed by its hygroscopic coating (this is the same type of crystal as was discussed in relation to crystal oscillators in Chapter 8).

Relative humidity can also be measured using these same sensor types, by calibrating the output accordingly. Alternatively, relative humidity can be measured using the psychrometric transducer shown; relative humidity is proportional to the dry bulb temperature, the temperature difference between the two bulbs and the barometric pressure (and can thus be determined by consulting a psychrometric lookup table).

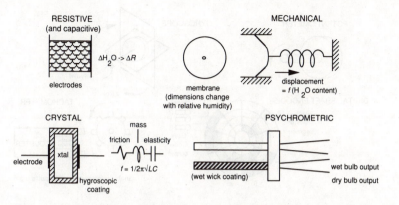

Figure 9.4 Humidity (moisture) sensors.

9.2.3 Position (velocity and acceleration)

Figure 9.5 shows a range of commonly encountered (linear) position transducers. The output coils of the Linearly Variable Differential Transformer (LVDT) are wound in opposition, such that movement of the slug induces currents which flow in the same direction, resulting in an induced voltage appearing across the output terminals. The variable inductance transducer utilizes the different abilities of iron and air to conduct a magnetic current (which is referred to as reluctance, the magnetic equivalent of electrical resistance).

In the capacitive transducer, varying the distance between the two plates affects its capacitance. The Hall effect transducer can be used to

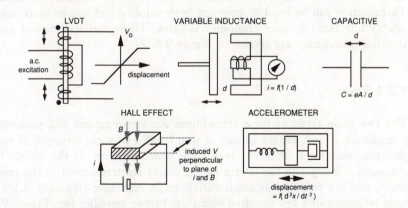

Figure 9.5 Position (velocity and acceleration) sensors.

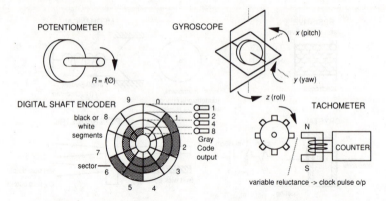

Figure 9.6 Angular position (velocity and acceleration) sensors.

measure magnetic field strength as well as displacement. In the case of the latter, the semiconductor slab is mounted in the air gap of a magnet (which is the technique used in Hall effect switches).

In the accelerometer depicted in Figure 9.5, the mass only moves when the reference frame is accelerating; at other times the spring–mass–damping system will be at rest.

Gyroscopes are used for measuring attitude (angular orientation). These days laser gyroscopes are rapidly replacing the more familiar three-degrees-of-freedom mechanical types.

Potentiometers (variable resistors) can be readily adapted for measuring angular position. Direct digital encoding of angular position is possible using a shaft encoder, as shown in Figure 9.6. Gray Code is preferred to Binary Coded Decimal (BCD) in such applications, since it provides greater accuracy; only one bit changes in moving from one sector to the next, as indicated.

The variation in the reluctance as a tooth passes by the magnetic detector is sensed and used to trigger a counter in the electronic tachometer. Tachometers can be used to measure both velocity and acceleration, and are readily interfaced to microcomputer systems. These various types of angular position transducers are shown in Figure 9.6.

9.2.4 Force

The two main types of force transducers are strain gauges and piezoelectric transducers. Strain gauges consist of thin lengths of wire, arranged in various patterns, and fixed (bonded) to a base which adheres to the object being measured. Changes in the length of the object are transferred to the resistive wires, and are reflected as small variations in resistance (typically 0.1% of a total resistance of a few hundred ohms). A bridge amplifier (see Figure 9.3) is usually necessary to amplify such small variations to levels better recognized

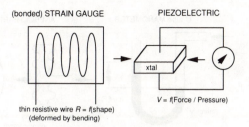

Figure 9.7 Force sensors.

by the measurement system. In fact, load cells are commonly used devices comprising both the bonded strain gauge and bridge amplifier, but which of course require external excitation (in the range 5–15 V DC). Semiconductor strain gauges are also available, exhibiting higher sensitivity and producing higher outputs than resistive gauges. However, their voltage outputs are non-linear and moreover they are temperature sensitive.

Piezoelectric force transducers are suited to dynamic force measurement, where the forces vary every few milliseconds or so (their upper frequency limit is of the order of 30 kHz). Piezoelectric materials develop a voltage perpendicular to the applied pressure, and are therefore classified as active transducers. Both types of force transducer are shown in Figure 9.7.

9.2.5 Pressure

There are many different types of pressure transducer available in the marketplace, several of which are shown in Figure 9.8. The strain gauges and piezoelectric transducers of Section 9.2.4 can also be used to measure pressure in practice.

In the capacitive type, variations in pressure alter the separation between the plates of the parallel capacitor, and hence its capacitance.

In the aneroid barometer, variations in pressure result in movement of the thin circular metal plate. U-tube manometers provide a primary measurement of pressure, expressed as a head of mercury in the tube.

Movement of the central diaphragm in the inductance bridge, due to the applied pressure differential, causes the inductances of the two coils to change, which can be measured using a bridge. Applying pressure to the bonded strain gauge will alter its resistance, which can be measured using a Wheatstone bridge, as mentioned previously.

Special techniques are required for measuring vacuums. The thermal conductivity type measures the conduction of heat from a central heated sensor through the mass of gas inside the vacuum to the outer container (which acts as a heat sink). The ionization type depends on the ionization of gas molecules

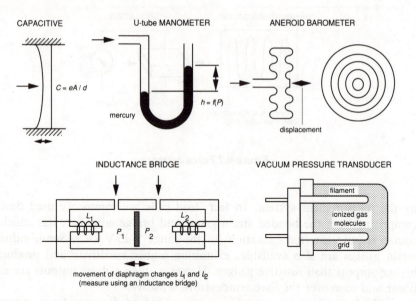

Figure 9.8 Pressure sensors.

to conduct electricity between an element and a grid, as indicated (similar to the arrangement in a vacuum tube amplifier).

9.2.6 Flow Rate Meters

The most widely used type of flow rate meter is the differential pressure drop meter, shown in Figure 9.9. Movement of the diaphragm or vane causes the indicator needle to move further towards full scale deflection. The amount of movement depends on the pressure differential between the two openings, which in turn is a measure of the flow rate between these two reference points. There are two common forms of this type of flow rate meter, namely the Venturi meter and the orifice plate. The advantage of pressure differential flow rate meters is their ability to reject transient pressure variations (noise) at both openings, however, they suffer from non-linearities.

Two other types of flow rate meters are also illustrated in Figure 9.9, these being the frequency type and the hot wire anemometer. In the frequency type, a toothed wheel is connected to the outer end of a shaft, and a propellor to the inner end. The flow rate is reflected in the rotational speed of the toothed wheel, which can be sensed using either magnetic (see Section 9.2.3) or optical means. The advantage of this type of sensor is that it can produce a digital output compatible with the control (measurement) computer.

In the hot wire flowmeter, the temperature of the hot wire provides an indication of the rate of flow of the liquid inside the pipe, since heat loss is roughly proportional to the square of the velocity.

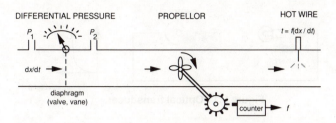

Figure 9.9 Flow rate meters.

9.2.7 Liquid Level

Two types of liquid-level transducer are illustrated in Figure 9.10. In the capacitive type the total capacitance (or conductance) between the two plates (wires) is the summation of the two individual capacitances, as indicated; the relative permittivity (e) and depth of both capacitors change with the level of liquid between the two plates.

In the resistive or float type of transducer, the moveable arm of a potentiometer floats on the surface of the liquid, which is readily reflected on the meter. Such level sensors require excitation, but can produce high-level outputs due to relatively large resistance swings.

Other types of liquid-level sensors include those based on force sensors which essentially measure the weight of the liquid in the container, thermometers which measure the heat transfer between two adjacent probes (heat transfer occurring more readily in a liquid rather than a gas), pressure transducers which measure the pressure difference between the top and bottom of a tank, and optical sensors (where light paths close to the liquid surface become scattered).

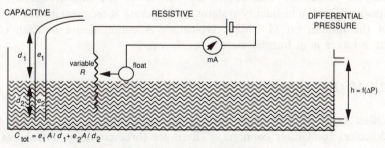

Figure 9.10 Liquid level transducers.

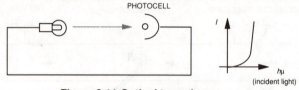

Figure 9.11 Optical transducer.

9.2.8 Optical

Photocells produce current flowing between anode and cathode proportional to the incident light. Photodiodes and phototransistors are semiconductor equivalents of photocells.

All diodes and transistors dissipate some of their energy as light, which is why they are usually enclosed in black plastic (or ceramic). Use is made of this property in LEDs, which are enclosed within clear rather than black plastic covers. Optical lenses are used to magnify the image, and red-coloured filters often added, since the human eye is most sensitive to this portion of the optical spectrum.

Infrared detectors operate in the same manner as photodetectors, except that they are sensitive to incident light of longer wavelength (lower frequency) than the visible portion of the spectrum.

Figure 9.11 shows a typical optical transducer. The mouse of Section 6.8.3 is an application which uses an optical sensor (specifically, motion of the ball produces rotation of x- and y-shafts, which is detected by photodetectors trained on optically encoded disks attached to the ends of both shafts).

9.2.9 Acoustic

Typical acoustic transducers are illustrated in Figure 9.12. Microphones are used as input sensors (either crystal, condenser or electrodynamic type), and loudspeakers as output sensors (either electrodynamic or electrostatic type). Electrodynamic sensors are more efficient than other types for both input and output. Ultrasonic transducers are similar to the high-frequency 'tweeter' speakers used in hi-fidelity systems, and operate at frequencies above the range of the human ear (1–5 MHz typically). A common use of such ultrasonic transducers is in burglar alarms, as shown.

9.2.10 Other Sensors

Other types of transducer include smoke, pollution and nuclear radiation detectors (or Geiger counters). There are three common techniques used to detect smoke, namely resistance change in gas sensors, changes in current

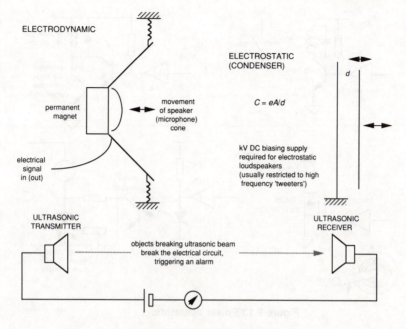

Figure 9.12 Acoustic transducers.

passing through an ionization chamber due to the slowing of alpha particles, and optical methods. Pollution detectors are based on the measurement of the oxygen content of the air (or water) in question using a spectrometer.

9.2.11 Power Actuators

There are many applications where output power needs to be boosted in order to drive high current electrical machinery. Typical of such power actuators are relays and solenoids, illustrated in Figure 9.13. A relay is capable of switching larger currents than the current required to operate its coil, with the added advantage that its output contacts are electrically isolated from its input winding. A relay's contacts can be normally open (n.o.), normally closed (n.c.), changeover, make before break and so on. A solenoid produces physical movement in response to an applied electrical voltage. They are typically used to open and close valves or operate switches, for example.

Even heavier current output drive capability is possible using thyristors which are capable of switching mains supplies (and higher) using much smaller trigger inputs. Large industrial AC motors can be controlled using devices such as the Silicon Controlled Rectifier (SCR). Other types of motor that lend themselves more readily to digital control are stepper motors, a typical one being shown in Figure 9.14. The outer, fixed part of the motor (stator) has

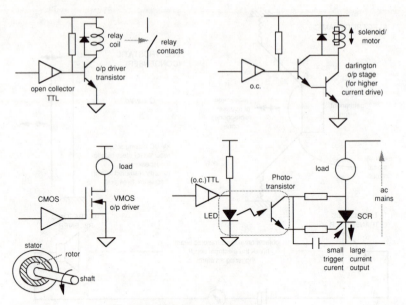

Figure 9.13 Power actuators.

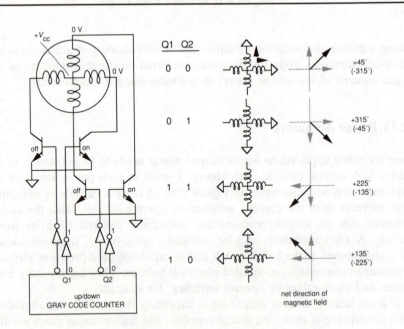

Figure 9.14 Stepper motor.

several coil windings (four in this particular example). Applying a voltage across these coil windings causes magnetic fields to be generated, which cause the inner, moving part of the motor (rotor) to turn, such that it becomes aligned with the resultant magnetic field. A shaft connected to the rotor provides motion (drive) output in response to an electrical input.

The stepper motor coils are under direct control of an output from a counter (which would be computer controlled in practice). A Gray code counter provides greater accuracy, since only one bit changes in going from one count to the next. Depending on the count, the resultant magnetic field applied to the rotor would lie at 45°, in one of four quadrants as indicated.

Stepper motors vary in resolution from 90° to 0.5° per step, with the ability to be positioned at rates of between 100 and 2000 steps/second. Stepper motors are admirably suited for accurate positioning tasks, but their major attraction is that they can be controlled directly from a computer.

9.3 SIGNAL CONDITIONING

We saw earlier how transducer outputs are often unsuitable for entering directly into a control or measurement system. The electrical signals produced by the transducer can require amplification, are often non-linear, and can have unwanted noise superimposed on them. In other words, the transducer signal outputs often need conditioning of some form or other.

Common signal conditioning functions include filtering (to remove unwanted noise and/or interference), attenuation or reduction of the signal level (to protect the input of the ADC), amplification (to boost the signal to an acceptable level), removal of non-linearities (to compensate for outputs from sensors such as thermocouples) and isolation. This latter consideration is extremely important in order to avoid unwanted ground loops and transient noise spikes. Differential or balanced inputs assist in this regard, since any noise common to both inputs will be ignored; only the *difference* between the two inputs will be passed through.

It might not be possible to remove all non-linearities through signal conditioning; sometimes it will be necessary to incorporate linearization routines in the A/D control software, as we shall see later in this chapter.

A big problem in industrial measurement and control systems is grounding. It is often assumed that ground potential is 0 V at all points around a factory. Unless the grounds are connected to a conducting rod inserted into the earth at these various points, this is not necessarily the case (even so, ground potentials themselves can vary from one location to another!). Indeed, grounding can amount to little more than connection to a metal chassis in which the equipment is housed, to the reference wire of a power supply, or simply to the common connection between input and output. In none of these

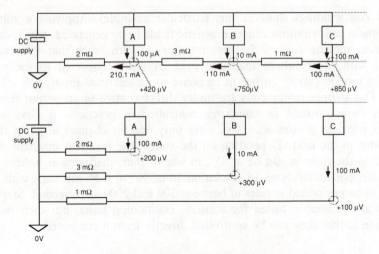

Figure 9.15 Ground (earth) loops.

cases is there any specific relationship to earth potential. Moreover, long interconnecting wires have a finite resistance, such that 'ground' potential can vary by several millivolts at different points around a site, as indicated in Figure 9.15. The accumulation of differences in ground potential can be alleviated somewhat by running separate earth wires back to a common point, however this increases cabling costs substantially.

The problems become more serious when connecting together independent items of equipment, each of which has its own power supply. In such systems, the commons of all supplies of the same size ($+5\,V$, $+12\,V$, $-12\,V$ and so on) can be tied together and then a heavy-gauge (low resistance) cable run between these different commons.

Problems can also result from the DC supplies themselves. Figure 9.16 shows the main components in a DC supply derived from the AC mains supply. Now while at first sight it might be assumed that the DC output in such a supply is constant, this is not in fact the case. Variations in output voltage can result from variations in the load connected to the output

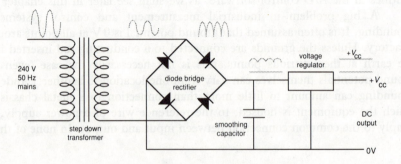

Figure 9.16 Power supply regulation.

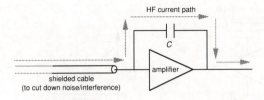

Figure 9.17 Use of a bypass capacitor.

terminals, as well as variations in the AC supply itself (where both voltage and frequency can vary over time). The regulation of a DC supply thus becomes an important consideration (the lower the variations in output voltage, the better).

Digital ground lines are usually quite noisy compared with analog ground lines, and can produce large current spikes (due to the sudden on-off/off-on switching). It is thus not a good idea to connect the two types of grounds together.

It is sometimes necessary to convert a unipolar signal to a bipolar one using an isolation amplifier; any noise or interference common to both inputs is removed. (This will be discussed more fully in our discussion of operational amplifiers.)

Besides DC and low frequency noise, high frequency (HF) noise can also present problems. Much can be done to alleviate HF noise by using bypass capacitors, as indicated in Figure 9.17. (At high frequencies, a capacitor acts as a short circuit and thus provides a signal path for signals to bypass the device around which it is connected.) Moreover, use of shielded cable can assist in preventing HF noise interfering with the desired signal on the line. In some applications, it may be necessary to shield the item of equipment in a wire mesh or metal enclosure in order to cut down on stray capacitive and/or inductive pickup, both of which can lead to HF noise. Proper insulation is also necessary in order to avoid leakage conductance. Even the layout of individual circuit components on printed circuit boards can be critical on occasion.

9.3.1 Operational Amplifiers

Operational amplifiers (op amps) are used extensively in signal conditioning. They originated in the days of valves, and were so named because they were used in analog computing circuits to perform mathematical operations such as addition, subtraction, differentiation and integration. These days they are fabricated in IC form. The op amp symbol and typical characteristics are shown in Figure 9.18. An op amp is a DC-coupled, high-gain, high-input impedance differential amplifier (it amplifies the *difference* between the signals appearing at its two inputs), which requires negative feedback in order to stabilize it and convert it into a useful circuit building block. Without

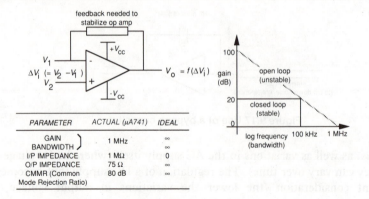

Figure 9.18 Operational amplifier (op amp).

feedback, it would tend to oscillate, being triggered into oscillation by the smallest transient noise spike or stray signal pickup.

It has two basic configurations, namely inverting and non-inverting, as shown in Figure 9.19. Because of its very high input impedance, hardly any current flows into its input terminals; virtually all of the current flows in the external components connected to the op amp. This greatly facilitates the use of op amps in signal conditioning circuits, since their overall behaviour can be entirely determined by the connected components.

In practice, op amps are non-ideal devices and suffer from offset currents and voltages, bias currents, drift of these currents and voltages with respect to time (and temperature), slew rate limiting, noise and power supply rejection. The input offset voltage is the input voltage required to produce zero output. Likewise, the input offset current is the difference between the currents flowing into the two input terminals in order to produce zero output, whereas input bias current is the *average* of these two input currents. Slew rate limiting is the inability of the op amp to keep pace with fast-changing large signal inputs; internal capacitance limits the rate at which the output can change. This can manifest, for example, as a triangular wave being produced in response to a high amplitude sine wave input (the op amp is unable to keep up with the steep slopes of the sine wave for large signal inputs, despite the input signal frequency being well within the op amp's bandwidth). Power supply rejection is the ratio of change in input offset voltage resulting from a change in one of the power supply voltages, expressed in decibels (20 $\log_{10}$ V_o/V_i (dB)).

We have already seen that some of the common signal conditioning functions needed with transducers are buffering (isolation), scaling (up or down), differentiation (rate of change), integration (averaging) and filtering

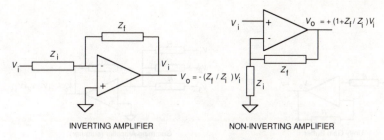

Figure 9.19 Inverter and non-inverting amplifier.

(removal of unwanted frequency components or noise). Circuits to perform these functions, together with other representative op amp circuits are shown in Figure 9.20.

Logarithmic amplifiers are useful when dealing with large dynamic signal ranges. Sample-and-Hold (S/H) circuits are necessary in applications where the input signal only appears for a short time, and must be stored for subsequent conversion to digital form. Signals can sometimes change during the time it takes an ADC to perform a conversion, depending on the sampling rate. In the S/H circuit shown, a negative pulse on the gate of the pMOS switch turns it on, which enables current to flow, charging the capacitor up to the input voltage. When the pMOS switch is turned off, charge cannot escape back through the switch to the input (the OFF resistance of the pMOS transistor being several million ohms, compared with an ON resistance of a few ohms). Likewise, charge cannot escape through the buffer amplifier (voltage follower), due to its extremely high input impedance. Thus, providing the capacitor can retain its charge, the sampled signal is held for as long as is required for the ADC to perform its conversion.

The gain, cutoff frequency and rolloff of active filters (so called because they are based on op amps, and thus *amplify* as well as filter) are determined by the values of the external resistor and capacitor values (and their configuration). It is also possible to cascade lower order filters in series in order to achieve steeper rolloffs. Moreover, different forms of filters can be fabricated by merely swapping component positions; band stop or notch filters are useful, for example, in deglitching circuitry, where unwanted noise spikes of a particular narrow frequency band can be removed.

Two more sophisticated devices (not shown in Figure 9.20) which often find use in signal conditioning are multiplexers and multipliers. Analog multiplexers or switches are often employed to take readings from several different sensors, so that a single ADC may be shared. Analog mixers or multipliers are useful in modulating a low frequency signal onto a high frequency carrier, and also in calculating quantities such as electrical power (since $P = V^2/R$).

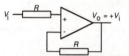

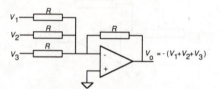

Unity Gain Buffer
(ISOLATION AMPLIFIER - output
isolated from input, due to high Z_i))

$V_o = +V_i$

Summing Amplifier (summer)

$V_o = -(V_1+V_2+V_3)$

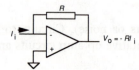

Current-to-Voltage Converter

$V_o = -RI_i$

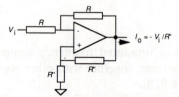

Voltage-to-Current Converter

$I_o = -V_i/R'$

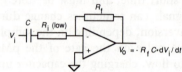

Differentiator (time rate of change)

$V_o = -R_f C \cdot dV_i/dt$

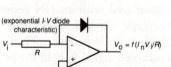

Integrator (averaging circuit)

$V_o = -(1/R_i C)\int(V_i)\, dt$

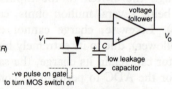

(exponential I-V diode characteristic)

Logarithmic Amplifier

$V_o = f(I_n V_i/R)$

voltage follower

$V_o = +V_i$

low leakage capacitor

-ve pulse on gate to turn MOS switch on

Sample-and-Hold (S/H)
(captures fleeting signals for subsequent processing)

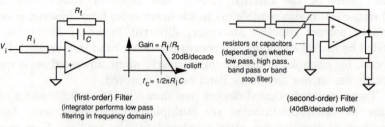

(first-order) Filter
(integrator performs low pass filtering in frequency domain)

Gain = R_f/R_1

20dB/decade rolloff

$f_c = 1/2\pi R_i C$

resistors or capacitors (depending on whether low pass, high pass, band pass or band stop filter)

(second-order) Filter
(40dB/decade rolloff)

Figure 9.20 Typical op amp circuits.

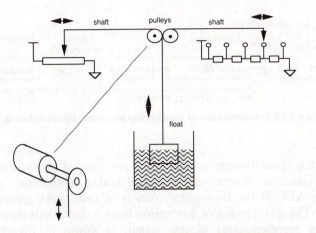

Figure 9.21 Analog and digital float systems.

9.4 ANALOG-to-DIGITAL CONVERSION

Figure 9.21 shows two liquid-level transducers, one analog and one digital. The analog instrument uses a continuously variable resistor connected via a pulley system to a float in a tank; the reading can take any value within the allowable range. In the digital liquid-level meter, the float connects to a shaft in a similar manner, but in this instance the shaft connects to a multiposition switch rather than a continuously variable resistor. Only a limited number of discrete positions are provided in the case of the latter. This multiposition switch can be likened to a digital computer, in that values can never be exact, but only *approximations* to their real (or actual) value exist; how good an approximation depends on the data bit width of the computer in question (8-, 16-, 32-bits and so on).

A computer processes data (information) in terms of digital representations of that data. In processing data collected from the real world, it first has to be converted into an electrical quantity, using a suitable transducer. It then has to be converted from an analog (or linear) electrical signal into a digital one, suitable for input to a digital computer (at TTL levels, say). A similar situation applies in the case of transferring such data over a digital communications channel. Figure 9.22 shows such a communications facility in block diagram form.

Prior to performing the necessary Analog-to-Digital (A/D) conversion, the incoming signal is first filtered in order to remove any unwanted high frequency noise (and/or interference). The signal is then sampled at regular intervals to convert the incoming continuous signal into a series of discrete levels. Each level has a corresponding digital code, and it is this binary representation which is actually transmitted down the channel. At the distant

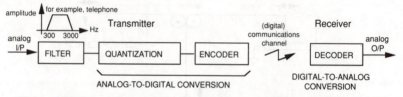

Figure 9.22 Transmission of analog signals over digital network.

receiver end, these discrete voltage levels are decoded into analog form in a continuous manner, to retrieve the original analog information.

The ADC at the transmitter consists of two stages: quantization and encoding. The quantization or conversion from a continuous input to a series of discrete representations of this signal, is shown in Figure 9.23. The quantizer has a limited resolution, such that the sinewave input becomes converted into the rather jagged waveshape shown; an 8-bit ADC can handle 256 discrete voltage levels, a 12-bit one 4096, and so on.

Obviously an incoming signal should ideally be either amplified or attenuated in order to make full use of the available resolution of the ADC (this is one reason for signal conditioning, as discussed in Section 9.3). It is possible to conceive of this digitized version of the incoming sinewave as consisting of the (wanted) sinewave itself, together with superimposed (unwanted) high frequency noise (resulting in the jagged effect indicated). Such unwanted noise is inherent in the quantization process itself and can never be removed altogether, only reduced to an acceptable level. (It should be mentioned that in a lot of applications this quantization noise is largely removed at the output of the DAC, due to the natural smoothing effect of the device which connects to it, for example, the loudspeaker in the case of digital music. Moreover, in the case of compact disk players, output filtering is incorporated into the device itself.) The encoder simply transmits these digital readings at the appropriate rate, with the decoder at the distant receiver reversing this process.

The rate at which the incoming waveform is sampled is not arbitrary, but is determined by the frequency spectrum of this incoming signal. It is, in fact, determined by the Nyquist Sampling Theorem, which states that the incoming analog signal must be sampled at a rate equal to or greater than twice the highest frequency component of the incoming signal (f_0). Figure 9.24 demonstrates the effect of various sampling rates on a simple sinewave input, in both the time and frequency domains.

The top pair show the sinewave (which has a single component only in the frequency domain). The next pair show the effect of sampling the sinewave at a rate equal to the frequency of the sinewave. The result will be a constant (or DC – zero frequency) value, varying in magnitude from zero to the peak value of the incoming sinewave, depending on the phase of the sampling signal

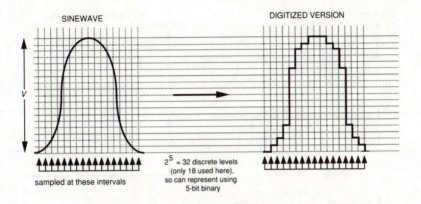

SINEWAVE

DIGITIZED VERSION

2^5 = 32 discrete levels (only 18 used here), so can represent using 5-bit binary

sampled at these intervals

Figure 9.23 Quantization process.

(in other words, whether it samples the peaks, zero crossings, troughs or whatever part of each successive cycle).

The middle pair show the effect of sampling the sinewave at a rate greater than its fundamental frequency, but still less than twice this value. The resulting waveform is a sinewave (or a rough approximation thereof), but whose frequency is much less than f_0.

The fourth pair show the effect of using a sampling frequency of $2f_0$. The resultant waveshape is a square wave whose frequency is the same as that of the incoming sinewave. The magnitude of this square wave can be anywhere from zero (sampling at the zero crossings) and the peak value of the original sinewave (sampling at successive peaks), depending on the phase relationship between the sampling frequency and the sampled waveform. This square wave might not appear to bear much relation to the original sinewave at first sight, but examination of this waveshape in the frequency domain reveals that the desired sinewave is indeed present (f_0), however, higher order harmonics are also present (a square wave can in fact be considered as comprising the fundamental frequency together with all the odd harmonics, of ever-decreasing magnitude). It is a simple matter to remove these unwanted higher order harmonics in practice, by cascading a low pass filter, as indicated.

The last pair show the effect of sampling at a rate considerably higher than $2f_0$; the unwanted higher order harmonics have decreased in magnitude, and the time domain representation of the sampled signal is beginning to look more like a 'sinewave'. Again, it should be emphasized that quantization noise can never be removed altogether; the sampled sinewave will always have a jagged appearance, however small, irrespective of the resolution of the ADC or the sampling rate.

In practice, both the sampling rate and number of quantization levels are compromises. The sampling interval cannot be too long, otherwise aliasing

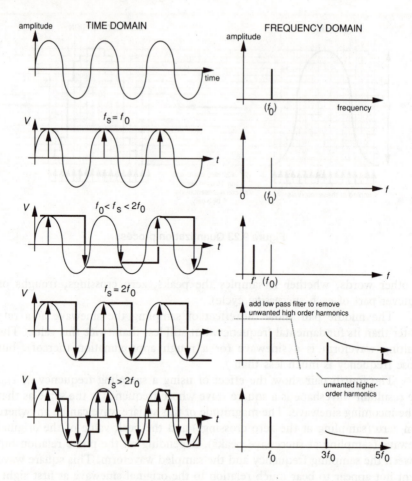

Figure 9.24 Effect of sampling frequency on quantized signal.

will result; on the other hand, if it is too short, this could result in too many samples for the available memory, and moreover increase the likelihood of unwanted high frequency noise being sampled. If the number of quantization levels is too few, then this could lead to errors (due to lack of resolution); too many levels has repercussions in terms of processing power (and hence cost).

9.5 D/A CONVERTERS

Figure 9.25 shows the internal construction of an analog (MOS) switch; application of a LO to its control input turns the upper MOSFET transistor

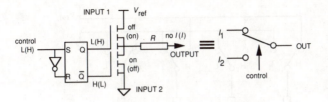

Figure 9.25 Analog (MOS) switch.

off and the lower one on, thus switching input 2 through to the output line (and similarly for the application of a HI signal to the control input). Such a switch could be used to multiplex (or share) two inputs between a single output, by sampling both at regular intervals.

This kind of switch is used in the DAC shown in Figure 9.26. The DAC uses a binary weighted resistor network; depending on which resistors are switched through to the reference voltage (V_{ref}), then a current flows through that resistor and into the input of the summing amplifier. This summing amplifier also acts as a current-to-voltage converter, producing a voltage output proportional to the sum of the current inputs. In the example shown, the binary input 1001_2 produces currents flowing in the resistors R and $8R$, which results in an output of $9R \star V_{ref}$ from the DAC.

In order to simplify interfacing, some DACs have onboard latches, which hold a binary input that might only appear momentarily. Figure 9.27 shows the interfacing of a typical DAC, the Analog Devices AD7524, to a (MC6800-style) microcomputer. The DAC produces a current output, which is converted into a voltage using an operational amplifier.

Op amps, as their name suggests, were originally developed to perform mathematical operations in analog computers. We saw earlier how their characteristics can be set by the external components connected to them, such as the resistor R_f in Figure 9.20. Their high input impedance means that they will not draw very much current from the circuit connected to it (and hence will not load it down).

In some applications the reference voltage can vary, which results in a multiplying DAC.

Figure 9.28 shows a typical application of a DAC. In many industrial situations, it is necessary to alter the setting on particular items of plant, in order not to overload them. By controlling such an item of plant through a DAC, it is possible to change this setting *gradually* rather than suddenly, as indicated. This can be readily achieved using appropriate control software.

Besides the Analog Devices AD7524, other microprocessor-compatible DACs include the Burr Brown (12-bit) DAC811 and (16-bit) DAC701, Motorola (8-bit multiplying) MC1408 and National Semiconductor (8-bit) DAC1000.

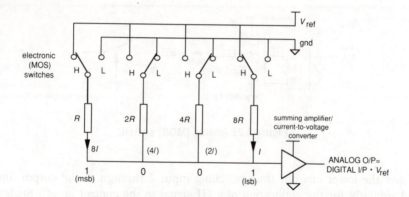

Figure 9.26 Digital to analog converter.

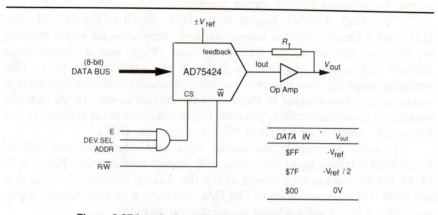

**Figure 9.27 Interfacing a DAC to a microcomputer
(courtesy of Analog Devices Inc.).**

DATA IN	V_{out}
$FF	$-V_{ref}$
$7F	$-V_{ref}/2$
$00	$0V$

Figure 9.28 Ramp generation using a DAC.

9.5.1 Errors

There are a number of different errors which can manifest in both DACs and
ADCs, and these are summarized in Figure 9.29. Resolution refers to the
smallest analog output which can be produced by the DAC (or alternatively
discriminated by an ADC). This is directly related to the number of bits used.
For example, the smallest output that a 12-bit DAC can produce is $V_{ref}/4096$,

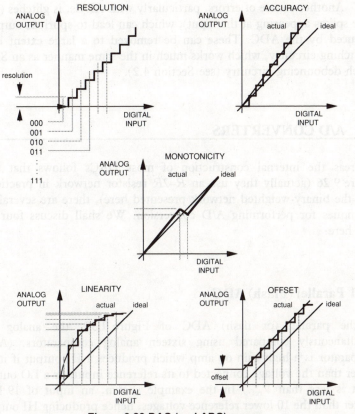

Figure 9.29 DAC (and ADC) errors.

whereas the smallest output that an 8-bit DAC can produce is $V_{ref}/256$ ($2^8 = 256$).

The accuracy of a DAC depends on the number of bits it uses, however this is limited in practice due to stability problems. For example 16 bits implies an accuracy of one part in 65 536, which is only achievable using laser-trimmed resistors. It is also possible that a DAC might produce unequal analog increments in response to equal increments in the digital input, resulting in non-linear behaviour. Alternatively, linear behaviour might be exhibited up to a certain digital value, at which point there is a sudden discontinuity, thus resulting in non-monotonicity. Zero offset is where the DAC produces a small but not insignificant output with no applied input; this offset is carried through all input settings of the DAC.

It takes a certain time to perform the D/A conversion, after which it takes additional time for the outputs to settle. These conversion and settling times are usually faster with DACs than with ADCs. The operating speed of D/A and A/D converters usually has a large bearing on their cost; video ADCs being rather expensive, for example.

Another source of errors, particularly with ADCs, is glitches (unwanted noise spikes appearing at the input), which can lead to spurious outputs being produced by the ADC. These can be removed to a large extent by adding deglitching circuitry, which works much in the same manner as an SR latch in switch debouncing circuitry (see Section 4.2).

9.6   A/D CONVERTERS

Whereas the internal construction of most DACs follows that shown in Figure 9.26 (actually they use an R–$2R$ resistor network in practice, rather than the binary-weighted network presented here), there are several different techniques for performing A/D conversion. We shall discuss four different ones here.

9.6.1 Parallel (Flash) ADC

In the parallel (or flash) ADC of Figure 9.30, the analog input is simultaneously compared using sixteen analog comparators. (An analog comparator is a high gain op amp which produces a HI output if its input is higher than the voltage connected to its reference input, or a LO output if the input is less than V_{ref}.) In the example shown, an input of 19 $V_{ref}/32$ is greater than the 10 lower reference voltages, hence producing HI outputs from the 10 lower comparators. A code converter (ROM lookup table) is then used to produce the corresponding digital output. The advantage of this type of ADC is its high-speed operation (typically < 50 ns), due to its inherent parallelism. Its main disadvantage is its limited resolution, since an n-bit ADC requires 2^n analog comparators.

9.6.2 Integrating ADC

The integrating type of ADC shown in Figure 9.31 is slow by comparison with the flash type, and also exhibits limited accuracy. The Voltage Controlled Oscillator (VCO) produces a pulse train output whose frequency is directly proportional to the analog voltage applied to its input. This pulse train output is strobed, using a fixed duration gating pulse, and the number of pulses counted. The counter output is latched, so that a digital representation of the analog input is held on the counter outputs following removal of the strobe pulse. The counter is then reset prior to performing the next A/D conversion.

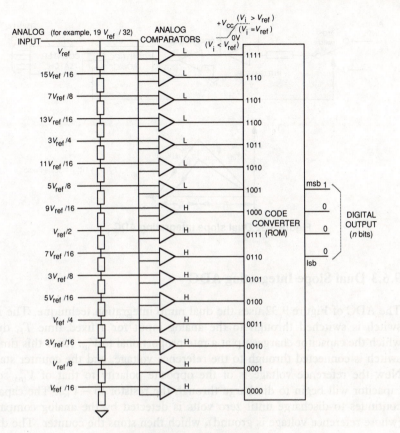

Figure 9.30 Parallel (flash) ADC.

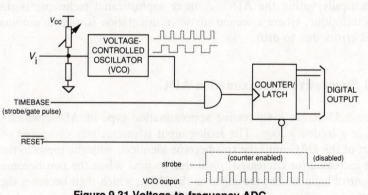

Figure 9.31 Voltage-to-frequency ADC.

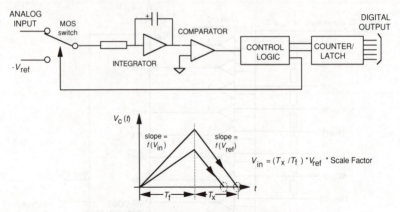

Figure 9.32 Dual slope integrating ADC.

9.6.3 Dual Slope Integrating ADC

The ADC of Figure 9.32 uses the dual ramp integration technique. The MOS switch is switched through to the analog input for a fixed time T_f, during which the capacitor charges up at a rate proportional to V_{in}. After this time the switch is connected through to the reference voltage, and the counter started. Now the reference voltage is of the opposite polarity to that of V_{in}, so the capacitor will begin to discharge through the resistor to $-V_{ref}$. The capacitor continues to discharge until zero volts is detected by the analog comparator (whose reference voltage is ground), which then stops the counter. The digital output is latched to the counter output at this time.

Simple triangulation shows that the time held in the counter (T_x) is directly proportional to the analog input. This type of ADC is slow but accurate. It is quite often used in digital multimeters, where the (BCD) counter drives an LCD display, and the counter reading can be scaled automatically within the ADC. A more sophisticated technique is the *quad ramp* technique, where a second up/down integration is used to automatically cancel errors due to drift.

9.6.4 Successive Approximation ADC

Figure 9.33 shows a successive approximation type of ADC, which uses a DAC in a feedback loop. The analog input is successively compared with the output of the DAC until the two become identical, with the input to the DAC being increased (or decreased) until this occurs. When the two become equal the control logic latches the input to the DAC, which then becomes the ADC output.

The ADC shown uses a PLA to control its operation (PLAs were

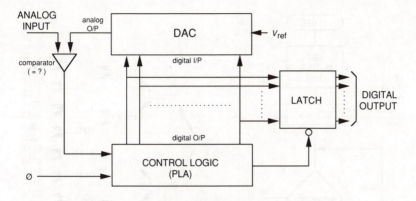

Figure 9.33 Successive approximation ADC.

discussed previously, in Section 2.6.3). An alternative (and simpler) controller would use a presettable up/down counter.

Figure 9.34 shows the binary search algorithm used in a successive approximation ADC. The controller output is initially set to the middle of its range (1000_2 for this 4-bit ADC). The comparator output is then tested to see whether the DAC output is higher or lower than the analog input. If it is higher, then the count should be decreased, and the msb cleared to zero (and conversely for lower). The next msb is then set HI, and the comparator output tested again. Depending on the result of this test, the second msb is either set or cleared. Two more tests are required to determine whether the two remaining bits should be HI or LO.

In this manner, the input to the DAC is successively changed in order to approximate better the analog input. Figure 9.34 shows the successive approximation of 1011_2 (which is reached after only three samples of the comparator output).

Only n tests are required for an n-bit ADC, so that fast conversion and settling times can be achieved with this type of ADC. It can also be readily extended for continuous output. However, it is susceptible to errors produced by noise spikes in the analog input signal.

9.6.5 Practical ADCs

Microprocessor-compatible ADCs incorporate three state outputs, so that they can be interfaced directly to a microcomputer bus; no additional interface logic is required. The ADC appears as a memory (or I/O) location, with separate controls being provided for each 8-bit byte. (Recall that ADCs typically provide between 8- and 16-bit resolution.) In interfacing to microprocessors, it should be emphasized that ADCs should either be polled or interrupt driven. The reason for this is the relatively long conversion and settling times inherent

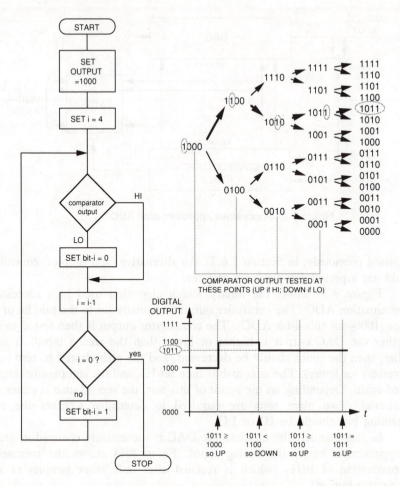

Figure 9.34 Binary search algorithm and search tree.

within the ADC (typically µs rather than ns). Thus, the CPU can be getting on with productive work while waiting for the ADC to complete its conversion, checking periodically (if polling), or performing other calculations until interrupted.

Calibration (lookup) tables are often included within the A/D control software in order that outputs can be read directly. It is also possible to increase the resolution of the A/D process without affecting its accuracy. One such technique is scaling, in order to utilize the full scale resolution of the ADC. Small values might need amplifying prior to inputting to the ADC. Alternatively, large values might need to be attenuated (scaled down), using a potential divider circuit, for example.

A second technique is shown in Figure 9.35 using a DAC together with

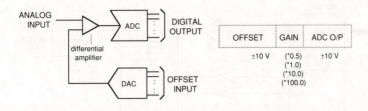

Figure 9.35 Increasing the resolution of an A/D conversion.

the ADC in order to provide a constant offset. Rather than input the entire analog value to the ADC, the *difference* between this value and the constant offset is used. This technique is useful for small variations about the constant offset value, since the gain of the differential amplifier can be adjusted to make full use of the resolution of the ADC. (However, care has to be taken in selecting a differential amplifier and DAC of sufficient accuracy.) Both the offset value and the gain can be under software control, as indicated.

The Analog Devices AD570 is a sucessive approximation type of ADC, with a conversion time of around 25 μs. There are three control lines on the AD570: bipolar select, data ready and blank and convert. Connecting the bipolar select input to ground selects unipolar operation, which is 0 to +10 V for supply voltages of +5 V and −15 V, as indicated.

Driving the blank and convert line LO places the TS outputs into the high impedance condition and commences a conversion. Upon completion of this conversion the data ready line will go LO, and the digital value will appear on the output pins. Pulling the blank and convert line HI blanks (three states) the outputs and readies the ADC for the next conversion.

Other common types of ADCs include the National Semiconductor ADC0804, Motorola MC6108 and MC10319 and Analog Devices CAV1220. Figure 9.36 shows the interfacing of the AD570 to a microcomputer, using a parallel interface chip (MC6821 PIA). Lowering control line CB2 starts the conversion process. When the conversion is complete, the lowering of data

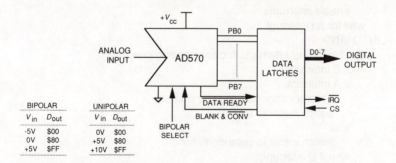

Figure 9.36 AD570 ADC interface signals (courtesy of Analog Devices Inc.).

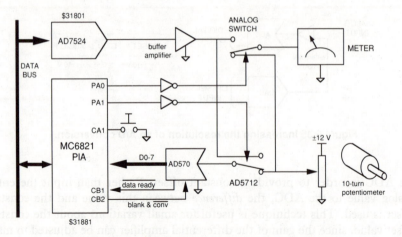

Figure 9.37 Interfacing an AD570 to a microcomputer .

ready can be used to interrupt the CPU or set a flag. The analog value can then be read by simply reading the PIA.

An AD570 is used together with an AD7524 DAC and AD5712 analog switches in the application shown in Figure 9.37. In this configuration, it is possible to switch the output from the DAC to either the meter or the input of the ADC. Similarly, the input to the ADC can be selected from either the potentiometer or the output of the DAC. The MC68000 routine which follows alternately displays the potentiometer reading (V_i) and its complement $(10\,\text{V} - V_i)$ on successive presses of the pushbutton connected to control input CA1. The corresponding algorithm is as follows:

```
MAIN:
    declare constants
    initialize:-
        interrupt handler,
        PIA data direction & control registers,
        enable interrupts
    wait for an interrupt
INT_HAND:
    disable further interrupts & clear pending one
    A or B interrupt?
    if A interrupt,
        if meter connected to potentiometer,
        switch meter to DAC
    else
        switch meter to potentiometer
    else if B interrupt,
        read ADC data register,
        find complement,
```

```
                    send complement to DAC,
                    reset DAC,
                    request another conversion
                else unidentified interrupt
            return to MAIN
```

This is the corresponding MC68000 code:

```
INIT:       move.l  #INTHAN,$70     ;MC68000 level 4 autovector
            move.b  #0,$31883       ;select PIA port A DDR
            move.b  #3,$31881       ;select PA0 & PA1 as outputs
            move.b  #0,$31887       ;select PIA port B DDR
            move.b  #0,$31885       ;select PB0-7 as i/p's (ADC)
            move.b  #5,$31883       ;port A data reg (& ints en)
            move.b  #1,$31881       ;switch pot to meter & ADC
            move.b  #$35,$31885     ;CB2 o/p, CB1 int enabled
                                    ;& start A/D conversion
            move.b  #1,flag         ;pot → meter if set
            move.l  #$2300,SR       ;enable interrupts ≥ level 4

MAIN:       bra     MAIN            ;wait for interrupt

INTHAN:     move.b  $31883,D3       ;port A interrupt?
            btst    #7,D3           ;pushbutton CA1?
            beq     B?              ;if not was it CB2?
            move.b  $31881,D3       ;clears p.b.int
            move.b  FLAG,D0         ;read 'pot → meter' flag
            cmp.b   #1,D0           ;if set then → CHANGE
            beq     CHANGE          ;
            move.b  #1,$31881       ;connect pot to meter
            move.b  #1,flag         ;and set flag
            bra     RETURN          ;
CHANGE:     move.b  #0,$31881       ;switch pot to ADC
            move.b  #0,flag         ;and clear flag
            bra     RETURN          ;
B?:         move.b  $31887,D3       ;port B that interrupt?
            btst    #7,D3           ;data ready from ADC?
            bne     DATA            ;if so input data from ADC
            jmp     ERROR           ;neither A nor B interrupted
                                    ;(error routine not included
                                    ;here)
DATA:       move.b  $31885,D4       ;read ADC output
            move.b  #$FF,D5         ;load maximum ADC output
            subq    D4,D5           ;complement (10 V − Vin)
            move.b  D5,$31801       ;send complement to DAC
            move.b  #$3D,$31887     ;reset ADC
            move.b  #$35,$31887     ;initiate next A/D
                                    ;conversion
RETURN:     rte                     ;return to main
                                    ;(wait for interrupt)
```

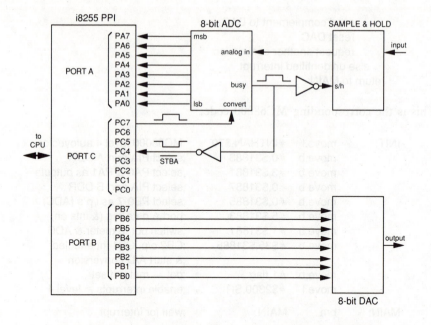

Figure 9.38 Interfacing an ADC and DAC to a i8086 using a i8255 PPI.

It should be noted in passing that the output from the DAC should be the same as the input to the ADC when both are connected together. In practice, however, losses and calibration errors may cause these values to differ. If such errors are appreciable, then they can be corrected either by using either a lookup table or a compensation algorithm (such compensation has not been included here for the sake of simplicity).

Figure 9.38 shows how an i8255 Programmable Peripheral Interface (PPI) could be used to interface to both an ADC and DAC. The ADC connects to port A, and the DAC to port B. Port A operates in mode 1, port B in mode 0, and port C is used to provide both a convert output (bit 7) and a strobe input (bit 4). The busy output from the ADC is triggered whenever bit 7 of port C is set, which in turn causes the (S/H) circuit to output a constant value (the input to the ADC has to remain constant during the A/D conversion process).

Interrupts are not used in this system, so that port A has to be polled by the i8086 software in order to determine when data is ready for inputting to the system.

The trailing edge of the busy output triggers the one-shot, which then produces a fixed-duration strobe signal for passing the digital value from the output of the ADC through to port A. (It simultaneously allows the (S/H) circuit to revert to sampling the changing input rather than holding the previously sampled analog value.) The output from port B is connected directly to the input of the DAC (handshaking is not used in this system). The appropriate i8086 assembler routine would be as follows (Y–C. Liu/G.A. Gibson, *Microcomputer Systems: the 8086/8088 Family, Architecture, Programming, and Design*, (2nd edn), © 1986. Reprinted by permission of Prentice-Hall, Inc., Englewood Cliffs NJ.):

```
INIT:    mov   DX,01003H    ;A1,A0 = 00 selects i8255 control reg
         mov   AL,B0H       ;A = i/p port (mode 1), B = o/p port
         out   DX,AL        ;(mode 0), C7 as o/p, C4 as strobe.
           :
           :

ADC:     mov   DX,01003H    ;A1,A0 = 11 selects i8255 control reg
         mov   AL,0FH       ;set bit 7 of port C (convert)
         out   DX,AL
         mov   AL,0EH       ;clear bit 7 of port C
         out   DX,AL
           :
           :

ADIN:    mov   DX,01002H    ;input status from port C (A1, A0 = 10)
POLL:    in    AL,DX        ;(programmed I/O, not using interrupts)
         test  AL,20H       ;strobe (bit 4) asserted (active LO)?
         jz    POLL         ;if not, keep polling until it is
         mov   DX,01000H    ;if so, input data from port A
         in    AL,DX        ;(A1,0 = 00)
           :
           :

DAOUT:   mov   DX,01001H    ;output to port B (A1,A0 = 01)
         out   DX,AL        ;(no handshaking used here)
```

9.7 A/D and D/A SUBSYSTEMS

ADCs and DACs come in many different forms, ranging from single ICs to complete board subassemblies for connection to various microcomputer busses. Typical of the latter are Analog Devices' μMAC-4000 (which uses RS232c or 20 mA current interfaces), Analog Devices' MACSYM (Measurement and Control System, available in either workstation or front-end processor form), Burr Brown's MP8xxx Multibus compatible I/O systems, and Data Translation's DT2821 board for the IBM PC/AT.

A typical board will have several I/O channels (typically 16 single ended or 8 differential), which multiplex (share) between a single ADC (or DAC). This ADC (DAC) will often be fabricated in hybrid form, rather than in a single IC package. Such hybrid circuits combine integrated transistors and discrete components within the same package, thereby providing heavier current capability.

The I/O board will also contain the necessary address decoding, timing and control circuitry necessary to interface to the CPU. Often these boards will also provide isolation between the CPU and the external system voltage levels. (Most industrial systems will interface to higher voltage relays which open and shut valves, turn motors on and off etc.) Such isolation protects the microcomputer from voltage transients (unwanted noise spikes) and equipment malfunctions, and moreover eliminates ground loops.

SUMMARY

In this chapter we have looked at the interfacing of microcomputers to the external (real) world. There is a fundamental difference between the real world and the world of the microcomputer in terms of the electrical signals which can exist in either. Within the (binary) computer these signals are restricted to TTL levels, whereas they can take any value in the real world.

We saw how transducers can be used to first convert real-world (analog) quantities into their electrical equivalent. Several different types of transducer were discussed, including temperature, humidity, position, pressure, liquid level, optical and acoustic. Active transducers are those which can produce their own electrical output, whereas passive ones rely for their operation on an external power supply. Input transducers are also known as sensors, while output transducers which produce movement of an external device are referred to as actuators.

Once the real-world quantity has been converted into electrical form, it may require signal conditioning prior to the A/D conversion proper. Signal conditioning, for example, could involve either amplification or attenuation of the incoming signal, in order to make full use of the available resolution. Operational amplifiers were discussed in relation to signal conditioning.

The first stage of the A/D conversion process is quantization, where the incoming signal is sampled at regular intervals, and a digital representation of this signal produced (the rate at which the input signal is sampled being determined by the Nyquist Sampling Theorem). Each digitized sample is encoded into a binary representation of that sample, after which it is in a form suitable for inputting to a computer.

We saw how DACs are fabricated using a resistor ladder network together with a summing amplifier. By way of contrast, a number of different techniques are used in the fabrication of ADCs. The types considered here included parallel (or flash), voltage-to-frequency, dual ramp (integrating) and successive approximation.

Interfacing typical DAC and ADC devices to microcomputers was discussed, and representative assembler routines presented.

REVIEW QUESTIONS

9.1   What is meant by the term transducer? Is it identical to sensor?

9.2   Why are stepper motors suitable for use as microcomputer peripheral devices?

9.3   Explain two methods of compensating for a thermocouple's non-linearity. (Hint: one hardware, and one software.)

9.4   What is meant by differential amplifier, and how is this related to common mode noise rejection?

9.5   What is meant by the term operational amplifier, and how are such devices useful in A/D conversion?

9.6   With reference to A/D conversion, what is quantization noise, and how can it be overcome?

9.7   What function does a sample-and-hold unit perform in A/D conversion?

9.8   Discuss the relative merits of the following types of ADCs: flash, voltage-to-frequency, integrating and successive approximation.

9.9   Sketch the flow chart and timing diagram for obtaining the output 6_{16} using a (4-bit) successive approximation ADC.

9.10   Explain how the resolution of A/D conversion can be increased, without sacrificing accuracy.

9.11   With reference to A/D and D/A subsystems generally, what is meant by the terms isolation and signal conditioning?

10

Mass Storage Devices

OBJECTIVES

Three types of mass storage device are treated in this chapter, namely magnetic tape drives, magnetic disk drives (both hard and floppy) and optical disk drives (CDROMs). Most attention is given to floppy disk drives and their associated controller chips.

Disk formatting is discussed, as well as the interfacing between both the host CPU and the disk drive unit. RAMdisks and Smart Cards are also covered.

10.1 INTRODUCTION

Semiconductor memory constitutes a computer's primary memory. Secondary storage usually comes in the form of a disk, whether that be floppy, Winchester or multiplatter hard disk. Archival storage is facilitated by means of magnetic tape (reel-to-reel, streaming tape cartridges or cassettes). The transition from primary through secondary to archival storage is characterized by decreasing cost per bit and increasing capacity, but at the expense of decreasing access speeds.

In this chapter, we shall concern ourselves firstly with magnetic tape, then with disk drives and their associated microprocessor support chips, and finally optical disk drives.

10.2 MAGNETIC TAPE

Figure 10.1 shows the basic construction of a reel-to-reel magnetic tape drive. It is very similar in operation to an audio magnetic tape drive, but operates at much faster speeds. As such, special tape tensioning mechanisms are required in order to prevent the tape either stretching or breaking; because data is packed so close together on the tape surface, the feed mechanism has to be capable not only of stopping at precise positions along the tape, but also of reaching full speed from a rest position very quickly.

The write head in Figure 10.1 is an electromagnet, which converts an electrical input into a stored magnetic pattern on the surface of the magnetically coated mylar tape. The read or playback head is mounted alongside the write head (indeed the same physical electromagnet can often serve for both reading and writing). Data is stored in parallel tracks along the length of the half-inch wide tape, at densities ranging from 800 to 6250 bits/inch, as indicated in Figure 10.2. Nine tracks are used, eight for data, and one for parity.

Data is stored as physical records, with the tape controller being responsible for the mapping between logical and physical records. Data is not stored along the entire surface of the tape, but is separated by Inter-Record Gaps (IRGs). The stored data takes up far less space than the IRGs, each of which accounts for around half an inch of the tape length.

Blocking is the technique whereby multibyte records are grouped together to make more efficient use of the storage capacity available on the tape. In the example shown in Figure 10.3, the records are grouped in blocks of 10 bytes.

The disadvantage of magnetic tapes is that they are a serial access medium; to find a particular record, the tape will either have to be rewound or fast forwarded from its current position. This leads to slow access times, on average. The main advantage of magnetic tape is the low cost per bit; tens of megabytes of data can be stored on a single tape.

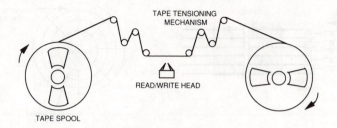

Figure 10.1 Magnetic tape drive.

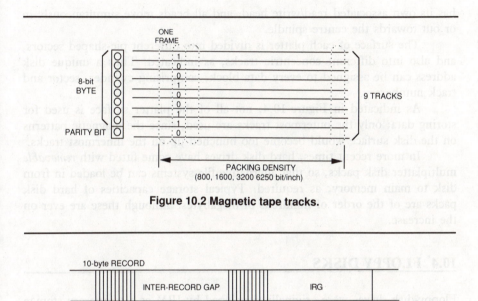

Figure 10.2 Magnetic tape tracks.

Figure 10.3 Multibyte records (blocking).

10.3 MAGNETIC DISK DRIVES

Magnetic disks have the advantage over magnetic tapes in that they are a random access storage medium rather than a serial one; any record or file can be accessed as fast as any other. They come in three main forms, namely hard disks, Winchesters and floppy disks.

The oldest type of disk drive is the hard disk, so called because the magnetic surface is coated on a rigid metallic disk. Figure 10.4 shows the construction of a multiplatter hard disk; six platters are connected to the same spindle, so that they are all aligned and spin at the same speed. Each surface

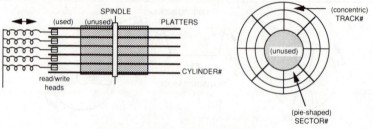

Figure 10.4 Multiplatter hard disk.

has its own associated read/write head, and all heads move simultaneously in or out towards the centre spindle.

The surface of each platter is divided into different pie-shaped sectors, and also into different concentric tracks, as indicated. Thus a unique disk address can be assigned to every data block, comprising cylinder, sector and track numbers.

As indicated in Figure 10.4, not all of the platter surface is used for storing data; only the outermost tracks are used, since the magnetic patterns on the disk surface would become too bunched up on the innermost tracks.

In more recent times, hard disk drives have come fitted with *removable* multiplatter disk packs, so that alternative file systems can be loaded in from disk to main memory, as required. Typical storage capacities of hard disk packs are of the order of hundreds of megabytes, although these are ever on the increase.

10.4 FLOPPY DISKS

Floppy-disk drives were originally developed by IBM as a temporary storage device for loading micro-(control) programs into some models of their IBM/370 computers, as well as into their model 3330 hard-disk drives. During the 1970s, manufacturers of home/hobby computers seized on these same floppy disks as being suitable as low-cost secondary storage devices for the small microcomputer systems they were developing. Storage capacities at that time were limited to between tens and hundreds of kilobytes. Mid 1980s capacities, by way of contrast, had increased to several Mbytes.

The earliest floppy disks – so-called *standard* floppies – were of 8″ diameter, but have been since superseded by 5¼″ *mini*floppies (the type used on the IBM-PC). During the mid 1980s, the Sony 3½″ disk became widely accepted, via such computers as the Apple Macintosh, Commodore Amiga and IBM-PS/2. This latter type of disk is housed inside a plastic protective jacket rather than a cardboard one.

The basic construction of a floppy-disk drive is shown in Figure 10.5. A DC motor is used to drive a spindle which rotates the disk at constant speed

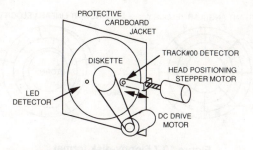

Figure 10.5 Floppy-disk drive.

(360 revolutions/minute for 8″ drives; 300 rpm for 5¼″). A second motor, a stepper type in this case, is used to move the read/write head in and out across the disk surface, one track at a time. (See Section 9.2.11.) Hard disks, by way of contrast, often use voice coils rather than stepper motors for increased speed.

The (floppy) disk itself is housed inside a protective (stiff) cardboard jacket, as shown in Figure 10.6. There are four holes in this cardboard jacket, each serving a different function. There is a large circular hole in the centre which allows the drive spindle to make contact with the disk and turn it around inside the jacket. The rectangular slot underneath the read/write head enables the head to make contact with the disk surface once it has been positioned over the desired track. There is a small index hole, under which a small hole in the magnetic disk passes once every revolution; this is used to find the first sector on each track. The fourth 'hole' is a notch on the side of the cardboard jacket which indicates whether it can be written to as well as read from. On 8″ diskettes this notch has to be present to 'write protect' it, whereas on 5¼″ diskettes it has to be covered. On 3½″ diskettes, a miniature plastic switch can be moved to cover (read/write) or to expose (read only) a rectangular hole in the plastic cover.

Not all manufacturers divide the disk surface up into tracks and sectors,

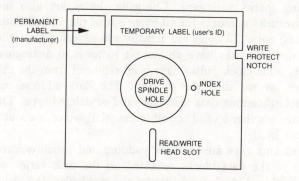

Figure 10.6 Floppy diskette construction.

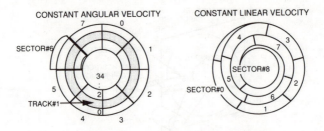

Figure 10.7 Floppy-disk format.

as discussed previously. An alternative to this constant angular velocity (CAV) scheme is the constant linear velocity (CLV) scheme; the two schemes are contrasted in Figure 10.7. A modification of this scheme is used on the Apple Macintosh computer, where concentric tracks rather than a spiral are used, which *approximates* CLV recording.

10.4.1 Disk Formatting

Disk formatting refers to the division of the disk surface into a regular pattern which acts as a template for subsequent data storage. The IBM 3740 and 37 standard formats are shown in Figure 10.8 (3740 is for single density disks; 37 for double density disks). The IBM 3740 format was used on the earlier 8″ disks, and more recently with the 5¼″ disks on the IBM-PC/AT.

The IBM 3740 standard allows for 128, 256, 512, 1024 or 2048 bytes per sector, with corresponding changes in the number of sectors per track. Thus most floppy disk controllers incorporate programmable formatting.

One complete track is shown in folded-out form in Figure 10.8. Not all of the available space will be used to store data; there is a lot of other information which needs to be stored apart from the data proper. Each of the 26 sectors comprises track and sector identification, together with their corresponding marks and gaps. Checksum bytes are also included. This additional overhead accounts for 60 bytes out of the 188 allocated for each of the 26 sectors; only 128 bytes are actually available for data storage.

The various marks have unique bit patterns to distinguish them from data (in fact, some clock pulses have been removed from the mixed data and clock stream, as we shall see shortly). The data address mark indicates whether the forthcoming data field is a valid or deleted type. The ID address mark indicates whether a valid or bad (corrupted) sector is about to pass under the read/write head.

The various gaps are used for padding and synchronization purposes. The lengths of the data blocks recorded on the disk varies with the exact rotational speed and clock frequency of the particular disk drive concerned. Thus, some padding is needed when attempting to read this same disk on a

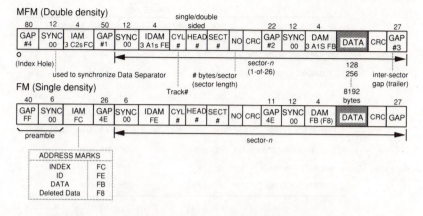

Figure 10.8 IBM 3740 and 37 floppy-disk formats.

different drive, one which has a slightly different speed and clock frequency. Moreover, data blocks are frequently overwritten, using slightly different clock speeds. The gaps provide additional bytes which can be used to synchronize the data recovery hardware. (We shall see more clearly how this is achieved in our discussion of phase-locked loops). Within each gap is a variable number of FFs and 6 bytes of 00s (the latter being sync trailers). Cyclic Redundancy Check (CRC) characters are added to facilitate error checking.

Once a disk has been initialized (formatted), only the data field and associated CRC characters can be altered thereafter.

It should be obvious from the above that formatted disk capacities are much less than unformatted ones. Figure 10.9 shows typical mid 1980s formatted capacities, together with the corresponding number of tracks. It should be emphasized that disk capacities, like memory chips, have a habit of increasing their capacities dramatically every year or two. Typical mid 1980s formatted capacities were 360 kbytes to 1.2 Mbytes (IBM-PC and IBM-PC/AT), and 400 kbytes or 800 kbytes (Apple Macintosh).

Commonly used IBM-PC formats use either eight or nine sectors per track, 512 bytes per sector and double density recording. This yields formatted capacities of 160 (180) and 320 (380) kbytes for single- and double-sided disks respectively. High-density disks use 80 tracks in total, 15 sectors per track, and rotate at 360 rpm, resulting in a capacity of 1.2 Mbytes.

The IBM PS/2 uses either 1 or 2 Mbyte disks (2 Mbyte disks use a second write protect notch, in the lower right corner, to distinguish them from 1 Mbyte disks). The Macintosh II disks, by way of comparison, can store 1.44 Mbytes of information.

The Floppy Drive High Density (FDHD) disk used in the Macintosh-IIx and Macintosh-SE/30 computers supports not only 400K and 800K Macintosh (CLV) formats, but also A/UX (Apple's implementation of UNIX), MS-DOS and OS/2 formats.

		(SINGLE-SIDED)								
		SINGLE DENSITY					DOUBLE DENSITY			
8" total # tracks = 77; 360 rpm	NO. BYTES/SECTOR	128	256	512	⋯⋯	4096	256	512	1024	⋯⋯ 8192
	NO. SECTORS/TRACK	26	15	8	⋯⋯	1	26	15	8	⋯⋯ 1
	TOTAL NO. BYTES	256K	296K	315K	⋯⋯	315K	512K	591K	630K	⋯⋯ 630K
5 1/4" total # tracks = 35 (40), 80; 300 rpm	NO. BYTES/SECTOR	128	256	512	1024	2048	256	512	1024	2048 4096
	NO. SECTORS/TRACK	16	8	4	2	1	16	8	4	2 1
	TOTAL NO. BYTES	72K	72K	72K	72K	72K	144K	144K	144K	144K 144K
3 1/2" total # tracks = 80; 300 rpm	NO. BYTES/SECTOR	128	256	512			256	512	1024	
	NO. SECTORS/TRACK	15	9	5			15	9	5	
	TOTAL NO. BYTES	154K	184K	205K			308K	368K	410K	

512
9   for IBM PC double-sided (40 tracks)
369K

Figure 10.9 Formatted disk capacities.

10.4.2 Data Encoding

Whether we refer to hard disks or floppy types, the information is stored on the disk surface in exactly the same manner. Figure 10.10 shows a typical read/write head, which is in the form of an electromagnet. A write operation involves applying a voltage to the electromagnet, which will induce a magnetic field through its coil windings, and in turn will induce a miniature magnetic domain in the magnetic coating on the disk platter. Depending on the polarity of the applied voltage, the magnetic domain will either be clockwise or counterclockwise orientated (or alternatively miniature north and south poles). Thus we have a binary storage element, which can be used for storing 1s and 0s in a computer system. A read operation involves sensing the orientation of the stored magnetic domain, as an induced current flowing through the coil, as indicated in Figure 10.10.

Magnetic disks (and tapes for that matter) are non-volatile storage media; they retain their stored data when power is disconnected from the disk drive. This property is due to the inherent hysteresis of the magnetic medium; it is a bistable device, and will reside in either of its two stable states until an electrical current is applied to shift it from one state to the other.

We have already noted that data is stored in serial form, either within a single track on a CAV disk, or within one long spiral on a CLV disk drive. In either case, it is essential that the bit pattern read from the disk is synchronized to the data clock. This system clock is actually stored along with the data on the disk surface, and is separated out from the mixed incoming data and clock bit stream during a read operation.

Figure 10.11 shows the encoding technique used on floppy disks. 200 ns

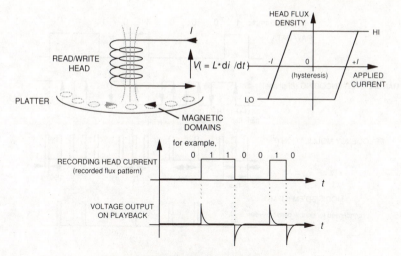

Figure 10.10 Magnetic recording.

clock pulses of $4\,\mu s$ period are mixed with the incoming data stream. A 1 is recorded as a 200 ns pulse in the middle of the clock period, whereas a 0 is not recorded as a pulse. This results in what is essentially an FM encoding technique; 0s are recorded as one frequency, and 1s as twice that frequency (the Kansas City Standard, for example, encodes 0s as 1200 Hz, and 1s as 2400 Hz). An alternative encoding technique, Manchester Encoding, is also included in Figure 10.11 for comparison.

A different encoding technique is used for double-density disks, which allows some of the pulses of the FM technique to be removed without loss of information. This technique is referred to as modified FM (MFM), and is also illustrated in Figure 10.11. A clock pulse only appears if a data pulse did *not* appear in the previous cell (window), and similarly does *not* appear in the current cell. Thus, the only clock pulses appearing in the example of Figure 10.11 are within the 000 portion of the data stream. The removal of 'redundant' clock pulses enables the pulse stream to be condensed, in fact to twice its previous density. The penalty paid, however, is the increased overhead necessary in regenerating these 'missing' clock pulses during a read operation. We saw in Figure 10.8 how the address marks consists of special bit patterns to distinguish them from data. These special patterns result from *deliberately* removing one or more clock bits.

Hard disks often employ a different encoding scheme yet again, this being Run Length Limited (RLL) encoding. In the 2, 7 RLL scheme, for example, the incoming data stream is encoded such that there are never less than two nor more than seven successive 0s. (MFM, by comparison, can be thought of as a 1, 3 RLL encoding scheme.) Different input sequences are encoded as either four, six or eight bits. For example, 01_2 becomes 0100_2, 101_2 becomes 100100_2, and 1100_2 becomes 00001000_2 (where 1 indicates the

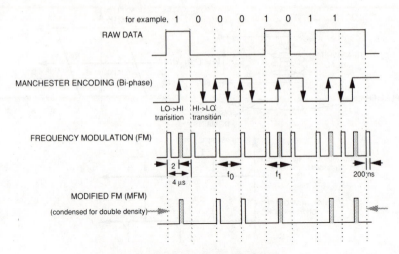

Figure 10.11 Encoding techniques.

presence and 0 the absence of a pulse). The relatively few 1s in the encoded bit stream means that the pulses can be compressed on to the hard-disk surface, thus resulting in higher storage densities.

10.4.3 Data Recovery

We have seen how data and clock information is stored together on the disk surface. In reading back this information from disk to memory, we therefore need some means of separating out the data bits from the clock stream. The key element which enables us to do this is the Phase-Locked Loop (PLL), illustrated in block diagram form in Figure 10.12.

A PLL consists of four component parts; a phase detector, low pass filter, voltage controlled oscillator and frequency divider. The phase difference between the incoming signal and the reference signal is generated and averaged out in the low pass filter to form a DC value proportional to this phase difference. This DC value is in turn used to produce a square wave output from the voltage controlled oscillator. This output is divided down to a frequency equal to the incoming frequency, and fed back to the phase detector input.

Following power-up, the PLL will change from its free-running frequency and latch onto the incoming signal frequency, maintaining a small but finite phase difference between the two. Thereafter, it will track small variations in the incoming frequency, either side of its nominal value. This makes it ideally suited for use in a disk-drive data recovery circuit, since the frequency of the recorded bit pattern can vary considerably in practice.

Figure 10.13 shows a simple type of exclusive-OR phase detector which

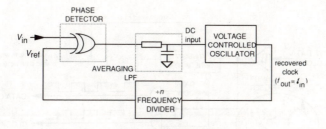

Figure 10.12 Phase-Locked Loop (PLL).

could be used in such a PLL. The top three waveforms show a reference voltage whose phase is very close to the incoming signal, together with the small output signal generated by the EXOR-gate. The lower two waveforms show the situation where the reference and incoming signals differ considerably in phase, such that a much higher DC or average output is generated by the EXOR-gate.

Figure 10.14 shows the use of a PLL in a disk-drive data separator circuit (after Stone (1982), reprinted by permission of Addison-Wesley). The raw mixed data and clock stream appearing at the input can appear as quite a noisy signal, hence the inclusion of the Schmitt Trigger to clean up these incoming pulses. Any incoming signal greater than $+2.4$ V is converted to $+5$ V, and likewise any signal less than $+0.4$ V is converted to 0 V (the Schmitt Trigger simply acts as a voltage comparator).

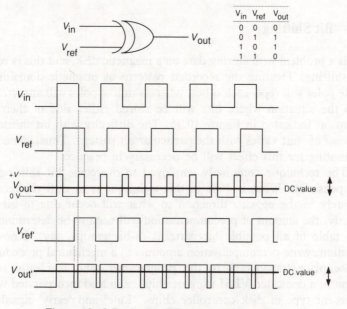

Figure 10.13 Exclusive-OR phase comparator.

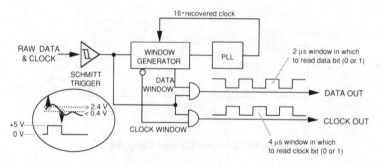

Figure 10.14 Data recovery.

The PLL in this data separator runs at 16 times the nominal clock frequency; eight counts correspond to a time window during which a clock pulse is expected, and eight counts to a data window (during which there may or may not be a pulse present). Thus the window generator of Figure 10.14 consists essentially of a simple 4-bit counter.

The only difficulty with this type of window generator is that an initial guess has to be made as to whether the incoming pulse is a data or clock pulse. There is a 50% chance of making a correct guess initially; if a wrong guess is made, this will show up as missing pulses in the 'clock' bit stream, so that the window generator simply swaps its two outputs internally (hence the need for sync bytes).

10.4.4 Bit Shifting

There is a problem with storing data on a magnetic disk, and this is referred to as bit shifting. Treating the recorded patterns as magnetic domains, we see that like poles will repel each other, whereas unlike poles will attract. This will lead to the situation where bits will be stored either side of their nominal positions, as indicated in Figure 10.15. The difficulty with bit shifting is that the *amount* of shift varies with the particular bit pattern. Thus, some means of compensating for this effect will be necessary in practice.

The technique commonly employed to overcome bit shifting is write precompensation. What is done in this technique is to shift the recorded bit deliberately in the *opposite* direction to what will occur due to bit shifting. Obviously, the amount of precompensation will need to be determined from a lookup table of all possible bit patterns (8-bit groups, say). Knowing this information, write precompensation amounts to a mechanical procedure which can take place transparent to the programmer, and is ideally suited for inclusion in a dedicated VLSI support chip, or indeed incorporated within the more recent type of disk controller chips. 'Late' and 'early' signals will be produced by this dedicated controller.

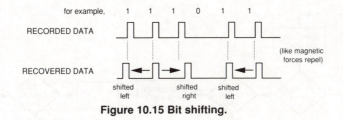

for example, 1 1 1 0 1 1

RECORDED DATA

(like magnetic forces repel)

RECOVERED DATA

shifted left   shifted right   shifted left

Figure 10.15 Bit shifting.

10.4.5 Error Checking

We have already seen that data is recorded in 128 (256, 512, or 1024)-byte blocks within each sector of a CAV disk. Two bytes of checksum information is also included in each sector, in the form of a CRC. This CRC is formed initially by dividing the data stream to be written to disk by a known standard divisor $G(x)$, and appending the resulting remainder as the CRC character(s). On playback, the data stream together with the CRC character(s) is divided by $G(x)$; if a non-zero result is obtained, then an error has been detected.

Figure 10.16 shows an example of how a single CRC character would be generated using $G(x)$ on the incoming data stream 10100011_2. In this case, the CRC character to be appended would be 0011_2, so that the bit pattern actually recorded would be 101000110011_2. In practice, more sophisticated generator polynomials are used, a typical one being $x^{16} + x^{12} + x^5 + 1$.

A typical disk read sequence is illustrated in Figure 10.17. The disk controller searches firstly for the ID address mark, and then once that has been detected, for the desired sector number on that particular track. A CRC check is performed to ensure that this sector ID information has not been corrupted, before initiating a search for the data mark. Once the data mark has been detected, a 128 (256, 512, 1024)-byte block is read out, followed by its corresponding CRC characters. Failure to verify either CRC check leads to an error routine, which could initiate a retry.

In the case of a 'soft' or temporary error (a dust particle on the disk surface perhaps), a retry would usually result in a successful read. In the case

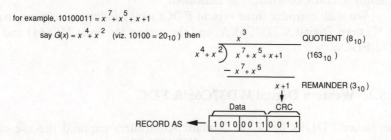

for example, $10100011 = x^7 + x^5 + x + 1$

say $G(x) = x^4 + x^2$ (viz. $10100 = 20_{10}$) then

$$x^4 + x^2 \overline{)\, x^7 + x^5 + x + 1} \quad \begin{array}{l} x^3 \quad \text{QUOTIENT } (8_{10}) \\ (163_{10}) \end{array}$$

$$\underline{-\ x^7 + x^5}$$

$$x + 1 \quad \text{REMAINDER } (3_{10})$$

Data   CRC

RECORD AS ◄— | 1010 | 0011 | 0011 |

Figure 10.16 CRC check.

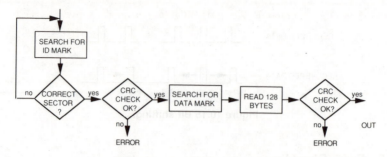

Figure 10.17 Typical read sequence.

of a 'hard' or irretrievable error (such as a surface imperfection or spurious magnetic field on the disk), then retries would produce the same result. After a dozen or so retries, the disk controller would mark that particular sector as bad, and inform the operating system accordingly.

10.5 FLOPPY-DISK INTERFACING

There are two groups of signals used to interface to a floppy-disk drive. The two primary signals are the serial read and write bit streams (of mixed data and clock). Other output signals from the drive include ready, write protect sensed, track#00 (outermost) detected, index pulse(s), and error bit sensed. Other input signals are the basic step pulses (one per track), step direction (in or out), load the head (onto the disk surface, in readiness for a read or write) and a write gate pulse (or a time window during which writing can take place).

Instead of having a CPU control such a floppy-disk drive directly, and have so much of its system resources tied up in disk overhead, it makes more sense to make use of a dedicated peripheral support chip, thus freeing the CPU for other, more pressing tasks. Such a peripheral support chip comes in the form of a Floppy-Disk Controller (FDC). Figure 10.18 shows the typical interface signals required between a CPU, FDC and disk drive.

Transferring files between memory and disk can often be speeded up by including a DMA controller, as indicated.

We shall consider three typical FDCs in the following sections, namely the Western Digital WD37C65/A, and the earlier Motorola MC6843 and Intel i8272 FDCs.

10.5.1 Western Digital WD37C65/A FDC

The earlier FD179x family of formatter/controllers required the use of two additional support chips, namely the WD1691 Floppy Support Logic and the WD2143 Clock Generator. The WD1691 provided data separation and write

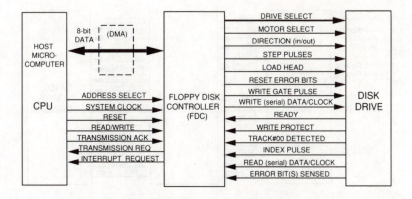

Figure 10.18 Disk-drive interface signals.

precompensation support for the WD179x. Later Western Digital FDCs, such as the WD279x, incorporated the PLL data separator and write precompensation onchip. Table 10.1 shows the characteristics of the WD279x family members. The WD179x (279x) FDCs supported both the IBM3470 FM (single density) and IBM34 MFM (double density) formats, with sector lengths of 128, 256, 512 or 1024 in both.

These devices have been superseded by the WD37C65/A Floppy Disk Subsystem Controller, which integrates a formatter/controller, data separator, write precompensation, data rate selection, clock generation and disk-drive interface drivers (receivers) on a single peripheral controller chip. Specific support for the IBM PC/AT is provided, via an inbuilt 12 MHz i80286 bus interface (which includes qualification of the interrupt request signal). Eight internal registers are provided, these being a main status register, four additional status registers, a control register, an operations register and data register. Figure 10.19 shows a typical WD37C65/A-based system.

Figure 10.20 shows the master status register. This register can be read at any time, and can be used to facilitate data transfers between the WD37C65/A FDC and the host CPU. The DIO and RQM bits indicate when data is ready and in which direction it is to be transferred on the data bus.

The WD37C65/A can be in one of three phases, namely command, execution or result. During the command phase, the FDC receives all the

Table 10.1 Western Digital WD279x family characteristics.

Characteristic	2791	2793	2795	2797
SINGLE DENSITY (FM)	yes	yes	yes	yes
DOUBLE DENSITY (MFM)	yes	yes	yes	yes
DATA BUS (True/Inverted)	true	inv	true	inv
SIDE SELECT OUTPUT	no	no	yes	yes
INTERNAL CLOCK DIVIDE	yes	yes	no	no

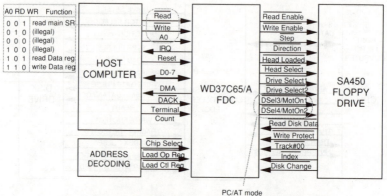

A0	RD	WR	Function
0	0	1	read main SR
0	1	0	(illegal)
0	0	0	(illegal)
1	0	0	(illegal)
1	0	1	read Data reg
1	1	0	write Data reg

PC/AT mode

**Figure 10.19 Western Digital WD37C65/A FDC
(courtesy of Western Digital Corp.).**

information necessary to perform a particular operation. During the execution phase, the FDC performs the operation it was instructed to do. After completion of the operation, status and other housekeeping information are made available to the host CPU. The data bytes sent to the WD37C65/A during the command phase are read out during the result phase in the order contained within the command table; the command code must be sent first, with the other bytes following in the prescribed sequence (no foreshortening of the command or result phases is allowed). Execution commences automatically following the sending of the last data byte in the command phase. Similarly, a command terminates following the last data byte read out of the result phase.

The four additional status registers ST0–3 are only available for reading during result phases, upon completion of a command. These registers are summarized in Figure 10.21.

The control register provides support logic which latches the two lsbs of the data bus upon the $\overline{\text{LDCR}}$ and $\overline{\text{WR}}$ becoming asserted. These bits are used to select the desired data rate, which in turn controls the internal clock generation.

The 8-bit data register stores data, commands, parameters and floppy-disk drive status information. The operations register provides support logic

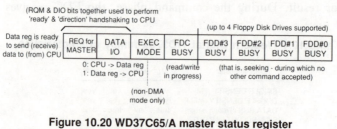

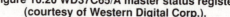

**Figure 10.20 WD37C65/A master status register
(courtesy of Western Digital Corp.).**

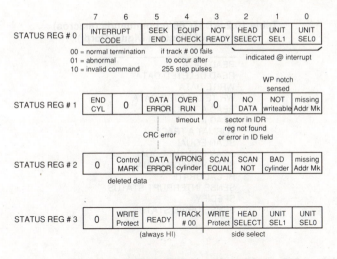

Figure 10.21 WD37C65/A status registers 0-3 (courtesy of Western Digital Corp.).

which latches the data bus following assertion of $\overline{\text{LDOR}}$ and $\overline{\text{WR}}$; it replaces the latched port in earlier floppy-disk subsystems used to control disk-drive spindle motors and selection of a particular drive (1-of-n, n being four typically).

Fifteen inbuilt macros (commands) are provided on the WD37C65/A, as indicated in Table 10.2. Each command is initiated by a multibyte transfer from the host CPU.

A sequence of nine bytes is required to place the FDC into read data mode, which loads the head (if not already loaded), waits for the head to settle, then begins reading ID address marks and fields. When the current sector number (stored in the ID register) matches the sector number on the diskette, the FDC reads data from the diskette to the disk controller, on a byte-by-byte basis. After one sector is read (and the CRC checked), the sector number is incremented and data read from the next sector onto the data bus; this constitutes a multisector read operation. A multitrack function allows the FDC to read data from both sides of a double-sided diskette. Should the FDC sense the index hole twice without finding the required sector, it sets the no data flag in status register #1, and terminates the read data command. An error in the CRC bytes is indicated by setting the data error flag in status register #1 (errors in the data field are indicated by the data error bit in status register #2). Encountering a deleted data address mark also terminates a read command.

A 9-byte sequence is also required to place the FDC into write data mode, which loads the head (if not already loaded), waits a predetermined head settling time, and begins reading ID fields. When a match is found, the FDC receives data from the host CPU on a byte-by-byte basis and outputs it to

Table 10.2 WD37C65/A commands (macros)
(courtesy of Western Digital Corp.).

READ DATA
READ DELETED DATA
WRITE DATA
WRITE DELETED DATA
READ A TRACK
READ ID
FORMAT A TRACK
SCAN EQUAL
SCAN LOW OR EQUAL
SCAN HIGH OR EQUAL
RECALIBRATE
SENSE INTERRUPT STATUS
SPECIFY
SENSE DRIVE STATUS
SEEK

the disk drive. After writing data into the current sector, the sector number is incremented, and the next data field written into; this constitutes a multisector write operation. This procedure continues until a terminal count signal is issued. The FDC reads the ID field of each sector and checks the CRC bytes; if a read error is detected, the data error flag of status register #1 is set and the write data command terminated.

A write deleted data command is the same as a write data command, except that a deleted data address mark is written at the beginning of the data field in place of the normal data address mark (F8 instead of FB for single density disks, as indicated previously in Figure 10.8). A read deleted data command is identical to a read data command, but with the following variation: when a data address mark is detected at the beginning of a data field and the SK-bit (bit 5 in the first command word) is LO, the data in that sector will be read, the control mark flag set in status register #2, and the command terminated. If the SK-bit is HI, that particular sector is skipped and the next one read.

A read track command is similar to read data, except that all sectors on a particular track are read as continuous blocks of data (even if errors in the ID or data CRC check bytes are detected). Multitrack or skip operations are not allowed with this command.

The read ID command enables the current head position to be determined. If the index hole is sensed twice without detecting a proper ID address mark, the missing address mark flag in status register #1 becomes set. Similarly, if no data is found, the ND flag in status register #1 is set.

Figure 10.22 shows the sequence of events which occur during a format track command. Following detection of the index hole, a template is written onto the diskette, comprising gaps, address marks, ID fields and data fields, as illustrated previously in Figure 10.8. Either system 3740 single density or system 34 double density format is used; the particular density in question is reflected in the N, SC, GPL and D command bytes, as indicated. Four data requests per sector are made by the FDC to the host CPU, for cylinder, head

PHASE	R/W	bit 7 bit 6 bit 5 bit 4 bit 3 bit 2 bit 1 bit 0	
COMMAND	W	0 MF 0 0 1 1 0 1	Command Codes
	W	x x x x x HS US1 US0	
	W	◄——N (# bytes / sector) ——►	bytes / sector
	W	◄——SC (# sectors / cylinder) ——►	sectors / track
	W	◄——GPL (gap length) ——►	gap 3
	W	◄——D (data pattern) ——►	filler byte
EXECUTION			FDC formats an entire track
RESULTS	R	◄——————ST0 ——————►	⎫ status information after
	R	◄——————ST1 ——————►	⎬ command execution
	R	◄——————ST2 ——————►	⎭
	R	◄——————C (cylinder #) ——————►	⎫
	R	◄——————H (head #) ——————►	⎪ (ID information has no meaning
	R	◄——————R (sector #) ——————►	⎬ for this particular command)
	R	◄——N (# bytes / sector) ——►	⎭

Figure 10.22 Format track command (courtesy of Western Digital Corp.).

and sector numbers, as well as the number of bytes per sector. This enables the diskette to be formatted with non-sequential sector numbers if so desired. The sector number (R) is updated following formatting of each sector, and the command terminated following detection of the index hole for a second time.

The scan command allows data being read from the diskette to be compared with data supplied from the main system, on a byte-by-byte basis. This continues until either the scan condition is not met (equal, low or high), the last sector is reached (end-of-track) or a terminal count signal is received. Should the scan condition not be met, the scan hit flag of status register #2 is set and the command terminated.

The seek command is used to move the read/write head from cylinder to cylinder, either in or out, with the stepping rate set previously by a specify command. No other commands can be issued while the WD37C65/A is involved with sending stepping pulses.

Recalibrate retracts the read/write head(s) to track #00, on both sides if so desired (if double-sided disk drives are in use).

The sense interrupt status command is used to determine the cause of a particular interrupt. Interrupts are cleared by reading (writing) data from (to) the FDC. Figure 10.23 shows the different interrupts which can be discriminated on the WD37C65/A FDC. A sense interrupt status command must be sent following a seek or recalibrate interrupt, otherwise the FDC will treat the next command as invalid. Sense drive status enables the present state of all four floppy-disk drives to be reflected in status register #3.

Figure 10.24 shows the interfacing of an MPI model 51/52 Flexible Disk Drive to an MC68000 CPU using a WD2797A FDC. The following MC68000 code describes how a diskette in such a system would be formatted, building up an image in memory as follows:

```
assemble track preamble information;
   for sector = 0 to MAXSEC do
      store sector image in memory;
   store track trailer information.
```

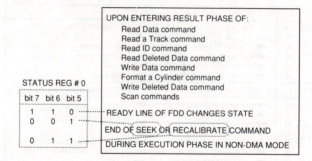

STATUS REG # 0

UPON ENTERING RESULT PHASE OF:
 Read Data command
 Read a Track command
 Read ID command
 Read Deleted Data command
 Write Data command
 Format a Cylinder command
 Write Deleted Data command
 Scan commands

bit 7	bit 6	bit 5	
1	1	0	⋯ READY LINE OF FDD CHANGES STATE
0	0	1	⋯
			END OF SEEK OR RECALIBRATE COMMAND
0	1	1	⋯ DURING EXECUTION PHASE IN NON-DMA MODE

Figure 10.23 Sources of interrupts (courtesy of Western Digital Corp.).

Interleaving is used in order to cut down seek times. If information is stored in sequential sectors, then a complete rotation of the disk would be necessary in order to move from sector n to sector $(n + 1)$. However, if the information is stored sequentially on every *second* physical sector, the read/write head only needs to be rotated two sectors before accessing the next logical sector. A simple yet effective scheme for mapping between logical and physical sectors is as follows: 1 3 5 7 . . . 2 4 6 8 . . .

DISK_FORMAT
  for track = 0 to MAX do
    build track image in memory
    write image to disk
    step_in

```
FORMAT:    move.b   #0,D0           ;starting @ track#00
           bsr      START           ;start the drive motor
           bsr      RESTORE         ;reposition R/W head over track#00
LOOP:      bsr      BUILD           ;build a track image in memory
           bsr      WRITE           ;format the track
           bsr      STEP__IN        ;move to next innermost track
           add.b    #1,D0           ;increment track count
           cmp.b    #34,D0          ;35 tracks done yet?
           ble      LOOP            ;if not, continue until there are
           bsr      RESTORE         ;if so, reposition R/W head
           move.b   #0,$30081       ;stop disk drive motor
           rts

START:     move.b   #$60,$30081     ;start disk drive motor
           move.l   #88000.,D1      ;initialize a 1/2 second timer (to
HALFSEC:   subq.l   #1,D1           ;allow motor to come up to speed)
           bne      HALFSEC         ;keep looping
           rts                      ;return after 1/2 second delay

RESTORE:   move.b   #7,$30001       ;FD2797A restore command
           bsr      DELAY           ;
```

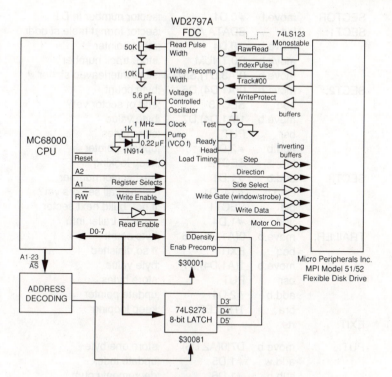

Figure 10.24 MC68000 FDD interface.

```
24µSEC:    move.b   $30001,D2      ;FDC command (status) register
           btst     #0,D2          ;test lsb of FDC status reg
           bne      24µSEC         ;if still busy, keep looping
           rts

DELAY:     move.w   #3688.,D3      ;initialize a 24 µs timer
MORE:      subq.w   #1,D3          ;
           bne      MORE           ;keep looping
           rts                     ;return after 24 µs

BUILD:     lea      TDATA,A1       ;track format table
           lea      BUFFER,A2      ;start addr of image buffer
           lea      INTLEAV,A3     ;intleave pattern start addr
           move.l   #0,D4          ;initialize table index
           move.l   #0,D5          ;initialize buffer index
HEADER:    move.b   0(A1,D4),D6    ;D6 = byte counter
           beq      SECTOR         ;end-of-track header?
           move.b   1(A1,D4),D7    ;byte stored in D7
           bsr      PUT            ;store count values
           add.b    #2,D4          ;update table pointer
           bra      HEADER         ;
```

```
SECTOR:     move.l    #0,D1               ;sector number in D1
SECT1:      lea       SDATA,A1            ;sector format table st addr
            move.b    #0,D4               ;reset pointer
            move.b    D0,TNUM             ;store track number
            move.b    0(A3,D1),SNUM       ;store interleaved sector #
SECT2:      move.b    0(A1,D4),D6         ;byte count
            beq       SECT3               ;end of sector yet?
            move.b    1(A1,D4),D7         ;byte value
            bsr       PUT                 ;store bytes
            add.b     #2,D4               ;update pointer
            bra       SECT2               ;keep looking
SECT3:      add.b     #1,D1               ;next sector number
            cmp.b     #14.,D1             ;finished all sectors yet?
            ble       SECT1               ;if not, build next sector
            add.b     #1,D4               ;point to trailer info
TRAILER:    move.b    0(A1,D4),D6         ;byte count
            beq       EXIT                ;if so, finished
            move.b    1(A1,D4),D7         ;byte value
            bsr       PUT                 ;store bytes
            add.b     #2,D4               ;update pointer
            bra       TRAILER             ;keep looping
EXIT:       rts

PUT:        move.b    D7,0(A2,D5)         ;store one byte
            add.w     #1,D5               ;update index
            sub.b     #1,D6               ;decrement count
            bne       PUT                 ;loop until finished
            rts

WRITE:      lea       BUFFER,A1           ;trailer info start address
INDEX:      move.b    $30001,D1           ;read FDC status register
            btst      #1,D1               ;index pulse?
            beq       INDEX               ;keep looping until detected
            move.b    #$F4,$30001         ;FD2797A write track command
            bsr       DELAY               ;24 µs delay
            bra       WAIT                ;wait for FDC interrupt
BYTE:       move.b    (A1)+,$30007        ;write byte to FDC data reg
WAIT:       move.b    $30001,D1           ;read FDC status register
            btst      #1,D1               ;data request bit set?
            bne       BYTE                ;if so, store next byte
            btst      #0,D1               ;if not, keep looping
            bne       WAIT                ;
            rts

STEP_IN:    move.b    #$57,$30001         ;FD2797A step command
            bsr       DELAY               ;24 µs delay
STP_LOOP:   move.b    $30001,D1           ;FDC Status Register
            btst      #0,D1               ;still busy?
            bne       STP_LOOP            ;keep looping until complete
            rts
```

TDATA:	.byte	40.,	$FF	;inter-sector gap – gap#4
				;(track preamble)
	.byte	6,	$00	;sync pulses
	.byte	1,	$FC	;Index Address Mark (IAM)
	.byte	26.,	$4E	;gap#1
	.byte	0		
SDATA:	.byte	6,	$00	;sync pulses
	.byte	1,	$FE	;ID Address Mark (IDAM)
	.byte	1		
TNUM:	.byte		$00	;track number
	.byte	1,	$00	;side number (double-sided)
	.byte	1		
SNUM:	.byte		$00	;sector number
	.byte	1,	$80	;sector length (128 bytes)
	.byte	1,	$F7	;two CRCs
	.byte	11.,	$4E	;gap#2
	.byte	6,	$00	
	.byte	1,	$FB	;data address mark
	.byte	128.,	$E5	;128 bytes of data
	.byte	1,	$FC	;two CRCs
	.byte	27.,	$FF	;inter-sector gap (gap#3)
	.byte	0		
BUFFER:	.even			
	.blkb	$1000		;4Kbyte block allocated here
INTLEAV:	.byte	1,5,9,13.,2,6,10.,14.,3,7,11.,15.,4,8,12.		

10.5.2 Motorola MC6843 FDC

The Motorola MC6843 FDC supports the IBM3470 single density format, but not the IBM34 double density one. It is designed to operate with an external 1 MHz PLL clock, in either polled or DMA modes (using an MC6844 DMAC in the case of the latter).

The MC6843 register set is shown in Figure 10.25. A total of 12 user-accessible registers are provided, as indicated. Like the FD279x and WD37C65/A FDC families, the MC6843 has a number of built-in macro commands to assist in writing disk driver software. These are summarized in Table 10.3. Both single sector and multisector reads and writes are possible. STZ positions the read/write head to the outermost track (track#00). The SEK command positions the head over the track specified by the contents of Current Track Address Register (CTAR), in readiness for a read (write) operation involving n sectors (where $n = $ CTAR – GCR). The RCR command is used to verify that correct data has written to the disk.

Free format reads and writes are also possible on the MC6843, where the user is able to define a format other than the IBM3470.

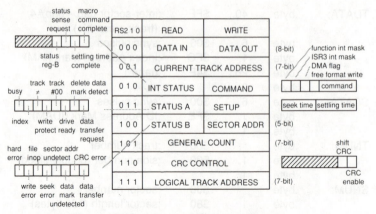

Figure 10.25 MC6843 FDC register set (courtesy of Motorola Inc.).

10.5.3 Intel i8272 FDC

Like the WD37C65/A and MC6843 FDCs, the Intel i8272 FDC has its own inbuilt set of macro commands, as well as being able to run in DMA mode (using an i2237 DMAC, for example). The i8272 supports both single-density and double-density formats (IBM3470 and IBM34 respectively), and can control up to four separate disk drives.

The i8272 FDC macro (command) set is summarized in Table 10.4. Each command is executed in a three-phase sequence, as follows: during the command phase, the CPU initiates a multibyte transfer to the FDC, which includes command and parameter information. Immediately following the transfer of the last command parameter, the FDC enters the execution phase, which is terminated when the last byte is read from (written to) disk. Following command execution, status information is made available to the CPU, after which the FDC is ready to enter a new command phase. During every result phase, individual status registers are made available for reading by the CPU.

Table 10.3 MC6843 macro commands (courtesy of Motorola Inc.).

Hex	MACRO	INSTRUCTION NAME
$2	STZ	SEEK TRACK#00
$3	SEK	SEEK
$4	SSR	SINGLE SECTOR READ
$5	SSW	SINGLE SECTOR WRITE
$6	RCR	READ CRC
$7	SWD	SINGLE SECTOR WRITE (with Delete Data Mark)
$A	FFR	FREE FORMAT READ
$B	FFW	FREE FORMAT WRITE
$C	MSR	MULTI-SECTOR READ
$D	MSW	MULTI-SECTOR WRITE

Table 10.4 Intel i8272 FDC command set(courtesy of Intel Corp.).

MT MFM SK	0 0 1 1 0				READ DATA
MT MFM SK	0 1 1 0 0				READ DELETED DATA
MT MFM	0	0 0 1 0 1			WRITE DATA
MT MFM	0	0 1 0 0 1			WRITE DELETED DATA
0 MFM SK	0 0 0 1 0				READ A TRACK
0 MFM	0	0 1 0 1 0			READ ID
0 MFM	0	0 1 1 0 1			FORMAT A TRACK
MT MFM SK	1 0 0 0 1				SCAN EQUAL
MT MFM SK	1 1 0 0 1				SCAN LOW OR EQUAL
MT MFM SK	1 1 1 0 1				SCAN HIGH OR EQUAL
0	0	0	0 0 1 1 1		RECALIBRATE
0	0	0	0 1 0 0 0		SENSE INTERRUPT STATUS
0	0	0	0 0 0 1 1		SPECIFY
0	0	0	0 0 1 0 0		SENSE DRIVE STATUS
0	0	0	0 1 1 1 1		SEEK

MT= multitrack selector
MFM/FM= mode selector
SK = skip (over data addr marks) flag

The specify command allows the head load/unload time and step rate time to be set. Seek causes the read/write head to be positioned over the specified track number. Recalibrate moves the head to track #00, after which the diskette can be initialized (writing the ID field, gaps and address marks for each sector). During a read/write operation, the FDC loads the head onto the disk surface, waits the specified load time, then begins reading the ID address marks and ID fields. When the sector address matches that specified during the command phase, the FDC transfers the data to memory. Sequential sectors will be read until the terminal count pin becomes asserted, either by the CPU or DMAC. Multitrack transfers are also possible.

Address line 0 is used to select between the main status register (0) and the data register (1). The main status register contains the status of each disk drive, as well as the FDC itself, as indicated in Figure 10.26. The four individual status registers are also shown in this figure. The read/write data register is used to transfer data, commands, parameter and status information.

Reading and writing of 'bad' sectors (those with hard errors on the disk surface) is possible using the read/write deleted data commands. Scan commands allow the data being read to be searched until a match is found.

10.6 HARD DISKS

Numerous developments have been made in recent years with hard-disk units, particularly for use with Personal Computers (PCs). Capacities in the 20–50 Mbyte range have become commonplace. Moreover, hard-disk units with removeable disk packs have proved popular. There are a number of different types of hard-disk drives; we shall consider Winchester and Bernoulli types here.

Winchester disks are multiplatter hard disks which use lightweight read/write heads that actually make contact with the disk surface when the disk drive is powered down. Contact with the disk surface while spinning

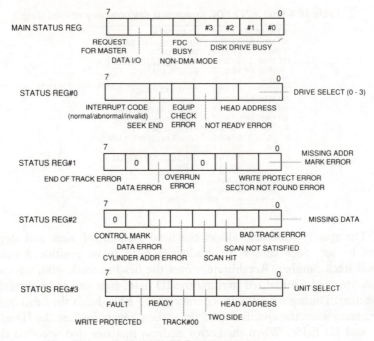

Figure 10.26 i8272 FDC status registers.

could lead to a 'head crash', where the magnetic coating becomes gouged from the disk surface, and the read/write head is also damaged. Some drives guard against such an eventuality by using a technique called auto-parking, where the read/write head is swung out of the range of the platters when not in use.

When the disk spins, the lightweight head is supported on a thin cushion of air. Because of the close proximity of the head to the disk surface, this results in larger signals being induced in the read/write head, which leads to higher storage capacities on physically small disks.

Figure 10.27 shows the construction of a typical Winchester disk drive. The actuator arm is mounted so that *angular* movement of the voice coil is translated to *linear* (track-to-track) movement of the read/write head. Very fast disk accesses are possible using this mechanism. Winchester disks were so named because the original ones were manufactured as dual units, each of 30 Mbyte capacity, and were said to resemble the twin cartridge Winchester rifle. Winchester disks are usually manufactured as sealed units, since the heads fly extremely close to the disk surface (a fraction of the wavelength of light in practice), and thus are very susceptible to minute dust particles. This increased susceptibility means that backups of information stored on disk are essential, often via streaming tape drives. The disks are usually quite rugged in construction as well.

In the Bernoulli drive of Figure 10.28, an air cushion is maintained

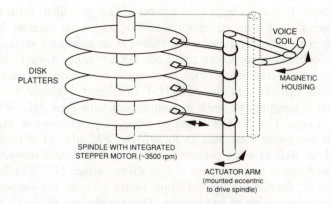

Figure 10.27 Winchester disk drive.

between the flexible diskette and the read/write head, with an air filter used to remove impurities. This type of disk drive depends on the Bernoulli lift principle, the same principle used to provide aeroplane lift (where, because of the convex shape of a plane's wing, a low pressure area is created on its upper side, thus lifting the plane into the air). As the disk spins near the rigid Bernoulli plate, air pressure causes the diskette to bend and make closer contact with the head. Should a drop in air pressure occur, the diskette simply falls away from the head, so that crashes become non-destructive. The penalty paid for such fail-safe crashes is wear and tear on diskettes, as a result of repeated bending.

Such hard-disk units require more sophisticated disk controller chips, two of which we shall consider briefly now.

The Intel i82062 and i82064 Winchester Disk Controllers specifically control the Shugart ST506 and ST412 drives (in both 5¼″ and 8″ form). A maximum transfer rate of 5 Mbit/second is possible. Sector lengths of between 128 and 1024 bytes are supported, as well as the possibility of using a seven byte sector extension for error correction purposes (using an external error

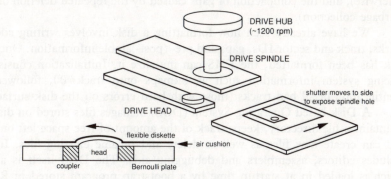

Figure 10.28 Bernoulli disk drive.

correction chip). The usual high-level commands are provided: restore, seek, read/write sector (with implied seek), scan ID, and write format. Multiple sector transfers are also supported. The i82064 is an enhanced version of the i82062, with onboard Error Correcting Code (ECC) (either 5- or 11-bit), and additional high-level commands (such as compute correction, set parameter).

Motorola manufacture the MC68454 Intelligent Multiple Disk Controller, which is designed to work in conjunction with their MC68459 Disk Phase Lock Loop. The MC68459 has an onboard programmable oscillator, and supports composite data rates up to 20 MHz. FM and MFM modulation is supported, as well as write precompensation and read data recovery. The MC68454 can be used to control up to four drives, either 5¼″ Winchester or floppy (single or double density). Multiple sector accesses are supported, as well as automatic handling of bad sectors. There is also inbuilt ECC, 4 Gbyte DMA capability and database management functions.

Advanced Micro Devices offer the Am9580 Hard Disk Controller and Am9581 Disk Data Separator. The latter chip acts as a serial data stream front-end processor, and incorporates its own PLL. Transfer speeds in the range 125 kbit/second through 1 Mbit-second (floppy) and 4–16 Mbit/second (Winchester) are supported. The Am9580 can be used to control up to four different drives (floppy or Winchester), and incorporates DMA capability and ECC. Dual sector buffers are included for data buffering, and a data format controller is also provided.

10.7 DISK OPERATING SYSTEM (DOS)

A File Management System (FMS) is an operating system facility which is used to perform all the tedious low-level disk operations on behalf of the user. It will provide such functions as opening (closing) files, copying, deleting, changing file names, reading (writing) files and so on. Typical functions handled by the FMS are the allocation of the appropriate number of sectors to a particular file, the writing of files into various sectors (contiguous or otherwise), and the compaction of gaps caused by the repeated deletion of files (garbage collection).

We have already seen how formatting a disk involves writing address marks, track and sector IDs, gaps and pre- (post-)amble information. Once the disk has been formatted, the FMS can initialize it. Initialization consists of placing system information such as bitmaps onto track#00, followed by identification of all bad tracks (those with hard errors on the disk surface).

A Disk-based Operating System (DOS) manages files stored on disk. It maintains a file directory, keeps track of the amount of free space left on disk and can create new files as well as delete and rename existing files. It also includes editors, assemblers and debugging aids. The DOS itself is a file, which is loaded in at startup time by a bootstrap program stored in ROM, hence the term booting up. (A bootstrap program is capable of loading itself

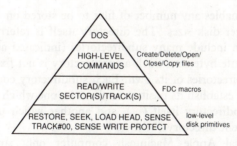

Figure 10.29 DOS hierarchy.

into RAM, hence it is able to 'pull itself up by its own bootstraps'.)

Figure 10.29 shows how a DOS is comprised of a hierarchy of modules. At the lowest level are the disk primitives supported by a disk controller chip such as the WD37C65/A, MC6843 or i8272 FDCs. The next level up involves the reading and writing of sectors (tracks), and is usually supported by inbuilt macros within the controller chips. The highest level is concerned with creating, deleting and changing the names of files. At the apex of the tree resides the DOS itself, which is usually concerned with more system functions than just disk I/O.

As a typical example of a DOS, let us turn our attention briefly to IBM's PC-DOS (originally developed by Microsoft as MS-DOS), used on its IBM PC and PC/AT computers. MS-DOS is an enhanced version of the earlier CP/M – Control Program for Microprocessors (which itself was an outgrowth of QDS – 'Quick-and-Dirty operating System').

Sectors of 512 bytes are used, with tracks on opposite sides of double-sided disks grouped together into cylinders. This effectively decreases disk access times, since two tracks can be read (written) without moving the read/write head (seek times are typically an order of magnitude longer than read/write times). An MS-DOS disk contains 40 cylinders (of two tracks each), with 9512 byte sectors per track.

A seven-sector directory is maintained on the first track, commencing on sector 6 (sector 4 on earlier eight sector/track disks). Each directory entry comprises 32 bytes, which contain the file name, (optional three character-) extension, attribute (hidden, user or system file), time and date of creation, number of the first occupied cluster (two consecutive sectors) and file size. Each directory sector can contain up to 16 file names, resulting in an overall maximum disk capacity of 112 files.

Two copies of a 2-byte file allocation table is maintained by MS-DOS. This table contains a pointer to the next cluster on the disk; FFFH indicates the last cluster in the file, whereas 0H indicates an unoccupied cluster. Deleted files have the first character of their file name changed to E5H, and all file allocation table entries are changed to zero.

More recent versions of MS-DOS incorporate a tree-structured directory which enables any number of files to be stored on disk, and is more efficient with larger disk sizes. The directory itself is referred to as the root directory, and can include many subdirectories (indicated as such by having bit 4 of the attribute byte set). Such a subdirectory is not fixed in length, and may contain subdirectories of its own. Each subdirectory contains two entries which enable it to establish its position in the tree, one which points to the first cluster in the subdirectory itself ('.'), and another which points to the first cluster of the parent directory ('..').

The original Apple Macintosh computer only supported flat file structures, but later versions supported a tree directory structure, in the form of the Hierarchical File Structure (HFS).

10.8 RAMDISK

A common I/O technique used on early computers was to 'fool' the CPU into thinking that a new peripheral device connected to the system was one for which a software driver already existed. This overcame the need to write a new I/O driver for each new device, so long as this driver could be made to simulate the already existing device. A similar reasoning lies behind the RAMdisk concept. Actually, there are two types of RAMdisk in common use. The first comes as a plug-in peripheral, which consists internally of semiconductor memory, but which interfaces to the computer as if it were a disk drive. As far as the OS is concerned, it acts as a fast, quiet disk drive.

The other type of RAMdisk is where an unused portion of main memory is made to look like a disk drive. This type of RAMdisk requires its own special software driver, and is only applicable in systems where there is plenty of spare memory (and as we all know, application programs tend to expand to consume whatever memory is available, so that less and less memory is in fact 'spare').

A typical example of where a RAMdisk is useful is in the IBM PC/AT, where 1 Mbyte of RAM is standard, but where the MS-DOS is restricted to 640K addressing. By having a portion of the 1 Mbyte RAM simulate a disk drive, this addressing limitation is readily overcome.

A RAMdisk makes use of freely available memory (either internal or external plug-in), in order to make this memory look like secondary disk storage. The OS is fooled into thinking that it is performing disk accesses, moving the read/write head to the correct 'position' in memory, loading the head onto the disk, and so on; whereas in reality it is accessing locations in semiconductor memory. In this manner, an already existing disk-driver routine can be utilized in interfacing what amounts to a very fast disk.

At initialization time (booting up), system utilities can be loaded from floppy disk into RAMdisk and thereafter accessed as required at much faster rates than would be possible from floppy disk. The main disadvantage with

RAMdisk is its volatility; unlike a disk drive, its contents will disappear following powering down of the system.

10.9 MAGNETIC CARDS

The proliferation of plastic credit cards during the 1970s and 1980s led to the development of the magnetic card as a suitable information storage medium for small computer systems. The standard credit card as used in Automatic Teller Machines (ATMs) has a magnetic stripe on its reverse side which is divided into three tracks, one each for the cardholder's name, their account number and account balance. A total of 40 characters are available for data storage.

The smartcard was first developed in France by Roland Moremo in 1974, and contains its own onboard processor and memory. More recent versions of the smartcard have been developed by Philips and GEC. The GEC smartcard, for example, contains a microcontroller and 256 kbytes of memory, as shown in Figure 10.30. Both chips are embedded within the plastic card, and moreover the card can be bent without breaking. (Recall from Chapter 2 that a silicon chip only amounts to few millimetres in size, and a thickness of a few tens of microns.)

A current loop is also buried within the plastic, whereby an electrical current can be induced by an electromagnet in a card reader, so that the card and reader do not have to make electrical contact for reading (writing). The GEC smartcard can handle data transfers at 9600 baud. The advantage of smartcards over magnetic stripe cards is that they are less prone to fraud; the Personal Identification Number (PIN) is stored within the card itself, along with credit limit information and records of previous transactions. Smartcards can also be used to gain privileged access not only to ATMs, but also to private or business premises, computer systems and so on. The Philips smartcard was adopted by the French government for electronic financial transactions. Note, however, that smartcards require information (such as available credit levels) from a centralized network in order to carry out transactions.

Recently, the Japanese have developed a super or very smartcard, which contains its own battery supply, miniature keyboard and LCD display, as illustrated in Figure 10.31. The I/O circuitry includes a controller for a

Figure 10.30 Magnetic smart card.

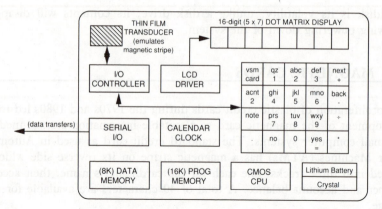

Figure 10.31 Super smartcard.

transducer used to emulate magnetic stripe signals, as well as high-speed data encryption circuitry.

Such very smartcards cards will no longer require telephone modem links to a host computer, since they will have all the necessary processing power onboard. Apart from their use in point-of-sale terminals, very smartcards will also be suitable for other functions, such as personal databases.

10.10 OPTICAL DISKS (CD-ROMs)

The type of disks discussed so far in this chapter have been of the magnetic type. We shall now turn our attention to optical disks. A lot of effort was expended by manufacturers during the mid 1980s in the wake of developments in the fields of both (analog) audio and video, namely with Compact Disks (CDs) and video disks.

The video disk was developed during the late 1970s. It stores video images as FM signals on a spiral track at a density of 16 000 tracks per inch, which amounts to hundreds of times higher storage capacity than floppy disks (and likewise tens of times higher density than Winchester disks).

In Section 10.4, we saw how, instead of maintaining a constant angular velocity, the disk speed of a CD-ROM is varied in order to maintain a constant recording density (and sector length) over the entire disk surface. The resulting blocks are then formed into a spiral, rather than into tracks and sectors, as with a magnetic disk drive. This has repercussions as far as disk file systems are concerned, since files will be distributed in *sequential* order on the disk surface. Constant Angular Velocity (CAV) disks readily support random file accesses, whereas CLV disks support sequential files.

Each successive turn of the (54 000-turn) spiral is spaced 1.6 microns apart on the 12 inch disk. The recording density is around 25 000 bits per

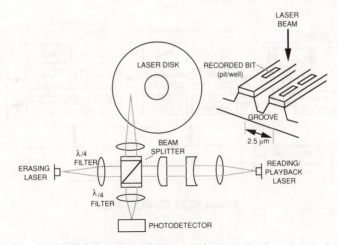

Figure 10.32 Optical disk (CD-ROM).

inch, which is an order of magnitude greater then magnetic disks. The positive-going half cycles of the FM signal are stored as pits or wells on the disk surface. A laser beam is trained on the grooves during playback to detect these pits for conversion back to video information. This same principle is used in digital optical disks, where the presence or absence of a pit indicates a 1 or a 0. This mechanism is illustrated in Figure 10.32.

The Sony CD was developed during the early 1980s. Up to 74 minutes of high-fidelity music can be recorded on a 12 cm disk. Computer manufacturers subsequently became interested in using these optical disks as mass storage media in computer systems. The CD-ROM first appeared during the mid 1980s, as a medium for distributing large databases, such as the Grollier Encyclopedia. Each 12 cm CD-ROM can store around 550 Mbyte of data, and support data accesses of around 176 kbyte per second. Compared with CDs, a CD-ROM has additional error correction built in, which reduces the uncorrectable error rate down to one in 10^{+13}. Figure 10.33 shows the internal construction of a typical CD-ROM.

What held up the widespread adoption of optical disks was their read-only nature. However, the development of first the Write Once Read Many (WORM) optical disk followed by the erasable (read/write) optical disk has pointed the way to the future (and perhaps to the death knell of magnetic disks?).

There are, at present, three different erasable optical systems under development. The first type uses a hybrid magneto/optical system, in which data is stored magnetically, on the same type of rigid polycarbonate platter as used in CD-ROMs. Data is rewritten by heating the magnetic surface of the disk with a laser, thereby reversing the magnetic domain stored there. The disadvantage of this type of disk is the relatively slow read/write time.

The NeXT computer incorporates a magneto/optical disk drive.

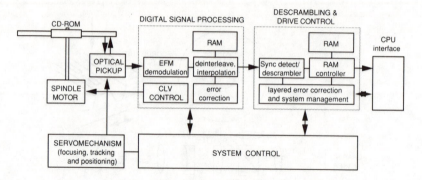

Figure 10.33 CD-ROM drive.

Rotational speed is 3000 rpm (10 times that of a CD-ROM), with an average seek time of around 96 ms. NeXT uses removeable 256 Mbyte cartridges, the one supplied originally containing the (Carnegie Mellon) Mach UNIX kernel and bundled software.

An alternative read/write optical disk is the phase charge type, where a tellurium-based film is switched between its (reflective) crystalline and (non-reflective) amorphous states upon the application of a laser. The most recently developed type of read/write disk is the dye polymer type, where data is stored as a series of non-permanent bumps on a dye polymer disk surface. A laser is used to create (remove) these bumps.

SUMMARY

In this chapter we have considered mass storage devices. We started with a discussion of magnetic tape, commonly used for archival storage. Tapes have a low cost per bit in terms of storage capacity, but suffer from slow access times due to their inherent serial access.

Magnetic disks offer random access mass storage, and thus are preferred as secondary storage devices, with programs (data) being loaded from disk to main memory as required. Both multiplatter hard disks and floppy-disk drives were considered. The formatting and data encoding (and recovery) of data onto floppy disks was treated in some detail. Bit shifting was explained, as was the technique used to overcome it, namely write precompensation. We saw how error correction is achieved using CRC checks.

The floppy disk controllers considered were the Western Digital WD37C65/A, Motorola MC6843 and Intel i8272. Some more recent 16/32-bit disk controllers were also briefly mentioned.

The functions of a disk operating system were discussed. Optical disks (CD-ROMs) were also introduced.

The interfacing to peripheral devices such as disk drives has been standardized somewhat by the upsurge of interest in the SCSI bus (discussed previously in Section 3.4.6).

REVIEW QUESTIONS

10.1 In relation to magnetic tape drives, what is meant by the terms record, inter-record gap and blocking?

10.2 Hard-disk units often use voice coil motors for positioning the heads over the desired track number, in order to decrease access times. What type of head positioning motor is more commonly encountered in low-cost floppy-disk drives?

10.3 What is meant by the term disk formatting?

10.4 Describe the IBM3740 and IBM37 floppy disk formats. Which is used for single-density and which for double-density diskettes?

10.5 Discuss the encoding and/or decoding of binary data to (from) the surface of a floppy disk.

10.6 Sketch encoded versions of $E6_{16}$ using both Manchester and MFM coding.

10.7 Why do you think sync pulses are encoded as 0s on a disk? and address marks as 1s?

10.8 What is meant by the term bit shifting, and how can it be overcome?

10.9 Assuming a disk drive uses a generator polynomial $g(x) = x^4 + x^2$, what CRC character is generated for the data 10100011_2?

10.10 What is meant by the term seek error? What other types of errors can occur with a disk drive?

10.11 Compare and contrast 8″ standard floppies, 5¼″ mini-floppies and 3½″ floppy disks, in terms of rotation speeds, number of tracks, number of sectors, number of bytes per sector and formatted capacities.

10.12 What common macros (commands) would be useful to have in a floppy disk controller?

10.13 What is meant by the term head crash? Is such an event catastrophic?

10.14 Explain the difference between a Winchester and a Bernoulli disk drive.

10.15 Explain the difference between a video disk, a compact disk, a CD-ROM and a WORM.

10.16 How does the formatting of a CD-ROM (optical disk) differ from that of a magnetic disk, and what repercussions does this have regarding file access mechanisms on both?

10.17 What is meant by the abbreviation DOS?

10.18 Rewrite the MC68000 formatting code given in the text assuming a MC6843 FDC is used in place of the WD2797. Repeat for an i8272 FDC. Rewrite this program in i8086 assembly code rather than MC68000.

Appendix A
Motorola MC68000 Family

A.1 MC68000 REGISTER SET

Motorola upgraded their first-generation MC6800 8-bit processor into the MC6809 during the late 1970s. The second-generation MC6809 also has an 8-bit architecture, but is capable of performing 16-bit operations. The first true 16-bit processor from Motorola came in the form of the MC68000, released in 1979. Internally, the MC68000 has a 32-bit architecture, but only 24 address lines and 16 data lines are brought out to the external world. Higher speed versions followed in the years 1980 through 1982. In 1982 a virtual memory version – the MC68010 – was released.

1984 saw the release of the full 32-bit processor in the 68000 family – the MC68020 – which incorporated such enhanced features as an on-chip instruction cache, coprocessor support and dynamic bus sizing. This was followed in 1987 by the release of the MC68030, which exhibited increased internal parallelism, on-chip instruction and data caches, as well as an on-chip (paged) memory management unit.

The 24 address lines of the MC68000 result in a 16 Mbyte direct addressing range, whereas the MC68020 (and MC68030) have a direct addressing range of 2^{32} or 4 Gbyte.

The MC68000 register set is shown in Figure A.1. There are sixteen 32-bit general-purpose registers (8 data and 8 address), a 32-bit program counter and a 16-bit status register. Address registers can also be used as stack pointers. (8-bit)Byte, (16-bit)word and (32-bit)longword manipulations are all supported on data registers, but only word and longword transfers are permitted with address registers.

The writing of position-independent code (the ability to both load and run programs anywhere in memory) is supported by virtue of its (PC) relative addressing modes and Load Effective Address (LEA) instruction. There are built-in (hardware) debugging aids, such as the TRAP instruction and TRACE facility. High-level language compiler development is facilitated by the ready availability of several general-purpose registers, the large direct addressing range and the MOVEM, LINK, UNLK, CHK and TRAPV instructions (see Section A.3).

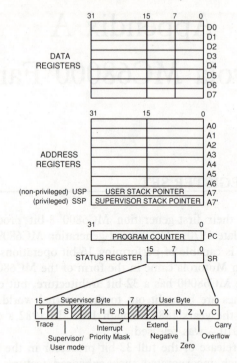

**Figure A.1 Programmer's model of Motorola MC68000
(Courtesy of Motorola Inc.)**

The writing of operating systems is facilitated by the ability to operate in either supervisor or user modes, user mode having restricted system access. The current operating mode is reflected in the S-bit of the status register. Operating System development is further facilitated by the TRAP, MOVEM, CHK and TAS instructions, vectored interrupts and built-in DMA support. Depending on whether the MC68000 is running in user or supervisor mode, either the User Stack Pointer (USP) or Supervisor Stack Pointer (SSP) will be the currently activated stack pointer.

The MC68000 status register comprises a supervisor byte and a user byte. The user (least significant) byte contains the condition codes – individual bits which flag the condition of the CPU at any particular instant. The four rightmost bits mirror the condition code bits of the earlier 8-bit MC6800 – negative/zero/overflow/carry. An extend bit has been added to the MC68000 status register, which is affected by the results of certain arithmetic, logical and shift/rotate instructions.

The single interrupt bit on the MC6800 has been expanded to three bits on the MC68000, resulting in seven possible interrupt levels, six of which can be masked off; level 7 cannot be masked off and thus functions as a non-maskable interrupt, whereas level 0 corresponds to no interrupts.

The T-bit indicates when the processor is running in (instruction-by-

Table A.1 MC68000 addressing modes (courtesy of Motorola Inc.).

	MODE	EFFECTIVE ADDRESS	EXAMPLE
DIRECT	DATA REGISTER DIRECT ADDR REGISTER DIRECT	EA=Dn EA=An	move.l A0,D1
ABSOLUTE	ABSOLUTE SHORT ABSOLUTE LONG	EA = (next word) EA = (next 2 words)	clr.b $1000
RELATIVE	(PC)RELATIVE + OFFSET (PC) RELATIVE + INDEX + OFFSET	EA = (pc)+d_{16} EA = (pc)+(Xn)+d_8	imp * +10 [*=current (PC)]
INDIRECT	(address) REG INDIRECT POSTINCR REG INDIRECT PREDECR REG INDIRECT REG INDIRECT + OFFSET indexed REG IND + offset	EA = (An) EA = (An);An<-An+N An <- An-N;EA=(An) EA = (An)+d_{16} EA = (An)+(Xn)+d_8	clr.b (A2) clr.w (A1)+ clr.w -(A1) clr.w -10(A2) clr.w $4(A0,A2)
IMMEDIATE	IMMEDIATE DATA QUICK IMMEDIATE	#xxx #1 - #8	move.b #$FF,D0
IMPLIED		(SR,USP,SSP,PC)	rts

instruction) Trace mode; in Trace mode an exception is generated after each instruction execution, which allows a debugger program to monitor the current program execution.

A.2 MC68000 ADDRESSING MODES

Fourteen addressing modes are available on the MC68000, as shown in Table A.1. These can be grouped together into six distinct types: register direct, absolute data, (program counter) relative, address register indirect, immediate and implied. By combining instruction types, data types and addressing modes, more than 1000 different instructions are supported in the MC68000.

MC68000 family instructions contain three types of information: the type of operation, the operand(s) on which it is to be performed, and the operand size (byte, word or longword). The operand address can be specified in terms of either a register or an Effective Address (EA), or alternatively can be implicit, depending on the instruction (the EA is the place from which the CPU either fetches an operand or stores a result). Instructions can extend in length from one to five words.

Most MC68000 instructions specify the operand location by using an EA, which consists of two 3-bit fields: the (addressing) mode field and the register field. Additional information, if required, is stored in the effective address extension (the next word(s)).

The address register indirect with displacement (offset) mode requires a 16-bit sign extended displacement. In the address register indirect with index mode, a 16-bit extension is used, which comprises an 8-bit signed (two's complement) extension together with the contents of an index register. Consider for example the instruction:

clr.b $10 (A1,A2)

Suppose A1 contains $230000 (hexadecimal), and A2 contains $FFFC_{16} (which is the signed binary representation of -4_{10}). The EA is found by adding together the contents of A1 and A2, together with the displacement $10. This calculation yields $23000C, which in this particular example indicates which memory byte is to be cleared.

Some MC68000 instructions make implicit reference to the program counter, system stack pointer, supervisor stack pointer, user stack pointer or status register. Typical examples include ANDI to SR (status register), JMP (program counter) and TRAP (supervisor stack pointer and status register).

A.3   MC68000 INSTRUCTION SET

The MC68000 assumes that memory is organized on a byte-addressable basis, with lower addresses corresponding to higher order bytes (the i8086, by way of contrast, employs byte swapping). Moreover, both instructions and multibyte data must be aligned on even byte boundaries (no such alignment is necessary with the i8086).

The MC68000 instruction set comprises eight different instruction types: data movement, integer arithmetic, logical, shift and rotate, bit manipulation, binary coded decimal, program control and system control.

A.3.1 Data Movement Instructions

The MOVE instruction provides the basic method of data acquisition (the transfer and storage of data) on MC68000 family processors. The various EA modes allow for manipulation of both data and addresses. Movement is always from a source to a destination, as indicated in the instruction field, with the condition code bits in the status register being set according to the outcome of this move.

Movement (of either data or addresses) can be from memory to memory, memory to register, register to memory or register to register. Data moves are possible on byte, word and longword operand sizes, but only word and longword moves are allowed when moving addresses.

Care has to be taken however in the use of MOVE instructions; most significant bits are not automatically cleared when using byte moves. For example move.b #123,D1 only affects the low-order byte of D1, whereas move.l #123,D1 clears the upper most significant bits to zero.

The different effects on memory and registers should also be noted; a

MOVE byte from a register to memory results in the least significant byte in the register moving into the most significant byte in memory. This is referred to as big-endian addressing (the i8086, by way of contrast, uses little-endian addressing).

MOVEM is a move multiple registers instruction. MOVEP is used to transfer data between a data register and alternate bytes of memory; it is useful in interfacing to 8-bit peripherals. The MOVEP instruction is useful when communicating to only one half of a 16-bit data bus.

MOVEQ is an inherently quicker method of moving 8-bit immediate data to a data register, rather than using moveb #xxx,Dn (where the 8-bit data is automatically sign extended to 32-bits, prior to the transfer).

The LEA instruction first calculates an effective address, using PC-relative addressing if required, and loads it into an address register. Since this results in loading the register with an address rather than data stored at a memory location (as movea.l #table,A0 would), then this facilitates the writing of position-independent code. PEA is a similar instruction, used for pushing an effective address onto the stack.

LINK and UNLK allow for the allocation and deallocation of additional stack space; LINK (and allocate stack) saves a pointer to the current workspace, and reserves a new one of specified size. UNLK reverses the operation, releasing the allocated stack space and restoring the pointer to the old one.

The EXG instruction exchanges the contents of two registers, while SWAP exchanges the least significant and most significant words within a specified register.

A.3.2 Integer Arithmetic Instructions

The four basic arithmetic operations are supported on MC68000 family processors: ADD, SUBtract, MULtiply and DIVide. Add and subtract are available for both address and data operations, using byte, word or longword operands (however, address operations are limited to 16- or 32-bit operands). All five condition code bits of the status register are affected by the results of ADD or SUB instructions, and all but the X-bit are affected by MUL and DIV (the C-bit is always cleared).

Data and address compare operations are also provided; compare does not affect the operands, just the appropriate condition code bits in the status register (it can be thought of as a SUB, but without the final storing of the result). The clear and negate instructions may be used on all three operand sizes.

Multiply and divide operations are possible in either signed or unsigned form, with each having slightly different effects on the condition code N-bit depending on the result. A word multiply produces a longword product, while a longword divided by a word yields a word quotient and a word remainder.

Built-in error checking is provided on division, with an attempt to divide by zero causing a trap, and overflow setting the V-bit of the status register (but leaving the original operands unaffected).

The extended instructions ADDX, SUBX, NEGX and EXT (sign extend) are used for multiprecision and mixed-size arithmetic. Floating-point arithmetic is supported via an MC68881(2) floating-point coprocessor (designed to operate with an MC68020(30)CPU).

The test operand instruction TST sets the condition codes as the result of a comparison of the operand with zero, but the result is not stored. The test and set instruction TAS is used for synchronization in multiprocessor systems, as a semaphore.

A.3.3 Binary Coded Decimal Instructions

Multiple precision arithmetic operations on (packed) BCD numbers are accomplished on MC68000 family processors using the add decimal with extend ABCD instruction, subtract decimal with extend SBCD, and negate decimal with extend NBCD. Both operands need to be located either in data registers or in memory. In the latter case, the operands are addressed using the predecrement addressing mode, which facilitates BCD arithmetic.

A.3.4 Logical Instructions

The four standard logical operators AND, OR, ExclusiveOR and NOT (invert), can be used on all three operand sizes. A similar set of instructions exist for immediate data, namely ANDI, ORI and EORI.

A.3.5 Shift and Rotate Instructions

Shift operations, both left and right, are available in arithmetic as well as logical form. Left shifts lead to the same result, but affect the condition code bits differently. (For example, the V-bit is always cleared for LSL, but is set if the msb changed at any time during the execution of ASL.) Right shifts differ inasmuch as ASR always replicates the most significant (sign) bit following each shift; LSR, on the other hand, always clears the msb. ASR and LSR again affect the condition codes differently.

Rotate instructions are available in two versions; one affects the extend bit of the status register (ROXL/R), the other does not (ROL/R).

All shift and rotate instructions can be used on either registers or memory. Register shifts and rotates can be used on all three operand sizes, and allow for a shift count in a data register. This shift count can be specified as the six least significant bits of a data register (giving a range from 0–63), or as immediate data (giving a range from 1–8). Memory shifts and rotates, on the other hand, can only be used on words, and only shifted (rotated) one bit at a time.

A.3.6 Bit Manipulation Instructions

The MC68000 provides several bit manipulation operations. In the bit test (BTST) instruction, the designated bit in the destination operand is reflected in the Z-bit of the status register (prior to any change); the bit itself remains unchanged. The bit number can be specified either as immediate data or as the contents of a data register. Likewise, bit clear (BCLR) clears the designated bit to zero, and bit set (BSET) sets it high. Bit change (BCHG), on the other hand, toggles the bit (sets it to the opposite of what it was previously). Bit manipulations can be performed on both registers and memory, with the bit number specified either in a data register or as immediate data; register operands are always 32 bits long, while memory operands are always 8 bits long.

A.3.7 Program Control Operations

Ordinarily, a program will continue execution from the next consecutive memory location, as indicated by the contents of the program counter. Programs can continue execution at a non-sequential memory address on an MC68000 by using either branch or jump instructions. Branches use the PC-relative addressing mode, where the address branched to is a specified number of bytes away from the current program counter location (in either a positive or negative direction). This two's complement displacement can be either 8 or 16 bits long, thus allowing for a range of ± 32 kbytes. Jumps, on the other hand, use absolute addressing modes, and as a result can relocate to anywhere within the entire 16 Mbyte address space (4 Gbyte on the MC68020,30).

Whereas jumps are unconditional (like the go-to construct in Fortran), branches can be either unconditional or conditional; conditional branches are what give a processor its decision-making capability (that is the ability to take one of several courses of action depending on what has taken place beforehand).

Branch on condition (Bcc) can be used with all the following conditions:

CC	carry clear	LS	low or same
CS	carry set	LT	less than
EQ	equal	MI	minus
GE	greater or equal	NE	not equal
GT	greater than	PL	plus
HI	high	VC	no overflow
LE	less or equal	VS	overflow

Decrement and branch on condition DBcc supports the writing of high-level language constructs (such as while . . . do loops in Pascal). So long as the condition is not met, the low-order 16 bits of the (data) counter register are decremented by one. If the result is −1, program execution continues at (PC). This is the loop termination condition. However if the result is not −1 execution continues at (PC) + 16-bit sign-extended displacement, usually negative, in order to yield a branch back to the start of the loop. On the other hand, if the condition is true, no operation is performed, and execution continues from the next sequential location in memory.

DBcc supports all 14 branch conditions shown previously for Bcc, as well as F(alse) and T(rue). Scc sets a byte to all 1s if the condition is true, or clears to all 0s if false.

With BSR and JSR (branch/jump to subroutine), the address of the next instruction in sequence is pushed onto the stack prior to making the branch/jump, and similarly the PC is popped from the stack following execution of RTS (return from subroutine).

A.3.8 System Control Operations

Any instructions which alter the context of the CPU naturally enough need to be used with care. Accordingly, system control operations are restricted to supervisor mode; inadvertent and unexpected results could eventuate if users were allowed access to these instructions (owing to spurious settings of the T-, S- and I-bits in the status register). The privileged group of MC68000 system control operations include loading a new value into the status register, logical operations on the entire status register, relocating the USP, return from exception RTE, RESET and STOP.

Reloading the condition codes, logical operations on the condition code bits and copying the contents of the status register are system control operations which are allowed both in supervisor and user modes. Likewise, CHK, TRAP and TRAPV are unrestricted.

MOVE USP is restricted because users should not be able to relocate stacks anywhere in memory (like overwriting the system stack, for instance; note that additional address checking against permitted bounds is required in order to prevent this from occurring altogether).

Under normal conditions, the CPU is involved with the execution of instructions; its only other possible states are halted or exception processing. Exceptions (to normal instruction execution) include interrupts, TRAP instructions and tracing. Care is thus required in exception handling, including return from exception (RTE); this is why RTE is a privileged instruction.

The RESET instruction causes a hardware reset of all external devices connected to the CPU; program execution then continues with the next instruction in sequence. A hardware reset, on the other hand, loads the SSP from locations $0 (most significant word) and $2 (least significant word), loads the PC from locations $4 and $6, then commences program execution from (PC).

STOP moves the immediate operand into the status register, advances the program counter to point to the next instruction, and then stops the fetch, decode and execution of any further instructions. The processor subsequently resumes execution when either a trace, interrupt or reset occurs (with trace only if the T-bit was set prior to execution of STOP, and with interrupts only if the incoming interrupt has a priority higher than the current mask).

CHK checks the low-order word in a register against a (two's complement) upper bound. An exception is generated if the register value is less than zero, or alternatively if it is greater than the upper bound.

The TRAP instruction initiates exception processing. The program counter and status register are placed onto the system stack, and execution continues from the address supplied. Exception processing is also initiated if the overflow bit in the status register becomes set during execution of a TRAPV instruction.

Traps are useful for implementing system calls from user programs, for example, to selected routines in a firmware monitor (software-in-ROM). A TRAP can generate 16 different exception vectors; for example, on Motorola's MEX68KECB single-board computer, TRAP#14 is used to provide such a system call function. The calling sequence is as follows:

```
move.b #[function no.],D7    ;256 functions available,128
trap #14                     ;of which are user defined
```

The 68KECB trap handler uses this function number to access the address of the desired routine in a lookup table, and then transfers control to that address. Most functions return to the user's program upon completion.

A.3.9 Multiprocessor Operation

There is one MC68000 instruction which executes an indivisible read–modify–write bus cycle, during which the CPU cannot respond to bus requests from external devices. Such bus cycles allow the CPU to read from a memory location and write back to that same location during a single cycle. This provides a secure means for intertask and interprocessor communication.

The only MC68000 instruction which uses such an indivisible cycle is test and set (TAS), which sets the N- and Z-bits of the status register according to the result of a byte test. The most significant bit of the operand is also set. Thus a semaphore facility is provided which allows for the synchronization of several system processes, or indeed processors, by using a memory location shared by both.

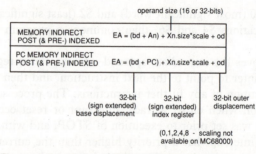

Figure A.2 Additional MC68020(30) addressing modes.

A.3.10 Additional MC68020 Instructions

The MC68020 CPU includes all the addressing modes and instructions of the earlier MC68000, and incorporates a couple of enhanced modes not available on the MC68000. For instance, word and longword offsets can be used with the indexed register indirect mode. Moreover, unlike the MC68000, operands are no longer required to align on even byte boundaries.

Two addressing modes not available on the MC68000 are memory and PC indirect with pre- (and post-) indexing, and these are shown in Figure A.2. The ability to multiply by a scaling factor (1, 2, 4 or 8) with these two modes further enhances their usefulness.

As far as the instructions proper are concerned, there are several enhancements over the earlier MC68000 instruction set. 32-bit signed and unsigned multiplies are supported (the MC68000 only supports 16-bit multiplies). Likewise, whereas the MC68000 only supports division of a 32-bit dividend by a 16-bit divisor, yielding a 16-bit quotient and 16-bit remainder, the MC68020 supports division of both 64- and 32-bit dividends by 32-bit divisors, producing 32-bit quotients and remainders.

A CMP2 instruction has been included, which enables the contents of a register to be compared with both an upper and lower bound in one operation, with the condition codes set according to the results of this comparison. (Recall that the MC68000 CMP instruction was capable of performing only a single comparison at a time.)

The MC68000 EXT instruction enables 8-bit bytes to be sign extended into 16-bit words, or alternatively 16-bit words to be sign extended into 32-bit longwords. The MC68020 EXTB instruction allows bytes to be sign extended into longwords.

The BCD instruction group has been expanded to include PACK and UNPK instructions for converting between BCD and byte encoded ASCII or EBCDIC strings.

The MC68020 bit field instructions are analogous to the bit manipulation instructions presented in Section A.3.6, but operate on fields of up to 32 bits rather than on single bits. They comprise bit field test and set, test and clear, test and change, insert, extract and find first one. All bit field instructions set the N- and Z-condition code bits prior to performing their respective operations; the msb of the field is copied into the N-bit, and the NOR of all bits in the field is written into the Z-bit.

Program control instructions have been enhanced in the MC68020. A Call Module instruction, and its counterpart Return from Module, allow previously developed software modules (possibly from a library) to be included readily in programs. Both instructions reference module descriptors, which contain control information for entry into a module. A module frame is created on the top of stack, and the current state saved in the frame. The immediate data in call#[data],[EA] specifies the number of argument bytes to be passed to the called module.

An additional return instruction has been included in the MC68020 set, namely the Return and Deallocate parameters. It is similar to the MC68000 RTS instruction in that it pulls a PC value from the stack, but it loads a different value into the stack pointer; the 16-bit displacement data is sign extended to 32-bits, then added to the SP (with the condition codes remaining unaffected).

Additional MC68020 system control instructions are Move Control Register, Breakpoint, CHK2 and TRAP on condition code. MOVEC is a privileged instruction, in which the control register is one of the following: SFC, DFC, CACR, CAAR, VBR, USP, MSP or ISP (MC68020 registers will be discussed in Section A.11.4). CHK2 checks whether the contents of a register (byte, word or longword) are within the range specified by an upper and lower bound.

Apart from the MC6800 TRAP instruction, the MC68020 also includes a conditional trap TRAPcc, which allows for traps on the 16 conditions mentioned previously in Section A.3.7. The BKPT instruction can also generate a trap; it facilitates the writing of debug monitors and real-time hardware emulators.

Apart from the MC68000 Test And Set instruction, the MC68020 also provides another read–modify–write instruction, namely Compare And Swap with operand. This instruction can be used to perform secure update operations on system control data structures in a multiprocessing environment. A dual Compare And Swap instruction is also provided.

As mentioned earlier, the MC68020 incorporates support for coprocessors, and hence includes 'test coprocessor condition' instructions in its instruction set. Allowance has also been made for user-defined coprocessor instructions in this instruction group.

A.3.11 Additional MC68030 Instructions

The MC68030 incorporates all of the previous MC68000 and MC68020 instructions, as well as new instructions to support its on-chip paged memory

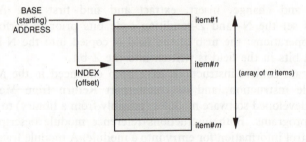

Figure A.3 MC68000 array support.

management unit. These latter instructions are a subset of the MC68851 Paged Memory Management Unit coprocessor.

A.4   MC68000,20,30 DATA STRUCTURES SUPPORT

MC68000 family processors provide support for the following data structures: arrays, stacks, queues and lists. Arrays are supported via the indexed addressing mode, while stacks and queues are supported by the address register indirect with postincrement (and predecrement) addressing modes. Lists are supported by the CAS and CAS2 instructions on the MC68020(30).

Figure A.3 illustrates the use of the indexed addressing mode, discussed previously in Section A.2, in indexing into an array of m (16-bit) items. The base address is stored in an address (pointer) register, and the index in a separate index register. Indexing into the array is achieved using an indirect register move with offset, following appropriate alteration of the index register.

A stack is a Last-In-First-Out (LIFO) list, with data being either pushed onto the stack or pulled from it. The system stack (address register 7) is used implicitly by many instructions. This is either in the form of the supervisor stack pointer (SSP) or the user stack pointer (USP), depending on whether the S-bit of the status register is set or cleared. During subroutine calls, for example, the program counter is saved on the active system stack. However, during exception processing, both the program counter and status register are saved on the supervisor stack.

As indicated in Figure A.4, the stack can either build down from high memory locations to low, or alternatively up from low to high. In the former case, the predecrement addressing mode is used to push items onto the stack, and the postincrement addressing mode to pull items from the stack. The reverse applies in the case of the latter, postincrement addressing is used to push items onto the stack, and predecrement addressing to pull items from it.

Byte data must be placed onto the stack in pairs when mixed with word or longword data to ensure that the stack does not become misaligned upon

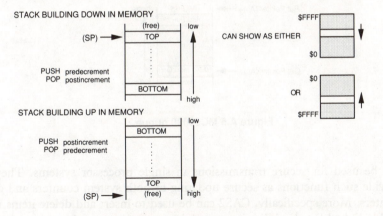

Figure A.4 MC68000 stack growth.

retrieval of the data. Again, word and longword accesses must be on word boundary (even) addresses.

Data workspace can also be allocated on the stack, immediately following the return address and saved registers. This is often necessary in structured high-level languages such as Pascal.

A queue is a First-In-First-Out (FIFO) list, and like the stack is readily implemented on MC68000 family processors. Queues can either grow up or down in memory: (An)+ addressing is used to grow a queue from low memory to high, whereas −(An) addressing is used to grow a queue from high memory to low. In either case, a register pair is required, since queues are pushed from one end and pulled from the other.

Figure A.5 shows a queue growing from low memory to high: after a put operation, the put address register points to the next available space in the queue; the get address register remains unchanged, and continues to point to the next item to be removed from the queue. Following a get operation, the get address register points to the next item to be removed from the queue, and the put address register remains unchanged (and points to the next available space in the queue). A similar procedure applies for the growing of a queue from high memory down to low, but using the predecrement addressing mode rather than postincrement.

For implementing a queue as a circular list buffer, the address register needs to be checked, and if necessary adjusted before the put or get operation is performed. This is done by subtracting the buffer length, in bytes (in other words, put and get operations are restricted to modulo-buffer_length).

It should be noted in passing that if the head and tail point to the same location, then we have a null or empty list.

We saw earlier how the MC68020(30) CAS and CAS2 instructions facilitate interprocessor communication in multiprocessing systems. They can

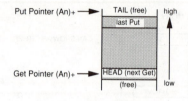

Figure A.5 MC68000 queue.

also be used for secure transmissions in single processor systems. They can provide such functions as secure updating of both system counters and global pointers. More specifically, CAS2 can be used to insert and delete items into a doubly-linked list. Each list entry contains a pointer not only to the next item, but also to the previous one.

The advantage of using the CAS2 instruction is that the swapping of Last and Next pointers can be achieved in one operation.

A.5   MC68000 PINOUT

Figure A.6 shows the functional diagram of the MC68000. Since it is a word-based machine, address line 0 does not appear on its pinout. The MC68000 is available in a 64-pin Dual In-Line (DIL) package, 68-pin chip carrier, quad pack and pin grid array form.

Address line 0 is an internal signal used within the CPU to address upper and lower bytes; it is replaced externally by the $\overline{\text{UDS}}/\overline{\text{LDS}}$ pair. The 23 address lines on the MC68000 allow for the direct addressing of 8 megawords of memory.

The MC68000 requires a single power supply (+5 V and ground), with two pins being provided for each power rail. The system clock can run at speeds in the range 4–16.7 MHz.

Five asynchronous bus control lines are provided on the MC68000. Address Strobe ($\overline{\text{AS}}$) is an output signal from the CPU to indicate a valid address currently appearing on the address bus. Read/$\overline{\text{Write}}$ (R/$\overline{\text{W}}$) is used in conjunction with the Upper and Lower Data Strobes ($\overline{\text{UDS}}/\overline{\text{LDS}}$) to indicate the type of transfer currently in progress (word or byte, reads or writes). $\overline{\text{Data}}$ $\overline{\text{Transfer Acknowledge}}$ ($\overline{\text{DTACK}}$) is a handshake signal returned from a peripheral (or memory) to the CPU to indicate that the data transfer has been successful.

Motorola incorporated synchronous peripheral support into the MC68000, thus enabling designers to take full advantage of the already existing MC6800 family of support chips upon first release of the MC68000. The relevant signals are E(nable/synchronizing) clock, Valid Memory Address and Valid Peripheral Address.

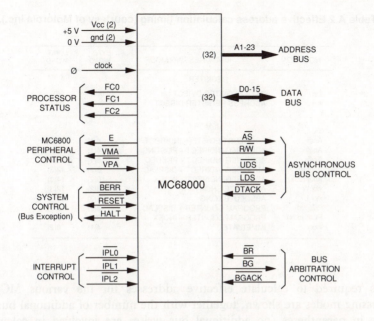

Figure A.6 MC68000 functional diagram (courtesy of Motorola Inc.).

The three Function Control lines FC0–2 indicate the current state of the processor (user/supervisor program/data space, or CPU space). The system control lines comprise $\overline{\text{BERR}}$, $\overline{\text{RESET}}$ and $\overline{\text{HALT}}$; both Reset and Halt are bidirectional, and thus can be asserted by either the CPU or a peripheral device. Bus Error ($\overline{\text{BERR}}$) is an input signal to the CPU which flags problems such as non-responding devices, failure to generate an interrupt vector number and illegal access as detected by a memory management unit. Depending on the relation between $\overline{\text{BERR}}$ and $\overline{\text{HALT}}$, an attempt could be made to re-execute the current bus cycle, or exception processing could be initiated (exception processing is discussed in Section A.8).

A.6 MC68000 INSTRUCTION FETCH, DECODE AND EXECUTE

MC68000 instructions contain information on both the instruction type and the location of the operand(s) on which this operation is to be performed. Operands can either be implicit (located in specific registers), located in general-purpose registers (data or address), or located in an effective address (pointed to by an address register). In the latter case, additional external memory fetches could be necessary in order to compute an instruction's effective address. This is indicated in Table A.2, where the numbers of clock

Table A.2 Effective address calculation timing (courtesy of Motorola Inc.).

NOTATION	ADDRESSING MODE	BYTE, WORD	LONG-WORD
	REGISTER		
Dn	DATA REGISTER DIRECT	0(0)	0(0)
An	ADDRESS REGISTER DIRECT	0(0)	0(0)
	MEMORY		
An@	ADDRESS REGISTER INDIRECT	4(1)	8(2)
An@+	ADDR REG INDIRECT + POSTINC	4(1)	8(2)
An@-	ADDR REG INDIRECT + PREDEC	6(1)	10(2)
An@(d)	ADDR REG INDIRECT + DISPLAC	8(2)	12(3)
An@(d,ix)	ADDR REG INDIRECT + INDEX	10(2)	14(3)
xxx.W	ABSOLUTE SHORT	8(2)	12(3)
xxx.L	ABSOLUTE LONG	12(3)	16(4)
PC@(d)	PROGRAM COUNTER + DISPLAC	8(2)	12(3)
PC@(d,ix)	PROGRAM COUNTER + INDEX	10(2)	16(4)
#xxx	IMMEDIATE	4(1)	8(2)

cycles required to calculate effective addresses for the various MC68000 addressing modes are shown, together with the number of additional bus read cycles in parentheses (no additional bus writes are involved in calculating effective addresses however). The direct addressing modes require no external bus reads, since the effective address is contained within the operand itself.

Instruction times include instruction fetch, operand read and operand write cycles. In the case of the move.w D0,D1 instruction, for example, the effective addresses are contained within the operand itself. This instruction therefore requires only a single fetch, and would execute in four clock cycles (assuming read and write cycle times take four clock cycles each). On the other hand, the move.w (A0),(A1) instruction would take 12 cycles to execute; two external bus reads are required in order to determine the addresses specified indirectly by A0 and A1, and a bus write is required for moving the result to the effective address (with each of these taking four clock cycles).

The MC68000 processor incorporates a two word tightly-coupled prefetch mechanism. This prefetching enhances performance, since an operand will already have been fetched while the instruction type is being decoded.

A.7   SYSTEM CONTROL

The Function Control lines FC0–2 indicate the current status of the processor to all connected peripherals, and is only meaningful when the address strobe $\overline{AS}$ is asserted. The most significant bit FC2 indicates whether the processor is involved with user (non-privileged) or supervisor (privileged) operations. The other two lines indicate whether program or data segments are currently active, or whether accesses to CPU space are in progress. This latter case is restricted to supervisor mode, and could involve interrupt acknowledge cycles, or breakpoints, coprocessor operations or module calls and returns in the case of the MC68020(30).

MC68000 family processors can be in one of three states: normally they will be fetching, decoding and executing instructions, but at times could be either handling exceptions or halted. An exception is a deviation from normal instruction execution, caused either internally by certain instructions, or externally by events such as interrupts, bus errors or a hardware reset. Exception processing provides the processor with an efficient context switch mechanism to handle unusual conditions. The HALT condition is an indication that a catastrophic hardware failure has occurred; a halted processor can only be restarted by an external RESET.

The S-bit in the status register indicates whether the CPU is in user or supervisor mode. In user (non-privileged) mode, certain instructions are not permitted, namely those which would result in alterations to the processor status (such as operations on the status register itself). No such restriction applies in supervisor (privileged) mode though. It is thus possible to maintain system integrity and security by discriminating use of these two modes. This greatly facilitates the development of operating systems, with users' application programs running in non-privileged mode.

The only way of moving from user to supervisor mode is during exception processing (using a TRAP instruction); as soon as the exception is processed, the CPU returns to user mode. Transition from supervisor to user can be achieved by using one of the MOVE (ANDI or EORI) to SR instructions, or by a return from exception RTE.

A.8 EXCEPTION PROCESSING

There are four steps involved in exception processing on MC68000 family processors: firstly the status register is copied internally by the CPU, the S-bit is set to indicate supervisor mode, and the T-bit cleared to inhibit tracing. Secondly, the exception vector is calculated; this tells the CPU whereabouts in memory to jump (or vector) in order to execute the appropriate exception handler routine. The current processor context is then saved, by placing the contents of the program counter and status register onto the supervisor stack. Lastly, the new processor context is found and the processor switches to instruction execution mode once more, beginning execution at the location indicated by the new program counter contents.

Exceptions can be generated either internally or externally. Externally generated exceptions are interrupts, bus error and reset (processor restart). Internally generated exceptions can be caused by certain instructions, address errors or tracing. The TRAP, TRAPV, CHK, and DIV instructions on the MC68000 can all generate exceptions as part of their normal execution

	VECTOR NO	(Hex)ADDR	TYPE OF EXCEPTION	
supervisor program space	0	0	RESET: initial SSP	
	1	4	RESET: initial PC	
supervisor data space	2	8	BUS ERROR	
	3	C	ADDRESS ERROR	
	4	10	ILLEGAL INSTRUCTION	
	5	14	DIVIDE-BY-ZERO	
	6	18	'CHK' INSTRUCTION	
	7	1C	'TRAPV' INSTRUCTION	
	8	20	PRIVILEGE VIOLATION	
	9	24	TRACE	
	10	28	UNIMPLEMENTED INSTRUCTION	
	11	2C	UNIMPLEMENTED INSTRUCTION	
	12	30	(unassigned-reserved)	
	13	34	COPRO. PROTOCOL VIOLATION	
	14	38	FORMAT ERROR	(68020, 30 only)
	15	3C	UNINITIALIZED INT. VECTOR	
	16-23	40-5C	(unassigned-reserved)	
	24	60	SPURIOUS INTERRUPT	
	25	64	LEVEL1 INT. AUTOVECTOR	
	.	.	.	
	31	7C	LEVEL7 INT. AUTOVECTOR	
	32	80	TRAP#00 INSTRUCTION	
	.	.	.	
	47	BC	TRAP#15 INSTRUCTION	
	48-63	C0-FC	(unassigned-reserved)	
	64-255	100-3FF	USER INTERRUPT VECTORS (192)	

(vector address = vector no. * 4)

Figure A.7 Exception vectors (courtesy of Motorola Inc.).

sequence. TRAPV results in the event of an arithmetic overflow occurring, CHK if a subscript is out of bounds, and DIV from an attempt to divide by zero. All three will force an exception if a runtime error is detected. The TRAPcc, cpTRAPcc, CHK2, CALLM, RTM and RTE MC68020(30) instructions will also generate exceptions.

TRAP is an inbuilt system call mechanism; 16 different traps are available (on the MEX68KECB single-board computer, for example, Trap #14 is used to implement supervisor calls). Traps can also be used to set breakpoints, as an aid in debugging programs.

Single-stepping of instructions is possible on MC68000 processors via the inbuilt TRACE mechanism, since an internal exception is generated immediately following each instruction. This can also prove useful in program debugging. Illegal instructions, attempted word fetches from odd addresses, attempted reads from (or writes to) unimplemented addresses and attempted privilege violations will also cause exceptions.

In the event of multiple exceptions occurring simultaneously, a three-tier priority exists, with RESET having priority, for example, over address errors, which in turn have priority over traps and interrupts.

The exception vectors (the starting addresses of each respective exception handler routine) are shown in Figure A.7. The first two vectors belong in the supervisor program space, and correspond to a 110_2 function

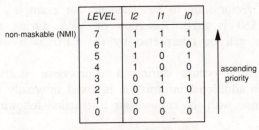

Figure A.8 Interrupt mask.

code, whereas vectors 2–255 are included in the supervisor data space
(FC = 101_2).

A.8.1 Interrupts

There are seven interrupt levels possible on the MC68000. These range in
priority from level 7 down to level 1, as shown in Figure A.8. An input of 000_2
on the IPL lines corresponds to no interrupt. The CPU does not respond
immediately to interrupts; they are made pending until detected in between
instruction executions. Interrupts will then only cause an exception if their
priority level is higher than the interrupt mask contained within the status
register (bits 8–10). Only levels 1–6 can be masked out; thus level 7 represents
the Non-Maskable Interrupt (NMI) on MC68000 family processors.

The address for the processor to jump to in response to a particular
interrupt can be derived in one of two ways; either the interrupting device can
supply an 8-bit vector number, or this vector number can be supplied
automatically by the processor. In either case, the CPU translates the vector
number into the corresponding exception vector simply by multiplying by
four. This exception vector contains the starting address of the appropriate
interrupt service routine. Autovectors reside in memory locations $64–$7C, as
indicated. Locations $100–$3FF are reserved for user-defined interrupt
vectors.

The MC68000 responds to valid interrupts in the following manner: the
processor is switched into privileged mode, the current contents of the status
register are saved on the supervisor stack, and tracing is suppressed. The CPU
fetches the appropriate vector number, outputs Interrupt Acknowledge (111)
on pins FC0–2 and the interrupt level on address lines A1–3. If the external
device is providing the vector number, then it does so on the lower byte of the
data bus (D0–7). The interrupting device further indicates that this is a valid
peripheral address by returning $\overline{\text{DTACK}}$ along with the vector number.

In the case of a peripheral device not initializing its vector number
following a reset, then it will use the uninitialized interrupt vector $0F. If no

device supplies a vector (due to bus timeout, for example), the spurious interrupt vector $60 is used. Assertion of $\overline{\text{VPA}}$ during the interrupt acknowledge cycle will be interpreted by the CPU as a request to use autovectoring.

If an interrupt occurs during a coprocessor instruction on a MC68020(30), then additional information is saved internally to enable the processor to continue with the coprocessor instruction following the return from exception.

A.9   ASYNCHRONOUS BUS CONTROL

The MC68000 uses an asynchronous bus, which means it can cater for peripherals of varying access speeds. It has the added advantage that data transfers are more definite since handshaking is an integral part of an asynchronous bus system.

The asynchronous bus control signals on the MC68000 are $\overline{\text{AS}}$, R/$\overline{\text{W}}$, $\overline{\text{UDS}}$, $\overline{\text{LDS}}$ and the $\overline{\text{DTACK}}$ handshake signal. The MC68000 is a word-based machine, but by using various combinations of the two data strobes it is also possible to perform byte transfers (both read and write). In the case of a byte write, the same data appears on both the upper and lower eight data lines. If neither data strobe is asserted, then no valid data appears on the data bus, irrespective of the signal activity on the R/$\overline{\text{W}}$ line. Address line 0 is an internal signal used within the MC68000, but it is not brought out to the outside world; resolution down to the byte level is achieved using $\overline{\text{UDS}}$ and $\overline{\text{LDS}}$.

The sequence of events for a word read is as follows: firstly R/$\overline{\text{W}}$ is set HI (for reading), and the corresponding function code (user or supervisor) placed on the FC0–2 pins. The address in question is placed on address lines A1–23 and $\overline{\text{AS}}$ asserted. Next $\overline{\text{UDS}}$ and $\overline{\text{LDS}}$ are both asserted. The peripheral (or memory) places its data on the data bus and asserts $\overline{\text{DTACK}}$. The data is then latched into the CPU, after which $\overline{\text{UDS}}$, $\overline{\text{LDS}}$ and $\overline{\text{AS}}$ are all negated. Finally, the peripheral (memory) removes its data from the bus and negates $\overline{\text{DTACK}}$. The processor then continues onto its next cycle. A similar procedure is followed for the writing of a word to a peripheral (or memory); similarly, a longword read/write would take two such cycles.

In the event of an MC68000 being connected to slow peripherals (or memory), wait states will automatically be inserted until the peripheral (memory) can respond with the desired information.

A.9.1 Bus Arbitration

Three lines on the MC68000 are devoted to bus arbitration, these being Bus Request ($\overline{\text{BR}}$), Bus Grant ($\overline{\text{BG}}$) and Bus Grant Acknowledge ($\overline{\text{BGACK}}$). These signals allow for the sharing of the system bus between the CPU and some

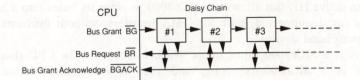

Figure A.9 Daisy chain bus arbitration.

other potential bus master, such as a DMA controller. The peripheral device first asserts $\overline{BR}$. At the completion of its current cycle, the processor asserts $\overline{BG}$, and upon receipt of this signal the peripheral device asserts $\overline{BGACK}$, which is a broadcast signal to all other potential bus masters (including the CPU) to indicate that this peripheral has temporary control of the bus. The peripheral negates $\overline{BR}$, the processor negates $\overline{BG}$ and three-states (disables) its connections to the system bus. Then the new bus master is free to carry out the transfers it desires. (It should be noted in passing that under such a bus arbitration scheme the external device effectively has a higher priority than the CPU.)

In systems with multiple bus masters, there needs to be some external arbitration scheme in order to determine which device should be given priority. One simple scheme is daisy chaining, which is shown in Figure A.9, where the $\overline{BG}$ signal from the MC68000 has to be offered first to each device further up the chain. The bus is only given to the requesting device if no other device further up the chain wants it at that particular time. Thus the closer the device is to the CPU, the higher is its priority.

A.10 INTERFACING TO SYNCHRONOUS PERIPHERALS

The earlier 8-bit MC6800 is a synchronous processor. It requires a two-phase non-overlapping clock, having a duty cycle (the proportion of time it is high) of around 40%. MC6800 peripherals expect a synchronizing E-clock together with a Valid Memory Address (VMA) signal, which indicates that valid information currently appears on the address bus. Data transfers in a MC6800 system are set up during the $\varnothing 1$ phase, but actually take place on the trailing edge of the $\varnothing 2$ or E-clock. Since the MC6800 uses a non-overlapping two-phase clock, then successive peripheral accesses can be carried out on successive E-cycles. Data Bus Enable (DBE) echoes $\varnothing 2$, and is used to provide the bus driving capability for actually writing to peripherals.

While the MC68000 is an asynchronous processor (and hence more versatile than the MC6800), it nevertheless can support MC6800-type synchronous peripherals as well as MC68000 asynchronous types. More specifically, it can supply both $\overline{VMA}$ and the synchronizing E-clock output, which runs at one tenth of the speed of the MC68000 system clock. $\overline{VMA}$ on the MC68000 differs from that on the MC6800 however in that it is active LO rather than active HI; this allows the MC68000 to place its buses into a high-impedance (or disconnected) state for DMA transfers, without inadvertantly selecting peripheral devices.

$\overline{\text{VPA}}$ is a MC68000 input signal which indicates to the CPU that the peripheral is a MC6800-style one, and that data transfers should be synchronized with the E-clock. It can be pulled HI by a pull-up resistor. The assertion of $\overline{\text{VPA}}$ during an interrupt acknowledge cycle indicates that autovectoring should be used for interrupts.

Synchronous support was built into the MC68000 to take advantage of the wide range of MC6800 support chips already available at the time of its release. The MC68020 and MC68030, being later entries into the marketplace, do not have this built-in synchronous support, but rely on asynchronous MC68000 peripheral (and coprocessor) support, both of which have become readily available in the intervening years. Typical of such asynchronous support chips is the MC68230 Parallel Interface/Timer chip, discussed in Chapters 4 and 8. Typical coprocessor support chips are the MC68851 Paged Memory Management Unit (PMMU) and the MC68881(2) Floating Point Unit(s) (FPU).

A.11 MC68020

The 32-bit MC68020 offers a number of enhancements over the earlier MC68000. Most notable are dynamic bus sizing, on-chip instruction cache and coprocessor support.

The earlier MC68000 had 23 address lines and 16 data lines brought out to the outside world, and was a physically large (64-pin) IC when manufactured in a Dual In-Line (DIL) package. Bringing out all 32 lines of address and data in such a DIL package for the MC68020 proved unfeasible. Instead, the MC68020 is fabricated in pin grid array or leadless chip carrier form.

Figure A.10 shows the MC68020 pinout in functional form. Unlike the MC68000, address line 0 is brought out on the MC68020. Thus there is no longer any need for two data strobes, so that $\overline{\text{DS}}$ and A0 together perform the function previously carried out by $\overline{\text{UDS/LDS}}$ (namely access down to the byte level).

The single asynchronous handshake $\overline{\text{DTACK}}$ line of the MC68000 has been replaced by two on the MC68020, namely $\overline{\text{DSACK0,1}}$. The other asynchronous bus control lines are $\overline{\text{ECS}}$, $\overline{\text{OCS}}$, $\overline{\text{DBEN}}$ and $\overline{\text{RMC}}$. $\overline{\text{ECS}}$ and $\overline{\text{OCS}}$ flag the start of a bus cycle. $\overline{\text{DBEN}}$ prevents external buffer contention while the R/$\overline{\text{W}}$ line is changing. $\overline{\text{RMC}}$ indicates that the current cycle is an indivisible read–modify–write cycle (used to implement semaphores in shared-memory multiprocessor systems).

Two additional interrupt control signals are provided on the MC68020,

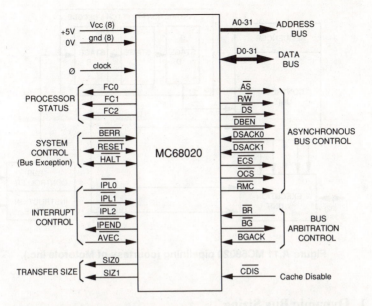

Figure A.10 MC68020 functional diagram (courtesy of Motorola Inc.).

namely $\overline{\text{IPEND}}$ and $\overline{\text{AVEC}}$. The former indicates a pending interrupt, while the latter can be used by a peripheral device to request the CPU to generate a vector number automatically.

It will be recalled that on the MC68000, operands have to be aligned on even byte boundaries. No such restriction applies with the MC68020, however, performance is maximized if data is aligned in this manner (since multiple bus cycles are required in the case of operand misalignment).

The MC6800 prefetching mechanism discussed in Section A.6 is taken a stage further in the MC68020. Each portion of Figure A.11 operates semi-independently of the other three. This leads to a high degree of concurrency, while at the same time maintaining synchronization between instruction execution and bus operation. The bus controller fetches instructions from the data bus and then loads them into the decode unit and on-chip cache. The sequencer and control unit manage the execution unit, internal busses and internal registers.

The performance of the MC68020 is further enhanced by the inclusion of a three-stage instruction pipe, also indicated in Figure A.11. The pipe allows the concurrent operation of up to three words of a single multi-word instruction, or of three consecutive single-word instructions. Instructions are loaded from either external memory or the on-chip cache during instruction prefetch into stage B. Instructions are passed from stage B to stage C, where any immediate data or extension words required by the control and execution units will already reside. Fully decoded and validated instructions will issue forth from stage D of the pipe.

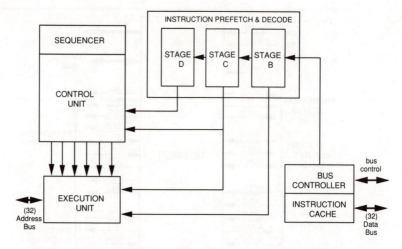

Figure A.11 MC68020 pipelining (courtesy of Motorola Inc.).

A.11.1 Dynamic Bus Sizing

The MC68020 Data Transfer and Size Acknowledge lines combine to indicate the size of the transfer currently taking place on the bus. Moreover, the number of bytes being transferred during the current bus cycle is indicated on the two SIZ lines. During an operand transfer cycle, the slave device signals its port size (8, 16 or 32 bits) and transfer status (complete or incomplete) using $\overline{\text{DSACK0,1}}$.

A.11.2 On-chip Instruction Cache

The MC68020 incorporates an on-chip instruction cache which further enhances system throughput. The principle behind using cache is that, in general, programs spend most of their time either in tight loops or within a few main routines. This phenomenon is referred to as locality of reference. Once these active code segments are loaded into cache, the processor does not need to make any more fetches from external memory, thus significantly improving program execution speed. Moreover, since external bus activity is greatly reduced, more bus bandwidth is made available for other bus masters, such as multiprocessors or DMA controllers. Performance is further improved by allowing the processor to make simultaneous accesses to cache and external memory.

As indicated in Figure A.12, the MC68020 on-chip cache is organized as 64 longwords, each of which has a 25-bit tag and a valid status bit. Each tag consists of the upper 24 address bits together with the FC2 bit. This

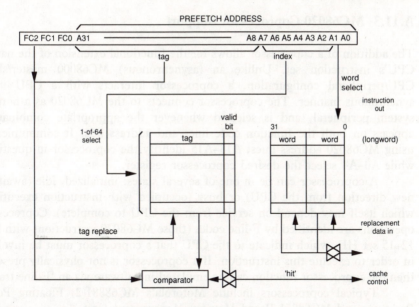

Figure A.12 MC68020 on-chip instruction cache (courtesy of Motorola Inc.).

effectively partitions the 4 Gbyte addressing range of the MC68020 into 256 byte blocks.

Assuming the cache is enabled, whenever an instruction fetch occurs it is first checked to see if the desired word is already present in the cache. This is done by first using address bits 2 to 7 to index into the cache, selecting one of the 64 entries therein. Then address bits 8–31 and FC2 are compared with the tag entry. If these are identical, then a cache hit results (providing the valid bit is set). Address bit 1 is then used to select which of the two stored words is required.

If there is no match, or if the valid bit is zero, then a cache miss occurs and the instruction is fetched from external memory. Moreover, since the MC68020 prefetches instructions as longwords aligned on even word boundaries, then *both* cache words will be updated, regardless of which word actually caused the miss.

Cache control is provided by the Move Cache Control Register (MOVEC) instruction. This privileged instruction allows the cache to be enabled, cleared or frozen (in which case the cache is enabled but cache misses do not result in entries being updated). Individual cache entries, contained in the cache address register, can also be cleared (Valid bit = zero).

An external Cache Disable ($\overline{\text{CDIS}}$) pin allows the cache to be disabled dynamically by external hardware, irrespective of the state of the enable bit in the cache control register.

A.11.3 MC68020 Coprocessor Support

The addition of a coprocessor allows for the functional extension of the native CPU's instruction set. Unlike an (asynchronous) MC68000 master/slave CPU/peripheral configuration, a coprocessor interacts with a CPU in a synchronous manner. The coprocessor connects to the MC68020 as a normal system peripheral, and is selected whenever the appropriate combination appears on both the function code lines and address bus. It communicates using MC68020 address lines; A13–A15 identify the coprocessor in question, while A0–A4 select the desired coprocessor register.

A coprocessor can be in one of several states: initialized, idle (awaiting new direction from the CPU) or busy (occupied with instruction execution, which itself may depend on service from the CPU to complete). Coprocessor operations are identified by F-line codes (those MC68020 instructions with bits 12–15 set HI), which indicate to the CPU that a coprocessor must be invoked in order to execute this instruction. If a coprocessor is not physically present, then the coprocessor function can be emulated in software via an 'F-line trap'.

Typical coprocessors include Motorola's MC68881(2) Floating Point Processor and MC68851 Paged Memory Management Unit.

A.11.4 MC68020 Register Set

The MC68020 includes all the MC68000 registers mentioned previously in Section A.1, as well as a number of additional special-purpose registers, as indicated in Figure A.13. The vector base register allows the MC68020 to support multiple exception vector tables, or alternatively to relocate one such table to a more convenient location. The alternate function code registers allow the supervisor to access any address space. Two registers are provided to control the operation of the on-chip instruction cache, namely the cache control and cache address registers. The four least significant bits of the cache control register allow either individual cache entries or the entire cache to be cleared, the cache contents to be frozen, and the cache to be enabled (disabled) under software control. A Cache Disable control input is included in the MC68020 pinout for applications where the cache can be disabled by hardware.

A.12 MC68030

The MC68030 is an enhanced 32-bit microprocessor which offers around twice the throughput of its predecessor, the MC68020. Increased internal parallelism results from its Harvard-style architecture (which allows for concurrent accesses of its separate data and address buses) and two clock cycle bus accesses. The MC68030 is shown in block diagram form in Figure A.14.

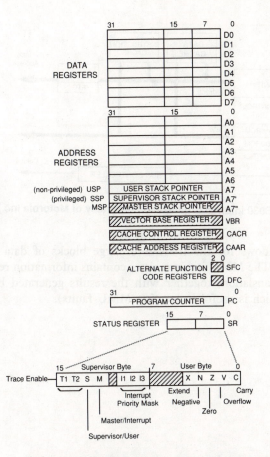

Figure A.13 Programmer's model of Motorola MC68020 (courtesy of Motorola Inc.).

Instruction execution can proceed concurrently with accesses to either or both of its on-chip caches, the on-chip MMU and the bus controller.

Two internal caches are provided on the MC68030, one for data and one for instructions, with both having a 64 longword capacity. Unlike the MC68020, these longwords are stored in a 16 × 4 array, rather than a 64 × 1 array. Address bits 2 and 3 together select one of the four longword blocks (and its associated valid bit). Moreover, since there are only 16 entries, the index is formed from A4–A7, rather than A2–A7, as on the MC68020.

The MC68030 incorporates an on-chip Paged Memory Management Unit (PMMU). Additional instructions have been included in its instruction set to control this MMU, and are in fact a subset of the instruction set of the MC68851 PMMU coprocessor. A CPU root pointer contains a descriptor to the first pointer to be used in a search of the translation table for the page descriptors corresponding to the current task. Transparent translation registers

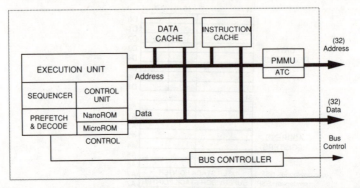

Figure A.14 MC68030 internal organization (courtesy of Motorola Inc.).

are used to define windows for the transfer of large blocks of data using untranslated addresses. The MMU status register contains information relating to a specific address translation, together with the results generated by the PTEST instruction (which is useful in locating MMU faults).

Appendix B
Intel iAPX86 Family

B.1   i8086 ARCHITECTURE

The first Intel 16-bit processor, the i8086, was introduced in 1979. It was based on the earlier 8-bit i8080 processor, and indeed could execute all i8080 instructions as a subset of its own instruction set. Added features included signed 8- and 16-bit arithmetic, efficient interruptible byte-string operations, improved bit manipulation and support for re-entrant code, position-independent code, dynamically relocatable code and multiprocessing.

Externally, the i8086 has 16 data lines and 20 address lines, which gives it a 1 Mbyte direct addressing capability, although this is divided into 64 kbyte segments, since the i8086 registers are only 16-bits wide. A separate 64 kbyte I/O space is also available, as shown in Figure B.1 (Intel processors use ported I/O, although memory-mapped I/O can also be used if so desired).

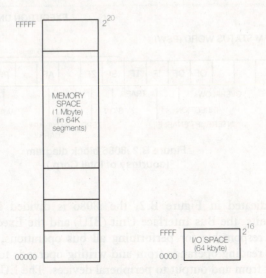

Figure B.1 i8086 memory and I/O address spaces.

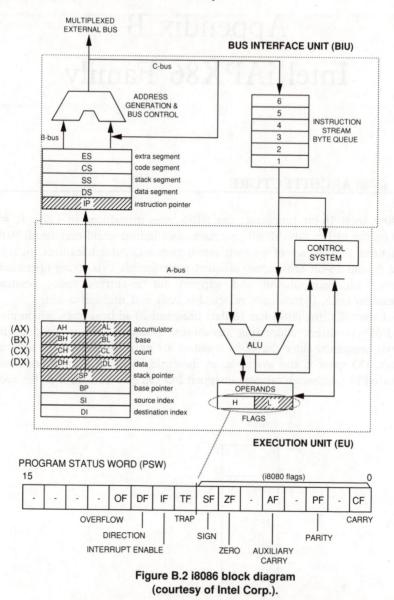

**Figure B.2 i8086 block diagram
(courtesy of Intel Corp.).**

As indicated in Figure B.2, the i8086 is divided into two separate processing units, the Bus Interface Unit (BIU) and the Execution Unit (EU). The BIU is responsible for performing all bus operations, such as fetching instructions, reading operands from and writing operands to memory, as well as data input from and output to peripheral devices. The EU is responsible for instruction execution. Both units operate concurrently, which results in more efficient use of the system bus as well as higher system throughput.

Two 16-bit register banks are provided in the i8086, one in the BIU and the other in the EU. Four registers in the EU bank (AX–DX) are general data registers. The remaining registers in this bank comprise two 16-bit memory base pointers (SP and BP) and two 16-bit index registers. The second register bank, in the BIU, consists of the instruction pointer and four segment registers, the latter allowing up to four 64 kbyte program or data segments to be accessed at any one time.

The 8-bit flag register of the i8080 was expanded into a 16-bit Program Status Word (PSW) in the i8086; the PSW includes the i8080 flags as its least significant byte. There are six read-only status flags, namely carry, (even) parity, auxiliary carry (from low nibble to high), zero, sign and overflow. There are three read/write control flags, namely trap, interrupt enable and direction. The direction flag determines whether string instructions automatically increment or decrement addresses, such that transfers occur either from low to high or from high to low addresses.

Other members of the Intel advanced processor (iAPX86) family include the i8088, i80186, i80286 and i80386. The i8088 is the 8-bit version of the i8086; it has a 16-bit internal architecture, but only 8 data lines and 20 address lines externally. The i80186, first introduced in 1982, incorporates the dozen or so ICs needed to form a minimum i8086 system onto a single chip. The i80286 extends the internal partitioning of the i8086, and incorporates on-chip memory management, but retains segmented memory addressing. This 16-bit processor was first introduced in 1983. It was not until 1986 that Intel's first offering in the 32-bit arena was forthcoming, in the form of the i80386.

Besides internal partitioning, Intel have also carried through the concept of external partitioning into all iAPX86 family members, via such coprocessors as the i8087, i8089, i80287 and i80387.

B.2 i8086 REGISTER SET

All four general-purpose data registers can be accessed either as a 16-bit word, or as two 8-bit bytes; in the former case the register is referred to as AX (BX, CX, DX), and in the latter as AL for the low-order byte and AH for the high-order one (and similarly for the other three data registers). All data manipulation instructions, such as ADD or AND, can be used on all registers, but some addressing modes are limited to certain registers. For example, CX is used to store the number of bytes being transferred in a string instruction, AX(AL) is used for I/O transfers, and DX is used to store I/O port addresses. These dedicated register functions are summarized in Table B.1.

The two pointer registers and two index registers are used for storing offset values for use by the BIU in calculating 20-bit addressing information. The stack pointer holds an offset which, when added to the stack segment register, points to the top-of-stack. The base pointer holds an offset which, when added to the segment stack, accesses data within the stack. The source

Table B.1 Dedicated i8086 register functions.

REGISTER	OPERATIONS ALLOWED
AX (AH+AL)	word multiply/divide, word I/O
AH	byte multiply/divide
AL	byte multiply/divide, byte I/O, translate, decimal arithmetic
BX	translate
CX	string operations, loops
CL	variable shift & rotate
DX	word multiply/divide, indirect I/O

and destination index registers hold offsets for calculating source and destination operands. They are used with the data segment register.

The 16-bit offsets contained within the stack pointer, base pointer, source index and destination index are used together with the segment registers to calculate 20-bit addresses, as indicated in Figure B.3. The segment referred to in this diagram is located within one of the four segment registers, except in the case of an I/O transfer, where no offset is involved, which means the i8086 I/O space is limited to 64 kbyte. The four segment registers are Code (CS), Data (DS), Stack (SS) and Extra (data – ES), and are illustrated in Figure B.4. Segments can be overlapped in order to make more efficient use of available memory.

The contents of CS identify which 64 kbyte code segment is currently active. All instruction fetches are made relative to CS, using IP as a 16-bit offset. ES is usually used for data storage, such as for destination addresses in string manipulations, in which case DI is used as the offset.

Relocatable programs can be written using these segment registers; however, their contents must be rewritten (usually by the operating system). It is easier to write dynamically relocatable code however if the segment registers are not used.

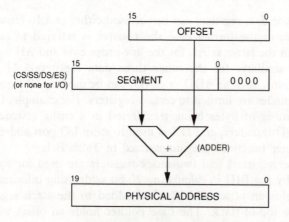

Figure B.3 Memory segmentation.

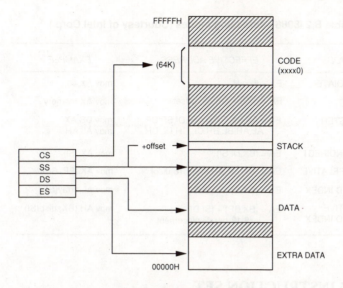

Figure B.4 i8086 segment registers.

B.3   i8086 ADDRESSING MODES

i8086 operand codes usually occupy the first byte of an instruction, although in a few instructions they can overlap into the second byte. In the latter case, a post byte is added, which indicates the addressing mode and location of the second operand, where applicable.

Table B.2 summarizes the addressing modes available on the i8086. In the immediate addressing mode, the 8- or 16-bit datum is contained within the instruction. In the direct (or absolute) addressing mode, the datum is located in the effective address specified by a 16-bit offset relative to DS. In the register addressing mode, the datum is contained within one of the 8- or 16-bit registers, as indicated. The effective address of the datum in the register indirect mode is contained within either BX, SI or DI (but not BP). The register relative mode allows an offset (of either 8 or 16 bits) from BX, BP, SI or DI; signed jumps in the range −128 to +127 bytes are thus possible with an 8-bit displacement.

In the based index addressing mode, the effective address is specified by summing the contents of an index register (SI or DI) with the contents of a base register (BX or BP). Relative based index mode is the same as the previous addressing mode, but also allows for a displacement (8 or 16 bits). Consider for example that (DS) = 10000H, (SI) = 2000H, (BX) = 0300H, and (8-bit) displacement = 40H. The effective address in the relative based index addressing mode would then be 2340H, relative to 10000H, or 12340H.

Table B.2 i8086 addressing modes (Courtesy of Intel Corp.).

MODE	EFFECTIVE ADDRESS	EXAMPLE
IMMEDIATE	EA = #xxxH	mov AX,#0
DIRECT	EA = (DS) + (16-bit) offset	mov AX,memory
REGISTER	EA = AX,BX,CX,DX,SI,DI,SP,BP AL,AH,BL,BH,CL,CH,DL,DH	mov DS,AX mov AL,AH
REG INDIRECT	EA = (BX,DI,SI)	mov AX,(SI)
REG RELATIVE	EA = (BX,BP,SI,DI)+(8,16)displ	mov AX,(BP).6
BASED INDEX	EA = (BX,BP) + (SI,DI)	mov AL,array(SI)
RELATIVE BASED INDEX	EA = (BX,BP) + (SI,DI) + (8,16-bit) displacement	mov AH,(BX).disp(SI)

B.4 i8086 INSTRUCTION SET

Memory in an i8086 system is organized as a contiguous list of bytes. Words are formed with the lower memory location constituting its least significant byte, and the upper memory location forming the most significant byte of the word. Unlike the MC68000, words are not required to align on even byte boundaries; words 00001H and 00002H are both valid in an i8086 system. However, programs will run faster if words *are* aligned, since the CPU will not be required to carry out two word fetches and extract the appropriate bytes of each.

Since addresses are stored with the least significant byte in the low-order memory position, then i8086 source listings will show addresses back to front. For example, for a source address of 1234H and a destination address of 5678H, these will actually be stored as 34H in location n, 12H in location $n + 1$, 78H in $n + 2$, and 56H in $n + 3$ (little-endian addressing, as discussed in Section 1.4).

The i8086 instruction set comprises eight different instruction types: data movement, arithmetic, logical, shift and rotate, block and string, program control, input/output and interrupts.

B.4.1 Data Movement Instructions

The i8086 MOV(e) instructions allow the transfer of data between registers and memory (or registers and registers), in either byte or word form (however suffixes are not used, as with MC68000 MOVE instructions). Note that transfers cannot take place between a source and destination which *both* reside in external memory. The PSW is not affected by any of the MOV instructions, except for POPF and SAHF, which load the flags explicitly. PUSH and POP implicitly use the stack pointed to by SP, with the stack growing down from high memory to low.

It should be noted that whilst immediate data can be moved into an effective address, it cannot be moved into a segment register. This is inconvenient, since it is often desired to load a constant value into a segment register. Likewise, there is no PUSH immediate instruction; constants must be first loaded into a register before they can be pushed onto the stack.

The XLAT instruction simplifies the implementation of look-up tables; (AL) can be used to access one of 256 table entries. The LEA, LDS and LES instructions allow a register to be loaded directly with a memory address. These instructions facilitate switching data segments by simultaneously initializing a base (or index) register together with a segment register, such as:

```
lds SI,STRING_POINTER
```

There is no corresponding instruction to initialize SP and SS however; this must be done in two steps, as follows:

```
mov   SS,SEG_BASE_ADDR
mov   SP,SEGMENT_OFFSET
```

(Interrupts are not allowed following a MOV SS instruction, since an interrupt service routine would store data in the wrong memory location, SS:SP being in a transition state at that time.)

B.4.2 Arithmetic Instructions

The i8086 CPU supports the addition, subtraction, multiplication and division of a number of different data types; signed and unsigned bytes and words, unpacked and packed decimal, and ASCII operands are all supported.

The PSW flags are set according to the result of each arithmetic instruction. Register(memory)-to-register, register-to-register(memory) and immediate-to-register(memory) operands are all allowed. In the case of the compare instruction (CMP), the flags are modified, but no result is stored.

Multiply and divide operations on bytes use AX as a double-length accumulator, whereas word operations use the AX:DX register pair. For example, a signed divide of AX by an 8-bit operand leaves an 8-bit quotient in AL and an 8-bit remainder in AH. CBW and CWD sign extend a byte in AL into a word in AX, and a word in AX into a double word in DX:AX respectively.

The decimal adjust instructions DAA and DAS store the result of an addition or subtraction in the low-order nibble of the byte in question; the high-order nibble is ignored. Decimal Adjust for Addition (Subtraction) performs a correction of the result in AL of adding (subtracting) two packed decimal operands, yielding a packed decimal sum (difference).

Similarly, the ASCII Adjust instructions AAA and AAS store the result in the low-order nibble, and add 0011_2 into the high-order nibble. Unpacked BCD (ASCII) Adjust for Addition performs a correction of the result in AL of adding two unpacked decimal operands, yielding an unpacked decimal sum (and similarly for ASCII Adjust for Subtraction).

B.4.3 Logical Instructions

Instructions are provided which allow the standard AND, OR, eXclusive OR and NOT operations on both bytes and words. Immediate operands are allowed as well as operands located in registers/memory. AND, OR and XOR all affect the flags, but NOT has no effect. TEST is the same as AND, but does not store a result; a conditional branch, depending on the state of the flags would normally follow a TEST instruction.

A common use of the AND and OR instructions is masking, whereas XOR is often used for 'flipping' bits.

B.4.4 Shift and Rotate Instructions

The four Shift and Rotate instructions available on the iAPX86 processor are logical shift (SHR/L), arithmetic shift (SAR/L), rotate (ROR/L), and rotate through the carry flag (RCR/L).

Each of these instructions can be carried out on either byte or word operands, in either a left or right direction, with the number of bits shifted being either one, or specified by a count in CL. The difference between SHR and SAR is that whereas the (most significant) sign bit is maintained for SAR, zeroes are loaded in from the left with SHR; there is no difference between SHL and SAL.

B.4.5 Block and String Instructions

A string is defined as a series of bytes or words which reside in consecutive memory locations. String instructions allow the movement of data from one block of memory to another, the scanning of an array for a specific entry, the comparison of two strings, or the initialization of a set of consecutive memory locations.

String instructions are one byte long, and implicitly use SI and DI to point to the source and destination strings respectively. Source strings are accessed by default via DS, and destination strings via ES, however a segment override prefix can be used to access source strings in a segment other than

DS, if so desired. Autoincrementing or autodecrementing is used with string instructions, depending on the direction flag DF. A repeat prefix can also be used, with the count stored in CX.

B.4.6 Program Control Operations

Instructions which allow a program to continue execution from a non-sequential memory address include JUMP, CALL and LOOP. Jumps can either be unconditional or conditional, in which case the PSW flags are examined in order to determine whether the jump is actually taken. The various jump conditions can either be single-bit, signed or unsigned.

Conditional jumps (Jcc, JCXZ) and Loop instructions (decrement and jump) are limited to jumps within ± 128 bytes of (IP). Unconditional jumps, by way of contrast, can be either intrasegment or intersegment. For intersegment jumps, either an 8-bit or 16-bit displacement from (IP) is allowed; the former limits jumps to a 256 byte range, whereas the latter allows jumps to any location within the current code segment (that is 64 kbyte). Intrasegment jumps alter the contents not only of IP but also of CS, and thus allow access to any location within the 1 Mbyte addressing range of the i8086.

The conditional jump instruction, JCXZ, uses CX as a count register, jumping to the specified address when the count decrements to zero.

The following branch conditions are supported in the i8086:

C	carry set	L (NGE)	less than (not greater than or equal to)
NC	carry clear	GE (NL)	greater than or equal to (not less than)
S	sign set	LE (NG)	less than or equal to (not greater than)
NS	sign clear	G (NLE)	greater than (not less than or equal to)
E (Z)	equal (to zero)	B (NAE)	below (not above or equal to)
NE (NZ)	not equal (to zero)	AE (NB)	above or equal to (not below)
O	overflow	BE (NA)	below or equal to (not above)
NO	no overflow	A (NBE)	above (not below or equal to)
P (PE)	parity (even)		
NP (PO)	no parity (odd)		

Entry to and exit from subroutines is provided via the CALL and RETurn instructions respectively. A CALL has the same options as a JUMP, but pushes a return address onto the stack before branching. This return address could involve IP, or both IP and CS, depending on whether an intrasegment or intersegment jump is involved. The RETurn instruction carries out this procedure in reverse, a return address being popped from the stack. RET *n* pops the return address, then adds '*n*' to SP. This is useful when passing parameters between main program and subroutine.

The LOOP instruction decrements CX, tests for a condition, then branches (or not) depending on the result of this test. Thus the LOOP instruction is seen to be equivalent to the following:

```
START:  mov  CX,n           =    START:  mov  CX,n
          :                                  :
          :                                  :
        dec  CX                            loop  START
        jnz  START
```

None of the JUMP, CALL or LOOP instructions affect the PSW flags. Separate instructions are included in the i8086 instruction set which allow the Carry, Direction and Interrupt flags to be set and cleared (as well as toggled in the case of CF).

Also included are HaLT, WAIT, ESCape and NOP. HLT stops the processor until it is either reset or an interrupt is received. WAIT suspends processing until the TEST line is activated; this allows the i8086 to synchronize itself to an external event, without requiring an interrupt. ESC is used to fetch instructions from an external coprocessor, such as the i8087 Numeric Processor. NOP is useful in debugging (where the programmer leaves a code segment to be filled in at some later time, padding it out temporarily with NOPs), and sometimes in 'padding out' time-critical instruction loops.

B.4.7 Input/Output, Interrupt and Trap Instructions

As already seen the i8086 has a 64 kbyte I/O addressing range. Moreover it uses ported I/O. I/O space is distinguished from memory space on the i8086 (memory-mapped I/O is still allowed on the i8086 however, in addition to the built-in ported I/O). Word (byte) I/O transfers take place via the AX (AL) register. Port addresses (8 or 16 bit) can either be specified in DX, or as immediate values.

The i8086 uses a two-level vectored priority interrupt scheme. The non-maskable NMI line has a higher priority than the maskable INTR line. Interrupts are only accepted on the INTR line if the IF bit has been previously set in the PSW.

Besides generating interrupts from external hardware, software interrupts (traps) are also possible on the i8086, using the INT instructions. The response of the i8086 to an interrupt is to first push the flags onto the stack, clear the TF and IF flags, and then branch to the appropriate interrupt service routine, using one of the 256 entries in the interrupt vector table (which resides in memory from 0–3FFH). INTO causes an interrupt if the overflow flag becomes set, whereas INT3 is used to replace executable instructions with breakpoints. IRET is used to return from an interrupt service routine to the main program.

LOCK is a prefix which can be used before any i8086 instruction in order to prevent DMA access during the execution of that particular instruction. It locks up the system bus and thus prevents the i8086 program from being interrupted.

Table B.3 Additional i80286 instructions (courtesy of Intel Corp.).

INSTRUCTION	OPERATION
PUSH #xxx	push immediate value onto STACK
PUSHA	push all registers (AX-DI) onto STACK
POPA	pop all registers (AX-DI) from STACK
IMUL #xxx	(signed) integer multiply with immediate data
INS source	input string from port-n to (AX,AH,AL)
OUTS dest	output string from (AX,AH,AL) to port n
REP INS/OUTS	transfer block of data between I/O & memory
ENTER procedure	creates a stack frame & pointers to previous
LEAVE	stack frames; also allocates dynamic storage
BOUND	checks index value against array bounds
CLTS	clear task switched flag
(protection)	(descriptor tables, access rights etc.)

B.4.8 Additional i80286 Instructions

The instruction sets of the more recently introduced members of the iAPX86 family are a superset of the earlier i8086 processor. The i80286 (and i80186) instruction set includes both enhanced versions of i8086 instructions, as well as new instructions.

Extensions to i8086 instructions include the immediate forms of PUSH and IMUL, PUSHA and POPA, and the privilege level restrictions on POPF and IRET. In the latter case, the i80286 must be in trusted/privileged mode rather than protected mode in order to execute either of these two instructions. PUSHA pushes all the registers AX–DI onto the stack (and likewise POPA pops them from the stack).

New i80286 instructions include the string input and output instructions INS and OUTS, the ENTER and LEAVE procedure instructions, and check index BOUND, as indicated in Table B.3. ENTER and LEAVE bring high-level language constructs to the assembly language level. ENTER 1024,2 would allocate 1 kbyte of dynamic storage on the stack, and set up a pointer to the previous stack frame in the stack frame that ENTER creates for this procedure. The 2 indicates the number of lexical nesting levels; up to 32 are allowed.

Instructions have also been included which support the built-in memory management capability of the i80286, such as CLear Task Switch flag (CLTS), Store Global Descriptor Table (SGDT), Load Task Register from register/ memory (LTR), and VERify write access (VERR).

Table B.4 i8086 Data types (courtesy of Intel Corp.).

DATA TYPE	COMMENTS
UNSIGNED INTEGER (byte, word)	+ 32-bit word on i80386
SIGNED INTEGER (byte, word)	+ signed 32 & 64-bit using i8087/80280/80387
(16 & 32-bit) POINTER	i80286 & i80386 only
STRING, ASCII	
(packed & unpacked) BCD	
BIT, BIT FIELD	i80386 only
(32 & 64-bit) SIGNED INTEGER FLOATING POINT (32,64,80-bit real)	using i80287/80387

B.4.9 Additional i80386 Instructions

The i80386 is object-code compatible with the earlier i8086 and i80286 CPUs. Both i8086 and i80286 software can run on the i80386. Moreover, i80286 and i80386 programs can run concurrently on the i80386. The i80386 also incorporates a virtual-86 mode, which creates a protected i8086 environment within the i80386 multitasking framework. Paging can also be used to give each virtual-86 task a 1 Mbyte address space anywhere in the i80386 physical address space.

The i80386 instruction set has been extended in two orthogonal directions over the earlier i8086 and i80286 processors. 32-bit versions of 16-bit instructions have been added to support 32-bit data types (the two earlier processors were both 16 bit). 32-bit addressing modes have been made available for all memory reference instructions.

Two additional segment registers are provided on the i80386: FS and GS. A load pointer to these two segment registers, as well as SS, has been included in the i80386 instruction set. The ability to MOV(e) with sign extension has been added, via the MOVSX and MOVZX instructions.

Table B.4 shows the data types supported by iAPX86 family processors. Strings are supported on all three processor generations. The i8086 and i80286 are 16-bit processors, and thus 32-bit integers are only supported on the i80386. The i80286 and i80386 support pointers, while bits and bit field support has been added to the i80386. Additional data types can be supported via numeric coprocessors, such as the i80287, in the form of signed 64- and 80-bit integers and reals.

Bit manipulation instructions, such as Scan Bit Forward (BSF) and Test Bit and Set (BTS), have been added to the i80386 instruction set. Insert and

Table B.5 Additional i80386 instructions. (courtesy of Intel Corp.).

INSTRUCTION	OPERATION
MOVSX,ZX	move with sign/zero extension
LFS,GS,SS	load pointer to FS,GS,SS
BSF	scan bit forward
BSR	scan bit reverse
BT	test bit
BTC	test bit & complement
BTR	test bit & reset
BTS	test bit & set
IBTS	insert bit string
XBTS	extract bit string
SETcc	conditional byte set (overflow, below, equal, below or equal, sign, parity, less, less or equal)

Extract Bit String instructions have also been incorporated, as shown in Table B.5.

The other main instruction group added to the i80386 instruction set is the conditional byte set group. The various conditions available are similar to the conditional jumps described earlier in Section B.4.6. Bytes can be set if the condition is either true or false. Typical of this instruction group is SET byte on Below (Not Above or Equal) SETB/SETNAE, and SET byte on Not Below (Above or Equal) SETNB/SETAE.

The i80386 also includes the additional i80286 instructions described in Section B.4.8.

B.5 i8086 PINOUT

The i8086 processor comes packaged in 40-pin DIL form. The limited number of pins in such a package led to Intel's decision to multiplex address and data lines on the same physical pins, as shown with AD0–15 in Figure B.5. The upper four address lines A16–19 are also multiplexed, but with status signals S3–S6. Data is read from or written to memory (or I/O devices) via AD0–15. Device identification information from an interrupt controller also travels via AD0–15. Address Latch Enable (ALE) indicates that address information is appearing on the multiplexed address/data lines (actually it is a LO-to-HI edge on ALE that indicates the start of a valid address).

Status line 7 or $\overline{\text{Bus High Enable}}$ ($\overline{\text{BHE}}$) enables data on the upper eight bits of the data bus. S6 is always LO. S5 reflects the interrupt enable flag in

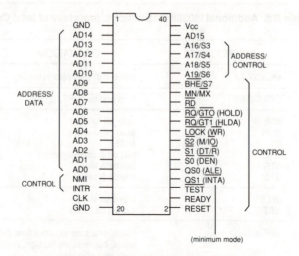

Figure B.5 i8086 pinout (courtesy of Intel Corp.).

the PSW. Status lines S4 and S3 indicate which of the segment registers was used to generate the physical address currently being outputted on the address lines (00 = Extra, 01 = Stack, 10 = Code [or none in the case of an I/O transfer], 11 = Data).

Status line 2 or M/$\overline{\text{IO}}$ indicates whether the current bus cycle is involved with a memory or I/O read/write. Status line 1 or Data Transmit/$\overline{\text{Receive}}$ (DT/$\overline{\text{R}}$) indicates the direction of the data transfer currently taking place. $\overline{\text{RD}}$ and $\overline{\text{WR}}$ indicate that a read or write bus cycle is currently in progress, respectively. Status line 0 or $\overline{\text{Data bus ENable}}$ ($\overline{\text{DEN}}$) is also asserted during a bus read cycle. READY is a handshake signal, which indicates a successful transfer between CPU and memory (I/O); it can be used to insert wait states when interfacing to slow memory (peripheral devices).

Interrupts are handled via the INTerrupt Request (INTR) and INTerrupt Acknowledge ($\overline{\text{INTA}}$) lines. Non-maskable interrupts are catered for via the NMI line. The $\overline{\text{TEST}}$ line can be polled by the WAIT instruction until it becomes asserted; this allows the CPU to be synchronized to an external event.

DMA capability is built into the i8086 via the HOLD and H(o)LD Acknowledge (HLDA). When the CPU asserts HLDA in response to a HOLD request, it simultaneously floats the bus, thus allowing an alternative bus master to take control of it.

Eight pins on the i8086 are dual purpose; their function depends on whether the CPU is running in minimum or maximum system configuration. The minimum mode functions are shown in parentheses in Figure B.5.

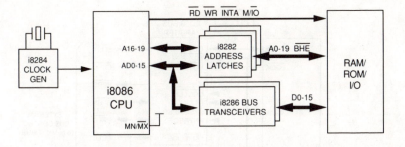

Figure B.6 Minimum system configuration (courtesy of Intel Corp.).

B.5.1 Minimum System Configuration

The MN/$\overline{\text{MX}}$ pin indicates whether the i8086 is operating in minimum or maximum mode. Other chips besides the i8086 CPU are required in order to form a minimum i8086 system.

Firstly, a system clock is required; this is the function of the i8284 clock generator in Figure B.6. Secondly, address latching is required. This is provided in the form of i8282s. The i8282s latch addresses appearing on the multiplexed address/data bus whenever the ALE output is active. Three such (8-bit) latches would be required for 20-bit addressing. Likewise, bus transceivers are required in order to pass data between the CPU and memory (or peripherals), a pair of 8-bit i8286 transceivers being shown in Figure B.6. Data appears on the multiplexed address/data bus whenever $\overline{\text{DEN}}$ is asserted.

The MN pin needs to be tied to the supply rail (that is, HI) for minimum mode operation.

B.5.2 Maximum System Configuration

Tying the MN/$\overline{\text{MX}}$ pin LO will cause the i8086 CPU to run in maximum mode. This facilitates the development of both multiprocessing and coprocessing systems. An i8086 processor in such a system will have access not only to its local resources, but also to global resources, via the system bus. This system bus could be Multibus, as indicated in Figure B.7.

Eight of the i8086 pins take on different functions when running in maximum mode configuration. $\overline{\text{WR}}$, M/$\overline{\text{IO}}$, DT/$\overline{\text{R}}$, $\overline{\text{DEN}}$, $\overline{\text{ALE}}$ and $\overline{\text{INTA}}$ are no longer produced by the i8086. Instead, status signals are output on status lines S0–S2 prior to the commencement of each bus cycle. These status signals are interpreted by an external controller, such as an i8288. Thus it is the i8288 and not the i8086 which produces the appropriate timing and control signals. These timing signals can then be used to interface directly to the system Multibus.

Figure B.7 also includes an i8289 bus arbiter. By incorporating the

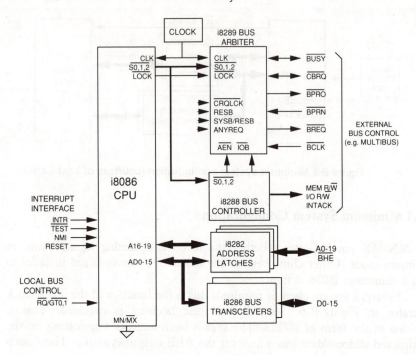

**Figure B.7 i8086 maximum mode configuration
(courtesy of Intel Corp.).**

external i8288 bus controller and i8289 bus arbiter, the CPU has been freed of
the task of generating multiprocessing signals. The Multibus bus exchange
signals so generated by the i8289 are bus busy ($\overline{\text{BUSY}}$), common bus request
($\overline{\text{CBRQ}}$), bus priority out ($\overline{\text{BPRO}}$), bus priority in ($\overline{\text{BPRN}}$), bus request
($\overline{\text{BREQ}}$) and bus clock ($\overline{\text{BCLK}}$). The i8086 itself generates the bus priority
lock ($\overline{\text{LOCK}}$) signal, using the $\overline{\text{WR}}$ line freed up by switching from minimum
to maximum modes. $\overline{\text{LOCK}}$ is activated by the LOCK prefix instruction, and
remains active until the next instruction is fetched from the queue.

These bus exchange signals ensure uninterrupted access to common (or
global) resources. The $\overline{\text{CRQLCK}}$ and ANYREQ inputs on the i8289 allow
lower priority bus arbiters to take control of the system bus. RESB,
SYSB/$\overline{\text{RESB}}$ and $\overline{\text{IOB}}$ can be used to arbitrate between local and global
resources.

The request/grant pins ($\overline{\text{RQ/GT0,1}}$) are used by other local bus masters
to force the CPU to release the local bus at the end of the processor's current
bus cycle, $\overline{\text{RQ/GT0}}$ having a higher priority than $\overline{\text{RQ/GT1}}$.

The QS0 and QS1 outputs allow external tracking of the internal i8086
instruction queue.

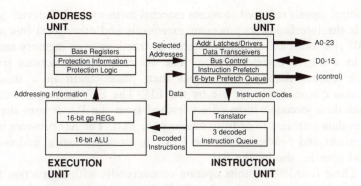

Figure B.8 i80286 block diagram (courtesy of Intel Corp.).

B.6 i80286

As already seen, more is required than an i8086 CPU to construct a minimum i8086 system. The i80186 processor, introduced in 1982, incorporates most of a minimum i8086 system onto a single chip. It is an enhanced version of the i8086 processor, which includes on-board clock generation circuitry, programmable timers, interrupt control, DMA control and programmable chip select circuitry. It replaces up to 20 ICs in an i8086 system. System throughput is roughly twice that of an i8086. Internally, the i80186 is functionally identical to an i8086, although its control microprogram has been altered so that the same instruction takes fewer clock cycles to execute. Its instruction set is a superset of the earlier i8086. The i80188, like the i8088, has an 8-bit external data bus, and uses a four instruction queue rather than a six.

The i80286 is an enhanced version of the i8086, which includes built-in memory management and protection. It is thus oriented towards multiuser and multitasking systems. It can access 2^{24} or 16 Mbyte of memory, compared with the 1 Mbyte addressing range of the i8086, although this is still segmented (the i80286 is limited to 1 Mbyte direct addressing range).

Separate address and data pins are provided on the i80286; multiplexing has been dispensed with in the i80286.

The block diagram of the i80286 is shown in Figure B.8. The internal partitioning of the earlier i8086 has been expanded upon in the i80286. There are four independent processing units within the CPU, the Address Unit (AU), Bus Unit (BU), Instruction Unit (IU) and the Execution Unit (EU). Each unit operates to both minimize bus requirements and maximize CPU throughput. Bus efficiency is more than double that of the i8086, owing to the pipelining techniques employed. This leads to higher bus throughput without requiring increased memory speed.

The BU performs all bus operations; it generates all of the address, data and control signals required to access external memory (or I/O devices). It also controls the interfacing to processor extensions and other local bus masters. The BU also looks ahead and prefetches instructions from memory and stores them in a 6 byte prefetch queue. The IU receives instructions from the prefetch queue, decodes them, and then places them in a three deep instruction queue, ready for use by the EU. The EU, as its name suggests, executes these decoded instructions fetched from the IU. It uses the BU to perform data transfers to or from memory (or I/O). The AU provides memory management and protection for the CPU; it translates logical addresses into physical ones for use by the BU.

These four i80286 units operate concurrently, with instruction fetches, decodes and executions overlapping. This pipelined architecture thus results in increased system performance.

External partitioning is continued in the i80286 family, with the upgrade of the i8087 into the i80287 numeric processor extension. The i80287 monitors instructions fetched by the i80286 CPU, and automatically executes any numeric instructions found. A special processor extension data channel within the CPU is used to request operand fetches and to store results of operations. Two processor extension lines allow the i80287 to indicate error and status conditions back to the i80286.

Figure B.9 shows the i80286 register set, which includes all i8086 registers, as well as a machine status word, task register and descriptor table registers.

The flags include all i8086 flags, as well as two new control bits, NTF and IOPL. NTF is the Nested Task flag, and bits 12 and 13 together form the I/O Privilege Level flag. Privileged instructions may only be executed if the current privilege level is higher than that contained within IOPL.

The MSW contains additional status bits specifically related to the built-in memory management capabilities of the i80286. The Protection Enable bit (PE) indicates whether the CPU is in real or protected mode. EM and MP are used with processor extensions, such as the i80287 numeric processor. The Task Switch bit (TS) is used to switch between tasks in a multiprocessing environment. Upon each task switch, the current machine status is stored in an area specified by a segment descriptor pointed to by the task register. The task register is then updated to point to the save area for the new task, and the new machine state loaded in.

The i80286 can operate in either real or protected addressing modes. In real mode, the CPU performs as an i8086; none of the additional i80286 registers are used. Following reset, an i80286 will power up in real mode. It can be switched to protected mode by simply clearing the PE bit in the MSW, however it can only be returned to real mode by a further system reset.

In protected or virtual addressing mode, the i80286 makes use of the segment descriptor registers, segment register extensions and task register in order to translate virtual addresses into physical ones. This is a fundamental function performed in memory management; another is memory protection,

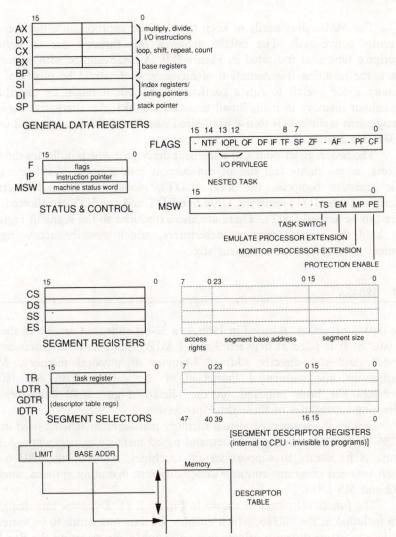

AX — multiply, divide, I/O instructions
DX
CX — loop, shift, repeat, count
BX — base registers
BP
SI — index registers/ string pointers
DI
SP — stack pointer

GENERAL DATA REGISTERS

FLAGS   - NT F IOPL OF DF IF TF SF ZF - AF - PF CF

F — flags
IP — instruction pointer
MSW — machine status word

STATUS & CONTROL   MSW   - - - - - - - - - - - - TS EM MP PE

TASK SWITCH
EMULATE PROCESSOR EXTENSION
MONITOR PROCESSOR EXTENSION
PROTECTION ENABLE

I/O PRIVILEGE
NESTED TASK

CS
DS
SS
ES

SEGMENT REGISTERS

access rights   segment base address   segment size

TR — task register
LDTR
GDTR — (descriptor table regs)
IDTR

SEGMENT SELECTORS

[SEGMENT DESCRIPTOR REGISTERS (internal to CPU - invisible to programs)]

LIMIT   BASE ADDR

Memory

DESCRIPTOR TABLE

Figure B.9 i80286 register set (courtesy of Intel Corp.).

where different segments of memory are designated as read only or read/write, and where access permissions can be restricted between the various system users (and indeed between different tasks originated by the same user). In a multiuser, multitasking system, two different tasks can appear to access the same logical address space. The MMU (in this case embedded within the i80286 CPU) performs the basic translation:

physical_addr = logical_addr + offset

The MMU thus needs to keep track of the appropriate offset for each currently active task. The i80286 achieves this through use of segment descriptor tables, as indicated in Figure B.9. A disadvantage with segmentation is the resulting fragmentation of memory; there could be plenty of free memory space overall to run a particular task, but it might be distributed throughout memory in many small unusable chunks. An alternative memory management technique is to use fixed-sized pages, and this is supported in the i80386 (see Section B.7).

The task register points to a segment descriptor which indicates the base address, access rights and size of the current task segment. The descriptor table registers comprise the local (LDT), global (GDT) and interrupt descriptor table (IDT) registers. Only one GDT and one IDT are allowed, but there can be several LDTs. There are also extensions to the segment registers that hold the current segment descriptors, which describe access rights, segment base address and segment size.

B.7   i80386

The i80386 processor, released in 1986, is a 32-bit enhanced version of the 16-bit i80286. It is rated at between 3 and 4 MIPS (millions of instructions per second), and can directly address 4 Gbytes of physical memory. More significantly, the segmented limitation of the earlier i8086 and i80286 processors has been removed on the i80386. Figure B.10 compares the addressing capabilities of these three processors.

Besides the segmented virtual memory management scheme used in the i80286, the i80386 also supports demand paged memory management. A new feature is its ability to support virtual machines, whereby the i80386 can switch between programs running under different operating systems, such as OS/2 and MS-DOS.

The functional pinout is shown in Figure B.11. Dynamic bus sizing has been included in the i80386, which enables the data bus width to be varied to interface to external device drivers more effectively. By asserting the $\overline{\text{Bus Size}}$ $\overline{16}$ line ($\overline{\text{BS16}}$), external hardware can instruct the CPU to perform transfers only on the lower 16 bits of the data bus.

The i80386 instruction set supports 8-, 16- and 32-bit transfers. The high order 30 bits of each address appear on address lines A2–31, with the relevant bytes indicated by $\overline{\text{BE0}}$–$\overline{\text{BE3}}$. A0 and A1 can be generated from these byte enable signals externally if so desired.

Assertion of the $\overline{\text{ADS}}$ line notifies external hardware that a normal bus cycle has commenced. W/$\overline{\text{R}}$, D/$\overline{\text{C}}$ and M/$\overline{\text{IO}}$ further distinguish this cycle, namely as a write (or read), data (or code) and memory (or I/O) respectively. Bus lock ($\overline{\text{LOCK}}$) is used in multiprocessing systems; it signals other bus masters that the CPU is performing a non-interruptable multiple bus cycle. Other bus masters can access the i80386's local bus by asserting HOLD; the

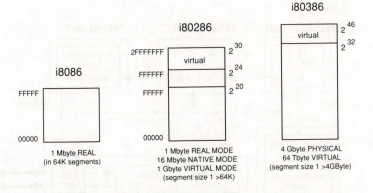

Figure B.10 Physical and virtual memory sizes.

i80386 grants access to the bus by asserting HLDA at the end of the current bus cycle.

Both pipelined and non-pipelined bus cycles are supported by the i80386; external hardware can dynamically enable pipelining by asserting the next address ($\overline{\text{NA}}$) line. $\overline{\text{READY}}$ is a handshake line which indicates that the external device has responded to the bus cycle. It also allows the insertion of wait states when interfacing to slow memory (I/O).

The interrupt lines on the i80386 are essentially the same as those on the i80286, with INTR and NMI being provided.

RESET places the i80386 in real mode, with interrupts disabled, and then fetches an instruction from location FFFFFFF0H. (Real mode has the same base architecture as the i8086, but with access to the 32-bit i80386

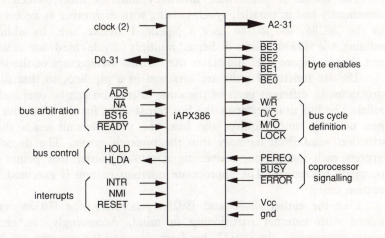

Figure B.11 i80386 functional diagram (courtesy of Intel Corp.).

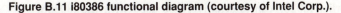

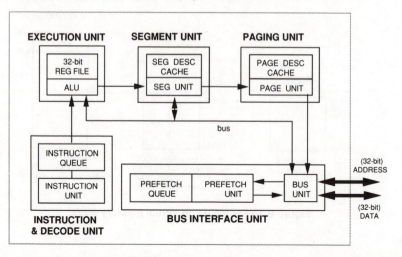

Figure B.12 i80386 internal architecture (courtesy of Intel Corp.).

registers; the addressing mechanism, memory size and interrupt handling are identical to real mode on the i80286.)

The i80386 coprocessor interface comprises PEREQ, $\overline{\text{BUSY}}$ and $\overline{\text{ERROR}}$. $\overline{\text{BUSY}}$ is asserted whenever the coprocessor is executing an instruction; the i80386 only passes a coprocessor instruction for execution after $\overline{\text{BUSY}}$ becomes negated. Synchronization with a coprocessor can be achieved using the WAIT instruction, which suspends activity until $\overline{\text{BUSY}}$ becomes inactive. $\overline{\text{ERROR}}$ is asserted by the coprocessor whenever it encounters an exception that needs to be handled by the operating system. PEREQ is used to implement the i80386 coprocessor protocol.

The i80386 is partitioned internally into six units, which operate autonomously and in parallel, synchronizing with each other as necessary. As with the i80286, the i80386 uses a pipelined architecture. In addition to pipelining, the i80386 utilizes dedicated multiply (divide) hardware as well as a barrel shifter. Figure B.12 illustrates the internal architecture of the i80386.

The six functional units are arranged in a pipeline, so that different instructions, or different parts of the same instruction can be operated on in parallel. The bus unit performs the bus transactions for the other five units. When no other unit requires the bus, the prefetch unit reads the next instruction word from memory into the prefetch queue. The decode unit interprets each instruction, converting it into a pointer that points to the appropriate microcode. The appropriate microinstruction is executed by the execution unit.

Like the earlier i8086 and i80286 processors, the i80386 was also designed with external partitioning in mind. Accordingly, an enhanced numeric coprocessor, the i80387, has been designed for use with the i80386. The earlier i80287 can alternatively be used with the i80386.

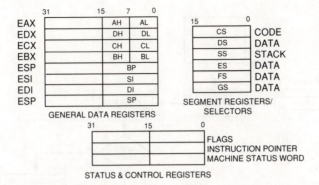

Figure B.13 i80386 register set (courtesy of Intel Corp.).

The i80386 can operate either in real or protected virtual address modes. In real mode the i80386 operates as a fast i8086, but with 32-bit extensions if so desired. Switching to protected mode allows access to the built-in segmented and paged memory management capabilities of the i80386.

Figure B.13 shows the i80386 register set. These registers are a superset of the earlier i8086, i80186 and i80286 register sets, just as i80386 instruction set is a superset of the instruction sets of these earlier processors.

The general registers EAX through ESP, the flags, instruction pointer and MSW have all been expanded from 16- to 32-bits, which reflects the 32-bit architecture of the i80386. The segment registers remain as 16-bit, however two additional segment registers have been provided: FS and GS. Two additional flag bits have been added, namely the Virtual Mode (VM) and Resume Flag (RF). The contents of all of these registers are task specific; they are automatically reloaded following every task switch.

The inbuilt MMU also appears in the i80386 pipeline, which serves to speed up address translation. Both paging and segmentation are supported within the i80386. Paging has certain advantages over segmentation. It results in less fragmentation of external memory, swap times are shorter, there are fewer restrictions on starting addresses and simpler replacement algorithms can be used. However, with paging the *internal* fragmentation increases as the page size increases (in an attempt to decrease the total number of descriptors); a much smaller number of descriptors is needed for large program or data spaces.

The i80386 segment unit performs address translations, and checks each access against segment protection attributes. The paging unit can be disabled by the operating system software. When it is disabled, the linear addresses produced by the segment unit pass through unaltered. When it is enabled, the paging unit translates these linear addresses into physical addresses, checking that accesses are consistent with page attributes. The paging unit incorporates a translation lookaside buffer, which is used to cache translation information

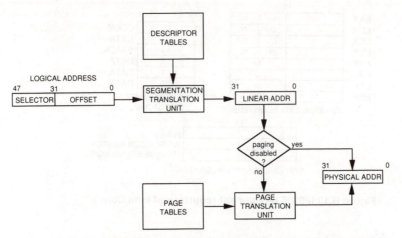

Figure B.14 i80386 cascadable segmentation and paging units (courtesy of Intel Corp.).

for the most recently used pages; this dramatically reduces the need to access memory-based page tables.

The i80386 segmentation and paging units are shown in Figure B.14. Translation from linear to physical addresses is illustrated in Figure B.15.

B.7.1 i80386SX

A scaled-down version of the i80386 was released by Intel in 1988. The i80386SX has a 32-bit internal architecture, but only 16 data and 24 address lines are brought out to the outside world (and in this respect is reminiscent of the MC68000). It is oriented towards the low end PC/AT market, and is intended to replace the i80286 as the system processor (although it is not pin compatible with the i80286). It operates at a clock speed of 16 MHz.

B.8 iAPX86 INSTRUCTION EXECUTION TIMING

All iAPX86 processors incorporate some form of pipelining and prefetch instruction queue. Thus while one instruction is executing, the next instruction in sequence is being decoded, and the following instruction is simultaneously being fetched from the queue.

The Bus Interface Unit (BIU) in an i8086 incorporates a 6-byte instruction (FIFO) queue in order to achieve internal pipelining (this being reduced to a 4-byte queue in the i8088). The BIU can look ahead to fetch the next sequential instruction whenever the EU has not requested it to perform reads or writes. Bytes loaded into the input end of the instruction queue are automatically shifted through the FIFO into the next empty location at the

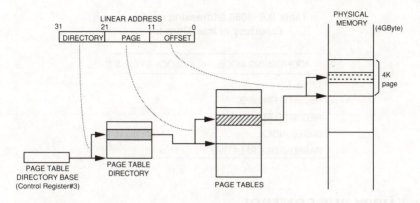

Figure B.15 i80386 linear to physical address translation (courtesy of Intel Corp.).

output end. The EU reads one instruction byte after the other from the queue output. The BIU also contains an address adder which converts 16-bit addresses into 20-bit ones using the segment registers and its 16-bit internal bus.

The EU fetches instructions from the output end of the instruction stream queue, decodes them, generates any necessary operand addresses, passes them to the BIU to perform any necessary reads (writes) to memory (I/O), then performs the specified operation on the appropriate operands. The EU also tests the status and control flags during instruction execution, and updates them according to the results of this execution.

Part of the instruction decoding process involves the calculation of an Effective Address (EA) whenever a memory operand is involved. The time taken to calculate this EA depends on the addressing mode employed. Table B.6 shows that it takes twice as long for the CPU to calculate an EA for the based index relative addressing mode as it does for the direct addressing mode, for example. The different times for the based index addressing mode correspond to the choice of index register, destination or source, with respect to the value in the base pointer (or alternatively SI or DI with respect to BX); likewise for the based index relative addressing mode.

Register-to-register transfers are faster than either memory to register or register to memory. In the latter case, extra time is required in order to store the result in memory. A range of times is possible for the MUL instruction group, because the execution time is data dependent. The same applies for DIVide and variable-bit SHIFT and ROTATEs.

Execution times for instructions which reference a full memory word vary depending on the alignment of the operand. If an operand is aligned on an odd address boundary, the CPU must spend four additional clock cycles to access the operand, compared to the case where it is aligned on an even address boundary.

**Table B.6 i8086 addressing modes
(courtesy of Intel Corp.).**

ADDRESSING MODE	# CLOCK CYCLES
DIRECT	6
REGISTER INDIRECT	5
REGISTER RELATIVE	9
BASED INDEX	7 or 8
BASED INDEX RELATIVE	11 or 12

B.9 iAPX86 BUS CONTROL

An i8086 read cycle commences with the simultaneous assertion of Address Latch Enable (ALE) and Memory/IO. The trailing edge of ALE latches the address information present on the multiplexed address/data lines AD0–15 into an external i8282/3 latch. A0 and $\overline{BHE}$ are used to access the low-order byte, high-order byte or word $\overline{BHE}$ enables data on the shared (multiplexed) lines AD8–15.

During the next clock cycle, the address is removed and the local bus is taken into its high impedance state, and the read strobe ($\overline{RD}$) is asserted. This causes the addressed device to enable its bus drivers onto the local bus. At some later time data becomes valid on the bus, after which the device asserts the ready line RDY. Wait states may need to be inserted here by the CPU when interfacing to slow devices. The CPU then negates the read line $\overline{RD}$, at which time the addressed device will three-state its bus drivers, relinquishing the local bus back to the i8086.

A write cycle similarly begins with the assertion of ALE and M/$\overline{IO}$. The device address is placed on AD0–15 during the first cycle and removed during the second, at which time the CPU places the data to be written on the bus.

When used in maximum mode, an external i8288 bus controller generates ALE, $\overline{DEN}$ and DT/$\overline{R}$ rather than the i8086, however their timing remains the same.

Each bus cycle in an i80286 consists of a send status T_s state, followed by one or more command states T_c. At maximum speed, the local i80286 bus will alternate between T_s and T_c, thus transferring a word of information every two processor clock cycles.

The read and write cycle timing of an i80286 closely follows that of an i8086, with the addition of the CODe/$\overline{INTerruptAcknowledge}$ line on the i80286 and the $\overline{MemoryReaDCommand}$ line on its associated i82288 Bus Controller.

Two classes of timing are possible on the i80386 processor, namely pipelined or non-pipelined, with the $\overline{NA}$ signal being asserted if pipelining is required during the next bus cycle. Furthermore, the bus width is dynamically selectable, at either 16 or 32. The $\overline{BS16}$ line is sampled near the end of each cycle to confirm the bus size for the current cycle. Termination of i80386 bus cycles depends on the reception of $\overline{READY}$ from the external device; wait states will be automatically inserted by the CPU until $\overline{READY}$ is detected. Another added feature of the i80386 over and above the i80286 is the inclusion of byte enable lines $\overline{BE0}-\overline{BE3}$, which are used in dynamic bus sizing and operand misalignment; they indicate when multiple bus cycles are required.

Apart from these added enhancements, read and write cycle timing for the i80386 follows a similar pattern to that discussed earlier for the i8086 and i80286 processors.

B.10 INTERRUPTS

Interrupts can be initiated on an i8086 either by external hardware or by software (using one of the INT instructions). Hardware interrupts can be either maskable or non-maskable; the former access the i8086 via the level-sensitive INTR line, while the latter do so via the (positive) edge-sensitive NMI line.

Upon receipt of an interrupt, control is transferred to a new program location. The appropriate location is contained within the interrupt descriptor table, which resides in memory at locations 0–3FFH. As seen in Figure B.16, each entry in this 256 element table is a 32-bit pointer to the appropriate interrupt service routine. Which particular interrupt service routine is jumped to depends on the 8-bit vector type which is placed on the bus by the interrupting device during the interrupt acknowledge cycle. Interrupts which arrive at the i8086 via the INTR line can be masked off by clearing interrupt enable flag IF. Further interrupts are disabled during the interrupt response sequence.

The response sequence is first to push the return address (in CS:IP) and flags onto the stack. $\overline{LOCK}$ is then asserted during the first bus cycle, which floats the bus, then a byte is fetched from the external device during the second. This byte indicates the interrupt type; it is subsequently multiplied by 4 and used by the CPU as a pointer to the appropriate interrupt service routine. This vector type could be provided by an external i8259 Programmable Interrupt Controller, for example. Type 3 and INTerrupt-on-Overflow, however, are single byte instructions.

The various interrupt vector assignments are as follows:

0	divide error
1	single step
2	non-maskable interrupt
3	INT instruction
4	INTO instruction
5–255	2 byte INT instructions and maskable external interrupts

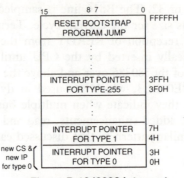

**Figure B.16 i8086 interrupt
descriptors
(courtesy of Intel Corp.).**

At the end of the interrupt service routine, a return from interrupt instruction IRET pops the return address and flags from the stack. The processor is returned to the state it was in prior to receiving the interrupt, and continues program execution from the next sequential instruction.

The interrupt mechanisms of the i80286(386) processors are the same as the i8086 interrupt mechanism just described. Their response to an interrupt is to save the current program location and the flags on the stack, then the 8-bit vector supplied to the processor is used to vector to the appropriate interrupt service routine. There are a couple of enhancements however, and these will now be elaborated upon.

Due to the inbuilt memory management capability of the i80286(386), the CPU can be operating in either real or protected mode. In real mode the processor behaves as an i8086, with the interrupt pointers stored in memory locations 0H–3FFH. In protected mode these pointers are contained within an Interrupt Descriptor Table (IDT), which can be loaded anywhere in memory, as indicated in Figure B.17.

The i80286(386) processors allow interrupts to cause a task switch directly. A task gate has two advantages over an interrupt gate. The first is that *all* processor registers are saved rather than just the flag register and CS:IP. Secondly, the new task is completely isolated from the task just interrupted; address spaces are isolated and the interrupt handling task is unaffected by the privilege level of the interrupted task.

When operating in real mode, an interrupt will automatically mask any further interrupts for the duration of the interrupt service routine. When operating in protected mode, the individual task gate for each interrupt service routine specifies whether or not INTR interrupts are to be masked during the execution of the interrupt service routine.

When simultaneous interrupt requests occur, these are processed in priority order, as follows:

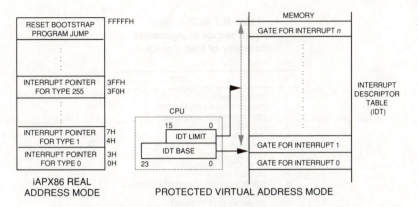

Figure B.17 i80286(386) interrupt descriptors (courtesy of Intel Corp.).

1. processor exception
2. single step
3. non-maskable interrupt
4. extension segment overrun
5. maskable interrupt request
6. INT instruction

In the i80386, exceptions as well as interrupts can alter the normal program flow. Now whereas interrupts handle asynchronous external events, exceptions are designed to handle instruction faults. Exceptions are treated as non-maskable interrupts, and can be classified as faults, traps or aborts.

Faults are detected before the execution of the faulty instruction, while traps are reported immediately following the offending instruction. A user-defined interrupt is an example of a trap. Aborts are exceptions for which the offending instruction cannot be precisely located; they are used to report serious system errors, such as a hardware fault or illegal table entries. The 8-bit vector supplied by the external device in the case of an INTR interrupt is supplied internally in the case of exceptions.

The i80386 interrupt vector assignments are shown in Table B.7. This figure is a superset of the i8086 table referred to earlier, with the additional entries reflecting the inbuilt memory management capabilities of the i80386. The i80286 table is identical to this table, but without the page fault and coprocessor error entries.

In either processor, a protection violation will cause an exception, which can be due to a program error or else constitutes an implicit request for service. Examples of the former include attempts to write into a ready-only segment or a violation of segment limits; an example of the latter is a stack overflow.

Table B.7 i80286(386)
interrupt vector assignments
(courtesy of Intel Corp.).

NO.	TYPE
0	DIVIDE ERROR
1	DEBUG EXCEPTION (S.STEP)
2	NON-MASKABLE INTERRUPT
3	(1-BYTE) 'INT' INSTRUCTION
4	'INTO' INSTRUCTION
5	ARRAY BOUNDS CHECK
6	INVALID OP CODE
7	DEVICE NOT AVAILABLE
8	DOUBLE FAULT
9	COPROCESSOR SEGMENT OVERRUN
10	INVALID TSS
11	SEGMENT NOT PRESENT
12	STACK FAULT
13	GENERAL PROTECTION FAULT
14	PAGE FAULT
16	COPROCESSOR ERROR
17-32	(reserved)
0-255	2-BYTE INTERRUPT

B.11 BUS ARBITRATION AND MULTIPROCESSING

The i8086 bus arbitration signals comprise HOLD and HLDA. Figure B.18 shows the connection of a DMA controller, such as an i8237, to a minimum mode i8086 system. Requests are received by the DMA controller and passed onto the CPU via the HRQ line. This request will be acknowledged following the completion of the currently executing instruction, at which time the CPU also switches the bus into its high impedance state.

DMA controllers improve system throughput by performing I/O and CPU tasks concurrently. This is achieved by utilizing previously unused CPU bus cycles, which can amount to more than 50% on an i8086. Concurrent operations can also be achieved using multiprocessor systems, which are catered for in i8086 maximum mode systems.

Three different types of multiprocessing systems are possible, namely tightly coupled, loosely coupled and coprocessor systems. In tightly coupled and coprocessor systems, the CPU and external processor are connected in master–slave configuration. Both the CPU and the extension processor share the same local memory (I/O), bus control logic and clock generator. Coprocessors are dependent on the CPU and interact directly with it. In a tightly coupled system the supporting processor is able to act independently of the CPU. Loosely coupled systems comprise several bus masters, each having access not only to its own local resources, but also to global (shared) system resources, via a system bus such as Multibus or Multibus-II.

Two important considerations in multiprocessing systems are bus contention and interprocessor communication. These are facilitated in i8086 maximum mode configuration by the inclusion of a LOCK facility, and by

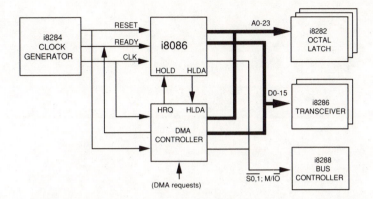

Figure B.18 DMA controller interface (courtesy of Intel Corp.).

flagging the instruction queue status, on pins QS0 and QS1. The single-byte LOCK prefix may be used to precede any i8086 instruction; it ensures that no other processor can gain control of the system bus until the locked instruction has finished. This is useful in implementing semaphores, which provide secure message passing between processes, and ensure that only one process accesses shared resources at any one time.

By examining the i8086 queue status (lines $\overline{S0-2}$), an external device can not only determine the currently executing instruction, but can also simulate an instruction execution sequence itself. This is necessary when an instruction needs to be executed by a coprocessor.

Typical iAPX86 family coprocessors include the i8087 Numeric coprocessor (NPX) and i8089 I/O processor (designed to operate with the i8086 CPU), the i80287 (designed to work with an i80286 host) and the i80387 (designed specifically for the i80386 CPU). In i80386 systems, an additional interrupt vector (#16) is included, to handle coprocessor errors more efficiently.

Additional bus arbitration logic is required in loosely coupled systems, in order to resolve potential bus contention; the host i8086 in each module is incapable of requesting bus accesses and recognizing bus grants. This additional bus arbitration logic is typically implemented in the form of an i8289 bus arbiter.

Simultaneous bus requests from different modules need to be resolved using an external priority controller, such as an i8289. This particular priority controller supports three different priority schemes, namely polling, daisy chaining and independent requests.

Multiprocessing systems based on the i80286(386) processor follow the same principles outlined above for the i8086. The external support logic has been upgraded with these more recent processors however, with the i82284 replacing the i8284 clock generator, the i82288 bus controller replacing the i8288, and the i8289 being superseded by the i82289 bus arbiter.

Figure B.15 DMA controller interface (courtesy of Intel Corp.)

Appendix C
Acronyms and Abbreviations

		Section
AC	Alternating Current	
ACIA	Asynchronous Communications Interface Adapter	5.4, 7.3
A/D	Analog-to-Digital	5.5, 9.4, 9.6
ADC	Analog-to-Digital Converter	7.3, 8.3.3, 9.4, 9.6
ADCCP	Advanced Data Communications Control Procedure	5.5
ALE	Address Latch Enable	B.5.1
ALU	Arithmetic and Logic Unit	1.2, 2.4
ANSI	American National Standards Institute	6.7.1, 7.5
AS	Address Strobe	A.5, A.9
ASCII	American Standard Code for Information Interchange	1.5, 4.1, 4.2, 5.3
ATLAP	Appletalk Link Access Protocol	5.7.4
ATM	Automatic Teller Machine	10.9
ATP	Appletalk Transaction Protocol	5.7.4
AU	Address Unit	B.6
A/UX	Apple Unix	10.4.1
Bcc	Branch on condition (instruction)	A.3.7, B.4.6
BCD	Binary Coded Decimal	
BG	Bus Grant	A.9.1
BGACK	Bus Grant Acknowledge	A.9.1
BHE	Bus High Enable	B.5, B.9
Bisync	Binary Synchronous (code)	5.5
BitBLT	Bit Block Transfer	6.7.1
BIU	Bus Interface Unit	B.1
BR(EQ)	Bus Request	3.3, A.9.1, B.5.2
BSR	Branch to Subroutine	A.3.7
BU	Bus Unit	B.6
CAD	Computer Aided Drafting	7.5
CAS	Column Address Strobe	2.6.2

CAV	Constant Angular Velocity	10.4, 10.10
CCITT	International Telegraph & Telephone Consulative Committee	5.2.2
CD	Compact Disk	10.10
CDI	Compact Disk Interactive	6.8.6
CD-ROM	Compact Disk Read Only Memory	6.8.6, 10.10
CFR	Cambridge Fast Ring	5.7.1
CGA	Colour Graphics Adapter	6.4
CLV	Constant Linear Velocity	10.4, 10.10
CMOS	Complementary Metal Oxide Semi-conductor	2.1, 2.3
CPU	Central Processing Unit	
CRC	Cyclic Redundancy Check	5.7.3, 10.4.1, 10.4.5
CRT	Cathode Ray Tube	4.1, 5.1, 6.2
CRTC	Cathode Ray Tube Controller	6.4.2
CS	Chip Select	4.2
CSMA/CD	Carrier Sense Multiple Access / Collision Detection	5.5
CTS	Clear To Send	5.2.2
D	D(ata)-type Flip Flop	2.5
D/A	Digital-to-Analog	5.5, 6.15, 9.5, 9.6
DAC	Digital-to-Analog Converter	9.5, 9.6
DARPA	(U.S. Department of) Defense Advanced Research Project Agency	5.7
dB	Decibel	9.3.1
DC	Direct Current	
DCB	Device Control Block	1.7
DCD	Data Carrier Detect	5.2.2
DCE	Data Communication Equipment	5.2
DDP	Datagram Delivery Protocol	5.7.4
DDR	Data Direction Register	4.2.1
DEN	Data Bus Enable	B.5
DIL	Dual-in-Line	A.5
DIN	Deutsch Industrie Normand	3.4.1, 3.4.2
DIP	Dual-in-line Package	A.5
DLE	Data Link Escape	5.5
DMA	Direct Memory Access	1.6.3, 3.3, 6.4.1, 8.4, A.9.1, B.10
DMAC	Direct Memory Access Controller	1.6.3
DOS	Disk Operating System	10.7
DPI	Dots per Inch	7.4
DRAM	Dynamic Read/Write Memory	2.6.2, 6.7
DSP	Digital Signal Processor	1.6.3

DSR	Data Set Ready	5.2.2
DTACK	Data Transfer Acknowledge	4.3.3, A.5
DTE	Data Terminal Equipment	5.2
DTR	Data Terminal Ready	5.2.2, 7.3
E	E(nable)-Clock	3.2.1, A.10
EA	Effective Address	A.2, B.3
EBCDIC	Extended Binary Coded Decimal Interchange Code	5.3
ECC	Error Correcting Code	10.6
EEROM	Electrically-Erasable (programmable) Read Only Memory	2.6.1
EGA	Enhanced Graphics Adapter	6.4, 6.6.4
EIA	Electrical Industries of Association of America	5.2.2
EISA	Extended Industry System Architecture	3.4.3
EL	Electroluminescent	6.6.3
Email	Electronic Mail	5.8
E(X)OR	Exclusive-OR	2.4, A.3.4
EPROM	(UV-) Erasable Programmable Read Only Memory	2.6.1
ETX	End of Transmission	5.5
EU	Execution Unit	B.1
FAX	Facsimile	6.8.5
FCL	Function Control Lines	A.1, A.7
FDC	Floppy Disk Controller	10.5
FDD	Floppy Disk Drive	10.4
FDHD	Floppy Drive High Density	10.4.1
FDM	Frequency Division Multiplexing	5.2.1
FET	Field Effect Transistor	2.8
FF	Flip Flop	2.5
FIFO	First-In-First-Out (buffer)	1.5, 5.5, A.4
FM	Frequency Modulation	5.4.4, 10.4.2
FMS	File Management System	10.7
FPU	Floating Point Unit	A.10
FSK	Frequency Shift Keying	5.2.1, 5.5
GDT	Global Descriptor Table	B.6
GKS	Graphics Kernel System	6.7.1
GSP	Graphics System Processor	6.7.1
HDLC	High-level Data Link Code	5.4.4, 5.5
HF	High Frequency	9.3
HFS	Hierarchical File Structure	10.7

HI	High	2.1
HLDA	Hold Acknowledge	B.5
HPIB	Hewlett Packard Interface Bus	3.4.5
HV	High Voltage	6.2
Hz	Hertz (cycles per second)	
iAPX	Intel Advanced Processor	B.1
IC	Integrated Circuit	2.8
I²C	Inter-IC (bus)	1.6.3
ID	Identification	10.4
IDT	Interrupt Descriptor Table	B.6, B.10
IEEE	Institute of Electrical and Electronic Engineers	3.4.5
INT(R)	Interrupt	4.3.2, A.8.1, B.4.7
INTA	Interrupt Acknowledge	B.5
I/O	Input / Output	
IP	Internet Protocol	5.7
IR	Instruction Register	1.2
IRG	Inter-Record Gap	10.2
IRQ	Interrupt Request	5.4.1, 8.3.1
IRT	Return from Interrupt	B.4.7
ISO	International Standards Organization	5.6.2
IU	Instruction Unit	B.6
Jcc	Jump on Condition (instruction)	A.3.7
JSR	Jump to Subroutine (instruction)	A.3.7, B.4.6
LAN	Local Area Network	5.7
LCD	Liquid Crystal Display	4.1, 7.6.1
LDR	Light Dependent Resistor	9.2
LDS	Lower Data Strobe	A.5, A.9
LDT	Local Descriptor Table	B.6
LEA	Load Effective Address (instruction)	A.3.1, B.4.1
LED	Light Emitting Diode	2.4, 4.1, 4.2
LIFO	Last-In-First-Out (buffer)	1.2
LO	Low	2.1
lsb	Least Significant Bit	
LSI	Large Scale Integration	1.1, 2.3.1
LVDT	Linearly Variable Differential Transformer	9.2.3
MACSYM	Measurement and Control System	9.7
MAR	Microinstruction Address Register	1.2
MCA	Micro Channel Architecture	8.4.3
MCGA	Multi-Colour Graphics Array	6.7

MDR	Microinstruction Data Register	1.2
MDS	Microprocessor Development System	preface
MFM	Modified Frequency Modulation	10.4.2
MIPS	Millions of Instructions per Second	B.7
MMU	Memory Management Unit	A.3.11, A.12, B.6
MN/MX	Minimum / Maximum	B.5.1
MODEM	Modulator / Demodulator	5.2.1
MOS	Metal Oxide Semiconductor	2.1
MOV	Move (instruction)	B.4.1
msb	Most Significant Bit	
MS-DOS	Microsoft Disk Operating System	8.5.2, 10.4.1, 10.7, 10.8, B.7
MSI	Medium Scale Integration	2.3.1
MSW	Machine Status Word	B.7
MUX	Multiplexer	2.4
NAU	Network Addressable Unit	5.6.1
NBP	Name Binding Protocol	5.7.4
NC	Normally Closed	4.2
NMI	Non-Maskable Interrupt	A.8.1, B.10
nMOS	n-type Metal Oxide Semiconductor	2.1
NO	Normally Open	4.2, 9.2.11
NOP	No Operation	1.3, 3.2.3
NPX	Numeric Coprocessor	B.10, B.11
NRZ	Non Return-to-Zero	5.4.4
NTSC	(U.S.) National Television System Committee	6.2
OC	Open Collector	3.1
OCR	Optical Character Recognition	6.8.5
Op Amp	Operational Amplifier	9.3.1
OS	Operating System	8.5.2, 10.7
OSI	Open Systems Interconnection	5.6.2
PABX	Private Automatic Branch Exchange	5.6.2
PAL	Programmable Array Logic	2.6.3
PC	Personal Computer	preface, 2.8, 3.4.3, 12.6
PCB	Printed Circuit Board	1.1, 1.3
PC-DOS	Personal Computer Disk Operating System	8.5.2
PCL	Peripheral Control Line	1.6.3
PIA	Peripheral Interface Adapter	4.3.1, 7.3
PIC	Priority Interrupt Controller	1.6.2
PI/T	Programmable Interface / Timer	4.3.3, 8.3.4, 8.4

PIT	Programmable Interval Timer	8.3.5
PixBLT	Pixel Block Transfer	6.7.1
PLA	Programmable Logic Array	2.6.3, 9.6
PLD	Programmable Logic Device	2.6.3
PLL	Phase Locked Loop	10.4.3
pMOS	p-type Metal Oxide Semiconductor	2.1
PPI	Programmable Peripheral Interface	4.3.2, 7.3
PROM	Programmable Read Only Memory	2.6.1, 2.6.3
PSW	Program Status Word	B.1, B.4.2
PTM	Programmable Timer Module	8.3.1, 8.3.2
RAM	Read / Write (Random Access) Memory	1.4, 2.6.2
RAS	Row Address Strobe	2.6.2
RC	Resistor-Capacitor	4.2
RDRF	Receive Data Register Full (flag)	5.4.1, 5.4.2
RF	Radio Frequency	5.2.1, 6.3
RGB	Red Green Blue	6.2, 6.3
RISC	Reduced Instruction Set Computer	2.4
RLL	Run Length Limited	10.4.2
RMX	Real Time Multitasking Executive	8.5.2
ROM	Read Only Memory	1.4, 2.6.1, 6.4
RPM	Revolutions Per Minute	10.4, 10.6
RT	Real Time	8.5
RTD	Resistance Thermal Device	9.2.2
RTE	Return from Exception	A.7
RTOS	Real Time Operating System	8.5.2
RTS	Request To Send	5.2.2
RTTY	Radio Teletype	5.2.1
R/W	Read / Write	1.4
Rx	Receiver	5.4
RxD	Receive Data (register)	5.4.1, 7.3
SCC	Serial Communications Controller	5.4.4
SCR	Silicon Controlled Rectifier	9.2.11
SCSI	Small Computer Systems Interface	3.4.6
SDLC	Synchronous Data Link Control	5.4.4, 5.5
S/H	Sample-and-Hold	9.3.1
SNA	Systems Network Architecture	5.6.1
SOH	Start-of-Header	5.5
SP	Stack Pointer	1.2, A.1, A.3.8, B.2
SPDT	Single Pole, Double Throw (switch)	4.2
SPST	Single Pole, Single Throw (switch)	4.2
SR	Status Register	1.2, A.1
SRAM	Static Read / Write Memory	2.6.2

SSI	Small Scale Integration	2.3.1
STX	Start-of-Transmission	5.5
SYNDET	Synchronous Detect	5.4.3
T	Toggle (type flip flop)	2.5
TCP/IP	Transmission Control Protocol / Internet Protocol	5.7
TCU	Timing & Control Unit	8.1
TDM	Time Division Multiplexing	5.2.1
TDRE	Transmit Data Register Empty (flag)	5.4.1, 5.4.2
TIFF	Tag Image File Format	6.8.5
TLB	Translation Lookaside Buffer	B.7
TS	Three State	3.1
TTL	Transistor-Transistor Logic	1.5, 2.3
TTY	Teletype	5.2.1, 6.1
Tx	Transmitter	5.4
TxD	Transmit Data (register)	5.4.1, 7.3
UART	Universal Asychronous Receiver / Transmitter	5.4, 7.3
UDS	Upper Data Strobe	A.5, A.9
USART	Universal Synchronous / Asynchronous Receiver / Transmitter	5.4.3
UV	Ultra Violet (light)	2.6.1
VCO	Voltage-Controlled Oscillator	9.6
VDT	Video Display Terminal	6.1, 6.4.1
VDU	Visual Display Unit	4.1, 6.1
VGA	Video Graphics Array	6.4
VIA	Versatile Interface Adapter	4.2.1, 8.3.3
VLSI	Very Large Scale Integration	1.1, 2.3.1, 2.5
VMA	Valid Memory Address	A.10
VPA	Valid Peripheral Address	A.10
VRAM	Video Read / Write Memory	6.7.1
WAN	Wide Area Network	5.8
WORM	Write Once, Read Many (disk)	10.10
XOR	Exclusive-OR	B.4.3
XTAL	Crystal	8.2, 9.2.2, 9.2.4

References and Further Reading

REFERENCES

Bradley D. (1984). *Assembly Language Programming for the IBM Personal Computer*. Englewood Cliffs NJ: Prentice-Hall.

Liu Y-C. and Gibson G. (1984). *Microcomputer Systems: the 8086/8088 Family – architecture, programming & design*. Englewood Cliffs NJ: Prentice-Hall

Nealon R.S. (1985). Ring communications protocols. *Internal Report*, Dept. of Computing Science, University of Wollongong

Stone H. (1982). *Microcomputer Interfacing*. Reading MA: Addison-Wesley

Tanenbaum A.S. (1987). *Operating Systems: design and implementation*. Englewood Cliffs NJ: Prentice-Hall

FURTHER READING

1 Microcomputer Architecture and Interfacing

Anceau F. (1986).*The Architecture of Microprocessors*. Reading MA: Addison-Wesley

Artwick B. (1980). *Microcomputer Interfacing*. Englewood Cliffs NJ: Prentice-Hall

Baer J-L. (1980). *Computer Systems Architecture*. Rockville MD: Computer Science Press

Gorsline G. (1986). *Computer Organisation: Hardware/Software*. Englewood Cliffs NJ: Prentice-Hall

Gray N. (1987). *An Introduction to Computer Systems*. Englewood Cliffs NJ: Prentice-Hall

Hordeski M. (1986). *Microcomputer Design*. Reston VA: Reston

Kirrmann H. (1983). Data Format and Bus Compatability in Multiprocessing. *IEEE Micro*, **3**(4), 32–47

Koopman P. (1987). Microcoded versus Hard-wired Control. *Byte*, **12**(1), 235–42

Leventhal L. (1978). *Introduction to Microprocessors: Software, Hardware, Programming*. Englewood Cliffs NJ: Prentice-Hall

Lorin H. (1982). *Introduction to Computer Architecture and Organization*. (2nd edn) New York: Wiley

Mano M. (1982). *Computer System Architecture*. Englewood Cliffs NJ: Prentice-Hall

Myers G.J. (1982). *Advances in Computer Architecture*. New York: Wiley Interscience

Osborne A. (1976). *An Introduction to Microcomputers Volume 1 – Basic Concepts*. Berkeley CA: Osborne & Associates

Tanenbaum A. (1984). *Structured Computer Organisation*. Englewood Cliffs NJ: Prentice-Hall

Thompson T. and Baran N. (1988). The NeXT Computer. *Byte*, **13**(12), 158–75
Toy W. and Zee B. (1986). *Computer Hardware/Software Architecture*. Englewood Cliffs NJ: Prentice-Hall
Wakerly J. (1981). *Microcomputer Architecture and Programming*. New York: Wiley

2 Hardware Building Blocks

Anceau F. (1986). *The Architecture of Microprocessors*. Reading MA: Addison-Wesley
Bartee T.C. (1985) *Digital Computer Fundamentals* (6th edn). New York: McGraw-Hill
Booth T.L. (1984). *Introduction to Computer Engineering: Hardware and Software Design* (3rd edn). New York: Wiley
Cirovic M. (1979). *Basic Electronics*. Reston VA: Reston
Ercegovac M. and Lang T. (1985). *Digital Systems and Hardware/Firmware Algorithms*. New York: Wiley
Fletcher W. (1980). *An Engineering Approach to Digital Design*. Englewood Cliffs NJ: Prentice-Hall
Greenfield J. (1983). *Practical Digital Design Using ICs*. New York: Wiley
Hill F. and Peterson G. (1978). *Digital Systems: Hardware Organisation and Design*. New York: Wiley
Holt C. (1978). *Electronic Circuits, Digital and Analog*. New York: Wiley
Horowitz P. and Hill W. (1980). *The Art of Electronics*. Cambridge: Cambridge University Press
Krutz R. (1980). *Microprocessors and Logic Design*. New York: Wiley
Mano M. (1984). *Digital Design*. Englewood Cliffs NJ: Prentice-Hall
Mano M. (1988). *Computer Engineering: Hardware Design*. Englewood Cliffs NJ: Prentice-Hall
McCluskey E.J. (1986). *Logic Design Principles, with Emphasis on Testable Semicustom Circuits*. Englewood Cliffs NJ: Prentice-Hall
Millman J. (1979). *Microelectronics: Digital and Analog Circuits and Systems*. New York: McGraw-Hill
Nashelsky L. (1983). *Introduction to Digital Technology*. New York: Wiley
Pasahow E. (1982). *Learning Digital Electronics Through Experiments*. New York: McGraw-Hill
Passafiume J. and Douglas M. (1985). *Digital Logic Design – Tutorials and Laboratory Exercises*. New York: Harper & Row
Prosser F. and Winkel D. (1987) *The Art of Digital Design*. Englewood Cliffs NJ: Prentice-Hall
Robinson P. (1987). Overview of Programmable Hardware. *Byte*, **12**(1), 197–203
Roth C. (1985). *Fundamentals of Logic Design*. St Paul MN: West Publishing
Shiva S. (1988). *Introduction to Logic Design*. Glenview IL: Scott, Foresman
Smith R.J. (1984). *Circuits, Devices and Systems* (4th edn). New York: Wiley
Tocci R. (1980). *Digital Systems, Principles and Applications*. Englewood Cliffs NJ: Prentice-Hall
Young G. (1980). *Digital Electronics – A Hands-on Learning Approach*. Rochelle Park NJ: Hayden

3 Microcomputer Bus Structure

Anceau F. (1986). *The Architecture of Microprocessors*. Reading MA: Addison-Wesley
Burton D. and Dexter A. (1979). *Microprocessor Systems Handbook*. Norwood MA: Analog Devices Inc.
Bywater R. (1981). *Hardware/Software Design of Digital Systems*. Englewood Cliffs NJ: Prentice-Hall

Cornejo C. and Lee R. (1987). Comparing IBM's Micro Channel and Apple's Nubus. *Byte*, **12**(12), 83–92
Dexter A. (1986) *Microcomputer Bus Structures and Bus Interface Design*. New York: Marcel Dekker
Hall D. (1986). *Microprocessors and Interfacing: Programming and Hardware*. New York: McGraw-Hill
Intel Corporation (1985). *Microcomputer Systems Handbook*. Santa Clara CA
Krajewskei R. (1985). Multiprocessing: an overview. *Byte*, **10**(5), 171–81
Motorola Incorporated (1984). *M68000 16/32-bit Microprocessor Programmer's Reference Manual* (4th edn). Austin TX
Protopapas D. (1988). *Microcomputer Hardware Design*. Englewood Cliffs NJ: Prentice-Hall
Triebel W. and Singh A. (1985). *16-bit Microprocessors: Architecture, Software and Interface Techniques*. Englewood Cliffs NJ: Prentice-Hall
Wilcox A. (1987). *68000 Microcomputer Systems: Designing and Troubleshooting*. Englewood Cliffs NJ: Prentice-Hall

4   Parallel Input/Output

Andrews M. (1982). *Programming Microprocessor Interfaces for Control and Instrumentation*. Englewood Cliffs NJ: Prentice-Hall
Artwick B.A. (1980). *Microprocessor Interfacing*. Englewood Cliffs NJ: Prentice-Hall
Cluely J.C. (1983). *Interfacing to Microprocessors*. Basingstoke, Hampshire: Macmillan
Coffron J.W. and Long W.E. (1983). *Practical Interfacing Techniques for Microprocessor Systems*. Englewood Cliffs NJ: Prentice-Hall
Craine J. and Martin G. (1985). *Microcomputers in Engineering and Science*. Reading MA: Addison-Wesley
Furht B. and Parikh H. (1986). *Microprocessor Interfacing and Communication Using the Intel SDK-85*. Reston VA: Reston
Georgopoulous C.J. (1985). *Interface Fundamentals in Microprocessor-Controlled Systems*. Hingham MA: Reidel
Hall D.V. (1986). *Microprocessors & Interfacing*. New York: McGraw-Hill
Intel Corporation (1985). *Microprocessor Components Handbook vols I & II*. Santa Clara CA
Lesea A. and Zaks R. (1977). *Microprocessor Interfacing Techniques*. Berkeley CA: Sybex
Leventhal L.A. (1978). *Introduction to Microprocessors: Software, Hardware, Programming*. Englewood Cliffs, NJ: Prentice-Hall
Liebson S. (1983). *The Handbook of Microcomputer Interfacing*. Blue Ridge Summit PA: Tab
Lipovski G.J. (1981). *Microcomputer Interfacing*. Lexington MA: Lexington
Money S. (1987). *Practical Microprocessor Interfacing*. London: Collins
Motorola Incorporated (1983). *Microprocessors Data Manual*. Austin TX
Protopapas D. (1988). *Microcomputer Hardware Design*. Englewood Cliffs NJ: Prentice-Hall
Rockwell (1985). *Data Book*. Newport Beach CA
Slater M. (1987). *Microprocessor-based Design, a Comprehensive Guide to Effective Hardware Design*. Mountain View CA: Mayfield
Staugaard A.C.Jr. (1982). *Microprocessor Interfacing*. Lexington MA: Heath
Triebel W.A. and Singh A. (1985). *16-bit Microprocessors: Architecture, Software and Interface Techniques*. Englewood Cliffs NJ: Prentice-Hall
Uffenbeck J. (1985). *Microcomputers and Microprocessors: the 808, 8085 and Z80 Programming, Interfacing and Troubleshooting*. Englewood Cliffs NJ: Prentice-Hall

5 Serial Input/Output

Arick M.R. (1987). *Data Communications: Concepts and Systems*. QED Inf. Sci. Inc.

Beauchamp K. (1987). *Computer Communications*. New York: Van Nostrand Reinhold

Black U. (1983). *Data Communications, Networks and Distributed Processing*. Reston VA: Reston

Bleazard G. (1982). *Handbook of Data Communications*. NCC Publications

Brooks L. (1984). Communication Protocols. *Dr. Dobb's Journal*, **9**(2), 26–9

Byers T. (1987). *Microprocessor Communications Support Chips*. North Holland: Elsevier

Campbell J. (1985). *The RS-232 Solution*. Berkeley CA: Sybex

CCITT (n.d.). *Recommendations V.29, X.21 & X.25*. International Telecommunications Union, Place des Nations, 1211 Geneva, Switzerland

Chou W. (1983). *Computer Communications Vol. 1 Principles*. Englewood Cliffs NJ: Prentice-Hall

Clifton C.S. (1986). *What Every Engineer Should Know About Data Communications*. New York: Marcel Dekker

Cole R. (1986). *Computer Communications*. Basingstoke, Hampshire: Macmillan

Electronic Industries Association (1969). *EIA Standard RS-232-C, RS422, RS423, RS449* EIA, Washington, DC. 1969(75)

Gofton P.W. (1985). *Mastering Serial Communications*. Berkeley CA: Sybex

Halsall F. (1985). *Introduction to Communications and Computer Networks*. Wokingham: Addison-Wesley

Halsall F. (1988). *Data Communications, Computer Networks and OSI*. Wokingham: Addison-Wesley

Held G. (1983). *Data Communications: a Comprehensive Approach*. New York: McGraw-Hill

Hopper A., Temple S. and Williamson R. (1987). *Local Area Network Design*. Reading MA: Addison-Wesley

Hopper A. and Needham R. (1988). The Cambridge Fast Ring Networking System. *IEEE Transactions Computers*, **37**(10), 1214–23

IBM (n.d.). Binary Synchronous Communications – General Information, IBM Synchronous Data Link Control – General Information. *IBM Publication nos. GA27-3004, -3093-2*. IBM Systems Development Division, Publications Center

IEEE (1985). *Logical Link Control – IEEE 802.2, CSMA/CD Access Method – IEEE 802.3, Token Bus Access Method – IEEE 802.4, Token Ring Access Method – IEEE 802.5*. Institute of Electrical and Electronic Engineers Press: New York, NY 10017 USA

Intel Corporation (1985). *Microprocessor Components Handbook vols I & II*. Santa Clara CA

Intel Corporation (1981). *Asynchronous Communication with the 8274 MPSC (AP134)* Santa Clara CA

Intel Corporation (1981). *Synchronous Communication with the 8274 MPSC (AP145)* Santa Clara CA

ISO (1985). *OSI documents 8236/7, 8822/3, 8824/5, 8571-4, 8831/3, 8649(3)/50(3), 9040/1* International Telecommunications Union, Place des Nations, 1211 Geneva, Switzerland

ISO (1981). *Network Service Using X25 and X21 TC97/SC5/N2743* International Telecommunications Union, Place des Nations, 1211 Geneva, Switzerland

Jennings F. (1986). *Practical Data Communications*. Oxford: Blackwell

Kahn R. (1987). Networks for Advanced Computing. *Scientific American*, **257**(4), 128–35

Kreager P. (1983). *Practical Aspects of Data Communications*. New York: McGraw-Hill

Loomis M. (1983). *Data Communications*. Englewood Cliffs NJ: Prentice-Hall

McNamara J.B. (1982). *Technical Aspects of Data Communications* (2nd edn). Bedford MA: Digital Equipment Corporation

Meijer A. and Peeters P. (1982). *Computer Network Architectures*. Rockville MD: Computer Science Press
Motorola Incorporated (1985). *Microprocessors Data Manual*. Austin TX
Motorola Incorporated (1981). *MC6854 – ADLC An Introduction to Data Communication*. Austin TX
Nichols E.A., Nichols J.C. and Musson K.R. (1982). *Data Communications for Microprocessors*. New York: McGraw-Hill
Rockwell (1985). *Data Book*.Newport Beach CA
Saal H. (1983). Local Area Networks. *Byte*, 8(5), 60–79
Schwartz M. (1987). *Telecommunication Networks: Protocols, Modelling and Analysis*. Reading MA: Addison-Wesley
Seyer M.D. (1984). *RS232 Made Easy*. Englewood Cliffs NJ: Prentice-Hall
Sherman K. (1985). *Data Communications – a user's guide*. Reston VA: Reston
Sloman M. and Kramer J. (1987). *Distributed Systems and Computer Networks*. Englewood Cliffs NJ: Prentice-Hall
Stallings W. (1985). *Data and Computer Communications*. Basingstoke, Hampshire: Macmillan
Stallings W. (1987). *Local Networks – an Introduction*. Basingstoke, Hampshire: Macmillan
Synertek Incorporated (1980). *SY6551 Asynchronous Communications Interface Adapter (ACIA)* (AN1) Santa Clara CA
Tanenbaum A. (1981). *Computer Networks*. Englewood Cliffs NJ: Prentice-Hall
Zilog (1985). *Data Book*. Campbell CA

6 Video Display Terminals

Adler G.J. (1985). Liquid-Crystal Displays. *Byte*, 10(7), 119–28
Coach K. (1984). Televisions as Monitors. *Byte*, 9(7), 171–6
Cruz A. (1984). Using the MC267x CRT set with the MC6809E. *Motorola Application Note AN–895* Austin TX: Motorola Inc.
Foley J. (1987). Interfaces for Advanced Computing. *Scientific American*, 257(4), 82–90
Hall D. (1986). *Microprocessors and Interfacing: programming and hardware*. New York: McGraw-Hill 1986
Hearn D. and Baker M. (1986). *Computer Graphics*. Englewood Cliffs NJ: Prentice-Hall
Intel Corporation (1985). *Microsystem Components Handbook vols I & II*. Santa Clara CA
Kane G. (1978). *CRT Controller Handbook*. Berkeley CA: Osborne/McGraw-Hill
Kavatsky J. (1979). A Low Cost CRT Terminal Using the 8275. *Intel Application Note AP-62*. Santa Clara CA: Intel Corporation
Killibrew C.R.Jr (1986). The TMS34010 Graphics System Processor. *Byte*, 11(13), 193–204
Krantz S. and Stanley J. (1986). *68000 Assembly Language*. Reading MA: Addison-Wesley
Melear C. and Browne J. (1981). Motorola MC6845 CRTC Simplifies Video Display Controllers. *Motorola Application Note AN-851*. Austin TX: Motorola Incorporated
Motorola Incorporated (1985). *Microprocessors Data Manual*. Austin TX
Nicholls B. (1987). Inside the 82786 Graphics Chip. *Byte*, 12(9), 135–41
Peterson R., Killebrew D., Albert T. and Guttag K. (1988). Taking the Wraps off the 34020. *Byte*, 13(9), 259–72
Shuford R.S. (1986). Two Flat Display Technologies. *Byte*, 10(3), 130–6
Smarte G. and Baran N. (1988). Face to Face. *Byte*, 13(9), 243–52
Thorne M. (1986). *Programming the 8086/8088 for the IBM, PC and Compatibles*. Reading MA: Addison-Wesley

7 Hard Copy Units

Cook R. (1987). Page Printers. *Byte*, **12**(10), 187–97

Furht B. and Parikh H. (1986). *Microprocessor Interfacing and Communication Using the Intel SDK 85*. Reston VA: Reston

Hall D. (1986). *Microprocessors and Interfacing: programming and hardware*. New York: McGraw-Hill

Hohenstein L. (1980). *Computer Peripherals for Minicomputers, Microprocessors, and Personal Computers*. New York: McGraw-Hill

Intel Corporation (1985). *Microprocessor Components Handbook vols I & II*. Santa Clara CA

Jansson L. (1987). Print Quality. *Byte*, **12**(10), 199–207

Kane G., Hawkins D. and Leventhal L. (1981). *68000 Assembly Language Programming*. Berkeley CA: Osborne/McGraw-Hill

Luft N.M. Color Printing. *Byte*, **12**(10), 163–75

Motorola Incorporated (1985). *Microprocessors Data Manual*. Austin TX

Motorola Incorporated (1982). The MC68230 Parallel Interface/Timer provides an effective Printer Interface. *Motorola Application Note AN854*. Austin TX

Osborne A., Kane J., Rector R. and Jacobson S. (1978). *Z80 Programming for Logic Design*. Berkeley CA: Osborne

8 Timers/Counters

Allworth S. and Zobel R. (1987). *Introduction to Real-Time Software Design*. Basingstoke, Hampshire: Macmillan

Bennett J. (1987). *68000 Assembly Language Programming, a structured approach*. Englewood Cliffs NJ: Prentice-Hall

Garrett P.H. (1987). *Computer Interface Engineering for Real Time Systems*. Englewood Cliffs NJ: Prentice-Hall

Hall D. (1986). *Microprocessors and Interfacing: programming and hardware*. New York: McGraw-Hill

Intel Corporation (1985). *Microsystem Components Handbook vols I & II*. Santa Clara CA

Isaak J. (1984). Designing Systems for R.T. Applications. *Byte*, **9**(4), 127–32

Lawrence P.D. and Mauch K. (1987). *Real Time Microcomputer System Design: an introduction*. New York: McGraw-Hill

Motorola Incorporated (1985). *Microprocessors Data Manual*. Austin TX

Savitsky S. (1985). *Real-Time Microprocessor Systems*. New York: Van Nostrand Reinhold

Signetics (1985). *Analog Data Manual*. Sunny Vale CA

Staugaard A.C.Jr. (1982). *Microprocessor Interfacing*. Lexington MA: Heath

Wyss C.R. (1983). A Conceptual Approach to Real-Time Programming. *Byte*, **8**(5), 452–62

9 A/D and D/A Conversion

Allocca J. and Stuart A. (1984). *Transducers: Theory and Applications*. Reston VA: Reston

Analog Devices (1984). *Data Acquisition databook vol. 1 – Integrated Circuits*. Norwood MA

Analog Devices (1984). *Data Acquisition databook vol. 2 – Modules/Subsystems*. Norwood MA

Andrews M. (1982). *Programming Microprocessor Interfaces for Control and Instrumentation*. Englewood Cliffs NJ: Prentice-Hall

Artwick B. (1980). *Microcomputer Interfacing*. Englewood Cliffs NJ: Prentice-Hall
Burr Brown (1984). *Product Selection Guide*. Tucson AZ
Burton D. and Dexter A. (1977). *Microprocessor Systems Handbook*. Norwood MA:
    Analog Devices
Clayton G.B. (1982). *Data Converters*. Basingstoke, Hampshire: Macmillan
Craine J. and Martin G. (1985). *Microcomputers in Engineering and Science*. Reading
    MA: Addison-Wesley
Furht B. and Parikh H. (1986). *Microprocessor Interfacing and Communication Using the
    Intel SDK 85*. Reston VA: Reston
Hall D. (1986). *Microprocessors and Interfacing: Programming and Hardware*. New York:
    McGraw-Hill
Lesea A. and Zaks R. (1978). *Microprocessor Interfacing Techniques*. Berkeley CA: Sybex
Leventhal L. (1978). *Introduction to Microprocessors: Software, Hardware, Programming*.
    Englewood Cliffs NJ: Prentice-Hall
Motorola Incorporated (1983). *Linear & Interface Integrated Circuits*. Austin TX
National Semiconductor (1984). *Data Conversion/Acquisition Databook*. Santa Clara CA
Norton H. (1969). *Handbook of Transducers for Electronic Measuring Systems*. Englewood
    Cliffs NJ: Prentice-Hall
Shiengold D. ed. *Transducer Interfacing Handbook*. Norwood MA: Analog Devices
Shiengold D. ed. *Analog-Digital Conversion Handbook*. Norwood MA: Analog Devices
Staugaard A.C. Jr. (1983). *Microprocessor Applications* Lexington VA: Heath
Sydenham P. (1977). *Transducers in Measurement and Control*. Armidale NSW:
    University of New England Press
Usher M. (1984). *Sensors and Transducers*. Basingstoke, Hampshire: Macmillan

10   Mass Storage Devices

Artwick B. (1980). *Microcomputer Interfacing*. Englewood Cliffs NJ: Prentice-Hall
Beims R. and LaViolette P. (1985). SCSI protocol and controller bus arbitration. *EDN*,
    21 March
Colomb S.W. 1986). Optical Disk Error Correction. *Byte*, **11**(5), 203–10
Freese R.P. (1988). Optical Disks Become Erasable. *IEEE Spectrum*, **25**(2), 41–5
Glass B. (1989). Hard disk interfaces. *Byte*, **14**(2), 293–7
Intel Corporation (1981). *Peripheral Design Handbook*. Santa Clara CA
Intel Corporation (1985). *Microsystem Components Handbook vols I & II*. Santa Clara
    CA
Intel Corporation (1981). Software Design and Implementation of Floppy Disk
    Subsystems. *Intel Application Note AP-121* Santa Clara CA
Kryder M. (1987). Data-Storage Technologies for Advanced Computing. *Scientific
    American*, **257**(4), 73–81
Laub L. (1986). The Evolution of Mass Storage. *Byte*, **11**(5), 161–72
Lesea A. and Zaks R. (1978). *Microprocessor Interfacing Techniques*. Berkeley CA: Sybex
Lohmeyer J. (1985). Use SCSI devices for multiprocessor, smart-I/O systems. *EDN*,
    January 24 1985
McIvor R. (1985). Smart Cards. *Scientific American*, **253**(5), 130–7
Motorola Incorporated (1985). *Microprocessors Data Manual*. Austin TX
National Semiconductor Incorporated (1983). *Interface, Bipolar LSI, Bipolar Memory,
    Programmable Logic Data Book*. Santa Clara CA
Rossi T. (1981). An Intelligent Data Base System Using the 8272. *Intel Application Note
    AP-116* Santa Clara CA: Intel Corp.
Roth J. (1986). *CDROMs*. Westport CA: Meckler
Shogase H. (1988). Pocket Banks. *IEEE Spectrum*, **25**(10), 35–9
Shuford R.S. (1985). CDROM's and Their Kin. *Byte*, **10**(11), 137–46

Sterling T. (1984). Theory of Disk Error Correction. *Byte*, **9**(9), 145–7
Thompson L.E. (1984). Floppy Disk Formats. *Byte*, **9**(9), 147–443
Thorne M. (1986). *Programming the 8086/8088 for the IBM PC and Compatibles*.
    Reading MA: Addison-Wesley
Western Digital Corporation (1987). *Data Book*. Irvine CA
Zoellick B. (1986). CD-ROM Software Development. *Byte*, **11**(5), 177–88

Appendix A

Bennett J. (1986). *68000 Assembly Language Programming: A Structured Approach*.
    Englewood Cliffs NJ: Prentice-Hall
Bramer B. (1987). *68000 Assembler Language Programming*. London: Edward Arnold
Clements A. (1987). *Microprocessor Systems Design: 68000 Hardware, Software and
    Interfacing*. Boston MA: Breton
Coffron J.W. (1983). *Using and Troubleshooting the MC68000*. Reston VA: Reston
Cramer W. and Kane G. (1986). *68000 Microprocessor Handbook* (2nd edn).
    Berkeley CA: Osborne/McGraw-Hill
Dr Dobb's Journal (1986). *Dr. Dobb's Toolbook of 68000 Programming*. New York:
    Brady
Driscoll F.F. (1987). *Introduction to 6800/68000 Microprocessors*. Boston MA: Breton
Eccles W.J. (1985). *Microprocessor Systems: A 16-bit Approach*. Reading MA: Addison-
    Wesley
Floyd R.W. (1983). The M68000 Educational Computer Board. *Byte*, **8**(10), 324–36
Ford W. and Topp W. (1988). *MC68000: Assembly Language and Systems Programming*.
    Lexington MA: Heath
Gill A., Corwan E. and Logar A. (1987). *Assembly Language Programming for the 68000*.
    Englewood Cliffs NJ: Prentice-Hall
Gorsline G.W. (1988). *Assembly and Assemblers: the Motorola MC68000 Family*.
    Englewood Cliffs NJ: Prentice-Hall
Greenfield J.D. and Wray W.C. (1988). *Using Microprocessors and Microcomputers: the
    Motorola Family* (2nd edn). New York: Wiley
Groepler P.F. and Kennedy J. (1984). The MC68020 32-bit microprocessor. *Byte*,
    9(11), 159–74
Gupta A. and Toong H-m.D. (1983). *Advanced Microprocessors*. Piscataway NJ: IEEE
    Press
Harman T.L (1989). *The Motorola MC68020 and MC68030 Microprocessors*. Englewood
    Cliffs NJ: Prentice-Hall
Harman T.L. and Lawson B. (1985). *The Motorola MC68000 Microprocessor Family:
    assembly language, interface design, and system design*. Englewood Cliffs NJ:
    Prentice-Hall
Jaulent P. (1985). *68000 Hardware and Software*. Basingstoke, Hampshire: Macmillan
Johnson T.L. (1986). A Comparison of MC68000 Family Processors. *Byte*, **11**(9),
    205–18
Johnson T.L. (1987). The RISC/CISC melting pot: classic design methods converge in
    the MC68030 microprocessor. *Byte*, **12**(4), 153–60
Kane G., Hawkins D. and Leventhal L. (1981). *68000 Assembly Language
    Programming*. Berkeley CA: Osborne/McGraw-Hill
Kelly-Bootle S. and Fowler B. (1985). *68000, 68010, 68020 Primer*. Indianapolis IN:
    Howard Sams
King T. and Knight B. (1987). *Programming the M68000* (2nd edn). Reading MA:
    Addison-Wesley
Krantz D. and Stanley J. (1986). *68000 Assembly Language: Techniques for Building
    Programs*. Reading MA: Addison Wesley

Mitchell H.J. (1987). *32-bit Microprocessors*. New York: McGraw-Hill
Morton M. (1986). 68000 Tricks and Traps. *Byte*, **11**(9), 163–72
Motorola Incorporated (1984) *M68000 16/32 bit Microprocessor Programmer's Reference
    Manual* (4th edn). Englewood Cliffs NJ: Prentice-Hall
Motorola Incorporated (1984) *MC68020 32-bit Microprocessor User's Manual*.
    Englewood Cliffs NJ: Prentice-Hall
Motorola Incorporated (1986). *Second Generation 32-bit Enhanced Microprocessor*.
    Motorola Technical Data. Austin TX
Scanlan L.J. (1981). *The 68000: Principles and Programming*. Indianapolis IN: Howard
    Sams
Skinner T. (1987). *Assembly Language Programming for the 68000 Family*. New York:
    Wiley
Starnes T.W. (1983). Design philosophy behind Motorola's MC68000. *Byte*, **8**(4),
    70–92
Wakerley J.F. (1981). *Microcomputer Architecture and Programming*. New York: Wiley
Wakerly J.F. (1989). *Microcomputer Architecture and Programming, the 68000 Family*.
    New York: Wiley
Wilcox A.D. (1987). *68000 Microcomputer Systems: Designing and Troubleshooting*.
    Englewood Cliffs NJ: Prentice-Hall
Williams S. (1985). *Programming the 68000*. Berkeley CA: Sybex

Appendix B

Abel P. (1987). *IBM-PC Assembler Language and Programming*. Englewood Cliffs NJ:
    Prentice-Hall
Coffron J. (1983). *Programming the 8086/8088*. Berkeley, CA: Sybex
Crawford J. and Gelsinger P. (1987). *Programming the 80386*. Berkeley, CA: Sybex
Fernandez J. and Ashley R. (1989). *Assembly Language Programming for the 80386*. New
    York: McGraw-Hill
Godfrey J.T. (1988). *IBM Microcomputer Assembly Language: Beginning to Advanced*.
    Englewood Cliffs NJ: Prentice-Hall
Gorsline G. (1985). *16-bit Modern Microcomputers: the Intel i8086 Family*. Englewood
    Cliffs NJ: Prentice-Hall
Gupta A. and Toong H. (1983). *Advanced Microprocessors*. Piscataway NJ: IEEE Press
Heywood S.A. (1983). The 8086 – an architecture for the future. *Byte*, **8**(6), 450–4
Intel Corporation (1983). *iAPX286 Hardware Reference Manual*. Santa Clara CA
Intel Corporation (1985). *iAPX286 Programmer's Reference Manual*. Santa Clara CA
Intel Corporation (1981). *iAPX88 Book*. Santa Clara CA
Intel Corporation (1985). *iAPX86/88,186/188 Hardware Reference Manual*. Santa Clara
    CA
Intel Corporation (1983). *iAPX86/88,186/188 Programmer's Reference Manual*. Santa
    Clara CA
Intel Corporation (1982). *Introduction to the iAPX286*. Santa Clara CA
Intel Corporation (1985). *Introduction to the 80386*. Santa Clara CA
Jourdain R. (1986). *Programmer's Problem Solver for the IBM PC, XT & AT*. New
    York: Brady (Prentice-Hall)
Liu Y-C. and Gibson G.A. (1986). *Microcomputer Systems: The 8086/8088 Family
    Architecture, Programming and Design*. (2nd edn). Englewood Cliffs NJ:
    Prentice-Hall
Miller A. (1986). *Assembly Language Techniques for the IBM PC*. Berkeley CA: Sybex
Mitchell H.J. (1987). *32-bit Microprocessors*. New York: McGraw-Hill
Morgan C.L. (1982). *8086/8088 16-bit Microprocessor Primer*. New York: Byte/McGraw-
    Hill

Morris N. (1988). *An Introduction to 8086/88 Assembly Language Programming for Engineers*. New York: McGraw-Hill

Morse S.P. (1980). *The 8086 Primer: an Introduction to its Architecture, System Design and Programming*. Rochelle Park NJ: Hayden

Morse S.P., Albert D.J. and Isaacson E.J. (1987). *The 80386/387 Architecture*. New York: Wiley.

Murray W. and Pappas C. (1986). *80386/80286 Assembly Language Programming*. Berkeley CA: Osborne/McGraw-Hill

Murray W.H. and Pappas C.H. (1989). *Assembly Language Programming Under OS/2^TM*. New York: McGraw-Hill

Norton P. (1986). *Peter Norton's Assembly Language Book for the IBM PC*. Englewood Cliffs NJ: Prentice-Hall

Rector R. and Alexy G. (1980). *The 8086 Book*. Berkeley CA: Osborne/McGraw-Hill

Scanlon L.J. (1986). *Assembly Language Subroutines for MSDOS Computers*. Blue Ridge Summit PA: Tab

Strauss E. (1986). *Inside the 80286*. Englewood Cliffs NJ: Prentice-Hall

Thorne M. (1986). *Programming the 8086/8088 for the IBM PC and compatibles*. Reading MA: Addison-Wesley

Triebel W. and Singh A. (1985). *16-bit Microprocessors: architecture, software and interface techniques*. Englewood Cliffs NJ: Prentice-Hall

Turpin R.W. (1987). *The 8086 and Assembly Language Programming*. Oxford: Blackwell

Uffenbeck J. (1987). *The 8086/8088 Family: design, programming and interfacing*. Englewood Cliffs NJ: Prentice-Hall

Wakerly J. (1981). *Microcomputer Architecture and Programming*. New York: Wiley

Wells P. (1984). The 80286 Microprocessor. *Byte*, 9(11), 231–42

Index